# THE EARTH IS RED

## The Imperialism of the Doctrine of Discovery

# THE EARTH IS RED

## The Imperialism of the Doctrine of Discovery

## ROBERTA CAROL HARVEY

SUNSTONE
PRESS

SANTA FE

Sunstone books may be purchased for educational, business, or sales promotional use.
For information please write: Special Markets Department, Sunstone Press,
P.O. Box 2321, Santa Fe, New Mexico 87504-2321.

Design › R. Ahl
Printed on acid-free paper
∞
eBook 978-1-61139-637-9

---

Library of Congress Cataloging-in-Publication Data

Names: Harvey, Roberta Carol, 1950- author.
Title: The earth is red : the imperialism of the doctrine of discovery / by
    Roberta Carol Harvey.
Description: Santa Fe, New Mexico : Sunstone Press, [2021] | Summary:
    "Historical and legal analysis of doctrine of discovery and how it
    facilitated the loss of indigenous lives, land, game and valuable
    natural resources"-- Provided by publisher.
Identifiers: LCCN 2021039696 | ISBN 9781632933584 (paperback) | ISBN
    9781611396379 (epub)
Subjects: LCSH: Conquest, Right of--History. | Conquest, Right of--Moral
    and ethical aspects. | Indians of North America--Land tenure--Law and
    legislation--History. | Indians of North America--Legal status, laws,
    etc. | Indians of North America--Government relations. | Imperialism. |
    Sovereignty.
Classification: LCC KZ3673.3 .H37 2021 | DDC 341.42--dc23
LC record available at https://lccn.loc.gov/2021039696

---

**WWW.SUNSTONEPRESS.COM**
SUNSTONE PRESS / POST OFFICE BOX 2321 / SANTA FE, NM 87504-2321 /USA
(505) 988-4418

# DEDICATION

To my beloved family for all their support:

Dag, DJ, Malin, Aaron, Marianne, Hadlie, Callan, Sander, Kennedie and Cooper

When I was a child, Daddy told me the Earth was red from the Blood of our People who fought for their land. I told my children the same story so they can tell their children the same story and it will never be forgotten.

# CONTENTS

# PREFACE

I am starting with this poem my son, Aaron, wrote for me, because it references a time before we referred to the 'New World' and North and South America in the Western Hemisphere and Indian peoples. Even though I would prefer to use other terminology I will, nonetheless, use these popular references. Please excuse the lengthy quotes in this article but I wanted our children to read the truth and not have it paraphrased. I hope this material can serve as a research and study guide.

## Canyon de Chelly, Navajo Nation

*I could hear the echoes of my running feet ricocheting off the canyon walls. A cold spring morning chilling my skin and making my nose run. Stillness like no other calm I've ever experienced. I wanted to live here a thousand years ago. I wanted to live here before anyone knew what Indian land meant. So I took a piece of the Earth and I carried it about on my travels. A piece of holy red Earth. A tangible reminder of where I came from and where I could always go. A sense of calm that no one can ever take away: a sense of belonging to the people.*

# 1

# DOCTRINE OF DISCOVERY

United States Supreme Court Chief Justice John Marshall, based on his analysis of custom, broadly proclaimed the "doctrine of discovery" as the supreme law of the land in 1823 in *Johnson v. M'Intosh*, 21 U.S. 543 (1823) (hereinafter "*Johnson*"). The doctrine of discovery incorporated the axiom that whichever European nation first 'discovered' land, then not ruled by a Christian prince or people, could claim ownership of the land as against other European nations, even if it was inhabited. The discovering Christian country acquired the 'fee simple absolute' title to the land, which is a term meaning the unlimited ownership interest in the land. As the fee simple absolute title is an estate of total ownership of land, two parties cannot claim it as to a parcel of land. One party would own the fee simple absolute unlimited estate and the other party would have a lesser interest—such as a right to lease or occupy.

The second component concerned the method which would be used to address the presence of inhabitants. The discovering country had to be given land by the Indians, purchase it or conquer them to acquire it. As to purchasing the inhabitants' interest in their land, the 'discovering country' secured the right of preemption over any land it discovered, occupied by non-Christians—the exclusive first right of refusal if they should choose to sell their right to the land, what Chief Justice Marshall construed as a right of 'occupancy'. If the inhabitants did not want to sell their 'occupancy' interest and the discovering country still wanted the land, it would have to be taken by force.

The third component of Chief Justice Marshall's unanimous decision in *Johnson* was a new 'term of art,' a 'legal fiction,' a definition of 'conquest.' A legal fiction is a fact assumed or created by courts, which is then used in order to help reach a decision or to apply a legal rule. Since conquest earned a conquering country dominion over land, 'discovery' was equated with conquest, even though no actual warfare occurred. Conquest could either be the generally understood term of the subjugation and assumption of control of a people by the use of military force or under this new legal fiction, by being the first 'discoverer.' An example of the use of military force would be the conquest of the Aztecs by Hernan Cortés and indigenous allies. An example of the legal fiction would be a colony where land was acquired from a tribe that was not conquered, such as by illegal squatting. Walter Echo Hawk, renowned federal Indian law expert, argues that 'discovery' cannot logically be equated with conquest.[1]

The ruling in *Johnson* is still the law today. Unless a treaty granted an Indian Nation its land in fee simple, which a few did, the Indians were only granted the right to occupy certain land, with the underlying fee simple absolute estate in the federal government. Thus, most Indian Nations only have the right to occupy their land, without the ability to sell, lease or develop the land or natural resources, without approval by the federal government.

This decision is critical to understanding the rights of Indians today. It eliminated their ownership of their land. Ownership is a key facet in developing and improving land. If one is only a 'tenant,' there is no incentive to invest in the land. Also, there is a grave anxiety and uncertainty created amongst tenants, as to if and when, their tenancy might be extinguished, with or without compensation or credit for any improvements.

This 'Indian land title of occupancy' facilitated the dispossession of Indian lands by European colonizing countries. It approved the use of conquest to expropriate Indian lands. It also reduced the sovereign rights of Indian Nations. They could not sell or alienate their land to anyone other than the purported 'discovering' country. Their inherent sovereign right to the supreme, absolute ability to govern themselves and their land was diminished—they lost the political right to deal commercially and diplomatically in the international arena with any country other than their 'discoverer,' and the right to the absolute ownership of their lands, along with the right to dispose of them as they decided.

## The Case Was Fraudulent

*Johnson* resulted from a feigned land dispute. It was an alleged land dispute between Thomas Johnson, a shareholder of the Illinois and Wabash Land Companies (hereinafter "United Land Company") and William M'Intosh, both allegedly claiming the same land, one under a purchase from the Indian Nations that owned it and the other from the federal government to whom the Indian Nations had ceded the land. The Illinois Land Company purchased land in 1773 from the Kaskaskia, Peoria and Cahokia Indian Nations. The Wabash Land Company purchased land in 1775 from the Piankashaw Indian Nation. The two companies thereafter merged, with a land base of 43,000 square miles, the size of New Jersey. The United States entered into questionable treaties with these Indian Nations to secure land cessions. M'Intosh, on April 24, 1815, acquired 12,000 acres of the ceded land from the federal government in a suspect transaction.

In 1991, University of Oklahoma Law Professor Lindsay G. Robertson found fifty years of corporate records of the United Land Company documenting the collusive effort to confirm title to the purchased Indian lands through the *Johnson* case. He published his findings in 2005 in *Conquest by Law, How the Discovery of America Dispossessed Indigenous Peoples of Their Lands*. These records are now in the University of Oklahoma's Law Digital Collection.[2] He summarizes his research as follows:

> This ... is a story of how a spurious claim gave rise to a doctrine—intended to be of limited application--**that itself gave rise to a massive displacement of persons and the creation of a law that governs indigenous people and their lands to this day**.[3] (Emphasis added.)

Under Article III of the U.S. Constitution, the Supreme Court may only hear actual cases or controversies. It does not render advisory opinions. Article III describes the type of cases that may be heard and limits its authority to certain cases. For example, the Supreme Court cannot adjudicate cases involving a political question which is in the domain of either the President or Congress. Also, it may only adjudicate claims where (1) the plaintiff has actually and personally suffered injury or harm in fact, (2) the injury or harm suffered by the plaintiff is fairly traceable to the defendant's actions and (3) the injury or harm would be capable of redress by the court.

Even though Johnson and M'Intosh stipulated their land claims overlapped, Eric Kades, Thomas Jefferson Professor of Law, William & Mary Law School (hereinafter "Professor Kades"), determined that there was no overlapping land dispute. His research found that the United Land Company's acreage was at least fifty miles from the closest M'Intosh holding.[4] There was no conflicting land claim to present to the U.S. Supreme Court. There was no actual case or controversy.

## Background of *Johnson* Case (1823)

In 1773 and 1775, in violation of the British Proclamation of 1763 prohibiting private Indian land purchases beyond the Appalachian Mountains, the Illinois and the Wabash Land Companies separately purchased land from Indians beyond the Appalachian Mountains. To circumvent the Proclamation of 1763, William Murray, Illinois Land Company's agent, used a forged opinion ostensibly written by Charles Pratt, the 1st Earl of Camden, the Attorney General for England and Wales, and Chancellor Charles Yorke, the Solicitor General for England and Wales. It appeared to allow the direct purchase of land from the Indian Nations. British Captain Lord, commander at Kaskaskia ... was not overawed by the weighty names and informed Murray that he "should not suffer him to settle any of the lands as it was expressly contrary to his Majestys Orders."[5] Nonetheless, Murray completed the purchase. Louis Viviat, as agent for Wabash Land Company, similarly purchased Indian land.

British officials after being informed of these purchases refused to recognize their legality. "...British officials aimed to prevent the speculators from establishing any settlement in consequence of 'those pretended Titles' and to authorize the local commander in the Illinois country to declare the 'King's disallowance of such unwarrantable proceedings.'" They instructed the commander at Kaskaskia "to delete from the public notary's register any of the proceedings relating to purchases already made and to declare publicly that they were invalid."[6]

It is important to note that the shareholders in the United Land Company were prominent businessmen and politicians: five of them had signed the Declaration of Independence, five had signed the U.S. Constitution, three were U.S. Supreme Court justices, two were governors, and Benjamin Franklin was a secret member.

## Original 1757 Opinion of Camden and Yorke Pertaining to British Colony of India

The original 1757 Opinion of Camden and Yorke pertained to the British Colony of India. A petition from the East India Company raised the question of title to land that the Company had conquered in Bengal, and evoked an opinion from Attorney General Pratt, later Lord Camden, and Solicitor General Yorke. The lawyers distinguished between two types of territory, that acquired by conquest, in which the crown had both sovereignty and title to the land, and that acquired by peaceful cession, in which the crown was sovereign but did not have proprietary rights. The critical sentence that applied to the second kind was as follows: "In respect to such places as have been, or shall be acquired by treaty, or grant from the Mogul, or any of the Indian Princes, or governments, Your Majesty's letters patent are not necessary, the property of the soil vesting in the Company by the Indian grants..."[7] Thus, in Bengal, for land acquired by peaceful cession, British citizens could make purchases directly from the Indian Moguls, Princes or governments.

## George Washington's 1773 Diary—Forged Version of Camden-Yorke Opinion

The forged version purportedly allowing the direct purchase of Indian lands by private parties is inscribed in George Washington's handwriting in the flyleaf of his 1773 Diary indicating his knowledge of the opinion, though not necessarily the forgery. The forgery deleted certain words to appear that it addressed Indian land in the colonies. The words "the Mogul" were deleted, though the forgery retained the phrase, "the Indian Princes or governments", turned "vesting in the Company" into "vesting in the Grantee," and omitted "as English settlements." Thus, in America, the forged opinion purported to make it lawful for British citizens to make purchases directly from the Indian Nations where the cession was peaceful, not resulting from conquest.

"The following is the forged opinion of the late Lord Chanceller Cambden, and Chanceller York, on Titles derivd by the Kings Subjects from the Indians or Natives.

"In respect to such places as have been, or shall be acquired by Treaty or Grant from any of the Indian Princes, or Governments, your Majestys Letters Patents are not necessary, the Property of the Soil, vesting in the Grantee by the Indian Grants, Subject only to your Majestys Right of Sovereignty over the Settlements, and over the Inhabitants as English Subjects who carry with them, your Majestys Laws wherever they form Colonies, and receive your Majestys Protection, by Virtue of your Royal Chartres."[8]

## Benjamin Franklin's Letter to His Son, William, July 14, 1773, regarding Forged Opinion

Benjamin Franklin also referenced the forged opinion as valid in regard to the purchase of Indian lands in America in a letter to his son, William.

The Opinion of Pratt and Yorke when Attorney and Sollicitor General is undoubtedly a good One, so far as it allows the Indian Power of Grant in their own Lands. It has been lately printed here at large in Bolts' Book on Indian Affairs. There are some small variations in your Extract. I gave the same Opinion to Mr. Wharton when he arrived here with respect to the Retribution Grant, and advised his not applying for a Confirmation, which thought not only unnecessary, but what would be attended with infinite Delay and Difficulty thro' the Chicane of Office.[9]

William Bolts' 'Book on Indian Affairs' noted by Franklin was on India—it attacked the system of English government in Bengal and did not contain the Opinion of Pratt and Yorke.[10]

This black market in Indian land was also supported by an informal culture that thought the British Proclamation of 1763, which prohibited the private purchase of Indian lands west of the Appalachian Mountains, exceeded the power of the British government. As stated by Walter Echo

Hawk, "The market was trading in the prospect of owning Indian land once the government displaced the Indians."[11] Certainly, one can see the incentive for removal of the Indian Nations.

The Indians owned their land and had the right to decide whom to sell it to, Franklin and others argued. The British government, with no claim to any property rights in the land, had no power to forbid its sale. The land speculators' dissatisfaction with the Proclamation was one of the first of many similar grievances that would lead to the American Revolution.

## United Land Company Petitions Various Government Bodies for Approval of Its Purchase of Indian Lands

The United Land Company petitioned British officials (offering John Murray, 4th Earl of Dunmore, known as Lord Dunmore, the opportunity to participate in subsequent transactions), the Continental Congress, the U.S. Congress, the State of Virginia and various land commissions for approval of the Indian land purchases, which was not granted. The reason the United Land Company sought Virginia's approval was that Virginia claimed jurisdiction over the land purchased by virtue of its sea-to-sea colonial charter. Lord Dunmore did write a letter to Lord Dartmouth speaking favorably of the United Land Company. Supreme Court Associate Justice James Wilson, the largest single investor in the United Land Company, with an interest totaling over 1,000,000 acres, drafted at least five of the memorials (i.e., petitions) to Congress and others seeking approval of the Indian land purchases. Wilson's substantial investments included banks, manufacturers, insurance companies and maritime ventures.[12]

## United Land Company Petitions Continental Congress

The United Land Company then petitioned the Continental Congress. They did not receive a favorable welcome. David Howell of Rhode Island, voicing the popular opinion, stated that land claims formed "the most complicated and embarrassing Subject .... Infinite pains are taken by a certain sett of men vulgarly called Land robbers [jobbers], or Land-Sharks to have it in their power to engross the best lands."[13]

## United Land Company's Congressional Memorials (Petitions)

The United Land Company was willing to seek approval from any of the array of possible governmental forums. So they then petitioned the newly established U.S. Congress. On November 3, 1781, the five-member congressional committee to which United Land Company's Memorial was referred issued its negative report. Among other things, the report refused the United Land Company's prayer to recognize its titles on certain grounds: (i) the purchases were made without a license, treaty or other proper act of notoriety; (ii) one of the company deeds contained only descriptions of territorial lines and did not touch on any tangible property; (iii) no notice of the purchases was given to the United States Agent for Indian Affairs at Fort Pitt; and (iv) the Six Nations also claimed the same lands in question.

On June 27, 1788, Congress, again reporting on the Memorial, came to a more favorable decision:

> ...considering all the Circumstances attending the purchases in question, in Case the same upon full investigation shall Appear to have been fairly conducted, and that on Account thereof the United States will be ultimately benefited by an exemption from the expence of purchasing the same Lands, your Committee are of the Opinion a reasonable Compensation in Land should be made to the said Companies.[14]

On July 1, 1788, Congress decided to postpone a vote on the report and its recommendations. As a result, no action was ever taken on the report.

## United Land Company Decides to Try U.S. Supreme Court

Even though the United Land Company was unsuccessful in its petitions, it thought it could win a case that the purchases from Indians were valid before the U.S. Supreme Court—if it controlled the case. Fifty years after the dispute arose, it filed its case. It wasn't until 1991 that it became known how they colluded to bring the case to the U.S. Supreme Court.

## Behind Scenes of *Johnson*

The United Land Company retained attorney and land speculator,

Robert Goodloe Harper, the son-in-law of one of the investors, to bring its ostensible federal case. Harper had successfully represented the defendant in *Fletcher v. Peck*, 10 U.S. 142 (1810), a feigned U.S. Supreme Court case regarding the Yazoo land fraud scheme in Georgia.

So Harper proceeded with fabricating the case for the United Land Company, based on a frontier claim, so that a decision at district court could be appealed directly to the U.S. Supreme Court, without an intermediary judicial appellate review requirement. Harper asked Judge Benjamin Parke of Indiana, the former legal counsel for the United Land Company, to hear the case. He refused due to his conflict of interest. Undeterred, Harper pressed on. Federal Judge, Nathaniel Pope, who had family ties to Johnson (Judge Pope's brother, John, was married to a niece of Johnson), agreed to hear the case.

For a plaintiff, Harper chose Thomas Johnson, an initial Wabash Land Company shareholder. Johnson was politically connected—a friend of George Washington who had appointed him to serve on the U.S. Supreme Court. Johnson's niece was married to the Secretary of State. For a defendant, Harper chose William M'Intosh who had a land warrant from the U.S. government, a conveyance of 'public lands' to a citizen, allegedly of the same land owned by Johnson pursuant to a purchase directly from the Indian owners. M'Intosh reportedly had a vendetta against Governor William Henry Harrison, of the Indiana Territory, and was willing to go along. Governor Harrison had sued M'Intosh for slander for publicly questioning the fairness of the future President's dealings with the Indians and won a judgment of $4,000. Governor Harrison described M'Intosh as "an arrant knave, a profligate villain, a dastardly cheat, a perfidious rascal, an impertinent puppy, an absolute liar and a mean cowardly person."[15]

The United Land Company planned and funded the entire court proceeding for the prosecution and the defense. A United Land Company corporate document evidences this expenditure.[16] The parties entered into an agreed Statement of Facts and Decision which limited the question before the Court to the validity of the English Proclamation of 1763 prohibition against private purchases of Indian lands from Indians beyond the Appalachian Mountains. Their claim was that it was not valid under British law as it was issued by King George III, not the

British Parliament. They argued a Royal Proclamation alone could not bind Indian Nations or British citizens. The parties stipulated to all other issues leaving this one question for the Court to resolve. **Answering this question alone would and should have settled this case**.

It was agreed that M'Intosh would win at the district court level. It was thought this would make the U.S. Supreme Court more sympathetic to Johnson. M'Intosh further waived his right to force the plaintiffs to post an appeal bond after they lost before the federal district court in Illinois and consented to the writ of error the plaintiffs filed in the Supreme Court in 1822.

What the United Land Company did not factor in was that the Chief Justice of the U.S. Supreme Court would be John Marshall, whose 240 square miles of family-owned land was purchased under state law, not directly from Indians. Even though the case afforded Chief Justice Marshall the opportunity to bolster the legitimacy of his family's land claims, along with those of many of his prominent colleagues, resulting in an undeniable conflict of interest in the outcome of the case, Chief Justice Marshall did not recuse himself from hearing the case. He had recused himself in previous cases in which he had an interest. Justice James Wilson also had a vested interest in the case and similarly failed to recuse himself. As President of the United Company in 1780, he was the largest single investor with an interest totaling over 1,000,000 acres.

Chief Justice Marshall's alleged particular interest in the case, that federal and state military veterans receive the land under the state land set-asides for bounty land for veterans in return for their military service in the Revolutionary War and/or Indian Wars, is questionable. Many of the veterans' land set asides were located within Indian Nations because the states fully expected the federal government to negotiate with the Indians to buy these lands. Most veterans, however, lacked the financial resources necessary to wait out the uncertainty, along with paying for surveying and moving to the unsettled land. It was legal for veterans to sell or exchange their military warrants which occurred frequently, resulting in only a few soldiers actually receiving title to bounty land. Prominent land speculators, including George Washington and Chief Justice Marshall, purchased these military warrants, for cents on the dollar, from veterans who lacked the financial resources to take advantage of them. For example, in Ohio, the 1,035,408 acres set aside within the Virginia Military District for veterans who served in the American Revolution or the Virginia Militia were patented to just 25 persons.[17] The 1,043,460 acres set aside within the U.S. Military District in Ohio for veterans who served in the Continental Army were patented to just 22 persons.

## Thomas Marshall's Land Speculation—Kentucky Surveyor (Daniel Boone Surveyor with Thomas Marshall)

In 1780, Thomas Marshall (U.S. Supreme Court Chief Justice John Marshall's father) purchased land in the Kentucky territory. He was a Licensed Kentucky Surveyor and worked with Daniel Boone, a Deputy Surveyor. Marshall's surveying services were in great demand due to the continual interest in acquiring land. Title could not be established without a survey.

### John Marshall

John Marshall sought opportunity closer to home. Born in western Virginia, he had strong family ties to Kentucky. "Marshall had a large personal and professional interest in Kentucky land," biographer Francis N. Stites wrote:

> A boom had followed passage of the Virginia land law of 1779, which offered some warrants to veterans upon proof of military service and allowed the purchase of others with depreciated paper currency. The establishment of title to the land required a complicated series of steps involving the location and survey of a tract and the filing of papers with the Virginia land office at Richmond. Conflicting claims abounded.[18]

Marshall was in a good position to help his father. R. Kent Newmyer wrote of the Virginia lawyer: "As a resident of Richmond, he was near the land office, where he could purchase treasury warrants for Kentucky land and continue to buy up military warrants. Marshall then sent the warrants to his father, who could locate them on specific tracts of good land, enter the title, and arrange for a survey, which by Virginia law was necessary for completion of title. ... Also, as a lawyer for officers, many of whom were his former comrades-in-arms, he was in a position to deal in land warrants, which very quickly become items of speculation during the postwar land boom. Marshall was well placed to garner a sizeable piece of the action; to buy at a discount and sell at a profit, or to sell a part to pay for the rest."[19]

Marshall also began to speculate on his own once he got out of the army. As an officer in the Continental line, he was entitled to an allotment of 4,000 acres. The title to his land claims in Virginia originated in the English crown. His brother-in-law, George Keith Taylor, was also involved in land speculation.

## Case Will Be Used to Set Precedent on Validity of Title as between Private Purchases of Indian Land and Purchases from Federal Government

It had taken fifty years for the persistent United Land Company to get its case to the Supreme Court. There was substantial interest in this case given the many land speculators who held titles from varying parties. The United Land Company could not have foreseen that Chief Justice Marshall would decide to expand this case to rule on pre and post-Revolutionary War British Crown/Federal and Indian land titles across the United States once and for all. There were no ndians as parties to the case nor anyone to represent their interests. Curiously, William Wirt, U.S. Attorney General in the Monroe and Adams presidential administrations and an Indian law advocate, was not asked by the U.S. to participate. It is uncertain why he did not participate. **This was probably a relief to the United Land Company and a letter referencing that he would not be participating in the case is in its correspondence.**[20]

In choosing to go beyond what was necessary to decide the case, Chief Justice Marshall stated that he knew he was going afield and why: "After bestowing on this subject a degree of attention which was more required by the magnitude of the interest in litigation...."[21]

## Three Cabinet Officials Knew Case Was 'Collusive'

Three of President Jefferson's Cabinet officials knew the case was 'collusive'—Attorney General Wirt, Secretary of State John Quincy Adams and Treasury Secretary William Crawford.[22] With three such high-ranking officials' knowledge of the fraud being propagated, most likely others were aware also. The United Land Company's correspondence evidences the knowledge of the officials of the collusiveness. They are specifically named in reference to the case and the word 'collusive' is underlined. Adams and Crawford were presidential contenders.

## Doctrine of Discovery Dogmatically Adopted by Chief Justice Marshall into Federal Law

Without citing any statutes or legal cases or other authority for his decision, Chief Justice Marshall's decision held that, under the European 'doctrine of discovery,' the land discovered in the 'New World' belonged to the 'discovering' sovereign, so long as there were no Christian sovereign or Christian inhabitants. The thirteen states, having defeated Great Britain in the American Revolution, succeeded to its title which was based on the doctrine of discovery.

The doctrine of discovery promulgated for the United States by Chief Justice Marshall was as follows:

> They (Indians) were admitted to be the rightful occupants of the soil, with a legal as well as just claim to retain possession of it, and to use it according to their own discretion; but their rights to complete sovereignty as independent nations were necessarily diminished, and their power to dispose of the soil at their own will to whomsoever they pleased was denied by the original fundamental principle that discovery gave exclusive title to those who made it.[23]

## Doctrine of Discovery Contested by Many

There were many who disagreed with Chief Justice Marshall's pronouncement of the 'Doctrine of Discovery.' In 1775, future President

John Adams unequivocally contested the 'doctrine of discovery,' stating that neither common law nor natural law supported it. His description of the impertinent and fantastical assumption of such authority as *delusionary* is unforgettable.

To the Inhabitants of the Colony of Massachusetts-Bay, 13 March 1775

> Discovery, if that was incontestible could give no title to the English king, by common law, or by the law of nature, to the lands, tenements and hereditaments of the native Indians here. Our ancestors were sensible of this, and therefore honestly purchased their lands of the natives. They might have bought them to hold allodially, if they would ... there was *no rule of the common law, that made the discovery of a country by a subject, a title to that country in the prince*. ... But there was another mist cast before the eyes of the English nation from another source. The pope claimed a sovereign propriety in, as well as authority over the whole earth. As head of the Christian church, and vicar of God, he claimed this authority over all Christendom; and in the same character he claimed a right to all the countries and possessions of heathens and infidels: a right divine to exterminate and destroy them at his discretion, in order to propagate the catholic faith. When king Henry the eighth, and his parliament, threw off the authority of the pope, stripped his holiness of his supremacy, and invested it in himself by an act of parliament, he and his courtiers seemed to think that all the right of the holy see, were transferred to him: and it was a union of these two the most impertinent and fantastical ideas that ever got into an human pericranium, viz. that as feudal sovereign and supream head of the church together, a king of England had a right to all the land their subjects could find, not possessed by any Christian state or prince, tho' possessed by heathen or infidel nations, which seems to have *deluded the nation* about the time of the settlement of the colonies.[29] (Emphasis added.)

In 1795, Representative Theodore Sedgwick spoke vehemently to his colleagues that this 'discovery doctrine' would result in a plunder of Indian lands:

"Two hundred years ago, he said, at the discovery of this country, when cupidity gave a right to possession, and all the cruelties of Spain were exercised upon the innocent inhabitants, which his mind shuddered to think of, this doctrine might have been held." But Sedgwick could not believe that "at the close of the eighteenth century, and in this place, doctrines of this kind would have been held. Were they to say to the savages in their own country, you have no right to any land? This, he said, *would be a principle of plunder which could never find advocates within those walls [Congress), hostile to, and destructive of, all security in property*."[30] (Emphasis added.)

In a letter from John Adams to William Tudor, Sr., dated September 23, 1818, Mr. Adams addressed the lack of confidence colonists had in the colony's Charter to convey Indian land based on the 'doctrine of discovery,' relying instead on purchasing Indian land.

> If, in our Search of Principles *We have not been able to investigate any moral phylosophical or rational foundation for any Claim of Dominion or Property in America, in the English Nation, their Parliament or even of their King*; if the whole appears a mere Usurpation of Fution Fancy and Superstition: What was the Right to dominion or Property in the native Indians?... These Reflections appear to have occurred to Our Ancestors and their general Conduct was regulated by them. *They do not Seem to have had any Confidence in their Charter, as conveying any Right, except against the King who Signed it. They considered the Right to be in the Native Indians. Our Ancestors ... considered the Indians as having Rights: and they entered into Negotiations with them, purchased and paid for their Rights and Claims whatever they were, and procured Deeds, Grants and Quit-claims of all their Lands.*[31] (Emphasis added.)

Of incredibly major significance is James Madison's reply to William Wirt, U.S. Attorney General for twelve years under Presidents James Monroe and John Quincy Adams, following his speech at Rutgers University on October 2, 1830:

> *I cannot but regret some of the Argumentative appeals which have been made to the minds of the Indians. What, they may say, have we to do with the Federal Constitution or the relations formed by it between the Union and its members. We were no*

*parties to the compact, and cannot be affected by it. And as to a charter of the King of England, is it not as much a Mockery to them, as the Bull of a pope dividing the world of discovery between the Spaniar[ds] and the Portuguese, was held to be by the nations who disowned and disdained his authority.* The plea, with the best aspect, for dispossessing Indians of the lands on which they have lived, is, that by not incorporating their Labour, and associating fixed improvements with the Soil, they have not appropriated it to themselves, nor made the destined use of its capacity for increasing the number, of the enjoyments of the human race. But this plea whatever original force be allowed to it, is here repelled by the fact, that the Indians are making the very use of that capacity which the plea requires, enforced by the other fact, that the claimants themselves, by their councils, their exhortations and their effective aids, have promoted that happy change in the condition of the Indians, which is now turned agains[t] them.[32] (Emphasis added.)

Further confirming his opposition to the 'doctrine of discovery,' Mr. Wirt, in a letter to James Madison, on October 5, 1830, stated it was an 'exquisite absurdity:"

The argument against the title of the Indians to their lands, compared with the argument in favor of our title to them, presents a most exquisite absurdity. It is said that they have no other title to those lands than having chased their game over them, or seen them from the tops of the distant mountains. And yet we contend that an English, Spanish– or french ship having sailed along the coast, or entered the mouth of a river, gives a complete title by discovery to the sovereign of the sailor, not only to the coast seen, but to the unseen interior up to the unknown heads of the rivers and even across to the Pacific![33]

In Congressional debates in 1830 regarding Indian removal which also addressed the 'doctrine of discovery,' there were senators and representatives who disagreed with the opinion expressed in *Johnson*. Mr. Jeremiah Evarts, from New York and affiliated with the American Board of Commissioners of Foreign Missions, challenged the doctrine of discovery as absurd and unsound. While King George II had granted the charter to James Oglethorpe for Georgia in 1733, Mr. Evarts questioned,

> But how could even a king grant "vast tracts of country, which neither he, nor any European, had ever seen"? Did a royal grant confer the right to dispossess the original inhabitants of a territory from their soil? The answer was unequivocally no. "But who will dare," Evarts asked, "to advocate the monstrous doctrine, that the people of a whole continent may be destroyed, for the benefit of a people of another continent?"[34]

Senator Theodore Frelinghuysen disputed the position that Indians did not own the land:

> It is a subject full of grateful satisfaction, Mr. President, that, in our public intercourse with the Indians, ever since the first colonies of white men found an abode on these western shores, we have distinctly recognised their title; treated with them as the owners, and in all our acquisitions of territory applied ourselves to these ancient proprietors, by purchase and cession alone, to obtain the right of soil. Sir, I challenge the record of any other or different pretension. *When or where did the assembly or convention meet which proclaimed, or even suggested to these tribes, that the right of discovery contained a superior efficacy over all prior titles. And our recognition was not confined to the soil merely. We regarded them as nations*—far behind us indeed in civilization, but still we respected their forms of government—we conformed our conduct to their notions of civil policy.[35] (Emphasis added.)

Ominously, Representative William Ellsworth (Conn.) countenanced what the specter of this rule of law, the 'doctrine of discovery,' could result in:

> What, sir, is this right of discovery? This right is often spoken of by those who are adverse to the claims of the Indians. Among the nations of Europe, it seems to be a principle of the law of nations, that, if the subjects of any king discover and enter upon new and unknown lands, they become a part of the dominions of that king. There is much that is arbitrary and fanciful about this right. But, be it reasonable or unreasonable, it is a mere political arrangement among nations, established to regulate their own conduct among

themselves, and has nothing to do with the prior possessors of the land.... If, because we are enlightened and civilized, by discovering this country we have acquired a right to drive off the Indians, or wrest from them their government, (which I consider the same thing,) then we may, if it becomes necessary, in order to secure our further advancement in knowledge and virtue, drive them into the western ocean, or even put them to death.[36]

The Hon. William W. Ellsworth, Representative from Connecticut stated:

As a nation, too, from the first, this government has admitted their independent existence, and their full right to the soil. Had it not been the established principle of this Government to recognise the Indian title?... We are estopped. We are convicted by our own conduct from the very beginning.[37]

As late as 1846, Abraham Alfonse Albert Gallatin, U.S. Minister to Great Britain, and Richard Rush, U.S. Attorney General, argued for the United States 'discovery' claim of the Oregon Territory in 1846 in its competition with Great Britain. The importance of their analysis regarding the doctrine of discovery cannot be overstated due to the possibility of war between England and France over competing 'discovery' claims to the Oregon Territory, which encompassed the present states of Oregon, Washington, Idaho, and parts of Montana and Wyoming, along with British Columbia. Congress voted for going to war if necessary to secure this vast land based on the drainage system of the Columbia River.

*At the time when America was discovered, the law of nations was altogether unsettled*. More than a century elapsed before Grotius attempted to lay its foundation on natural law and the moral precepts of Christianity and, when sustaining it by precedents, he was compelled to recur to Rome and Greece. It was, in reality, a new case, to which no ancient precedents could apply, for which some new rules must be adopted. *Gradually, some general principles were admitted, never universally, in their nature vague, and often conflicting. For instance, discovery varies, from the simple ascertaining of the continuity of land, to a minute exploration of its various harbors, rivers, etc.; and the rights derived from it may vary accordingly, and may occasionally be claimed to the same district by different nations.*[38] (Emphasis added.)

As stated by Messrs. Huskisson and Addington, British Commissioners, in 1846, when disputing the United States 'discovery' claim to the Oregon Territory: *"Upon the question how far prior discovery constitutes a legal claim to sovereignty, the law of nations is somewhat vague and undefined."*[39] (Emphasis added.)

## No Legal Precedent for Doctrine of Discovery

In *Johnson*, Chief Justice Marshall could not cite any legal precedent whatsoever in enunciating the doctrine of discovery for the United States as the supreme law of the land. There was none. As noted by future president John Adams in his March 13, 1775, presentation to the Inhabitants of the Massachusetts Bay Colony:

> Colonization is Casus omissus at common law. There is no such title known in that law. (1.A case omitted; a situation not provided for.)[40]

As Professor Cleveland observed:

> Chief Justice Marshall did not expressly cite any international law authorities. In fact, his opinion is nearly devoid of citation support. His invocation of the doctrine of discovery is also problematic from an international law perspective. As noted above, the discovery doctrine had fallen into disfavor, even among European powers, by the time Marshall wrote. The opinion appears motivated more out of a sense of necessity than an effort to accurately represent international law....[41]

Also as noted by Professor Berman:

At any rate, "the ambiguity of the Court's reasoning in *Johnson* on the nature of aboriginal rights was fundamental and extreme."[42]

As noted by Professor Kades, the basis for the holding in *Johnson* was custom. Phrases like 'understood by all,' 'exercised uniformly,' and 'universal recognition,' appeal to long-established practice, not to any specific constitutional, statutory, or common law rule.[43] Yet custom simply fails as a justification for his decision as there was no uniform exercise of the doctrine of discovery.

In *The Imperialism of John Marshall: A Study in Expediency*. George Bryan wrote about Justice Story's opinion of *Johnson*:

[M'Intosh] involved a flat question of right and wrong. It was a decision which seems to have altogether ignored property rights which had solemnly vested. ... We are then to inquire whether or not the conscience of the world will today respond affirmatively to the proposition that discovery and conquest alone give a title as against owners and occupants of property ... whether, in a word, that which is morally wrong can be legally and politically right.[44]

Chief Justice Marshall's arbitrary pronouncement of a 'great and broad rule' instead created a maelstrom of divergent opinions on what his opinion meant. This tension/ambiguity about Indian land title continues to allow for the misconstruction of the nature of the land rights of Indian Nations. The evolution of the definition of Indian title in cases after *Johnson* led to the conclusion that the aboriginal title amounted to no more than a defeasible right of occupancy which if divested by the United States might not even be compensable.

Nine years later in a subsequent case, *Worcester v. Georgia*, 31 U.S. 515 (1832), Chief Justice Marshall definitively recanted his prior promulgation of the 'discovery doctrine' and instead stated:

The extravagant and absurd idea that the feeble settlements made on the sea coast, or the companies under whom they were made, acquired legitimate power by them to govern the people, or occupy the lands from sea to sea did not enter the mind of any man.[45]

This recantation of the Doctrine of Discovery, by none other than Chief Justice Marshall himself, is the best evidence of its falsity.

## Chief Justice Marshall Trumps Government's Preemptive Right to Purchase Indian lands with Outright Ownership of Indian Lands by Virtue of 'Discovery'

Chief Justice Marshall formulated a new customary concept of Indian land title in *Johnson*. Indians had only a right of occupancy in land that they held at the will of the government, not a fee simple title that could be conveyed. Prior to Chief Justice Marshall's decision in *Johnson*, the government had possessed only an exclusive right of first refusal if the Indians decided to sell land. The Indians owned the land. The preemption right had not carried with it title to the land to which the right was claimed.

In an opinion dated September 12, 1791, Attorney General Edmund Randolph, advised President Washington regarding the preemptive right of the federal government to purchase Indian lands.

The constitution is the basis of federal power. This power, so far as the subject of Indians is concerned, relates:

    1. To the regulation of commerce with the Indian tribes.

    2. To the exclusive right of making treaties.

    3. To the right of preemption in lands.[46]

While serving as President Washington's Secretary of State, Jefferson confirmed his understanding of "our right in the Indian soil" in notes of his conversation with George Hammond in 1792: "[a] right of preemption of their lands; that is to say, the sole and exclusive right of purchasing from them whenever they should be willing to sell."[47]

Also, Chief Justice Marshall's pronouncement was a complete departure from President Washington's assurance to **over 1000 Indians and their leaders in 1793**, at negotiations between the Western Indian Confederacy and the appointed U.S. Commissioners, that they owned their lands, and the government would not confiscate them without compensation:

> We only claim ... the right to pre-emption, or the right of purchasing of the Indian Nations disposed to sell their lands, to the exclusion of all other White People whatever.[48]

Similarly, in an opinion from Secretary of State Jefferson to President George Washington in 1793 he wrote:

> I considered our right of pre-emption of the Indian lands, not as amounting to any dominion, or jurisdiction, or paramountship

whatever, but merely in the nature of a remainder after the extinguishment of a present right, which gave us no present right whatsoever, but of preventing other nations from taking possession, and so defeating our expectancy; that the Indians had the full, undivided and independent sovereignty as long as they choose to keep it, and that this might be forever.[49]

Chief Justice Marshall's determination that discovery inured to the discovering country the absolute dominion over the discovered land, the full ownership even if inhabited, grossly departed from the prior government's right of preemption only in Indian lands. His opinion was not universally shared.

## Chief Justice Marshall Falsely Asserted that All European Countries Adhered to 'Discovery' as Basis for Ownership of Indian Land in 'New World'

Significantly, in his 1803 biography of George Washington, Chief Justice Marshall falsely asserted that the powers of Europe estimated the right of the natives at nothing, referring to Spain, France, England, Holland and Sweden. While Spain and France may have accorded no regard to Indian rights, England, Holland and Sweden did. The facts directly contradict Chief Justice Marshall's allegation based on the incontrovertible evidence of colonial purchases from Indians and treaty negotiations for cessions. He also expressly details the controversies over discoveries between the competing nations confirming the lack of uniformity in understanding and conformity to the alleged postulates of the doctrine of discovery. While his opinion in *Johnson* states that one of the reasons for the various European nations adhering to the 'discovery doctrine' was "to avoid conflicting settlements, and consequent war," it is clear from his own analysis that this did not occur. England defeated Holland and Sweden's claims, but conflicting claims remained with France and Spain which resulted in a number of wars.

Specifically, Chief Justice Marshall stated:

In settling this continent, the powers of Europe, estimating the right of the natives at nothing, adopted, for their own government, the principle, that those who first discovered and took possession of any particular territory, became its rightful proprietors. But as only a small portion of it could then be reduced to actual occupation, the extent of country thus acquired was not well ascertained. Contests respecting prior discovery, and extent of possession, arose among all the first settlers. England terminated her controversy with Sweden and with Holland, by the early conquest of their territories; but her conflicting claims with France and with Spain, remained unadjusted.[50]

## Chief Justice Marshall's Categorization of Uniform Law of 'Discovery' Is Fraudulent

While Chief Justice Marshall posed the doctrine of discovery as universally accepted, this was categorically false. It varied arbitrarily and capriciously within a country and between countries over time.

Justice Joseph Story, a lawyer, jurist, and prolific writer of legal treatises, was one of the most renowned constitutional scholars in American history who served on the U.S. Supreme Court from 1811–45. He challenged Chief Justice Marshall's opinion in *Johnson* that the doctrine of discovery was universally accepted:

> The European nations found little difficulty in reconciling themselves to the adoption of any principle, which gave ample scope to their ambition, and employed little reasoning to support it....They were content to take counsel of their interests, their prejudices, and their passions, and felt no necessity of vindicating their conduct before cabinets, which were already eager to recognise its justice and its policy.[51]

Charles Royce, with the Bureau of Ethnology, complied an exhaustive and outstanding study of Indian land cessions from 1784-1894. He concluded that the United States' alleged position regarding the doctrine of discovery was not as formulaic as stated by Chief Justice Marshall in *Johnson*:

> In these statements the court, of course, speaks only from the legal point of view or theory, for it is well known that in their practical dealings with the natives the nations of Europe, and the United States also, often failed to carry out this theory.[52]

Indian land was accepted by gift, obtained by purchase, illegal squatting or conquest, not by a mere sighting of the land and concomitant claim of sovereignty and ownership.

The crux of Chief Justice Marshall's decision rested on his unfounded assertion that the 'custom' of the European countries in the 'New World' was to assert ownership of land by the sovereign based on its 'discovery.' This 'custom' must be explored to determine if it was universally recognized or exercised uniformly.

When actual practices are analyzed, it becomes obvious that customary behavior simply did not mirror the assumption that a sovereign owned 'discovered' land. The papal bulls or royal charters which were drafted in Europe before colonial settlement took place did not consider local conditions.

There are several reasons why a European power would acknowledge the Indian's ownership of their land and choose to purchase it, rather than relying on 'discovery' by the sovereign. First, the English, Dutch and Swedes did not want to be equated with the image of the Spanish conquistador or the Black Legend. The Spanish conquest of Indians, extermination by the millions and enslavement was considered base and barbaric, certainly not to be emulated. Second, purchasing land provided security and reduced the possibility of Indian conflict. Third, and more importantly, given European countries reliance on law and written documentation, a purchase documented by a deed served to prove ownership to another potential claimant. This became more important to the English after the Dutch and Swedes used documented purchases of Indian land to disavow English ownership of land wedged between New York and Massachusetts. By purchasing land and securing a fee simple title through a deed which could be recorded in the colony, it made it a simple matter for proving up a claim. Fourth, ownership by Indians made it possible to purchase incredibly vast tracts of land. "Possession" then did not have to coincide fully with "habitation." By purchasing land and securing a fee simple title through a deed, which was well-known under English law, a few land speculators could possess huge areas. Fifth, the speculators, by proving ownership, could profit by selling parcels of this land for a higher price. Sixth, as 'discovery' was honored in the breach by European countries, as evidenced by continual war between them over what constituted a legitimate claim, the potential for destructive war could be lessened by a written document as a proof of grant or purchase.

Chief Justice Marshall's opinion in regard to Indian land tenure lacked the nuances revealed in studying the different colonies. If the doctrine of discovery had been uniform and countries simply confiscated the Indians lands, as a matter of right, the variation in the methods used to acquire land would not be so prevalent.

### *Johnson* Illicitly Diminished Sovereignty of Indian Nations

In a vague argument, Chief Justice Marshall found that while 'discovery' did impair Indian rights, it was justified because 'discovery' vested a fee simple estate to their lands in the discovering sovereign. Thus, the Indians became tenants and lost their sovereign rights to own and control their land because of a questionable custom, not substantiated by any law.

In challenging the semantic change to the Indian Nation's land title, Senator Frelinghuysen pointed out the absurdity of such a proposition. *Indians had played no role in formulating the doctrine of discovery and, as such, there was no legal basis for applying it to them and in any way impairing their sovereignty.* He surmised the real reason for the change was greed.

> I am aware that some writers have, by a system of artificial reasoning, endeavored to justify, or rather, excuse the encroachments made upon Indian territory; and they denominate these abstractions the law of nations, and, in this ready way, the question is despatched. Sir, as we trace the sources of this law, we find its authority to depend either upon the conventions or common consent of nations. And when, permit me to inquire, were the Indian tribes ever consulted on the establishment of such a law? Whoever represented them or their interests in any Congress of nations, to confer upon the public rules of intercourse, and the proper foundations of dominion and property? The plain matter of fact is, that all these partial doctrines have resulted from

the selfish plans and pursuits of more enlightened nations; and it is not matter for any great wonder, that they should so largely partake of a mercenary and exclusive spirit towards the claims of the Indians.[53]

Similarly, Senator Peleg Sprague in his speech during the Senate debate on the Indian Removal Act declared that 'discovery' conferred no right against the native inhabitants such that their rights could not be affected, defeating the proposition that it could be used to diminish their sovereign rights. "Discovery, Sir, confers no claim or right against the natives—the persons discovered—but only as between discoverers."[54]

Yet, Chief Justice Marshall in *Johnson*, but not in his subsequent opinion on the same issue in *Worcester*, specifically applied the doctrine of discovery to the Indians, divesting them of their lands.

### If 'Discovery' Wasn't Adequate to Establish Dominion over Indian Lands, Chief Justice Marshall Added Conquest to Menu of Options

Chief Justice Marshall further explicitly stated in *Johnson* that the U.S. had derived their title by conquest. "Conquest gives a title which the Courts of the conqueror cannot deny..."[55] It is uncertain what conquest occurred. If he is referring to the American Revolution, President Washington explicitly refuted this in 1793.

Future president John Adams, in a message in 1775 to the Inhabitants of the Colony of Massachusetts-Bay. contested the argument that the 'New World' had been conquered.

> It is not a conquered, but a discovered country. It came not to the king by descent, but was explored by the settlers. It came not by marriage to the king, but was purchased by the settlers, of the savages. It was not granted by the king of his grace, but was dearly, very dearly earned by the planters, in the labour, blood, and treasure which they expended to subdue it to cultivation.[56]

Thomas Jefferson in his Notes questions the veracity of conquest:

> That the lands of this country were taken from them by conquest, is not so general a truth as is supposed. I find in our historians and

records, repeated proofs of purchase, which cover a considerable part of the lower country; and many more would doubtless be found on further search. The upper country we know has been acquired altogether by purchases made in the most unexceptionable form.[57]

Justice Story reiterated this point in his *Commentaries*:

§ 153. The Indians could in no just sense be deemed a conquered people, who had been stripped of their territorial possessions by superior force. They were considered as a people, not having any regular laws, or any organized government; but as mere wandering tribes. They were never reduced into actual obedience, as dependent communities; and no scheme of general legislation over them was ever attempted.[58]

Chancellor Kent also considered the concept of occupancy to have been derived from a 'pretension' melding 'discovery' into conquest.[59]

In an analysis of what constituted 'conquest,' Representative Smith in a Congressional speech at a later date maintained that the right of conquest was simply a false doctrine, "founded on a principle, maintained by arbitrary governments alone, that power gives right." If one glanced at his neighbor's field, Smith asked rhetorically, and saw that his fellow was not as skilled at cultivation, did one then possess the right to drive him from the premises and take the land for himself? The rhetoric of "proper usage" of the soil, Smith asserted, was a mere pretext for theft.[60]

Further Representative Ellsworth found the attributes of conquest lacking in the historical treatment of land cessions by Indians:

...the fact of a victorious conflict—taking possession as conquerors, instituting a government as such, and driving out the enemy or receiving him as a dependent subject. But none of all this, surely, is true of these southern tribes. All the wars between them and us have terminated in formal treaties, leaving them in possession of their territory, distinctly acknowledging their independent existence, and guarantying to them their possessions.[61]

Conquerors do not buy land or enter into land cession treaties from the conquered.

## Ignoring Indian Rights, Chief Justice Marshall Postulated that Doctrine of Discovery was Justifiable Measure to Avoid War between European Settler Colonial Countries

Chief Justice Marshall went on to explain another purpose of the doctrine of discovery. In order "to avoid conflicting settlements, and consequent war," European countries adopted the principle that "discovery gave title to the government by whose subjects, or by whose authority, it was made, against all other European governments, which title might be consummated by possession."[62] The 'discovery doctrine' dismally failed in this regard based on the numerous colonial wars between Spain, France and England in the first half of the nineteenth century based on competing claims in the 'New World,' even as to possessed territory. Chief Justice Marshall's allegation that it was customarily adhered to by the discovering European countries is belied by the facts which are incontrovertible.

France, England, Holland and Sweden refused to defer to Spain's 'discovery' of the 'New World' as affirmed by the papal donation, which Spain of course considered valid. Also, they rebuffed each other's factually known 'discoveries,' such as Spain's discovery of the mouth of the Mississippi River. Most importantly, if there was a uniformly respected 'discovery doctrine,' Queen Anne's War (1702–1713), King William's War (1689–97), the Seven Years War (aka French and Indian War), the War of 1812 and the Mexican American War fought over competing territorial claims, along with the many other Indian battles, massacres and wars, would never have occurred. Many lives were tragically lost as a result of the muddiness of the 'doctrine of discovery,' not its clarity. Unfortunately, Indians became entangled in many of these European conflicts and rivalries.

In *Johnson*, Chief Justice Marshall referred to the "magnificent purchase of Louisiana," as evidence of the derivative title acquired from France under the 'discovery doctrine.' He observed that it "was the purchase from France of a country almost entirely occupied by numerous tribes of Indians, who are in fact independent. Yet, any attempt of others to intrude into that country, would be considered an aggression which would justify war."[63] What Chief Justice Marshall failed to reveal was the dispute between Spain, France, England and the United States over the extent of the Louisiana Territory which would result in ongoing controversy and skirmishes, the War of 1812 and the Mexican American War. His decision made it appear that the 'discovered' Louisiana Territory boundaries were undisputed and crystal clear.

Also, the litigation between colonies and later states over lands covered under their colonial charters evidence the uncertainty of what lands were considered 'discovered.' The Connecticut-Pennsylvania Territorial Dispute over their conflicting charter claims and that of New Hampshire, Massachusetts and New York evidence this. Also, there was extensive litigation between colonist themselves over the lands they individually owned.[64]

In reality, the European countries concocted their own ideas of what 'discovery' meant and used them to justify their colonization of the 'New World.' The European states based their claims against each other on whatever theory was most appropriate to their interests.

## Chief Justice Marshall Relied on Ample Compensation to Indian Inhabitants of Civilization and Christianity Disdaining U.S Bill of Rights Separation of Church and State

For Chief Justice Marshall, dispossessing the Indians of their ownership in their lands was a boon to them as they received civilization and Christianity in return as adequate compensation:

> ...they made ample compensation to the inhabitants of the new, by bestowing on them civilization and Christianity...[65]

In his satirical rebuttal of *Johnson*, Justice Story presupposed this exchange more than sufficient consideration:

> They were bound to yield to the superior genius of Europe, and in exchanging their wild and debasing habits for civilization and Christianity they were deemed to gain more than an equivalent for every sacrifice and suffering.[66]

There were Indians that had converted to Christianity, but they were ignored in Chief Justice Marshall's analysis. Missionaries were active all along the east coast. Puritan missionary, John Eliot, believing that the Christian faith would grow through a Christian lifestyle, commissioned the building of planned settlements for his 'praying Indians.' By 1674, there were fourteen such settlements. While the numbers of conversions in Great Britain's colonies did not rival Mexico's, they were probably more realistic. In Mexico in 1543, the Catholic Church counted nine million indigenous converts.[67] The Twelve Franciscan friars who arrived in 1524 were each credited with over 1,000,000 conversions.

Nothing was said of the methods that would be used in converting Indians to Christianity that resisted, such as slaughtering their forces in one-sided warfare, eradicating their sovereignty, dispossessing their lands, destroying their villages, homes and possessions, enslavement and taking them into captivity.

The United States and states thus held title to Indian lands under *Johnson*, a case postulating that inculcating Christian religious dogma was a part of the compensation Indians received for their land. Even though the U.S. Constitution was predicated on separation of church and state and freedom of religion, Christianity, as a favored religion, was incorporated into Chief Justice Marshall's decision. While directed at Congress, the prohibition in the First Amendment applied to the judiciary as well: "Congress shall make no law respecting an establishment of religion, or prohibiting the free exercise thereof..."[68]

## Brutish Stereotype Employed by Chief Justice Marshall to Justify Indian Dispossession of Land

In attempting to justify a falsely premised opinion, Chief Justice Marshall countenanced this dispossession of Indian lands by 'discovery' by dehumanizing Indians. A brutish stereotype of Indians was thus written into the supreme law of the land by Chief Justice Marshall in the U.S. Supreme Court's first Indian law case: Indians were deemed to be inferior savages based on their character and religion.

> [The] character and religion of its inhabitants afforded an apology for considering them as a people over whom the superior genius of Europe might claim an ascendency.[69]

Supreme Court Justice Story detailed the alleged deficiencies among Indians which permitted European nations to claim an absolute dominion over the whole territories afterwards occupied by them, not in virtue of

39

any conquest of, or cession by, the Indian natives, but as a right acquired by 'discovery.'

> As infidels, heathens, and savages, they were not allowed to possess the prerogatives belonging to absolute, sovereign, and independent nations. The territory over which they wandered, and which they used for this temporary and fugitive purposes, was, in respect to Christians, deemed as if it were inhabited only by brute animals.[70]

> [T]he European nations paid not the slightest regard to the rights of the native tribes. They treated them as mere barbarians and heathens, whom, if they were not at liberty to extirpate, they were entitled to deem mere temporary occupants of the soil... The right of discovery, thus asserted, has become the settled foundation, on which the European nations rest their title to territory in America; and it is a right, which, under our governments, must now be deemed incontestable, however doubtful in its origin, or unsatisfactory in its principles... [The Indians] ... have been deemed to be the lawful occupants of the soil, and entitled to a temporary possession thereof, subject to the superior sovereignty of the particular European nation, which actually held the title of discovery.[71]

For many European states and their settler colonists, Indians went well beyond 'fallen men;' they were described as violent in nature, without any discipline or industry, uncivilized in their personal habits and a worshipper of the devil. It started early and is evidenced by this statement from a Plymouth Colony colonial settler upon their 'New World' arrival, when the indigenous inhabitants were confronted with the dilemma whether (i) to form an alliance with the Plymouth colonists, who might protect the Wampanoag Indians from a neighboring warring Indian Nation, the Narragansetts, or (2) try to put together a tribal coalition to drive out the colonists. According to William Bradford's account of his encounter with the Indians and their leader, Massasoit, "they got all the Powachs of the country, for three days together in a horrid and devilish manner, to curse and execrate them with their conjurations, which assembly and service they held in a dark and dismal swamp."[72] This dehumanization allowed for horrific acts to be committed against Indians.

## Chief Justice Marshall Denies U.S. Incorporation of Indians as Impossible based on His Epithet of Their Savagery

The usual practice of assimilating conquered people as citizens of the conquering government was not possible with 'fierce savages,' according to Chief Justice Marshall.

> But the tribes of Indians inhabiting this country were fierce savages, whose occupation was war, and whose subsistence was drawn chiefly from the forest. To leave them in possession of their country was to leave the country a wilderness; to govern them as a distinct people was impossible, because they were as brave and as high spirited as they were fierce, and were ready to repel by arms every attempt on their independence.[73]

His characterization of Indians does not correspond with the earlier statements of both Presidents Jefferson and Madison and other parties.

President Jefferson extolled the Indians advances in 'agriculture and household manufacture.' In his message of November 1808, he informed the Congress that:

> [W]ith our Indian neighbors the public peace has been steadily maintained; and generally from a conviction that we consider them as a part of ourselves, and cherish with sincerity their rights and interests... Husbandry and household manufacture are advancing among them--more rapidly with the Southern than the Northern tribes from circumstances of soil and climate.[74]

President Madison in his First Annual Message to Congress of November 1809, testifies to the gradual improvement of the Indians: 'With our Indian neighbors,' he remarks, 'the just and benevolent system continued toward them, has also preserved peace, and is more and more advancing habits favorable to their civilization and happiness.'[75]

## Chief Justice Marshall Refused to Consider Principles of Abstract Justice

In his opinion which cited no authorities, Chief Justice Marshall expressly refused to consider other principles:

> We will not enter into the controversy, whether agriculturists, merchants, and manufacturers, have a right, on abstract principles, to expel hunters from the territory they possess, or to contract their limits.[76]

This followed his earlier pronouncement that it would be necessary...

> ...in pursuing this inquiry, to examine, not simply those principles of abstract justice, which the Creator of all things has impressed on the mind of his creature man, and which are admitted to regulate, in a great degree, the rights of civilized nations, whose perfect independence is acknowledged; but those principles also which our own government has adopted...[77]

Chief Justice Marshall never made an inquiry into any principles of justice. According to Echo-Hawk, the fact that Chief Justice Marshall decided that the Supreme Court was unconstrained by justice or principles of abstract justice led to an ethically suspect outcome.[78]

## Censoring Chief Justice Marshall

Three months after the *Johnson* decision, Thomas Jefferson complained to Justice William Johnson regarding Chief Justice Marshall: "This practice of Judge Marshall, of travelling out of his case to prescribe what the law would be in a moot case not before the court, is very irregular and very censurable."[79] Without judicial rules regarding recusal due to conflicts of interest or basing a decision on the narrowest legal issue presented or anyone empowered to check the Chief Justice's behavior, he was free to range as arbitrarily and as dogmatically as he chose.

## Notes

1. Echo-Hawk, Walter. *In the Courts of the Conqueror: The 10 Worst Indian Law Cases Ever Decided*. Fulcrum Publishing, 2018: 79.

2. Robertson, Lindsay G. *Conquest by law: How the discovery of America dispossessed indigenous peoples of their lands*. Oxford University Press, 2005.

3. Ibid.

4. Kades, Eric. "The Dark Side of Efficiency: *Johnson v. M'Intosh* and the Expropriation of American Indian Lands." *University of Pennsylvania Law Review* 148.4 (2000): 1092.

5. Baule, Steven M. *Protecting the Empire's Frontier: Officers of the 18th (Royal Irish) Regiment of Foot during Its North American Service, 1767–1776*. Ohio University Press, 2014: 125.

6. Kades, Eric. "History and Interpretation of the Great Case of *Johnson v. M'Intosh*." *Law and History Review* 19.1 (2001): 83.

7. Sosin, Jack M. "The Yorke-Camden Opinion and American Land Speculators." *The Pennsylvania Magazine of History and Biography* 85.1 (1961): 38-49.

8. George Washington Papers, Series 1, Exercise Books, Diaries, and Surveys 1745-99, Subseries 1B, Diaries 1748-1799: Diary, January 1 - December 31, 1773.

9. "From Benjamin Franklin to William Franklin, 14 July 1773,"

*Founders Online,* National Archives, https://founders.archives.gov/
documents/Franklin/01-20-02-0165. [Original source: *The Papers of
Benjamin Franklin*, vol. 20, *January 1 through December 31, 1773*,
ed. William B. Willcox. New Haven and London: Yale University
Press, 1976, pp. 300–314.] (accessed online November 2, 2020).

10. Bolts, William. *Considerations on India Affairs: Particularly
Respecting the Present State of Bengal and Its Dependencies*. Vol. 3. J.
Almon and P. Elmsly, 1775.

11. Echo-Hawk, Walter. *In the Courts of the Conqueror: The 10 Worst
Indian Law Cases Ever Decided*. Fulcrum Publishing, 2018: 61.

12. Mikhail, John. "James Wilson, Early American Land Companies,
and the Original Meaning of Ex Post Facto Law." *Geo. JL & Pub.
Pol'y* 17 (2019): 79, 94.

13. David Howell to William Greene, April 29, 1785, Burnett, ed.,
*Letters of Continental Congress*, VIII, 106-107.

14. Carter, Clarence Edwin, and John Porter Bloom, eds. *The
territorial papers of the United States*. Vol. 1. US Government Printing
Office, 1934: 115-116.

15. Robertson, Lindsay G. *Conquest by law: How the discovery of
America dispossessed indigenous peoples of their lands*. Oxford
University Press, 2005: 52.

16. Letter from Brinton to Ingersoll, 02/26/1822. Illinois Wabash
Land Company. https://digital.libraries.ou.edu/IWLC/paper.
asp?pID=52&doc_type=Corr (accessed online November 14, 2020).

17. Knepper, George W. *The official Ohio lands book*. Auditor of State,
2002.

18. Cullen, Charles T., Francis N. Stites. "John Marshall: Defender of
the Constitution." (Library of American Biography.) Boston: Little,
Brown. 1981: 22.

19. Newmyer, R. Kent. *John Marshall and the Heroic Age of the
Supreme Court*. LSU Press, 2007: 37.

20. Letter from Ingersoll to Gratz et al, 02/11/1823.

https://digital.libraries.ou.edu/IWLC/paper.asp?pID=185&doc_type=Corr (accessed online November 14, 2020).

21. *Johnson v. M'Intosh*, 21 U.S. 543, 604 (1823).

22. Letter from Ingersoll to Gratz et al, 02/19/1823.

https://digital.libraries.ou.edu/IWLC/paper.asp?pID=186&doc_type=Corr (accessed online November 14, 2020).

23. *Johnson v. M'Intosh*, 21 U.S. 543, 574 (1823).

24. "To John Adams from Benjamin Lincoln, 11 September 1793," *Founders Online*, National Archives, https://founders.archives.gov/documents/Adams/99-02-02-1472. (accessed online November 28, 2020); Answer to Speech by the Commissioners (Aug. 16th, 1793), reprinted in AMERICAN STATE PAPERS, 1 INDIAN AFFAIRS 356 (1832).

25. Ibid.

26. Banner, Stuart. *How the Indians lost their land: Law and power on the frontier*. Harvard University Press, 2005: 134.

27. Ibid., p. 135.

28. Ibid.

29. "VIII. To the Inhabitants of the Colony of Massachusetts-Bay, 13 March 1775," *Founders Online*, National Archives, https://founders.archives.gov/documents/Adams/06-02-02-0072-0009. [Original source: *The Adams Papers*, Papers of John Adams, vol. 2, *December 1773–April 1775*, ed. Robert J. Taylor. Cambridge, MA: Harvard University Press, 1977, pp. 327–337.] (accessed online November 12, 2020).

30. Gales, Joseph. The Debates and Proceedings in the Congress of the United States: With an Appendix Containing Important State Papers and Public Documents, and All the Laws of a Public Nature. United States, Gales and Seaton, 1849: 900.

31. "From John Adams to William Tudor, Sr., 23 September 1818," *Founders Online, National Archives*, https://founders.archives.gov/

documents/Adams/99-02-02-6993 (accessed online November 12, 2020).

32. "James Madison to William Wirt, 2 October 1830," *Founders Online,* National Archives, https://founders.archives.gov/documents/Madison/99-02-02-2171 (accessed online November 18, 2020).

33. "William Wirt to James Madison, 5 October 1830," *Founders Online, National Archives*, https://founders.archives.gov/documents/Madison/99-02-02-2175 (accessed online November 12, 2020).

34. Evarts, Jeremiah. *Essays on the Present Crisis in the Condition of the American Indians*. Perkins & Marvin, 1829, No. XVI: 57.

35. Speech of Mr. Frelinghuysen, of New Jersey, delivered in the Senate of the United States, April 6, 1830, on The Bill For An Exchange Of Lands With The Indians Residing In Any Of The States Or Territories And For Their Removal West Of The Mississippi, p. 10.

36. Speeches on the Passage of the Bill for the Removal of the Indians, Delivered in the Congress of the United States, April and May, 1830, Perkins and Marvin. 1830: 138-139.

37. Speeches on the Passage of the Bill for the Removal of the Indians, Delivered in the Congress of the United States, April and May, 1830, Perkins and Marvin. 1830: 139.

38. Gallatin, Albert, The Oregon Question. New York: Bartlett & Welford, 1846. Number V, p. 27.

39. Twiss, Travers. *The Oregon Territory, Its History and Discovery: Including an Account of the Convention of the Escurial: Also, the Treaties and Negotiations Between the United States and Great Britain, Held at Various Times for the Settlement of a Boundary Line: and an Examination of the Whole Question in Respect to Facts and the Law of Nations*. New-York: D. Appleton, 1846, Chap. XVI: 121.

40. "VIII. To the Inhabitants of the Colony of Massachusetts-Bay, 13 March 1775," *Founders Online*, National Archives, https://founders.archives.gov/documents/Adams/06-02-02-0072-0009. [Original source: *The Adams Papers*, Papers of John Adams, vol. 2, *December 1773–April 1775*, ed. Robert J. Taylor. Cambridge, MA: Harvard

University Press, 1977, pp. 327–337.] (accessed online November 12, 2020).

41. Cleveland, Sarah H. "Powers inherent in sovereignty: Indians, aliens, territories, and the nineteenth century origins of plenary power over foreign affairs." *Tex. L. Rev.* 81 (2002): 1, 33.

42. Berman, Howard R. "The concept of aboriginal rights in the early legal history of the United States." Buff. L. Rev. 27 (1977): 659.

43. Kades, Eric. "The Dark Side of Efficiency: *Johnson v. M'Intosh* and the Expropriation of American Indian Lands." *University of Pennsylvania Law Review* 148.4 (2000): 1098.

44. Bryan, George. *The Imperialism of John Marshall: A Study in Expediency*. Stratford Company, 1924.

45. *Worcester v. Georgia*, 31 U.S. 515, 545 (1832).

46. "To George Washington from Edmund Randolph, 12 September 1791," *Founders Online,* National Archives, https://founders.archives.gov/documents/Washington/05-08-02-0367. [Original source: *The Papers of George Washington*, Presidential Series, vol. 8, *22 March 1791–22 September 1791*, ed. Mark A. Mastromarino. Charlottesville: University Press of Virginia, 1999, pp. 524–526.] (accessed online November 10, 2020).

47. Thomas Jefferson, Notes of a Conversation with George Hammond, June 3, 1792, in 17 THE WRITINGS OF THOMAS JEFFERSON 322, 328 (Andrew Lipscomb & Albert Ellery Bergh eds., libr. ed. 1903).

48. "To John Adams from Benjamin Lincoln, 11 September 1793," *Founders Online,* National Archives, https://founders.archives.gov/documents/Adams/99-02-02-1472 (accessed online November 10, 2020).

49. "Notes on Cabinet Opinions, 26 February 1793," *Founders Online,* National Archives, https://founders.archives.gov/documents/Jefferson/01-25-02-0251. [Original source: *The Papers of Thomas Jefferson*, vol. 25, *1 January–10 May 1793*, ed. John Catanzariti. Princeton: Princeton University Press, 1992, pp. 271–274.] (accessed online November 10, 2020).

50. Marshall, John. *The Life of George Washington-Volume 1*. Chap. X, 1807.

51. Story, Joseph. *Commentaries on the Constitution of the United States*. 1873, Vol. 1, Chapter 1, § 4.

52. Royce, Charles C. "Indian land cessions in the United States." *Eighteenth annual report of the Bureau of American Ethnology, 1896-1897* (1902): 529; Congress of the United States, April and May, 1830, Perkins and Marvin. 1830: 529.

53. Speeches on the Passage of the Bill for the Removal of the Indians, Delivered in the Congress of the United States, April and May, 1830, Perkins and Marvin. 1830: 6.

54. Speeches on the Passage of the Bill for the Removal of the Indians, Delivered in the Congress of the United States, April and May, 1830, Perkins and Marvin. 1830: 36.

55. *Johnson v. M'Intosh*, 21 U.S. 543, 588 (1823).

56. "XII. To the Inhabitants of the Colony of Massachusetts-Bay, 17 April 1775," *Founders Online*, National Archives, https://founders. archives.gov/documents/Adams/06-02-02-0072-0014. [Original source: *The Adams Papers, Papers of John Adams*, vol. 2, *December 1773–April 1775*, ed. Robert J. Taylor. Cambridge, MA: Harvard University Press, 1977, pp. 373–380.]

(accessed November 12, 2020). *Johnson v. M'Intosh*, 21 U.S. 543, 573 (1823) (accessed online November 10, 2020).

57. Notes on the State of Virginia by Thomas Jefferson

https://avalon.law.yale.edu/18th_century/jeffvir.asp (accessed online November 12, 2020).

58. Story, Joseph. *Commentaries on the Constitution of the United States*. 1873, Vol. 1, Chapter 1, §153: 102.

59. Kent, James, and Charles M. Barnes. *Commentaries on American law*. Lecture 50, Of the Foundation of Title to Land, Little, Brown, 1884.

60. Register of Debates, H. of R., 20th Cong., 1st Sess., 1543-1544.

61. Speeches on the Passage of the Bill for the Removal of the Indians, Delivered in the Congress of the United States, April and May, 1830, Perkins and Marvin. 1830: 139-140.

62. *Johnson v. M'Intosh*, 21 U.S. 543, 573 (1823).

63. Ibid., p. 587.

64. "United States Senate and House of Representatives The Connecticut-Pennsylvania Territorial Dispute. Editorial Note: The Connecticut-Pennsylvania Territorial Dispute," *Founders Online*, National Archives, https://founders.archives.gov/documents/ Jefferson/01-06-02-0369-0001. [Original source: *The Papers of Thomas Jefferson*, vol. 6, *21 May 1781–1 March 1784*, ed. Julian P. Boyd. Princeton: Princeton University Press, 1952, pp. 474–487.] (accessed online November 18, 2020).

65. *Johnson v. M'Intosh*, 21 U.S. 543, 573 (1823).

66. Story, Joseph. *Commentaries on the Constitution of the United States*. 1873, Vol. 1, Chapter 1, §4: 24.

67. The Sixteenth Century: Age of the Convento

http://www.colonialmexico.net/the-sixteenth-century-age-of (accessed online November 12, 2020).

68. U.S. CONST., First Amendment.

69. *Johnson v. M'Intosh*, 21 U.S. 543, 573 (1823).

70. Story, Joseph. *Commentaries on the Constitution of the United States*. 1873, Vol. 1, Chapter 1, §4: 24.

71. Story, Joseph. *A familiar exposition of the Constitution of the United States*. TH Webb & Company, 1842, §5: 13-14.

72. Real Adventure with the Pilgrim Settlers: William Bradford, Miles Standish, Squanto, Roger Williams. San Francisco: H. Wagner Publishing Co. Bulla, Clyde Robert (1954).

73. *Johnson v. M'Intosh*, 21 U.S. 543, 590 (1823).

74. "From Thomas Jefferson to United States Congress, 8 November

1808," *Founders Online, National Archives*, https://founders.archives.gov/documents/Jefferson/99-01-02-9054 (accessed online November 12, 2020).

75. https://millercenter.org/the-presidency/presidential-speeches/march-4-1809-first-inaugural-address (accessed November 12, 2020).

76. *Johnson v. M'Intosh*, 21 U.S. 543, 588 (1823).

77. Ibid., 572.

78. Echo-Hawk, Walter. *In the Courts of the Conqueror: The 10 Worst Indian Law Cases Ever Decided*. Fulcrum Publishing, 2018: 72.

79. "From Thomas Jefferson to William Johnson, 12 June 1823," *Founders Online,* National Archives, https://founders.archives.gov/documents/Jefferson/98-01-02-3562 (accessed online November 12, 2020).

# 2

# PAPAL INFLUENCE

From the early part of the fourteenth century, it was generally accepted that the entire globe was the property of God and, as such, distributable by the Pope as His delegate on earth. Prior to 337, Christianity was a persecuted and oppressed faith. Its postulates—the crucifixion, death and resurrection of Christ—were considered illegal superstitions under Roman law. This changed with Roman Emperor Constantine's conversion to Christianity. The Church's influence and power grew as it enjoyed imperial favor, ordained as the official religion of the Roman empire.

The Church claimed authority from God through Jesus Christ who designated His apostle Peter as "the rock upon which my church will be built."[1] Peter was regarded as the first Pope, the head of the Church, and all others as his successors were endowed with the same divine authority. The hierarchal structure imbued in Catholicism supported a solid organizational system. The Pope headed the Church; Cardinals served as administrators of the Church; Bishops and Archbishops governed as ecclesiastical superiors over a cathedral or region; and, Priests performed ecclesiastical duties for a parish.

Canon law was developed and decrees published which were binding on the entire Church membership. A papal bull, a document sealed with the insignia of the pope, from the Latin word bulla, was not only a binding, enforceable document, it addressed doctrine universal to the Church. In 494, Pope Gelasius I impressed on Emperor Anastasius, the primacy of papal power: "[a]lthough you take precedence over all mankind in dignity... Nevertheless, you piously bow the neck to those who have charge of divine affairs..."[2] What made this system ironclad was the

Church's infallibility proclaimed in 1090 by Pope Gregory VII in Dictatus Papae, The Dictates of the Pope: "That the Roman church has never erred; nor will it err to all eternity, the Scripture bearing witness."[3]

Emperors and empresses, monarchs, landowners and high officials seeking papal favor endowed the Church with treasure and land, and it became hugely wealthy. In addition, the Church collected a tithe of 10% of its members income, either in cash or goods. The Church was an economic juggernaut and acted as a financier and lending agent as well.

E. de Vattel, a prominent eighteenth-century scholar of international law, notes the immense sums raised through tithes and indulgences in Book I, Chapter XII. of *Piety and Religion*:

> § 155.10... ... Over every affair of life they extended their authority, under pretence that was conscience. They obliged new-married husbands to purchase permission to lie with their wives the first three first nights after marriage.

> § 156. Money drawn to Rome. This burlesque invention leads us to remark another abuse ... the immense sums which bulls, dispensations, &c., annually drew to Rome, from all the countries in communion with her. How much might be said on the scandalous trade of indulgences![4]

Religious and secular leaders waged a struggle for control during the Middle Ages. In 1077, Pope Gregory VII excommunicated King Henry IV for usurping the Pope's authority and appointing his own bishops. His Papal Bull, First Deposition and Banning of Henry IV, dated February 22, 1076, stated: "I withdraw ... from Henry ... who has risen against thy church ... the rule over ... the Germans and over Italy.... And I forbid any one to serve him as king."[5] With the severe penalty of losing his kingdom facing him, Henry IV trekked across the Alps to beg forgiveness, kneeling in the snow for three days to demonstrate his penitence. The Pope welcomed him back, cementing a short-lived win. Less than three years later, Henry IV deposed Pope Gregory VII, who later died in exile in 1085.

The Bull Unam sanctam, promulgated by Pope Boniface in 1302, reasserted the Church's primacy as follows:

We are informed by the texts of the gospels that in this Church and in its power are two swords; namely, the spiritual and the temporal. ... However, one sword ought to be subordinated to the other and temporal authority, subjected to spiritual power.[6]

Justice Story commented on the impact of the papacy as follows:

The Papal authority, too, was brought in aid of these great designs; and for the purpose of overthrowing heathenism, and propagating the Catholic religion, Alexander the Sixth, by a Bull issued in 1493, granted to the crown of Castile the whole of the immense territory then discovered, or to be discovered, between the poles, so far as it was not then possessed by any Christian prince.[7]

## No Second 'Discovery'

The lands of the numerous indigenous nations populating the western Hemisphere from time immemorial were not 'discovered' by European explorers. As noted by Travers Twiss in 1846, an English jurist who served as the Queen's Advocate-General, 'discovery' can only be made once.

There can be no second discovery of a country. In this respect title by discovery differs from title by settlement. A title by a later settlement may be set up against a title by an earlier settlement, even where this has been formed by the first occupant, if the earlier settlement can be shown to have been abandoned.[8]

Secondly, a second or subsequent discovery cannot by its nature be equated with a first discovery. "A title by second discovery cannot, from the nature of the thing, be set up against a title by first discovery. The term "second discovery" itself involves a contradiction, and where the discovery has been progressive, "further discovery" would seem to be the more correct phrase."[9]

## Indigenous Peoples Present in the Pre-Columbian Americas

North, Central and South America were highly populated prior to European voyages from Europe. There was an astounding multiplicity of civilizations and cultures, ranging from the nomadic peoples of the southern pampas and the North American plains to the high civilizations of the Andes (the Incas) and the central valley of Mexico (the Aztecs). Anthropologists estimate the presence of more than 350 major indigenous groups. There could be no 'discovery' of this area by European explorers. Europeans did not 'discover' a 'New World.' It was already inhabited by numerous peoples that established homelands, governments, economies that included broad trading routes, and varying ways of life. Though colonial settler histories of the Western Hemisphere contain scant reference to this significant part of indigenous history, it is an undeniable fact.

Christopher's Columbus Journal corroborates the extensive indigenous population present in Hispaniola, such that a claim of 'discovery' is false:

> Thursday, 11 October. The crew of the Pinta ... [and] the Nina saw ... signs of land...near a small island, one of the Lucayos, called in the Indian language Guanahani. Presently they descried people, naked, and the Admiral landed in the boat, which was armed...[10]

In 1500, Queen Isabella terminated Columbus's governorship because of his mistreatment of natives and her fears of papal retribution.

Similarly, when French King Francis I commissioned Jacques Cartier to "go to the New Lands" and discover "certain islands and lands, where it is said he should find rich quantities of gold and other rich things," it was easier said than done. Cartier's efforts to establish settlements in Canada were defeated by the indigenous population already living there.[11] Again, this history substantiates the indigenous population presence such that a claim of 'discovery' simply cannot be made.

England's awareness of indigenous inhabitants is evident from Philip Amadas and Arthur Barlowe's encounter with indigenous people at Roanoke Island. Amadas and Barlowe arrived July 13, 1584 and four days after their arrival they were visited by indigenous peoples:

[T]here came unto us divers boates, and in one of them the Kings brother, accompanied with fortie or fiftie men, very handsome and goodly people, and in their behaviour as mannerly and civill as any of Europe. His name was Granganimeo, and the king is called Wingina, the country Wingandacoa, and now by her Majestie Virginia. ... hee made all signes of joy and welcome, striking on his head and his breast and afterwardes on ours, to shewe wee were all one, smiling and making shewe the best he could of all love, and familiaritie. ... We found the people most gentle, loving and faithful, void of all guile and treason, and such as lived after the manner of the Golden Age.[12]

Again, England's confirmation of the indigenous inhabitants prevent a 'discovery' of a 'New World.'

In May of 1626, Dutch West India Company representative Peter Minuit met with local Lenape Indians to purchase the rights to the island of Manhattan. Similarly, Andres Lucasse, along with Sweden's representative, Peter Minuit, purchased land from the Lenni Lenape (Delaware) and Susquehannock Indians in a formal ceremony on March 29, 1638, with the presence of five native leaders—Mattahorn, Mitatsemint, Eru Packen, Mohomen and Chiton.

Clearly, no claim of 'discovery' by any of these European countries could be made to a 'New World' which was already populated by a multitude of indigenous peoples across the breadth of the Western hemisphere.

## Western European Monarchs

From the time Columbus first arrived in the Americas in 1492, western European monarchs relied on a variety of methods to assert their territorial claims. These included papal grants and royal charters. While Spain relied on 'discovery' and papal grants because of their political influence over the Pope, France and Britain relied more on royal charters and occupation; and Holland and Sweden purchased lands from Indians and required a deed. To refute Marshall's claim of a universal 'doctrine of discovery,' the policies of the western European monarchs will be analyzed.

## Relationships to Indigenous Peoples Varied

Each colonizing country had to decide how it would relate to the Indian inhabitants. Spain and France simply used coercion and force to expropriate Indian land, though France appeared to sustain a more amicable relationship. France's focus was on the economically lucrative fur trade; the fur trappers and traders intermarried with the Indians creating strong political alliances. The French population never compared numerically to Britain's settlers growing population which focused on families and agriculture.

The thirteen colonies differed in method in establishing functional relationships with the Indians. Royce concluded that:

> *In fact, the theory in regard to the Indian tenure was not precisely the same throughout ... those of one colony looking chiefly to meeting the claims of the Indians, while the main object in other cases was to obtain as much land as possible...*[13]
> (Emphasis added.)

To see what was exported to the 'New World,' one need only consider the machinations of England and France to control the continent of Europe. Having depleted their own backyard, the battle for empire and its accessories—power and wealth—would now be waged in the western hemisphere.

British official, Peter Wraxall in 1754, encapsulated the core of politics of this era: "To preserve the Ballance between us and the French is the great ruling Principle of the Modern Indian Politics."[14]

Notes

1. Matthew 16:18-19.

2. Gelasius I on Spiritual and Temporal Power, Robinson, James
Harvey. *Readings in European history*. Wildside Press LLC, 2008: 72-
73.

3. Gregory VII, Dictatus Papae, Translated in Ernest F. Henderson,
*Select Historical Documents of the Middle Ages* (London: George Bell
and Sons, 1910): 366-367.

4. de Vattel, Emerich. *The Law of Nations or the Principles of Natural
Law Applied to the Conduct and to the Affairs of Nations and of
Sovereigns*. Carnegie Institution of Washington, 1916. Book I, Chap.
XII, §155.10, §156.

5. Gregory VII, Reg. III, No. 10 a, translated in Ernest F. Henderson,
*Select Historical Documents of the Middle Ages* (London: George Bell
and Sons, 1910): 376-377.

6. English translation of 'Unam' is taken from a doctoral dissertation
written in the Dept. of Philosophy at the Catholic University of
America and published by CUA Press in 1927.

7. Story, Joseph. *Commentaries on the Constitution of the United
States*. 1833, Book 1, Chapter 1, §5.

8. Twiss, Travers. *The Oregon Territory, Its History and Discovery:
Including an Account of the Convention of the Escurial: Also, the
Treaties and Negotiations Between the United States and Great
Britain, Held at Various Times for the Settlement of a Boundary Line:*

*and an Examination of the Whole Question in Respect to Facts and the Law of Nations*. New-York: D. Appleton, 1846, Chap. VIII: 121.

9. Ibid.

10. Columbus, Christopher. *The Diario of Christopher Columbus's First Voyage to America 1492-1493*. Abs. Bartolomé de Las Casas. Trans. Oliver Dunn and James E. Kelley, Jr., Norman: U of Oklahoma P, 1989, p. 59.

11. Knecht, Robert Jean. *Francis I*. Cambridge University Press, 1984: 336.

12. Hakluyt, Richard. The Principal Navigations, Voyages, Traffiques and Discoveries of the English Nation. 3 vols. in 2. London, 1599-1600: 330-331.

13. Royce, Charles C. "Indian land cessions in the United States." *Eighteenth annual report of the Bureau of American Ethnology, 1896-1897* (1902): 563.

14. Richter, Daniel K. *Facing east from Indian country: a native history of early America*. Harvard University Press, 2009: 164.

# 3

# SPAIN'S IMPERIALISM

The conquest of the Moors by Spain in 1492 marked the end of the last Iberian Islamic state. With the marriage of Ferdinand II (Aragón) and Isabella (Castile) came the ascent of Castile-Aragón as the most powerful kingdom on the Spanish peninsula. These new monarchs' unification of Spain resulted in the rigid imposition of Catholicism over the disparate kingdoms in the Iberian Peninsula. Castile, León, Aragón and Granada each had distinct languages, histories, systems of governance and bodies of law.

In an effort to capitalize on the Reconquista and to re-establish a Spanish identity after 800 years of being a conquered people by the Moors, the monarchs imposed a rigid, invasive indoctrination of its population. The judicial system of the Catholic Church started what became known as the Inquisition whose aim was to combat heresy. It was a partnership of the Church and Crown to eliminate any diversity in thought or among peoples. The total number of people who were processed by the Inquisition throughout its history was approximately 150,000. Through repression, Spain was to be unified by Catholicism, government and the re-integration of the pure blood of the Spaniard as central to its superior status in Europe.

Pope Innocent IV's papal bull, Ad extirpanda of 1252, explicitly authorized and defined the appropriate circumstances for the use of torture by the Inquisition for eliciting confessions from heretics. By 1256, inquisitors were given absolution if they used instruments of torture. When the Inquisitors, the Santo Oficios, arrived in a city or town, their first act was to read a statement of the Edicts of Faith, along with a list of illicit beliefs and practices. Violators could confess and be redeemed though punishment and neighbors and employers were compelled to spy and inform on each other.

The first Inquisitor General, Tomas de Torquemada, from a Jewish family that converted to Christianity (a 'converso'), initiated a propaganda campaign against the Jews. In 1492, he persuaded the Catholic monarchs to expel all Jews who refused to be baptized. The Edict of the Expulsion of the Jews (1492) accused Jews of perverting and enticing Christians to Judaism "which has redounded to the great injury, detriment, and opprobrium of our holy Catholic faith." At first, Jews were separated from the Spanish population but then they were ordered "to depart and never to return." They could not export gold or silver or coined money. Any violation would result in the penalty of death and the confiscation of all their possessions ... without further trial, sentence or declaration.[1] This negative perception of Jews was included in Vattel's The Law of Nations: §20. Bad custom of the ancients. "The Jews especially placed a great part of their zeal in hating all nations; and, as a natural consequence, they were detested and despised by them in turn."[2]

Also, Converted Moors (moriscos) were suspect. Their land was confiscated. In 1567, a decree prohibited the use of the Arabic language and Muslim names and dress. In the identification of what was 'Spanish,' language, dress and cuisine came under scrutiny and were lauded as orthodox or suppressed as heretical. Edicts of Faith, issued regularly by the Inquisition, criminalized Arabic cultural habits. This policing of practices was left to the Inquisition.

Also, during the sixteenth century, identification by one's purity of Spanish blood (limpieza de sangre) was employed by the state to promote political centralization and Catholic militancy. Blood purity statutes, first instituted in Toledo in 1449, were promulgated throughout Spain, differentiating those of Spanish blood from Jews and Moors who were banned from holding governmental positions ("todo oficio e beneficio publico") on the basis of their being of 'impure blood.' Institutions like religious brotherhoods, churches, cathedrals, individual trade unions, schools, universities and city governments established their own "limpieza de sangre" policies.

Eventually an Edict for the Expulsion of the Moors was decreed by

King Philip III on April 9, 1609, condemning them as "hypocrites and eternal enemies of the Divine and Humanity alike," subjecting them to punishment for their crimes and misdeeds. They were given three days to depart. It is estimated that over 300,000 Moriscos were expelled.[3]

Carlos Fuentes, in *The Buried Mirror*, notes that when Spain needed all of its economic resources to sustain its new European position and its overseas empire, it deprived itself of many of its most economically active citizens and was laid open to exploitation by German and Italian financiers.[4]

Spanish Catholicism was a frightening combination of the concepts of 'limpieza de sangre' and the Inquisition. Spain considered herself divinely imbued with the defense of the Catholic faith. The virulent attack of anyone 'not of pure Spanish blood' or Catholic would have horrendous consequences for indigenous peoples. Using the pretense of Christianity justified the conquest, enslavement, confiscation of land and property and extermination of millions of indigenous peoples.

## Spain Asserted Right of Pope to Convey to Catholic Monarch Lands 'Discovered,' Not Then in Possession of Christian Prince or People

With Pope Eugene IV having granted certain lands in Africa to Portugal, Spain hoped to use its favored position with Pope Alexander VI, a member of the Borgia family of Spain, to capture its share of any lands it might discover. Christopher Columbus, after twice petitioning King Ferdinand II and Queen Isabella for approval for a voyage to explore for a new route to the Indies, secured their permission. He was also authorized to discover and subdue lands undiscovered by any Christian prince or inhabited by Christians. Upon his successful return to Spain, her Catholic monarchs quickly sought the Pope's grant to them of the land 'discovered.'

By the Bull Inter caetera of May 3, 1453, clarified thereafter to Spain's advantage, the Pope granted to Ferdinand II and Isabella and their descendants all lands lying west of a line joining the North and the South Poles, 100 leagues west of the Azores, so long as they had not already been seized by any other Christian Prince. Lands east of the line were awarded to Portugal.[5]

Spain and Portugal's dispute over which lands were actually conveyed to it was resolved in the Treaty of Torsedillas, ratified by the Pope.

The language in the Bull Inter caetera made it clear that the Pope regarded his grant as giving the Spanish monarchs full power of sovereignty and dominion over the territories 'discovered,' with the primary objective of spreading Christianity. The indigenous inhabitants' sovereignty and dominion were completely ignored. The Church further ceded all of its authority in the 'New World' to the Spanish Crown in three famous bulls. The first bull, Inter caetera, in 1493 delegated the exclusive privilege of Christianizing and civilizing the natives to the Spanish monarchs. A second bull in 1501, Eximae Devotionis, extended to the Spanish monarchs all rights of royal patronage, including the selection of all persons for ecclesiastical offices and the right to collect and use for itself all ecclesiastical tithes throughout its dominions. Still another bull, Universalis Ecclesiae, issued in 1508 by Pope Julius II, declared the King of Spain to be the head of the Church in Spain and its empire.[6] The Pope wholly abdicated his authority to the temporal, secular authority of the Spanish monarchy.

In a decree ('cedula') King Philip II sent to his viceroy in Spanish America, he forthrightly proclaimed:

> ...the right of the ecclesiastical patronage belongs to us throughout the realm of the Indias-both because of having discovered and acquired that new world, and erected there and endowed the churches and monasteries at our own cost ... and because it was conceded to us by bulls of the most holy pontiffs, conceded of their own accord.[7]

The King's appointment of missionaries assured that they were agents of the government of Spain. One scholar graphically noted that this "easy means of acquiring an honorable position and comfortable livelihood attracted such large numbers that in 1655 the town council of Mexico City implored Philip IV to send no more monks, as more than six thousand were without employment, living on the fat of the land."[8]

Spain rapaciously stole indigenous lands. It considered its right to claim sovereignty and dominion over all lands as absolute, according no rights to the Indians. In 1501, Governor Nicolás de Ovando initiated the system of 'encomienda.' Literally translated as "charge, commission, or patronage," the encomienda granted groups of Indians to Spanish 'encomenderos,' to use as forced labor.

Queen Isabella's "Decree on Indian Labor" in 1503 also authorized this use:

> I have now been informed that because of the excessive liberty allowed the said Indians, they run away from the Christians and withdraw from any intercourse and communication ... I order you, Our Governor ... to compel the Indians to work on their (Spanish) buildings, to mine and collect gold and other metals, and to work on their farms and crop fields; and you are to have each one paid...[9]

## Laws of Burgos (1512) Coerce Indian Subjugation

In 1512, King Ferdinand II promulgated the Laws of Burgos, the first colonial legislation, to regulate relations between Spaniards and the conquered Indians, ostensibly to ensure the material and spiritual welfare of the Indians. They approved the use of force to subjugate Indians and remove them from their lands:

> [N]othing has sufficed to bring the ... Indians to a knowledge of our Faith (necessary for their salvation), since by nature they are inclined to idleness and vice, and have no manner of virtue or doctrine ... [you are to] remove the ... Indians to the vicinity of Spaniards. ... I command you ... to have the lodges of the said villages burned.[10]

## Papal Permission to Use Force for Catholic Conversion

Intra arcana, a papal bull issued in 1529 by Pope Clement VII to Charles V, authorized the use of arms, if necessary, to convert Indians to Catholicism:

> We trust that ... you will compel and with all zeal cause the barbarian nations to come to the knowledge of God ... not only by edicts and admonitions, but also by force and arms, if needful...[11]

## Theologians' Views

Spanish theologians were the worst in confirming the right of Indians to their lands and then retracting it by creating huge loopholes for the Catholic monarchs. The loopholes included: first, since the 'New World' was unoccupied by Christians it was 'vacant land' and could be appropriated—terra nullius; secondly, Christians had a duty to convert non-Christians which required them to confiscate heathen lands; thirdly, the Law of Nations afforded them the right to engage in trade, regardless of the interest of the Indians; and, lastly, if land was not being cultivated, it could be lawfully settled without interference. Conversely, the Indians were obligated to receive the Pope's missionaries, the trade expeditions and the settler colonists, and any resistance or hostility to the European presence was a just basis for war.

Pope Innocent IV affirmed, in 1245 in Commentaria Doctissima in Quinque Libros Decretalium, that all rational creatures, Christian or pagan, had the right under natural law to own property and to govern themselves. This view was contested by Hostiensis, an Italian canonist, who asserted that only those who recognized Christ could hold property, otherwise their sovereignty could be eliminated and their land and possessions expropriated. Spain's discoveries, affirmed by Pope Alexander, relied on theologians such as Hostiensis. Aristotle's doctrine of the natural inferiority of certain peoples would be employed to justify Spain's domination and enslavement of Indians as consistent with natural order.

## Theologians: Vitoria, Gentili, Suárez, Sepúlveda, Oviedo and Rubios

Franciscus de Vitoria, Professor of Theology at the University of Salamanca, would argue simultaneously (1) that the Indians of North America were neither chattels nor beasts but human beings entitled to own land and respect; and (2) if the Spaniards, after resorting to all moderate measures, could not attain security among the Indians, they might lawfully seize their cities, reduce them to subjection, take away their property and depose their former rulers and set up new ones.

Vitoria denied that title to lands in the 'New World' could be claimed by papal grant or that mere 'discovery' could vest title in the 'discovering' sovereign where the territory 'discovered' was already inhabited:

> [T]here is another title which can be set up, namely, by right of discovery ... Now the rule of the law of nations is that what belongs to nobody is granted to the first occupant ... so, as the object in question (New World) was not without an owner, it gives no support to a seizure of the aborigines any more than if it had been they who had discovered us.[12]

Even if the aborigines in question were "as inept and stupid as alleged, still dominion can not be denied to them, nor are they to be classed with the slaves of civil law because they are not of unsound mind, but have ... the use of reason. ... [t]hey have polities which are orderly arranged and they have definite marriage and magistrates, overlords, laws, and workshops, and a system of exchange, all of which call for the use of reason; they also have a kind of religion."[13] Also, he considered the Pope to have spiritual, not secular power; with none over the Indians. Citing St. Thomas (Secunda Secundae, qu. 10, art. 8) for authority, he concluded "that unbelievers who have never received the faith, like Gentiles and Jews, are in no wise to be compelled to do so."[14]

Unfortunately, he proceeded in a complete reversal regarding Indian rights to list how Spain could exercise total dominion: (1) Christians have a right to preach the Gospel; (2) Spaniards have a right to travel to the 'New World' and to sojourn there so long as they do no harm; (3) they may carry on trade among the Indians, so long as they do no harm to their own country, by importing goods which the Indians lack, and exporting gold and silver and other articles in which the Indians abound; and (4) the Pope could entrust to the Spaniards alone the task of converting the Indians and engaging in trade.

Samuel von Pufendorf, a German jurist and historian, attacked Francisco Vitoria's justification for the Spanish treatment of American Indians by challenging the rights he claimed for Spaniards arriving in the 'New World':

First is the Spaniard's right of travel through Indian lands. Pufendorf responds:

It is crude indeed to try to give others so indefinite a right to journey and live among us, with no thought of the numbers in which they come, their purpose in coming, as well as the question whether...they propose to stay but a short time or settle among us permanently.[15]

Second is the right of Europeans to engage in free trade. Pufendorf states that he has failed to discover such a freedom of trade which cannot be limited by rulers if the well-being of the state demands it, much less a one as thrusts foreigners upon a people without permission and against their will.[16]

Pufendorf argues that one must first consider the Spanish motives for trade suggesting that they may be unjust or immoderate. He argues this last point by employing a metaphor:

Suppose I had given some one of my neighbours the privilege of entering my garden as often as he wishes, and of sampling my fruit; when later another man burst in and decides to break down the trees, to expel me and make an uninvited stay in my garden, I will surely have the right to close my gate to him.[17]

In regard to conquest, Italian Alberico Gentili, Regius Professor of Civil Law at Oxford, argued that under natural law if Indians were conquered, they could be forced to relinquish their sovereignty or be crushed: "the cause of the Spaniards is just when they make war upon the Indians, who practised abominable lewdness even with beasts, and who ate human flesh, slaying men for that purpose."[18]

Francisco Suárez, a Spanish Jesuit priest, philosopher and theologian, a leading figure of the School of Salamanca, and regarded as a great scholar in line with St. Thomas Aquinas, posited that the Pope could distribute the land of non-Christians, use force to coerce the indoctrination of Catholicism and, if necessary, protect its emissaries by war.

Juan Ginés de Sepúlveda, a scholar of Aristotle, used Aristotelian philosophy to support his ideology of racial hierarchy and to demonize native Americans, not entitled to the land 'discovered' by Spain. He served as Emperor Charles V's official chaplain and royal historian and authored Democrates Alter (or, On the Just Causes for War against the Indians) in which he claimed Indians had no sovereignty or rights to property. He issued four main justifications for war against certain Indians. First, if their natural condition deemed them unable to rule themselves, it was the responsibility of the Spaniards to act as masters. Second, Spaniards were entitled to prevent cannibalism as a crime against nature. Third, the same went for human sacrifice. Fourth, it was important to convert Indians to Christianity.

For doctrinal support, he relied on the work of Gonzalo Fernández de Oviedo y Valdés (1478–1557), a Spanish colonialist and historian, and Juan López de Palacios Rubios, a member of the Council of Castile, which advised King Ferdinand II.

Oviedo's blatant racism against Indians is uncontroverted:

> [They are] naturally lazy and vicious, melancholic, cowardly, and in general a lying, shiftless people. Their marriages are not a sacrament but a sacrilege. They are idolatrous, libidinous and commit sodomy. Their chief desire is to eat, drink, worship heathen idols, and commit bestial obscenities. What could one expect from a people whose skulls are so thick and hard that the Spaniards had to take care in fighting not to strike on the head lest their swords be blunted? ... In prudence, talent, virtue, and humanity they are as inferior to the Spaniards as children to adults, women to men, as the wild and cruel to the most meek, as the prodigiously intemperate to the continent and temperate, that I have almost said, as monkeys to men.[19]

Rubios authored the Requerimiento which demanded Indians to immediately convert to Catholicism or face annihilation:

> [W]e ask and require that you ... acknowledge the Church as the ruler and superior of the whole world and the high priest called Pope and in his name the king and that you consent [they] preach to you ... [I]f you do not do this or if you maliciously delay ... we shall make war against you ... and shall take away your goods and shall do to you all the harm and damage that we can ... and we protest that the deaths and losses that shall accrue from this are your fault.[20]

The first known Spanish leader to use the Requerimiento (requirement) was Pedrarias D'vila near Santa Marta in 1514. According to American historian Lewis Hanke, it was used in a number of dubious circumstances:

> "The Requirement was read to trees and empty huts when no Indians were to be found. Captains muttered its theological phrases into their beards on the edge of sleeping Indian settlements, or even a league away before starting the formal attack, and at times some leather-tongued Spanish notary hurled its sonorous phrases after the Indians as they fled into the mountains. Once it was read in camp before the soldiers to the beat of the drum. Ship captains would sometimes have the document read from the deck as they approached an island, and at night would send out enslaving expeditions, whose leaders would shout the traditional Castilian war cry 'Santiago!' rather than read the Requirement before they attacked the near-by villages."[21]

## Dominican Friars Silenced for Disclosing Atrocities Committed by Conquistadors

Particularly disturbed were a group of Dominican priests. Antonio de Montesinos denounced the "cruel and horrible servitude" to which Amerindians were being reduced. In a sermon accusing encomenderos of sinful behavior toward Indians and threatening to withhold confession and absolution from colonists who mistreat natives, he preached:

> The message [is] that you are all in mortal sin, that you live in it and will die in it, because of the cruelty and oppression with which you treat these innocent people. Tell me, by what right do you hold these Indians in such cruel and horrible servitude? By what authority did you make unprovoked war on these people, living in peace and quiet on their land, and with unheard-of savagery kill and consume so great a number of them?[22]

Bartolomé de las Casas, a 16th-century landowner, Dominican priest, bishop and advocate for indigenous peoples, disclosed the atrocities in his book, *A Short Account of the Destruction of the Indies*:

> The Indies were discovered in the year one thousand four hundred and ninety-two. ... And of all the infinite universe of humanity, these people (Indians) are the most guileless, the most devoid of

wickedness and duplicity, the most obedient and faithful to their native masters and to the Spanish Christians whom they serve. They are by nature the most humble, patient, and peaceable, holding no grudges, free from embroilments, neither excitable nor quarrelsome. These people are the most devoid of rancors, hatreds, or desire for vengeance of any people in the world. ... in the forty years that have passed, with the infernal actions of the Christians, there have been unjustly slain more than twelve million men, women, and children. ... Their reason ... is to acquire gold, and to swell themselves with riches in a very brief time and thus rise to a high estate.[23]

The King ordered Montesinos and his fellow friars to be silenced, which was supported by the superior of the Dominicans in Spain.

## Sublimus Dei: Prohibiting Enslavement and Forced Conversion of Indians

Nonetheless, a bull, Sublimus Dei (On Prohibiting the Enslavement and Forced Evangelization of Indians), was promulgated, decreeing that Amerindians were not to be deprived of their liberty or the possession of their property: "The said Indians and all other people who may later be discovered by Christians, are by no means to be deprived of their liberty or the possession of their property, even though they be outside the faith of Jesus Christ..."[24]

## Pope Paul III Retracts Penalties for Violating Sublimus Dei in Papal Letter: Non indecens videtur (1538)

Under pressure though from Emperor Charles V, Pope Paul III succumbed to the Emperor's diatribe that the punishment of excommunication or interdict for violating Sublimus Dei, contained in a contemporaneous Apostolic Brief (Pastorale official), was injurious to the imperial right of colonization and harmful to the peace of the Indies. **The Pope retracted the ecclesiastical censures in another papal letter,** Non Indecens Videtur, dated June 19, 1538.

In Non indecens videtur, Pope Paul III wrote,

> It does not seem to us improper if the Roman Pontiff...revoke, correct, or change those [dispositions] ... *from whom they were extorted by stealth at a time when he was engaged in other matters* and that it caused disruption to the peaceful state of the islands of the Indies ...Accordingly, by virtue of Apostolic authority, we revoke, invalidate, and annul the previous letter(s) and whatever is contained in it (or them).[25] (Emphasis added.)

Thus, the sanctions for excommunication for violating Sublimus Dei were removed, leaving it without any penalties or enforceability. The Dominican friars were blamed for extorting the Apostolic Brief (Pastorale official) from the Church.

### New Laws of the Indies, 1542

In 1542, the King issued a set of pro-Indian laws—so pro-Indian that they had to be revoked in Mexico and in Peru due to settler opposition, where the viceroy was killed when he attempted to enforce them. The 1542 laws forbade the enslavement of Indians, abolished all servitude by Indians to encomenderos, prohibited any further encomiendas from being granted, obliged all royal and church officials to surrender their rights to tribute from the Indians and specified that all existing private encomiendas would become the property of the crown upon the death of the present holder. The royal emissary, Francisco Tello de Sandoval, suspended them in the face of the violent opposition.[26]

### Urbanization of New Spain

As mining and commercial agriculture became the lifeblood of the Spanish, a whole new urban development fostered the economy. Coming from an Iberian tradition of town dwelling, the Spanish were quick to lay out new settlements as administrative, religious and commercial centers for the territories they occupied. Even with this spread of development across New Spain, the vast majority of Spaniards (estimated at over 95%) lived in central Mexico, not the outlying areas of California, Arizona, New Mexico and Florida.

## Chancellor Kent and Vattel Consider Conquest of Mexico and Peru Atrocious Injustices

In his Commentaries on American Law (1826–1830), Chancellor James Kent, renowned jurist and author of a landmark treatise on American common law wrote, citing Vattel as in agreement: "... the conquest of the half civilized empires of Mexico and Peru was a palpable usurpation, and an act of atrocious injustice..."[27]

Montaigne wrote:

> Whoever set the utility of commerce and trading at such a price? So many cities razed, so many nations exterminated, so many millions of people put to the sword, and the richest and most beautiful part of the world turned upside down, for the traffic in pearls and pepper![28]

Spain was one country that absolutely adhered to its sovereignty and dominion over peoples and lands 'discovered,' so long as they were not inhabited by Christians.

Notes

1. Ferdinand II, King of Aragón and Isabella I, Queen of Castile, March 31, 1492, Edict of the Expulsion of the Jews, translated by Edward Peters, in Documentos acera de la expulsión de los Judíos, edited by Luis Suárez Fernández, pp. 391-95 (Valladolid: Consejo Superior de Investigaciones Cientificas, 1964.)

2. de Vattel, Emerich. *The Law of Nations or the Principles of Natural Law Applied to the Conduct and to the Affairs of Nations and of Sovereigns.* Carnegie Institution of Washington, 1916, §20: 273.

3. Cowans, Jon, ed. King Philip III. "Decree of Expulsion of the Moriscos," *Modern Spain: A documentary history.* University of Pennsylvania Press, 2003.

4. Fuentes, Carlos. *The buried mirror: Reflections on Spain and the New World.* Houghton Mifflin Harcourt, 1999: 82.

5. [Inter Caetera, 1493, https://www.papalencyclicals.net/Alex06/alex06inter.htm] (accessed online November 17, 2020).

6. Editorial: Church and State in Latin America, J. E. W., Jr., Journal of Church and State, Volume 8, Issue 2, Spring 1966, pp. 173, 174.

7. Ibid., p. 175.

8. Ibid., p. 179.

9. Parry, John Horace, and Robert G. Keith, eds. *New Iberian World: The Andes.* Vol. 4. Times Books, 1984.

10. Ronan, Charles E. "The Laws of Burgos of 1512-1513. Royal Ordinances for the Good Government and Treatment of the Indians. Translated, with an Introduction and Notes, by Lesley Byrd Simpson.

(San Francisco: John Howell, 1960)." *The Americas* 17.4 (1961): 404-405.

11. Translation from: https//suburbanbanshee.wordpress.com/2015/09/28/intra-arcana-the-good-bits/ (accessed online November 5, 2020).

12. de Vitoria, Francisco. *Francisci de Victoria De Indis et De ivre belli relectiones*. Carnegie Institution of Washington, 1917:139.

13. Ibid., p. 128.

14. Ibid., p. 145.

15. von Pufendorf, Samuel Freiherr. *De jure naturae et gentium*. Book III, Chapter III, §9, ex officina Knochiana, 1759.

16. Ibid.

17. Ibid.

18. Green, Leslie C. *The law of nations and the new world*. University of Nebraska Press, 1989:49.

19. Hanke, Lewis. *The Spanish struggle for justice in the conquest of America*. Southern Methodist University Press, 1949: 11.

20. Parry, John Horace, and Robert G. Keith, eds. *New Iberian World: The Andes*. Vol. 4. Times Books, 1984: 288.

21. Hanke, Lewis. *The Spanish struggle for justice in the conquest of America*. Southern Methodist University Press, 1949: 17; https://www.pbs.org/conquistadors/devaca/lascasas_02.html

22. Ibid.

23. de Las Casas, Bartolomé. *The devastation of the Indies: A brief account*. JHU Press, 1992: 31.

24. https://www.papalencyclicals.net/paul03/p3subli.htm (accessed online November 5, 2020).

25. Parish, Helen Rand, Harold E. Weidman, and Bartolomé de las Casas. *Las Casas en México: historia y obra desconocidas*. Fondo de cultura económica, 1992: 303 –305, 310-312.

26. Stevens, Henry. *The New Laws of the Indies for the Good Treatment and Preservation of the Indians*. London: Priv. print. at the Chiswick Press, 1893.

27. Kent, James, and Charles M. Barnes. *Commentaries on American law*. Lecture 50, Of the Foundation of Title to Land. Vol. 1. Little, Brown, 1884.

28. Garber, Daniel, and Steven Nadler. "Oxford Studies in Early Modern Philosophy: Volume 2." (2004): 11.

## 4

## FRANCE'S IMPERIALISM

Official French exploration of the 'New World' lagged some thirty years behind Spain, beginning in the reign of Francis I. France claimed all of Canada and Louisiana based on its 'discovery,' when Indians occupied almost the entire area. As a Catholic ruler, Francis I was restricted by the Papal Bull Inter caetera which granted newly found lands east of the Azores to Spain and excluded the rest of Christian Europe from entering them without permission. In 1533, King Francis I met with Pope Clement VII to 'reinterpret' the Bull, thus protecting France's 'discovery.' By 1540 though, Francis I openly challenged not just the scope of Inter caetera but its legitimacy, asserting that popes had no power to distribute lands among kings and asking "to see Adam's will to learn how he had partitioned the world." Having rejected papal grants as a basis for a valid title, Francis I also discounted 'discovery' without settlement, stating that 'passing by and discovering with the eye was not taking possession.'[1]

Thus, notwithstanding, Chief Justice Marshall's allegation of the binding 'doctrine of discovery,' France voluntarily, knowingly and willfully violated it and reformulated it. Of course, Spain refused to concur in any modification.

In fact, France's refusal to concede to Spain's vast territorial claim in the 'New World,' was considered by Spain's Emperor Charles V as "a direct contravention of the treaty between us and the said King of France and contrary to the grace and concession granted by the Apostolic See to the Kings of Castile and Portugal for the said conquest." He appealed to the King of Portugal to join with him to:

...resist and destroy them.... And should they meet with the ships of the said Jacques or any other Frenchman sailing with a fleet bound to the said Indies, let them engage and destroy them, since the intention of these Frenchmen is known; and let all the men taken from their ships be thrown into the sea, not saving any one person, for this is necessary as a warning against the undertaking of similar expeditions.[2]

The Portuguese were unwilling to commit to this endeavor. However, Spain did send out two reconnaissance ships but was unable to locate the French.

Francis I granted letters patent to Sieur Demonts, in 1603, constituting him Lieutenant General, with the authority to extend the power of the French over the country he discovered and its inhabitants, to give laws to the people, to treat with the natives, and enforce the observance of treaties, and to parcel out and give title to lands, according to his own judgment.

The French royal commission to Marquis de Tracy (November 19, 1663) bestowed on him the government of Canada, containing the following passage, which indicates reliance on the power of arms rather than on peaceful measures:

Sieur de Prouville Tracy Our Lieutenant General [is] authorized ... to invade either the continent or the Islands for the purpose of seizing New Countries or establishing New Colonies ... to subdue, subject and exact obedience from all the people of said Countries ... to extend and preserve said places under Our authority and obedience.[3]

An example of French dominion asserted over the Indians, which was analogous to the Spanish Requerimiento, is the following: In June 1671, Simon-François Daumont de Saint-Lusson gathered together fourteen First Nations tribes that had come from 100 leagues (some 400 kilometers) around the Jesuit mission at Sault-Ste-Marie. The interpreter, Nicolas Perrot, allegedly read a document in the native language claiming all the territories so far discovered, and those to be discovered, in the name of the King of France.

From the 1680s, de la Salle established a ring of forts through the St. Lawrence and Great Lakes regions, along the Mississippi to the Gulf.

However, the French American territories would remain under-settled in comparison to their British rivals, given the focus on fur trading. Their lack of emphasis on agriculture prevented them from using the encroachment on Indian lands approach by decimating the subsistence game habitat.

A patent was given by Louis XV to the "Western Company" in August 1717 granting "all the lands, coasts, ports, havens, and islands which compose our province of Louisiana." ... Also,

> SEC. VI. The said company shall be free ... to negotiate and make alliance in our name with all the nations of the land, except those which are dependent on the other powers of Europe ... and in case they insult her she may declare war against them, attack them or defend herself by means of arms, and negotiate with them for peace or for a truce.[4]

Again, notwithstanding the 'doctrine of discovery,' France afforded no recognition of Spain's earlier 'discovery' of the Mississippi River by Hernan de Soto in 1541. Under an obscure 'axiom' of the Law of Nations, any sovereign 'discovering' the mouth of a river earned the entire river drainage.

Notes

1. Knecht, Robert Jean. *Francis I*. Cambridge University Press, 1984: 340.

2. Love, Ronald S. Maritime Exploration in the Age of Discovery, 1415-1800. United Kingdom, Greenwood Press, 2006: 151.

3. Royce, Charles C. "Indian land cessions in the United States." *Eighteenth annual report of the Bureau of American Ethnology, 1896-1897* (1902): 547-548.

4. Royce, Charles C. "Indian land cessions in the United States." *Eighteenth annual report of the Bureau of American Ethnology, 1896-1897* (1902): 545-546.

# 5

# ENGLAND'S IMPERIALISM

Even England, characterized by Marshall as an unequivocal supporter of the 'doctrine of discovery,' departed from the principle when it suited its national purpose. England was a Catholic nation under the rule of Henry VII (1485–1509), during much of Henry VIII's (1509–1547) reign and for the period 1685–1688 under James II. When the Pope refused to grant Henry VIII a divorce from Catherine of Aragón, Henry VIII completely severed the English Church from the Catholic Church. Rather than the Pope, the King would be the spiritual head of the English Church. The Anglican Church became the official church in England in 1559.

Without regard to the papal donation to Spain, King Henry VII, in 1496, granted letters patent to John Cabot and his sons to discover countries then unknown to Christian people, and to take possession of them in the name of the King of England. Subsequent grants to others were made thereafter.

> [T]o find, discover and investigate whatsoever islands, countries, regions or provinces of heathens and infidels, in whatsoever part of the world placed, which before this time were **unknown to all Christians** And that the before-mentioned John and his sons or their heirs and deputies may **conquer, occupy and possess** whatsoever such towns, castles, cities and islands by them thus discovered that they may be able to conquer, occupy and possess, as our vassals and governors lieutenants and deputies therein, **acquiring for us the dominion, title and jurisdiction** of the same towns, castles, cities, islands and mainlands so discovered.[1] Emphasis added.

In response to Spain's claims to the 'New World' based on the 'papal donation,' Queen Elizabeth announced in 1580 that:

> [S]he would not persuade herself that the Indies are the rightful property of Spain only on the ground that the Spaniards have touched here and there, have erected shelters, have given names to a river or promontory, acts which cannot confer property......this donation of what does not belong to the donor and this imaginary right of property ought not to prevent other princes from carrying on commerce in those regions or establishing colonies in places not inhabited by the Spaniards. Such action would in no way violate the law of Nations, since prescription without possession is not valid.[2]

England thus reformulated the doctrine of discovery.

**Real Property Common Law of England**

There was a common basis for English colonists in their familiarity with English common law and its application to real property. As presented by William Blackstone, renowned English jurist:

> They enjoyed the rights and privileges of British born subjects; and the benefit of the common laws of England; and all their laws were required to be not repugnant unto, but, as near as might be, agreeable to the laws and statutes of England.[3]

Real property law was highly developed in England. The estates concerning real property were clearly distinguished and the conveyance of real property was of critical import as to form, given property's limited availability and value. Real property is unique because of the multiple rights associated with each parcel, commonly referred to as a "bundle of rights." A fee simple title is the absolute ownership in land which includes all of the elements: possession, control, exclusion, enjoyment and disposition.

The bundle of rights includes:

The right of possession.

Possession of real property is a matter of physical fact, not a right. As stated in Black's Law Dictionary, possession is "the fact of having or holding property in one's power." It may be lawful or not. Either way, it is the physical fact, the fact of having or holding the property in one's power, that constitutes possession.[4]

The right of control: The ability to control the use of the land so long as the use is legal, for example, agriculture, mining, industrial uses, etc.

The right of exclusion: The right to exclude others, to determine who can enter the land.

The right of enjoyment: Enjoyment refers to the right of an occupant of real property to enjoy and use the premises in peace and without interference.

The right of disposition: The right of disposition allows for the transfer of ownership of one's land—this includes many forms such as a lease, an easement, use, etc.

Prior to the arrival of the European colonizing countries, Indians possessed all of these indicia of ownership.

To transfer real property under English law, there must be a *competent grantor* and a grantee capable of taking title. The physical document conveying the title to land to the new owner, the grantee, is a deed. The deeds by which Indians sold land were written in English and typically worded the same as the deeds by which English colonists sold land, conveying the same type of ownership enjoyed by the English – a fee simple if all of the ownership interest was to be transferred.

William Blackstone, renowned English jurist, described delivering a deed to a buyer as "the most solemn and authentic act that a man can possibly perform, with relation to the disposal of his property; and therefore a man shall always be estopped by his own deed, or not permitted to aver or prove any thing in contradiction to what he has once so solemnly and deliberately avowed."[5]

Blackstone further elucidated the language necessary to convey a fee simple which is critical in determining the estate received: a grant with the wording '**to the grantee and his heirs**' creates a fee simple.[6]

The norm for acquiring Indian land by the settler colonists in the thirteen colonies was to purchase it and a receive a deed to record with the colonial administration. Given their desire for stability in their land ownership, they were hesitant to merely rely on what some of them considered, an imaginary 'Doctrine of Discovery.'

This practice is confirmed by Justice Story in his *Commentaries*:

> § 174 (4) From a very early period of their settlement the colonies adopted an almost uniform mode of conveyance of land, at once simple and practicable and safe. The differences are so slight, that they became almost evanescent. All lands were conveyed by a deed, commonly in the form of a feoffment, or a bargain and sale, or a lease and release, attested by one or more witnesses, acknowledged or proved before some court or magistrate, and then registered in some public registry.[7]

## Nemo Dat Rule

A person cannot convey more than what they own, though they may convey less than the full bundle of sticks—the Nemo Dat Rule. 'No one gives what they do not have' as a legal principle means that the purchase of a possession from someone who has no ownership right to it also denies the purchaser any ownership title. "I make no doubt," affirmed the minister Christopher Toppan, that the Indians "have as full, and firm a Right, to their Lands as any white men have to theirs."[8] To the colonists, the Indians were considered sovereigns with dominion over the soil and if the colonists wanted their land, they had to purchase it. As to the fee ownership of their lands, Indians constituted 'competent grantors.'

## Crown Entered into Treaties with Indian Nations

England and almost all of the Thirteen Colonies, recognizing the sovereignty of the Indian Nations, entered into peace and cession treaties with them. The Protocol of Indian Treaties as Developed by Benjamin Franklin and Other Members of the American Philosophical Society describes them as follows:

These Indian treaties were public events usually held in White trading posts, forts, towns, and cities; they lasted for days, sometimes weeks, and were attended by hundreds of people, both White and Indian. (For instance, more than 500 Indians attended the treaty at Easton in 1758, and more than 2,000 attended at Fort Niagara in 1764). ... The delegations were led in person by the highest officials—on the White side by representatives of the Crown, the governors, and superintendents of Indian affairs of the relevant colonies (later the territories of the United States); and on the Indian side by sachem chiefs from the Grand Council of the Six Nations and from chiefs' councils of other nations and tribal factions.[9]

According to Felix Cohen, the practice of entering treaties for Indian land expressed three critical premises:

(1) that both parties to the treaty were sovereign powers; (2) that the Indian tribe had a transferable title to the land under discussion; and (3) that the acquisition of Indian lands could not be left to individual colonists but must be controlled by the larger institution of government, or the Crown itself.[10]

## Law of Nations regarding Treaties

The acknowledgement of the sovereign status of Indian Nations is confirmed by the understanding under the Law of Nations regarding the status of the parties to treaties. Vattel states that treaties are made "between sovereigns who acknowledge no superior on earth."

§219. Treaties are sacred between nations.

...Between bodies politic,—between sovereigns who acknowledge no superior on earth,—treaties are the only means of adjusting their various pretensions,—of establishing fixed rules of conduct,—of ascertaining what they are entitled to expect, and what they have to depend on.[11]

§221. He who violates his treaties, violates the law of nations.

He who violates his treaties, violates at the same time the law of nations; for he disregards the faith of treaties,—that faith which the law of nations declares sacred; and, so far as depends on him, he renders it vain and ineffectual. Doubly guilty, he does an injury to his ally, he does an injury to all nations, and inflicts a wound on the great society of mankind.[12]

## Indian Leaders Considered Sovereigns of Soil

In numerous treaty conferences held between the highest-level of Crown and colonial officials and Indian leaders, Indian Nations were considered the sovereign owners of their land. The credibility of the sovereignty of the Indian tribes is recognized by Justice Story:

> § 3. There is no doubt, that the Indian tribes, inhabiting this continent at the time of its discovery, maintained a claim to the exclusive possession and occupancy of the territory within their respective limits, as sovereigns and absolute proprietors of the soil. They acknowledged no obedience, or allegiance, or subordination to any foreign sovereign whatsoever; and as far as they have possessed the means, they have ever since asserted this plenary right of dominion, and yielded it up only when lost by the superior force of conquest, or transferred by a voluntary cession.[13]

In a meeting, at Fort Augusta, in November 1763, the Governor of Virginia recognized the leaders from the Chicasah, Upper and Lower Creek, Chactah, Cherokee and Catawba Indians as royalty - 'emperors or kings:'

> ...we shall not interfere with you in the choice or appointment of your emperors or kings, but whenever you shall agree amongst yourselves upon the election or choice of an emperor, we shall be ready to confirm such choice.[14]

## Conference with Eastern Indians, Ratification of Peace, Falmouth in Casco-Bay, July and August 1726, Loron (Penobscot Abenaki Spokesman) (*Penobscot Abenaki Nation Exercised Sovereign Control over Their Land by Restricting Entry—Ability to Restrict Entry is Considered Primary Attribute of a Fee Simple Title*)

We desire that no Houses or Settlement may be made to the Eastward of Pemmaquid, or above Arrowsick; As for the Penobscutt Tribe in particular, we don't know that ever they Sold any Lands, That's all we have to say. ... We can't find any Record in our Memory, nor in the Memory of Our Grand-Fathers, that the Penobscutt Tribe have Sold any Land ...[15]

**Treaty, Lancaster, Pennsylvania, Commissioners for Provinces of Virginia and Maryland, with Indians of Six Nations, Court House at Lancaster, June 26, 1744; Canassatego (Onondaga Spokesman) (*Onondaga Nation Claimed Sovereign Ownership of Their Land*).**

The Governor of Maryland claimed some of their land by possession.

Canasateego 'When you mentioned the affair of the land yesterday, you went back to old times, and told us you had had the province of Maryland above one hundred years in comparison of the length of time since our claim began—since we came out of the ground? For we must tell you that, long before one hundred years, our ancestors came out of this ground, and their children have remained here ever since. You came out of the ground beyond the seas; but here you must allow us to be your elder brothers, and the lands to belong to us long before you knew anything of them.'[16]

**Court House Chamber, Lancaster, June 30, 1744, Commissioners of Virginia, Deputies of Six Nations; Gachradodow, Iroquois Spokesman (*Claim Sovereignty and Lack of Conquest by British*)**

THO' great Things are well remembered among us, yet we don't remember that we were ever conquered by the Great King, or that we have been employed by that Great King to conquer others; if it was so, it is beyond our Memory. We do remember we were employed by Maryland to conquer the Conestoges, and that the second time we were at War with them, we carried them all off.[17]

When New York Governor Dongan insisted that the Iroquois were subjects of the English crown and could not make treaties with France without their permission, Hotrewati declared "that they acknowledged no one as their master; they had received their lands from the Great Spirit and had never been defeated in war by either the English or the French."[18]

## Conference with Northern Indians, Lancaster, August 19, 1762: Thomas King, Chief of Oneidas, Spokesman (*Oneida Nation Exercised Sovereign Control over Their Land by Restricting Entry*)

> I will tell you one Thing, you are always longing after my Land, from the East to the West; you seem to be longing after it. Now I desire you will not covet it any more ... I desire you to go no further than Nixhisaqua (or Mohenoy) ... You may remember that GOD gave us this Land, and you some other; yet I have parted with some of it to you.[19]

## April 26, 1768, Minutes of Conference, Fort Pitt, Six Nations, Delawares, Shawanese, Mohickons, Munsies, 1103 Indians Present, besides Women and Children (*Delaware and Shawanese Nations Claim Ownership of Their Land, Complained to Official Authorities regarding Unauthorized Entry and Settlement*), Beaver, Delaware Spokesman:

> It is not without Grief that we see our Country settled by you, without our Knowledge or Consent ...

> *Nymwha, Shawanese Spokesman, Claimed Rightful Ownership of Their Land*: They are also uneasy to see that you think yourselves Masters of this Country, because you have taken it from the French, who you know had no Right to it, as it is the Property of us Indians.[20]

### James Wilson and Indian Policy

Another player in the formation and execution of Congress' Indian policy was James Wilson, known for land speculation and his term as a Supreme Court Justice. Together with New Yorker's James Duane, Philip Schuyler, Philip Livingston and Virginian Patrick Henry, Wilson was one of five original members of a committee appointed to determine what steps should be taken "for securing and preserving the friendship of the Indian Nations," a body which later became the permanent Committee on Indian Affairs.

Led by Wilson an important peace treaty was negotiated with the western Indian Nations at Fort Pitt in late October 1775. Nine of the twenty-two Indiana Company proprietors (land speculators) met at Fort Pitt for several days beginning on September 21, 1775. This led to a rumor by Thomas Walker and three other Virginians who wrote a letter to Thomas Jefferson, alleging that "a certain eminent Gentleman" who has "greatly interested himself in this affair"[21] was taking the opportunity to promote the interests of Pennsylvania in its long-standing border dispute with Virginia. A similar claim was made in 1776 by Edmund Pendleton to the Virginia Delegates in Congress. Pendleton informed them: "You should be on your guard as to one of your brethren in Congress who was an Indian Commissioner last Summer at Fort Pitt, who stands charged by all the Gentlemen then present of directing every Speech and treaty with the Indians to the particular emolument of Pensylva.; and [doing] many things unworthy [of] his Public Character."[22]

**Six United Nations Deed of Cession to Crown at Fort Stanwix in 1768 Contained Crystal Clear Legal Language Necessary To Convey Fee Simple Title**

The Six United Nations Deed of Cession to King George III at Fort Stanwix in 1768 contained crystal clear legal language (1) confirming the Six Nations as the '*true and absolute Proprietors of the Lands*;' and (2) conveying a fee simple absolute title. The Deed reads in part:

> AND WHEREAS His said Majesty has at length given Sir William Johnson orders to compleat the said Boundary Line between the Provinces and Indians ... *who are the true and absolute Proprietors of the Lands*...

WE the said Indians HAVE for us and our Heirs and Successors granted bargained sold released and confirmed and by these presents DO Grant bargain sell release and confirm unto our said Sovereign Lord **King George the Third, his heirs and successors**, to and for his and their own proper use and behoof for ever ... [23] (Emphasis added.)

The consideration paid the Six United Nations for the Deed of Cession to King George III, made on November 5, 1768, was £10,460 7. 3. sterling.

Clearly a fee simple was conveyed based on the use of the words unto King George and his heirs. It is wholly unlikely that King George would have considered that he was receiving a usufructuary interest.

Two legal title opinions written in 1775 confirm that the interest conveyed by the Six Nations at Fort Stanwix was a fee simple absolute estate. One of the opinions is a concurring opinion by Benjamin Franklin, a learned scholar, and Patrick Henry, a renowned jurist of the day. An opinion of title is a legal opinion which attests to the validity of the ownership of a parcel of property. It generally documents the legal description of the property being conveyed, current ownership of the property and the manner in which the title is held (e.g., fee simple, lease, etc.).

### Counsellor DAGGE's Opinion on the Indian Grant of Lands to William Trent, and others, viz.

In the case under consideration, I am of opinion that the Indians of the Six Nations appear to have been entitled to the lands in question from pre-occupancy, or from conquest, but however their right accrued, they are acknowledged in express words by the deed of cession to the crown, made at Fort Stanwix, November 5th, 1768, to have been at that time *the true and absolute proprietors* of the lands in question; and so they were also acknowledged to be in the publick negociations between England and France, in the year 1755, and so also, as is stated in the case, several treaties of peace and commerce entered into with particular nations of Indians by England consider and treat the natives or occupiers as the lawful possessors and owners of the countries they respectively occupy. *Lincolns Inn, 20th March*, 1775. (Signed) HENRY DAGGE.

### Serjeant GLYNN's Opinion

I Entirely concur with Mr. Dagge in his opinion on this case. ... In this case the supreme power of the country resided in the sellers (Six Nations). *Philadelphia, July 12th,* 1775. (Signed) B. FRANKLIN. *Philadelphia, July 29th*, 1775. (Signed) P. HENRY, jun. [from principles which appear to me very clear][24]

### *Johnson* Case Factually Wrong in Stating Indian Land Title Is Mere Occupancy

Chief Justice Marshall's opinion unequivocally stating that the nature of Indian title is mere occupancy, not ownership, is simply not evidenced by the factual history regarding land transactions by British colonists. The Crown and colonists would certainly have been concerned if they were told that all they had purchased from the indigenous owners was the mere right to occupy the land they purchased. In fact, in one instance when this was asserted, here is the adamant response:

Andros rejected land claims based on what he called "pretended Purchases from Indians," on the ground that "from the Indians noe title cann be Derived." The sudden change in policy aroused a storm of protest from New Englanders. If purchase from the Indians could not serve as the root of a valid land title, declared a group of prominent Bostonians, then *"no Man was owner of a Foot of Land in all the Colony."*[25]

Notes

1. Skelton, Raleigh Ashlin. *The Cabot voyages and Bristol discovery under Henry VII*. Routledge, 2017: Document 18.

2. Cheyney, Edward P. "International Law under Queen Elizabeth." *The English Historical Review* 20.80 (1905): 660.

3. Blackstone's Commentaries on the Laws of England, Book the Second - Chapter the Twentieth: Of Alienation by Deed, p. 295.

4. Black, Henry Campbell, et al. *Black's law dictionary*. Vol. 196. St. Paul, MN: West Group, 1999.

5. Blackstone's Commentaries on the Laws of England, Book the Second - Chapter the Seventeenth: Of Alienation by Deed, p. 296.

6. Blackstone's Commentaries on the Laws of England, Book the Second - Chapter the Seventh Of Freehold States, Of Inheritance.

7. Story, Joseph. 1 *Commentaries on the Constitution of the United States*. §174(4) (1st ed. 1833).

8. Banner, Stuart. *How the Indians lost their land: Law and power on the frontier*. Harvard University Press, 2005: 28.

9. Wallace, Anthony F. C. and Powell, Timothy B., "How to Buy a Continent: The Protocols of Indian Treaties as Developed by Benjamin Franklin and Other Members of the American Philosophical Society" (2015): 254.

10. Cohen, Felix S. *Handbook of federal Indian law: With reference tables and index*. US Government Printing Office, 1942: 47.

11. de Vattel, Emerich, *The Law of Nations or the Principles of*

*Natural Law*, 1797, trans. Charles G. Fenwick (New York: Oceana Publications for the Carnegie Institute, 1964) § 219.

12. Ibid., §221.

13. Story, Joseph. 1 *Commentaries on the Constitution of the United States*. §3 (1st ed. 1833).

14. JOURNAL of the proceedings of the SOUTHERN CONGRESS at Augusta: from the arrival of the several GOVERNORS at Charles-Town, South-Carolina, the first day of October, to their return to the same place, &c. the twenty-first day of November, 1763. http://name.umdl.umich.edu/N07603.0001.001 (accessed online November 21, 2020).

15. The Conference with the Eastern Indians, at the ratification of the peace, held at Falmouth in Casco-Bay, in July and August, 1726. Massachusetts. Lieutenant Governor (1716-1730: Dummer). Massachusetts. General Court. House of Representatives. Boston: Re-printed by S. Kneeland, by order of the Honourable House of Representatives, 1754.

https://quod.lib.umich.edu/e/evans/N05687.0001.001/1:5?rgn=div1;view=fulltext.] (accessed online November 21, 2020).

16. Kalter, Susan, ed. *Benjamin Franklin, Pennsylvania, and the First Nations: The Treaties of 1736-62*. University of Illinois Press, 2010: 94.

17. Ibid., p. 106.

18. Fenton, William Nelson. *The great law and the longhouse: A political history of the Iroquois Confederacy*. Vol. 223. University of Oklahoma Press, 1998: 261.

19. Hazard, Samuel, ed. *Colonial Records of Pennsylvania*. Vol. 8. T. Fenn & Company, 1852: 747.

20. Ellis, Franklin, and Hungerford, Austin N.. History of Washington County, Pennsylvania: With Biographical Sketches of Many of Its Pioneers and Prominent Men. United States, Unigraphic, 1882: 144.

21. "To Thomas Jefferson from Thomas Walker and Others, 13 September 1775," *Founders Online*, National Archives, https://founders.archives.gov/documents/Jefferson/01-01-02-0124. [Original source: *The Papers of Thomas Jefferson*, vol. 1, *1760–1776*, ed. Julian P. Boyd. Princeton: Princeton University Press, 1950, pp. 244–245.] (accessed online November 21, 2020).

22. "From Edmund Pendleton to the Virginia Delegates in Congress, 15 July 1776," *Founders Online*, National Archives, https://founders.archives.gov/documents/Jefferson/01-01-02-0184. [Original source: *The Papers of Thomas Jefferson*, vol. 1, *1760–1776*, ed. Julian P. Boyd. Princeton: Princeton University Press, 1950, pp. 462–465.] (accessed online November 21, 2020).

23. Deed Determining the Boundary Line between the Whites and the Indians [Plantations General, Vol., 30, V.S.] O'Callaghan, E. B. (Ed.). (1857); *Documents Relative to the Colonial History of the State of New York, vol. 8.* Albany, NY: Weed, Parsons, and Co., 111, 136.

24. "Endorsement of Legal Opinions on Land Titles Obtained From the Indians, 12 July 1775," *Founders Online*, National Archives, https://founders.archives.gov/documents/Franklin/01-22-02-0061. [Original source: *The Papers of Benjamin Franklin*, vol. 22, *March 23, 1775, through October 27, 1776*, ed. William B. Willcox. New Haven and London: Yale University Press, 1982, pp. 102–103.] (accessed online November 21, 2020).

25. Banner, Stuart. *How the Indians lost their land: Law and power on the frontier*. Harvard University Press, 2005: 41-42.

# 6

# HOLLAND'S AND SWEDEN'S LAND PURCHASES

The laws of the Colony of New Netherland expressly provided that "[t]he Patroons of New Netherland, shall be bound to purchase from the Lords Sachems in New Netherland, the soil where they propose to plant their colonies, and shall acquire such right thereunto as they will agree for with the said Sachems."[1]

Hugo Grotius, a renowned Dutch scholar and lawyer, was retained by the Dutch East India Company, to support its claims in the 'New World.' In 1608 he published, anonymously, Mare Liberum (Freedom of the Seas), asserting that the Dutch possessed the right to sail to the East Indies. At the same time, he rejected claims to the 'New World' based on mere 'discovery' or papal or royal grant:

> Infidels cannot be divested of public or private rights of ownership merely because they are infidels, whether on the ground of discovery, or in virtue of a papal grant, or on grounds of war.
>
> [D]iscovery per se gives no legal rights over things unless before the alleged discovery they were res nullius.[2]

In 1625, in De Jure Belli ac Pacis (The Law of War and Peace), Grotius stated that "**discovery applies to those things which belong to no one,**" and decried as "shameless" efforts to claim "by right of discovery what is held by another, even though the occupant may be wicked, may hold wrong views about God, or may be dull of wit." As to what could be lawfully occupied, Grotius enumerated places uncultivated and animals not yet possessed, such as uninhabited islands, wild beasts, fishes and birds.[3] (Emphasis added.)

In 1663, Peter Stuyesant, a Dutchman, advised the Directors of Amsterdam, to get an "'Acte, Commission, Patent or Letter' over Long Island as under Dutch jurisdiction because 'sealed with their High Mightinesses' Great seal, at which an Englishman commonly gapes as at an idol, it would, in our opinion, help matters somewhat."[4]

Thus, the records of the Dutch West India Company show that patents issued to Dutch settlers "conferred the ultimate right of ownership only after the grantees had first acquired title by individual purchase directly from the Indians."[5]

Wholly disregarding the purported 'doctrine of discovery,' Holland voluntarily, knowingly and willfully refused to concede to it.

## Sweden Required Purchase from "Rightful Lords" (Indian Inhabitants)

Hoping to capitalize on fur and tobacco trading opportunities, Sweden established a colony between England's claim to Virginia and the Dutch claim to New Amsterdam. Sweden established a historical practice of entering politically-based treaty relationships with Indian Nations who they recognized as sovereign entities and purchased the land they settled from the native owners. They gave no countenance whatsoever to the idea that the 'New World' had been 'discovered' by other European countries, such that their settlement was precluded.

The policy of the Swedes was explicitly set forth in the "Instructions to Governor Johan Printz," written in Stockholm and dated August 15, 1642. The Governor of New Sweden was instructed to "bear in mind that the wild inhabitants of the country" are "its rightful lords." Also, the boundaries of land purchased from the inhabitants were to be specified so as to respect the 'contract' entered into with them.[6]

## Notes

1. Royce, Charles C. "Indian land cessions in the United States." *Eighteenth annual report of the Bureau of American Ethnology, 1896-1897* (1902), Reprinted at Royce at 577.

2. Grotius, Hugo. *The freedom of the seas, or, The right which belongs to the Dutch to take part in the East Indian trade*. The Lawbook Exchange, Ltd., 2001:7.

3. Grotius, Hugo. *Hugo Grotius on the law of war and peace*. Cambridge University Press, 2012, Book 2, Chapter 22, On Unjust Causes Of Wars, §IX.

4. O'Callaghan, Edmund Bailey. *Documents relative to the colonial history of the State of New-York*. Vol. II. Weed, Parsons, printers, 1861: 488.

5. Watson, Blake A. "John Marshall and Indian Land Rights: A Historical Rejoinder to the Claim of Universal Recognition of the Doctrine of Discovery." *Seton Hall L. Rev.* 36 (2005): 519.

6. Sipe, Chester Hale. *The Indian wars of Pennsylvania, including supplement*. Arno Press, 1971: 62.

7

# ENGLISH COLONIAL PRACTICES

There were three types of British colonies: Crown, Charter and proprietary. Their purchasing practices of Indian land were similar.

A Crown or Provincial colony was an overseas territory under the direct authority of the British Crown. The colony was administered by a governor appointed by the Crown. At the start of the American Revolution the following were Crown colonies: New Hampshire, Massachusetts (originally Charter), New York (originally Proprietary), New Jersey (originally Proprietary), Virginia, North Carolina (originally Proprietary), South Carolina (originally Proprietary) and Georgia.

Charter colonies, also known as corporate colonies or joint stock companies, included Rhode Island, Providence Plantation, and Connecticut; Massachusetts began as a charter colony in 1684, but became a provincial colony in 1691. A joint stock company was a project in which investors would buy shares of stock in building a new colony. Depending on the success of the colony, each investor would receive some of the profits in proportion to the number of shares he bought. Charter colonies were governed by political corporations created by letters patent, giving the grantees control of the land and the powers of legislative government. If charter colonies were unable to govern or were in financial need due to Indian wars, the Crown could recall their charter or the colony could surrender it to the Crown. The Crown would then govern and pay expenses.

Proprietary colonies were grants of land in the form of a charter, or a license to rule, for individuals or groups. The land was titled in the proprietors' name, not the king's. The proprietors possessed full governing authority. As proprietary colonies, The Carolinas, New Jersey, Maine, Maryland, New Hampshire, New York and Pennsylvania were devised through hereditary proprietorship. By the 1720s, certain of the proprietors were forced to yield their political privileges and powers to the Royal Crown, making all but three—Maryland, Pennsylvania and Delaware—royal colonies. After the Revolution, these three former proprietary colonies paid the heirs to the Calvert, Penn and Grandville estates minimal amounts for the confiscated lands.

In the earliest years of colonization, the English lacked the military superiority to implement a policy of conquest of the Indian Nations. However, this changed as immigration skyrocketed, the colonial population doubling almost every 25 years in the 1700s. Even after the English population increased to the point where conquest would have been feasible, taking the Indians' land by force would have required sacrificing the lives of thousands of English colonists and would have been very costly. "Let now any soldier or politician consider the enormous endless expence of all this conduct," reasoned Thomas Pownall in his treatise on colonial administration, "and then answer to what profitable purpose such measure leads." It was far cheaper in money and in lives to maintain cordial relationships with the Indians, by purchasing land rather than seizing it.[1]

The "principle Care" of initial colonial policy was "to cultivate and maintain a good Understanding with all the Indians," the Pennsylvania Gazette declared in 1736. To that end, "nothing hath contributed more than the Practice of purchasing their Claims to Lands."[2] By the eighteenth century, the English colonists well-established practice of purchasing Indian land was the norm. The Indians owned their land and if the colonists wanted it, they would have to buy it. This view of Indian property rights was never unanimous. One can find opinions to the contrary, including some by people powerful enough to put them into usage.

Vattel, a prominent eighteenth-century scholar of international law, noted the colonial practice of purchasing Indian land, even though it may not have been required:

> Section 210. Colonies. [W]e can not but admire the moderation of

the English Puritans who were the first to settle in New England. Although they bore with them a charter from their sovereign, they bought from the savages the lands they wished to occupy.[3]

William Penn reported in 1685 that "I have made seven Purchases" of land from the Indians in Pennsylvania, "and in Pay and Presents they have received at least twelve hundred pounds of me." James Glen, the governor of South Carolina between 1738 and 1756, noted that he had "made a considerable Purchase from that Indian Nation," the Cherokees, "of some of those hunting Grounds." Glen "had the Deeds of Conveyance formally executed in their own Country, by their head Men, in the Name of the whole People, and with their Universal Approbation and good Will." Nathaniel Crouch reported the same of New Jersey: "The English that are setled here buy the Lands of the Natives, and give them real satisfaction for the same." The Creek leader, Alexander McGillivray, declared at the end of the colonial period, "no title has ever been or pretended to be made by his Britannic Majesty to our lands except what was obtained by free Gift or by purchase for good and valuable Considerations." William Johnson, superintendent of Indian affairs through the 1750s and 1760s, concurred. It was a "well judg'd Policy," he concluded, that the English government "have always made an Indian Purchase the Basis or Foundation of all Grants."[4]

Chief Justice Marshall's opinion in regard to Indian land tenure lacked the nuances revealed in studying the different colonies. If the doctrine of discovery had been uniform and countries simply confiscated the Indians lands, as a matter of right, the variation in the methods used to acquire land would not be so prevalent.

## Virginia's (1607) Colonial Practice Pertaining to Indian Land

King James I's First Charter of Virginia, dated April 10, 1606, and second Charter, dated May 23, 1609, granted full and complete right in the land, "in free and common socage."[6]

There were numerous Indian Nations inhabiting the areas where the southern colonies were established. Notwithstanding this, there is no reference to the rights or title to land of the existing Indian inhabitants in the Charters granting the land to individual proprietors or land companies.

98

Some of the Charters did reference the propagation of Christianity to the Infidels and Savages. Nonetheless and without regard to the alleged English dominion over Indian lands as a result of 'discovery' and the granting of a charter or proprietary interest, numerous purchases of Indian lands by the colonists or colonial governments routinely occurred.

In 1609, Smith purchased land of Powhatan in return for the colony's protection against the Manakin Indians and an unspecified quantity of copper. The Virginia Company used various arguments justifying their right to take Indian lands, such as the need to convert the Indians which could only be done with daily interaction, they were infidels and that there was plenty of land. Regardless, they purchased the land from Paspehay, one of their 'kings,' for copper.

In 1653, the Commissioners of Northhampton County were empowered to buy land from Indians on the conditions that the majority of Indians agreed and the terms were just. Unfortunately, this led to fraud so a new Act was passed on March 10, 1655 to remedy this situation.

The first declaration of general policy in respect to Indian lands is found in the act of March 10, 1655, which is as follows: Act. 1. What lands the Indians shall be possessed of by order of this or other ensueing Assemblyes, such land shall not be alienable by them the Indians to any man de futuro ...[7] This statute does not question the ownership of Indian lands or purchasing them; it only seeks to protect Indians from frauds and injustices.

Similarly,

> All the Indians of this collonie shall and may hold and keep those seates of land which they now have, and that no person or persons whatsoever be suffered to entrench or plant upon such places as the said Indians claime or desire until full leave from the Governour and Councill or com'rs.[8]

Virginia was a huge colony, encompassing what is today West Virginia, Kentucky, Indiana and Illinois, and portions of Ohio and Western Pennsylvania, purportedly extending to the Pacific Ocean, according to its Charter. Settlers were inevitably drawn to the fringes of the colony. Daniel Boone played a central role in the exploration of what is now Kentucky. As a militia volunteer at Ft. Duquesne, part of Braddock's

Campaign over control of the Ohio Valley and leading Cherokee raids in 1759, his military experience gave him an edge in settling the vast part of western Virginia. With Colonel John Todd, Colonel Robert Patterson and Colonel Stephen Trig and 175 Kentucky militia he organized retaliatory raids against the numerous Indian Nations in the area: the Shawnee, Delaware, Chippewa, Mingo, Miami, Ottawa and Wyandot. Later, he was elected to the Fayette County General Assembly. This background led to him being a part of the frenzied land speculation.

Judge Richard Henderson of North Carolina, the employer and backer of Daniel Boone, promoted the settlement of the Kentucky region and claimed ownership to a vast unsettled tract there. He organized a group of land grabbers under the name of 'The Transylvania Company.' Ignoring the British interdiction against Indian land purchases, he obtained from the Cherokees in 1773 about one-half of the present State of Kentucky, and immediately began settling the land. Henderson purchased land from the Cherokee on March 17, 1775 who were represented by Little Carpenter and Dragging Canoe.

Officials taking depositions from parties who had purchased land from Indians also evidence the colonial practice of purchasing Indian land.

## II. Depositions concerning Claims to Lands under Purchases from the Indians [April 1777–October 1778]

We have this day met at the Court House of Mecklenburg County ... That the Deponant in the month of March 1775 was present at a Fort at Watauga at a time when a Treaty was held between the said Richard Henderson and others on the one part and the Chiefs of the Cherokee Nation consisting of Occonostoto the little Carpenter and all the other Chiefs as this Deponant understood, at which Treaty about twelve hundred of the said Nation attended and in the course of the Treaty which continued several days that the said Treaty was conducted with the greatest regularity, order and sobriety....[9]

## Massachusetts' (New England, 1620; Plymouth, 1629; Massachusetts Bay, 1629) Colonial Practices Pertaining to Indian Land

By a 1620 Charter to New England,[10] a 1629 Charter to Colony of New Plymouth[11] and a subsequent 1629 Charter to Massachusetts Bay, King Charles II granted the area of what would become Massachusetts to various parties.[12] Massachusetts accepted Indian land by gift and purchase and recognized the Indians as proprietors.

John Carver (Governor of Plymouth Colony) and his associates entered into a league of peace with Massasoit who freely gave them certain lands. The Wamponoags hoped to forge an alliance with the colonists against the more powerful Narragansetts. It is important to note that one of the articles of the Treaty stated that King James would esteem of Massasoit as "**his friend and ally**."[13] (Emphasis added.) This reference unquestionably documents that the English did not consider the Indians under their sovereignty or their land under their dominion. Massasoit was to be a friend and ally.

Governor Winslow, in a letter dated May 1, 1676, stated as follows: "I think I can clearly say, that before these present troubles broke out, the English did not possess one foot of land in this colony but what was fairly obtained by honest purchase of the Indian proprietors. We first made a law that none should purchase or receive of gift any land of the Indians, without the knowledge of our court. And lest they should be straitened, we ordered that Mount Hope, Pocasset, and several other necks of the best land in the colony, because most suitable and convenient for them, should never be bought out of their hands."[14] His letter makes clear that Plymouth recognized the Indians as proprietors of the land and that no purchases were to be made without court consent. It further demonstrates the practice of respecting the Indian title to valuable lands, which were to remain in Indian ownership.

It is stated by Reverend T. M. Harris, in his account of Dorchester, that the first settlers were kindly received by the aborigines, who granted them liberty to settle; "but at the same time they were careful to purchase the territory of the Indians;" also that "for a valuable consideration they bought a tract of land from what is now called Roxbury brook on the west to Neponset river..."[15]

Records indicate purchases of land from Indians in the following communities: Dorchester, Barnstable, Nantucket, Sandwich, Marshpee, Truro, Raynham, Haverhill, Hopkinton, New Bedford, Compton, Middleborough, Rehoboth, Wrentham and others.

After settling Plymouth, Robert Cushman, an organizer of the Mayflower voyage in 1620 and agent of the New Plymouth Colony, wrote three distinct answers to the question he knew others would pose: "what right have I to go live in the heathens' country?" The first was Christianity. Englishmen ought to convert the Indians, but conversion was impossible "unless we go to them or they come to us; to us they cannot come, our land is full; to them we may go, their land is empty."[16] The task of Christianizing the Indians thus required settling on their land.

Cushman's discussion of relative population densities brought him to his second reason the English could occupy North America: "their land is spacious and void." The Indians did not use all the land available to them. "They are not industrious," Cushman explained, "neither have art, science, skill or faculty to use either the land or the commodities of it, but all spoils, rots, and is marred for want of manuring, gathering, ordering, etc."

But after twice justifying a simple seizure of the Indians' land, Cushman noted that neither course was required. Seizure of the Indians' land had not been required as Chief Massasoit had given the English the land. Massasoit **"hath promised and appointed us to live at peace where we will in all his dominions, taking what place we will, and as much land as we will."** Cushman assured readers that this fortunate transaction had not **"been accomplished by threats and blows, or shaking of sword and sound of trumpet."** Emphasis added. The Plymouth settlers were a small group far from home and in no position to take land by force. Cushman admitted that "our faculty that way is small, and our strength less."[17]

The theory held by the Puritan colonists of Massachusetts Bay in regard to the Indian right to land varied, at times, from the other colonies in Massachusetts. It was enacted into law in 1633 and provided that "what lands any of the Indians in this jurisdiction have possessed or improved, by subduing the same, they have just right unto..." Similarly, it was held, that all land not occupied by the Indians as agriculturists, lay open to any that could or would improve it.[18] This is in accord with John Locke's theory that only land cultivated and enclosed was open for settlement. The Puritans relied on Biblical scriptures, such as Ephron the Hittite's right to Maehpelah, to justify their agriculturist policy. "[A]s men and cattell increased, they appropriated some parcells of ground by enclosing and peculiar mannrance, and this in tyme got them a civil right."[19]

### New Hampshire's (1623) Colonial Practice Pertaining to Indian Land

In 1629, Charles granted to the Council of New England, Sir Ferdinando Gorges and Captain John Mason the area that came to be known as New Hampshire.[20] New Hampshire purchased land from Indian owners, as well.

### Maryland's (1634) Colonial Practice Pertaining to Indian Land

In 1632, King Charles granted a Charter to Caecilius Calvert, Baron of Baltimore for the colony of Maryland. His Charter included the right to grant lands in the province and wage war on the "barbarous Nations."[21] Under Section 4 of an act of June 22, 1786, the governor was authorized to purchase Indian lands ... and to take a deed for same. This was the pattern for other such transactions. By various statutes, Maryland set aside specific land for various groups of Indians compelled to move to the interior of the colony due to the growth in the colonist population.[22]

### Connecticut's (1635–36) Colonial Practice Pertaining to Indian Land

In 1662, King Charles II granted a Charter to John Winthrop et al. for the area of Connecticut, with the right to invade and destroy the Natives.[23] Winthrop was the first governor of the Massachusetts Bay Colony and a chief figure among the Puritans. William Holmes purchased land to settle Connecticut in 1633 from the original Indian owners of said land, who had been ousted by the Pequot Indians. This accounted for the Pequots antagonism which resulted in a subsequent war. Numerous other similar purchases are of record from the original proprietors of the country, the Indians. In addition, Benjamin Trumbull, in his History of Connecticut, catalogued the Indian Nations in the colony and the land they owned. [24]

In 1640 laws were enacted by both Connecticut and New Haven prohibiting all purchases from the Indians by private persons or companies without the consent of their respective general courts. Also, Indians were given the right to bring suit to recover lands reserved by them or sequestered for them and the defendant or tenant was prohibited from pleading possession as a defense. This prevented settlers from gaining an advantage by squatting on Indian land. Tracts for Indians to cultivate were set aside and laws passed to protect them from injury and insult.

### Rhode Island's (1636) Colonial Practice Pertaining to Indian Land

King Charles II granted a Charter to Rhode Island and the Providence Plantations in 1663 to the Governor and Company of the English Colony.[25] In 1636, Roger Williams and his twelve companions were granted certain land from Oanonicus, chief of the Narragansett's: "all that neck of land ... that they might sit down in peace upon it and enjoy it forever." Here, as Williams observed to his companions, "The Providence of God had found out a place for them among savages, where they might peaceably worship God according to their consciences; a privilege which had been denied them in all the Christian countries they had ever been in."[26]

As Williams denied the right of the King to the lands, but believed it to be in the Indian occupants, the colony's policy was to purchase land from the Indians for consideration. Stringent provisions were enacted against unauthorized purchases from Indians. Also, as in Connecticut, Indians were given the right to bring suit to recover lands reserved by them or sequestered for them and the defendant or tenant prohibited from pleading possession as a defense.

An example of a 1646 deed contains the following grant:

I Ousamequin ... for and in consideration of full satisfaction in wampum, cloth and other commodities received at present; doe give, grant, sell and make over unto Roger Williams and Gregory Dexter ... all my right and interest of all that parcell or tract of land ...[27]

Approval for purchases from the 'true owners' was given by the General Court. In one such approval, dated June 17, 1662, it is noted:

The Court doe grant free liberty and leave to the petitioners and their sayd associates to make purchase of the natives within this jurisdiction, and to buy of them that are true owners ...[28]

Williams in general deplored the acquisitive nature of the New England colonists, and feared that "Land will be (as now it is) as great a God with us English as God Gold was with the Spaniards."[29]

## North Carolina's (1663) Colonial Practice Pertaining to Indian Land

By Charter dated March 24, 1663, the area that came to be known as Carolina was granted to Edward, Earl of Clarendon and others by King Charles II.[30] In general, the transactions with Indian Nations in regard to lands were entered into by individual colonists, except if a separate colony was to be established. The first recorded purchase was near Albemarle for a consideration of £200 sterling. The sale was commemorated with a turf of the earth with an arrow shot into it taken by the colonists. Another colony at Newbern was recorded as purchased and paid for by Graffenried.

While there are not many purchases recorded, they can be ascertained from official correspondence. The Instructions relating to the settlement of The Province of Carolina to Sir William Berkeley (1663) clearly recognize the individual colonists purchase of lands from the Indians and the problems that can be created for the colony. Similarly, in a letter to the same person, dated September 8, 1663, it is noted that "that the people that are there have bought great tracts of land from the Indians, which if they shall injoye will weaken the plantation."[31]

In 1715, an act was passed by the general assembly to restrain "the Indians from molesting or injuring the inhabitants of this government and for **securing to the Indians the right and property of their own lands**." The fourth section of this act is as follows:

> And whereas there is great reason to believe that disputes concerning land has already been of fatal consequence to the peace and welfare of this colony, Be it further enacted, by the authority aforesaid, That no white man shall, for any consideration whatsoever, purchase or buy any tract or parcel of land claimed, or actually in possession of any Indian, without special liberty for so doing from the Governor and Council.[32]

Again, in an effort to prevent encroachments on Indian lands, an act was issued in 1748 to preclude encroachment on Tuscarora Indian Nation lands.

In 1761 the British government, recognizing the conflicts arising from individual purchases of Indian land, issued instructions to the governors of the several American colonies, including North Carolina, South Carolina and Georgia, and the agent for Indian affairs in the southern department, forbidding purchases of land from the Indians without first having obtained a license to this effect.

Due to the costs incurred in fighting the Cherokees in 1860–1862, the proprietors of Carolina decided that, if the colony was to be protected at the expense of England, its government ought to be vested in the Crown. The proprietors were no longer able to absorb the costs of protecting the colony; considerable sums of paper money had been issued for which there was no backing. The Crown took control of Carolina.

The scant documentation in North Carolina's records concerning purchases of Indian lands may also be a result of the Indians present in the area. Based on a study by Mr. James Mooney, with the Bureau of American Ethnology, he sadly wrote:

> War, pestilence, whisky and systematic savage hunts had nearly exterminated the aboriginal occupants of the Carolinas before anybody had thought them of sufficient importance to ask who they were, how they lived, or what were their beliefs and opinions.[33]

Nonetheless, the historical record clearly evidences the acknowledgement of Indian land ownership and purchases of their land.

## New York's (1664) Colonial Practice Pertaining to Indian Land

There were numerous Indian Nations inhabiting the areas where the northern colonies were established.

Purchasing practices varied—the English purchased Indian land as individuals or through the colonial government. **English settlers declared "that wee would purchase the land as wee are Englishmen."**[34] (Emphasis added.)

Written permits to settlers to purchase land from Indians was granted by Colonel Richard Nicolls who at times represented himself as Governor, under his Royall Highnesse the Duke of York. The fraud which occurred in certain purchases is seen in the extract below:

> Under the preceding Governor Fletcher, large grants had been made to individuals based on pretended purchases from the Indians. "For example, a considerable portion of the Mohawks' land was obtained by fraudulent and unauthorized purchases, and the grants, notwithstanding the protests of the Indians, were confirmed by Governor Fletcher."[35]

There were those who viewed purchasing Indian land as a way to maintain peace. In 1674, for example, New York's Council insisted that although it was "the usuall practice" for New Yorkers acquiring land "to give their Indians some recompence for their land & so [the landowner] seems to purchase it of them, yet that is not done for want of sufficient title from the King," the king being the land's true owner. Paying the Indians was a matter of "prudence & christian charity lest otherwise the Indians might have destroyed the first planters," not a recognition that the Indians owned the land.[36]

Yet, high-ranking British officials such as James, the Duke of York, the future King of England, instructed the colony's lieutenant governor that "when opportunities shall offer themselfes (as I am informed they frequently doe) for purchaseing great tracts of land for Me from the Indians, for small sumes," he should seize the chance to do so. The Duke of York is a title of nobility in the Peerage of the United Kingdom.

Since the 15th century, it has, when granted, usually been given to the second son of English monarchs. James, was the younger son of King Charles I. When Charles died in 1685, James ascended to the throne, though he was later deposed.[37]

Also, the official recognition of the Indian's ownership and the intention to act upon it is indicated in instructions, dated August 31, 1697, to the Earl of Bellomont. He was to purchase "great tracts of land for His Majty from the Indians for small sums."[38]

James Macauley in the History of the State of New York (1829), Vol. ii, p. 260, stated that Indian lands were purchased by the settlers with the consent of the agent of the Earl of Sterling and thereafter by municipal authorities or by individuals or companies acting on their own behalf.[39] As the method of obtaining Indian title was neither uniform nor systematic, future land title disputes resulted.

In 1698, the Earl of Bellomont, New York's new governor, asked the colony's attorney general, James Graham, about "the Methods of making grants of Land since the settlement of the Government under the Crown of England," Graham had no trouble providing an answer. The land first had to be purchased from the Indians.

> If the lands were not purchased of the Indians then a petition was made to the Governor and Councill for a License to purchase the same. Then there was an order for a purchase in the presence of the Magistrates of the County where the land lay ...[40]

In Stuart Banner's comprehensive study of colonial land acquisitions, he stated:

> The colonial government could grant licenses to purchase, and it could ratify purchases already made, but it could not dispense with the requirement of a purchase from the Indians. By the middle of the eighteenth century, New York required that lands purchased from Indians be first surveyed, by a government surveyor, in the company of Indians from the selling nation, to avoid subsequent disputes. Land purchasing had become a routine matter. ... Colonial officials in New York thought of themselves not as conquerors but as bargain shoppers, waiting for the Indians to put their land on sale.[41]

## New Jersey's (1664) Colonial Practice Pertaining to Indian Land

On July 24, 1664, James, Duke of York, granted to Lord Berkeley and Sir George Carteret the area which would come to be known as New Jersey.[42] Purchasing Indian land became a matter of controversy in New Jersey due to a dual purchasing requirement. First, the patent had to be purchased from the Crown. Second, the land had to be purchased from the Indians. In 1687, the Proprietors of East New Jersey complained of being "forced to buy every Acre over again at a considerable rate from the Indians, who daily raise the price of land as they understand our want of it."[43]

Governor Carteret's procedure of settlers purchasing Indian lands from the Indians or if previously purchased, paying their proportionate share was replaced in 1677 by a statute requiring the colony's commissioners to negotiate any purchase and consideration for Indian lands. This type of legislation did not address the estate in land held by the Indians but was a method to administer land ownership and avoid future disputes over land titles.

In 1703 the following act was passed which explicitly confirmed that Indians held various estates in their lands, including the fee:

> ...Whereas, several ill disposed persons within this province have formerly presumed to enter into treaties with the Indians or natives thereof, and have purchased lands from them ... Sec. 1. ... That no person or persons whatsoever, forever hereafter, shall presume to buy, take a gift of, purchase in fee, take a mortgage, or lease for life or number of years, from any Indians or natives for any tract or tracts of lands ...[44]

Royce concludes that all Indian lands were purchased from the Indians and if there were subsequent disputes the colony would re-purchase the land.

## Pennsylvania's (1682) Colonial Practice Pertaining to Indian Land

On February 28, 1681, a Charter for the Province of Pennsylvania was granted to William Penn by Charles II.[45] The policy adopted by Penn was to extinguish claims, and to give satisfaction to the natives for their possessory rights, rather than to fix definite and accurate boundaries of the lands purchased. One example was the 'Walking Purchase' where the land conveyed was to be that covered by a man walking a day and a half. This purchase was later to lead to claims of fraud when Penn's sons re-enacted the walk to re-determine the acreage.

While Penn made it a point to purchase Indian lands, he, nevertheless, was concerned with making a profit. The estimate below is an example of the substantial value to be made in acquiring and re-selling Indian lands. In the issue of May 26–29, 1759, The London Chronicle published a historical review of Pennsylvania which included an estimate of Penn's profit: Total in Pennsylvania Currency: £15,875,500. In Sterling, about Ten Million!

> That the Reader may form some Judgment of the Profits made by this Monopoly of Land in America in Favour of the House Of Penn, we shall just mention, that the Land is first purchased of the Indians, and none but the Proprietors are allow'd to purchase of the Indians within the Limits of their Grant: The Indians of late Years have somewhat rais'd their Price; and for the last great Purchase in 1754, which was of about Seven Millions of Acres, they demanded (how much do you think?) no less than 2000 Dollars amount at Seven and Sixpence Currency each, to Seven Hundred and Fifty Pounds.[46]

## Delaware's (1682) Colonial Practice Pertaining to Indian Land

James, the Duke of York, gave Delaware to William Penn in 1682 who wanted the land to secure his own colony of Pennsylvania.[47] At first the two colonies were joined and shared the same legislative assembly. After 1701, Delaware was given the right to its own assembly. However, both colonies shared the same governor. It was not until 1776 that Delaware was declared separate from Pennsylvania. Delaware purchased land from Indian owners, as well.

## South Carolina's (1719) Colonial Practice Pertaining to Indian Land

South Carolina became a separate colony in 1719. In 1739, when South Carolina passed legislation requiring government approval of land purchases from the Indians, the measure was intended to allow for the recording and administration of purchases. Also, the legislation was enacted in part to protect the Indians from being defrauded, such purchases being generally obtained from Indians by unfair representations, fraud and circumvention, or by making them gifts or presents of little value, by which practices, resentments and animosities were arose amongst the Indians towards the inhabitants of this Province. The other problem with private land purchases, the legislature explained, was that the Indians did not really own the land they were selling. The land was instead owned by the Crown. Sales by the Indians "tend to the manifest prejudice of his Majesty's just right and title to the soil of this Province."[48] This procedure for purchasing Indian land was contradictory if Indians did not own the land. If the colony intended to assert dominion over the land based on a 'discovery' claim, it would not have enacted procedural requirements to acquire Indian land.

According to Mills in the Statistics of South Carolina (1826), the first public deed of conveyance found on record is dated March 10, 1675. The territory was purchased by the Proprietors of the colony. It is clear from the language of the Deed that it was drafted by the colonists as the language is that of England, not the Indian Nation. This is important because the Indians are referred to as "natural born heirs and sole owners and proprietors" of the land ceded.

> ...Know ye, that we the cassiques, natural born heirs and sole owners and proprietors of greater and lesser Casor ... doe, for us, ourselves and subjects and vassals, demise, sell, grant, and forever quit and resign, the whole parcels of land [description follows] ... for and in consideration of a valuable parcel of cloth, hatchets, beads, and other goods and manufactures ...[49]

On November 25, 1707, an act was passed to prevent encroachment by colonists on Yamasee Indian Nation lands and to remove same.

Royce notes that while "the policy pursued by the South Carolina colony in regard to the Indian title was based—impliedly, at least—on an acknowledgment of this title... a large area in this state, as in North Carolina, does not have recorded treaties or purchases from the Indians."[50] This may have been the result of the presence of small Indian Nations, with the exception of the Catawba. Also, the Catawba were greatly reduced in numbers as a result of internecine warfare.

South Carolina, though, actively engaged in Indian enslavement. Indians were kidnapped, sold and kept in captivity in the British colonies or were exiled to places as far away as the West Indies. As late as 1708 the native population furnished a quarter of the whole body of slaves owned in South Carolina.

## Georgia's Colonial Practice Pertaining to Indian Land

On June 9, 1732, King Charles II granted a Charter to certain Trustees for the colony of Georgia.[51] On May 29, 1733, Governor Oglethorpe entered into a treaty with the Lower Creeks. The Indians later complained to Oglethorpe of encroachment by colonists on lands reserved to the Creeks. They planted corn, grazed their cattle and begin a plantation with Negro slaves. Governor Oglethorpe had these squatters removed promptly.

A statute was enacted in 1757 or 1758 acknowledging the abuses in colonists pretending to have made purchases of Indian land and requiring purchase through the municipal government:

> Whereas the safety, welfare, and preservation of this province of Georgia doth, in great measure depend on the maintaining a good correspondence between his majesty's subjects and the several nations of Indians in amity with the said province: And whereas many inconveniences have arisen, from private persons claiming lands, included in the charter granted to the late honorable trustees for establishing the colony of Georgia by his present majesty, and since reinvested in the crown under pretense of certain purchases made of them from the Indians, which have given occasion for disputes with those people ...[52]

Governor Oglethorpe wrote to the trustees on September 5, 1739, confirming the Creek Nation's declaration to and possession "of all the Land as far as the River Saint Johns and their Concession of the Sea Coast, Islands and other Lands to the Trustees."[53]

As concluded by Royce, in the transactions reviewed, clearly the ownership of the Indians to the lands they claimed was honored and the colony purchased lands desired. Governor Oglethorpe took decisive action to prevent squatters from invading Indian lands.

## Evidence of Colonial Policy of Purchasing Indian Land

Three indicators evidence that the purchase of land from Indians was extremely common. The first is the vast number of surviving deeds (written in English) by which Indians sold their land to English colonists. "Every Man that pretended to Propriety, had gotten his Right by Purchase from the Natives," a group of New Jersey colonists recalled in 1747; "without which purchase, the People there would hiss at the person pretending Property."[54] A second indicator that purchase was a British colonial norm for acquiring Indian land is in the colonial statutes regulating the purchasing process, requiring private purchasers acting on their own account to obtain permission from the colonial government before buying Indian land. The first such statute was enacted in Massachusetts in 1634. Most of the other colonies followed suit. Their common enactment makes it clear that land was purchased from the Indians. Their purpose was to (1) facilitate purchasing; (2) standardize a methodology and communicate it to the public; (3) administer the recording of such purchases to prove up ownership; and (4) regulate the market to prevent fraud. A third indicator is that colonial officials often judicially enforced Indian property rights against the competing claims of colonists. New England court records are full of property disputes, many involving Indian property owners and the Indians were treated the same as English litigants. In certain statutes, squatters were prohibited from relying on possession as nine-tenths of the law. This patent evidence belies Chief Justice Marshall's assertion that Indians were not considered as owners of their lands.

## Many of European Colonists Themselves Considered Indians as Owners of Land

Many European colonists themselves considered Indians as owners of the land. In his substantial research on this subject, Stuart Banner collected the following information:

The early Maine settler Christopher Levett arrived in 1623 with the belief that the Indians owned Maine by "a natural right of inheritance, as they are the sons of Noah." An early governor of New Haven declared that the Indians "were the true proprietours of the land (for we found it not a vacuum)."[55]

The English "settled by the Indians consent and good liking, and bought the Land of them, that we settle on, which they conveyed to us by Deed under their Hands and Seals," Thomas Budd explained in 1685. By 1691 the Massachusetts minister John Higginson mocked "the Popish Principle, that Christians have a right to the Lands of Heathen," a principle that might suit Catholics but one "disowned by all Protestants."[56]

Robert Morden's Geography Rectified (1693) described how the residents of New England "purchased their Lands of the Sachems, which were the heads; and the eldest of the Indian Families, the Antient Proprietors" of the land. By 1728 Daniel Dulany was incredulous when he "heard it asserted, that Maryland is a Conquered Country," an assertion "which, by the By, is false." Maryland, he implied, like the other colonies of British North America, was a purchased country. In Connecticut, explained Lord Saye, one of the colony's original patentees, settlers "purchased the land from the natives," because the Indians were "the acknowledged and right owners thereof."[57]

David Dunbar reported from Maine in 1730, for example, that the inhabitants all traced their ownership back to Indian deeds from the previous century. Without regard to the social status of Indians, the Scottish writer Robert Ferguson insisted they possessed "Title unto, and Property in what was anciently and originally theirs," because "the point of Right and Property is the same in the Poor that it is in the Rich, and in the Weak that it is in the Strong." Even James Glen, the expansionist governor of South Carolina in the mid-eighteenth century, was adamant that the Indians were the "Original possessors and Proprietors of the Lands and Countries they Inhabit."[58]

Jeremiah Dummer scoffed in 1721, "that we have any Claim upon the Foot that we were Christians, and they Heathen," was something that "no Body will say." "Neither yet is it lawfull for Christians, to usurpe the goods and lands of Heathens," insisted Samuel Purchas, a British cleric and ardent supporter of colonization, "for they are villains not to us; but to our and their Lorde."[59]

In the words of his biographer Edwin Gaustad, Roger Williams, an assistant to the pastor at Plymouth,

> ...questioned the very right of the English to occupy land that properly belonged to the Indians. What was it about Christendom, Williams wondered, that empowered Christian kings to give away land that wasn't even theirs? English colonization was nothing more than "a sin of unjust usurpation upon others' possessions." Indians owned the land before Europeans arrived; they would continue to own the land until appropriate purchases or agreements had been made.[60]

Even the ministers who preached sermons to the Virginia Company spoke of it. In his sermon delivered in February 1609, William Crashaw observed that the "first and fundamentall objection to the new colony in Virginia is the doubt of lawfulnes of the action. Was it right to take land from the Indians? ... *A Christian may take nothing from a Heathen against his will, but in faire and lawfull bargaine,*" Crashaw explained. ... The lesson, Crashaw concluded, was that the Virginia colonists must "take nothing from the Savages by power nor pillage, by craft nor violence, neither goods, lands nor libertie." How then was the colony to acquire the land it would need? Crashaw had an answer. "We will exchange with them for that which they may spare, and we doe neede," he asserted, "and they shall have that which we may spare, and they doe much more need." Fortunately the Indians had plenty of land to spare, "in so much as a great part of it lieth wild & inhabited of none but the beasts of the fielde, and the trees." Nevertheless, Crashaw affirmed, the colonists would have to buy it.[61] (Emphasis added.)

Daniel Gookin declared in 1674 that a patent from the king was enough for an Englishman to claim property rights in North America, but he recognized that it made no difference, because "the English had the grant of most of the land within this jurisdiction, either by purchase or donation from the Indian sachems and sagamores, which were actually in possession, when the English first came over."[62]

William Symonds, a minister, sermonized on the same theme. "There is one scruple, which some, that thinke themselves to be very wise, do cast in our way," Symonds noted. "The countrey, they say, is possessed by owners, that rule, and governe it in their owne right: then with what conscience, and equitie can we offer to thrust them, by violence, out of their inheritances?"[63]

Another factor was equally important. Land was abundant, and it was usually cheap. Roger Pederick informed his wife in 1676 of the ready availability of land—"the Natives were as willing to sell as we were to Buy; and there is Land enough bought." Robert Wade, another New Jersey colonist, agreed that the Indians "are very willing to sell their land to the English." The Scottish settler Gavin Laury reported that the Indians "do not refuse to sell Land."[64]

## Some Colonists Argued that Indians Did Not Own Their Lands

Evidence of those who challenged the Indians right of ownership can also be found. Their arguments included: (1) it was God's will, including that Indians were being decimated by smallpox and other diseases; (2) the land was vacant—not settled (vacuum domicilium); (3) the land was physically unoccupied; (4) Indian land rights were limited to land they cultivated and enclosed; (5) Indians were non-Christian; (6) Indians were not human but rather savage beasts; and (7) war was justified to confiscate their lands.

## Vacuum Domicilium and God's Will Argument

Over the course of time, the concept of terra nullius was extended by European lawyers and philosophers to include lands that were not in the possession of 'civilized' peoples or were not being put to a proper 'civilized' use according to European definitions of the term.

Samuel Purchas argued that Englishmen could rightfully seize Indian land because God intended land to be cultivated, and this land was "unmanned wild country, which they [the savages] range rather than inhabite."[65]

On January 3, 1633, John Winthrop wrote to John Endicott, his predecessor as governor of the Massachusetts Bay Colony, with a responsive argument to Roger Williams' claim that the Crown did not own the land. He argued it was God's will, that God was pleased to give it to the colonists and God was behind the Indian population decline:

> But if our title be not good, neither by Patent, nor possession of these parts as vacuum Domicilium nor by good liking of the natives, I mervayle by what title Mr. Williams himselfe holdes. & if God were not pleased with our inheritinge these partes, why did he drive out the natives before us? & why dothe he still make roome for us, by diminishing them as we increase?... If we had no right to this lande, yet our God hathe right to it, & if he be pleased to give it us (takinge it from a people who had so longe usurped upon him, & abused his creatures) who shall controll him or his terms?[66]

His reference to the diminishment of the natives may be the smallpox and other diseases that were having a catastrophic impact on Indians who had no immunity.

John Cotton, a Boston minister and contemporary of Winthrop and Williams, also embraced the emergent international law doctrine of vacuum domicilium, writing that, "[i]n a vacant soyle, hee that taketh possession of it, and bestoweth culture and husbandry upon it, his Right it is."[67]

Samuel von Pufendorf, a German jurist and historian, known for his defense of natural law, served as a professor of natural law at Heidelberg and Lund in Sweden. In his work on natural law, The Law of Nature and of Nations, 1672, he wrote that 'vacant' or unoccupied land must not automatically be assumed open for appropriation even when there are no plans on the part of the people who claim it to divide it into parcels, for it is perfectly legitimate that an agreement amongst a group of people render the ownership of their property to be communal.

And so we have not sinned against the law of nature in entirely doing away with primitive community, nor have backward peoples in retaining to this day many of its features.[68]

## Cultivation and Enclosure Argument

Some colonists argued that Indians had to cultiate and enclose land to claim it. John Winthrop, in a decidedly un-Christian manner, stated: The "savage people" had not enclosed or improved it, and due to smallpox, "God hath consumed the natives with a miraculous plague, whereby the greater part of the country is left void of inhabitants."[69]

Even William Penn, who was scrupulous about purchasing Indian land, declared that the Indians lacked any claim to "Waste, or uncultivated Country."[70]

Future president John Adams vehemently disagreed that Indians could be dispossessed of uncultivated lands in a letter to Philip Mazzei, June 26, 1786:

> The insinuation of the Abby Raynal, mentioned [in your] Letter of the 17th that "the Savages were to be dispossessed of Lands which they would not cultivate" is injurious. ... The first settlers of New England, as well as of the other parts of America were scrupulous to purchase the [title of the] Indians, wherever they planted—In a course of many years practice in the Courts of Law I have had a great oppertunity of knowing this fact—There is scarcely a suit concerning Land, in which the titles & Pretensions are not traced back to Indian Deeds—[71]

## Actual Occupation Argument

Many concluded that the only place to draw the line was at actual occupation. The Indians were the owners of the land upon which they were physically present, but the rest was open for settlement. "If any Countrey be not possessed by other men," Samuel Purchas argued in 1625, "every man by Law of Nature and Humanitie hath right of Plantation." And the same principle applied to a land that was partially

118

possessed, as he understood North America to be. "If a country be inhabited in parts thereof, other parts remaining unpeopled, the same reason giveth liberty to other men which want convenient habitation to seat themselves, where (without wrong to others) they may provide for themselves."[72]

The Massachusetts minister John Cotton affirmed that "God makes room for a People" when "he makes a Countrey, though not altogether void of Inhabitants, yet void in that place where they reside. Where there is a vacant place, there is liberty for the Son of Adam or Noah to come and inhabit, though they neither buy it, nor ask their leaves."[73]

While Indians could not own lands they did not occupy, the United States, under a different standard it promulgated, could own the massive Louisiana Territory though unpopulated by its citizens. Similarly, it could claim ownership of the broad Oregon Territory.

## Non-Christians Argument

A few argued that Indian land could be taken because Indians were non-Christians. As Virginia was "voide of Christian inhabitants," William Strachey asked, "may it not then be lawfull nowe to attempt the possession of such lands?"[74]

Cotton Mather, a New England Puritan minister, countered this argument. Though he stereotyped the Indians "infinitely barbarous," he refused to deny their property rights. He preached that "the Indians had not by their Paganism so forfeited all Right unto any of their Possessions" that the English could simply take their land. No Indian land could be settled, Mather explained, "without a fair Purchase and Consent from the Natives."[75]

Vitoria, relying on the scholarship of St. Thomas, contended that ownership and dominion are based on either natural or human law and they are not destroyed by want of faith.

> The proposition is also supported by the reasoning of St. Thomas, namely: Unbelief does not destroy either natural law or human law; but ownership and dominion are based either on natural or on human law; therefore they are not destroyed by want of faith. ...

119

Hence it is manifest that it is not justifiable to take anything that they possess from either Saracens or Jews or other unbelievers as such, that is, because they are unbelievers; but the act would be theft or robbery no less than if it were done to Christians.[76]

## Beasts Argument

Robert Gray's sermon, A Good Speed to Virginia, published in 1609, affirms the proposition that lands can rightfully be taken from the Indians due to their character:

> ...by reason of their godless ignorance, & blasphemous Idolatrie are worse than those beasts which are of most wilde and savage nature ... [They] have no interest in it [the land] because they participate rather of the nature of beasts than men. ... Some affirm, and it is likely to be true, that these savages have no particular propriety in any part of parcel of that country, but only a general residency there, as wild beasts in the forest; for they range and wander up and down the country without any law or government, being led only by their own lusts and sensuality. There is not meum and tuum [mine and thine] amongst them. So that if the whole land should be taken from them, there is not a man that can complain of any particular wrong done unto him.

But then he goes on to say, the land is their rightful inheritance which they have been willing to sell to the colonists such that force is not needed to take their land.

> But the answer to the foresaid objection is that there is no intendment to take away from that by force that rightfull inheritance which they have in that Countrey for they are willing to entertaine us, and have offered to yeelde into our handes on reasonable conditions more land then we shall be able this long time to plant and manure...[77]

He concludes though in his sermon that their lands may be taken if needed.

## Force Is Justifiable Argument

William Symonds, a clergyman, while not challenging the Indians ownership of their land, concluded that it could be taken by force:

> [It is wrong to suppose that] "it is not lawfull to invade the territories of other princes, by force of sword," when in fact human history was largely a catalogue of invasions and wars, with the winners taking the land of the losers. The English had every right to seize Virginia by force.[78]

Repeatedly, legal theorists proclaimed that there was no just basis for a war when it was merely to acquire territory.

## Indians Have Concept of Property

While it was alleged that Indians had no notion of property rights such that their land could be confiscated, there were those who challenged this view.

In 1629, John Winthrop assumed that "This savage people ruleth over many lands without title or property ... for they enclose no ground, neither have they any cattel to maintayne it, but remove their dwellings as they have occasion." Other colonists' accounts confirmed that the Indians in fact did allocate property rights in land. "Each household knoweth their owne lands & gardens," John Smith reported of the Indians near Jamestown. "They all know their severall landes, and habitations, and limits, to fish, fowle, or hunt in." The Virginia minister, Alexander Whitaker, affirmed that the Indians "observe the limits of their owne possessions, and incroach not upon their neighbours dwellings."[79]

Edward Winslow, the Governor of Plymouth colony, concurred that every Indian Nation knew its territory. The sachem allocated land amongst them for farming. In Pennsylvania, William Penn characterized the Indians "exact Observers of Property." John Lawson, explorer, surveyor, land speculator, fur trader, naturalist, ethnographer and writer, observed that the Indians in North Carolina "have no Fence to part one anothers Lots in their Corn-Fields; but every Man knows his own, and it scarce ever happens, that they rob one another of so much as an Ear of Corn."[80]

Benjamin Trumbull's lengthy analysis, in his History of Connecticut, undeniably demonstrates that Indians were aware of the lands that made up their Nation, as were the colonists, whether they were used for agriculture, hunting and gathering, or other purposes. Trumbull was a representative to the Connecticut General Assembly. Later he served as the Governor of Connecticut Colony (1769–1776) and then after the War of American Independence, as the Governor of the state of Connecticut (1776–1784).

## Colonists and British Royal and Crown Officials Purchased Vacant Lands from Indian Owners without Regard to Cultivation Evidencing Rightful Ownership of Indian Owners to Land Whether Cultivated or Not

While Indian title to uncultivated areas used for hunting and gathering was questioned, imperial and colonial officials normally recognized the Indians as owners of their entire territories, including hunting grounds and other uncultivated areas. In 1665, a visiting British royal commission reminded the Massachusetts General Court that "**no doubt the country is theirs till they give or sell it, though it be not improved**." In New York, Governor William Cosby authorized the purchase from "the Native Indian proprietors" of "fifteen thousand acres of Vacant Land." New York lieutenant governor John Nanfan proudly reported his purchase of "a tract of land 800 miles long and 400 miles broad" from the Five Nations to the Board of Trade in 1701.[81] (Emphasis added.)

The Earl of Egremont, secretary of state, emphasized in 1763 the importance of "*guarding against any Invasion or Occupation of their Hunting Lands, the Possession of which is to be acquired by fair Purchase only*." In 1693, even John Winthrop, who earlier had recognized Indian property rights only in cultivated land, purchased from two men, named Webomscom and Nodowahunt, an enormous tract (more than three hundred square miles) near the Massachusetts–Connecticut border, apparently without inquiring into how much of the land was in cultivation.[82] (Emphasis added.)

## Benjamin Franklin's Indian Policy regarding Purchases from Indian Sovereigns

According to Anthony Wallace and Timothy Powell, the principles of Benjamin Franklin's Indian policy grew out of a European Enlightenment view of world history.

> The basic elements of this perspective, as interpreted by British officials in Franklin's time, were: Natural law justifies, and the idea of progress predicts, the replacement of "savage" hunters and gatherers and village gardeners, who subsist on land that yields them a slender harvest, by agriculturists who farm intensively by advanced methods and thereby can support larger numbers of "civilized" people. It is preferable, because it is more just and more economical, for civilized countries to acquire Indigenous land by peaceful means rather than by war. *Indigenous land is owned collectively by its aboriginal occupants, who are recognized as self-governing sovereign nations, that may sell land voluntarily.*[83] (Emphasis added.)

Benjamin Franklin challenged Britain's claim to America purported to have resulted from the doctrine of discovery in the article On Claims to the Soil of America, printed in The Public Advertiser, March 16, 1773. First, the land in America was possessed by Indians prior to England's arrival; second, the land was purchased from the Indians or conquered recognizing their dominion; third, papal donative authority is a pretense; fourth, the mere sighting of coastal land was insufficient; fifth, arrival on land unseen by the inhabitants cannot operate to divest Indians of their land; and sixth, symbolic possession by branding a post or planting a flag did not equate to the assumption of dominion or sovereignty over the land or its inhabitants.

> ...unless Great Britain had a Property in the Lands of America before the Colonists went thither, it does not appear how they could take Lands of her to hold on any Terms. Now the Fact is well known, that Britain had not a Foot of Land in New-England; and that when the first Settlers went into that Country, they found it possessed by various Tribes of Indians, from whom they either purchased or conquered what they now enjoy. European Nations have indeed pretended, some, that the Pope could give them a Right to the Lands of America; others, that, sailing along a Coast

there, landing on some Beach unseen by the Natives, and branding a Post with the Arms of their own Country, created a Right to as much of the internal Territory as they should afterwards think proper to claim. But "one would hardly imagine" as your Writer says, "that such Nonsense could find Advocates."[84]

## Prominent Colonial Era Businessman Defended Sovereign Title of Indian Nations to Their Lands, with Right to Sell Their Lands

Prominent businessmen formed land syndicates to purchase Indian land from the Indians who they considered held title. These included, for example, the Asylum Company of Pennsylvania (Robert Morris, financier of the American Revolution was shareholder), the Holland Land Company, the Illinois Company, the North American Land Company, the Ohio Company, the Transylvania Company, The Walpole Company and the United Land Company.

The Ohio Company, a land speculation company owned by Virginians, was given a huge land grant by the British government in 1749. The Company sent out surveyors to explore the country, amongst them the young George Washington. The Ohio Company was immediately in conflict with the French who claimed the whole Ohio River Valley under the doctrine of discovery and were building forts to reinforce their claim. In order to protect themselves from military retaliation, the Ohio Company built several forts.

As members of the economic elite, the Ohio Company of Associates and John Cleves Symmes offered large and rapid influxes of revenue into the federal coffers in exchange for millions of acres of federal land, which was highly appealing to Congress. The Ohio Company demanded the creation of a territorial government staffed with Company directors which Congress assented to. The Ordinance of 1787 was enacted creating the Northwest Territory and filling four of its five offices with members from the Company. It gave them executive, legislative and judicial control of the area. This would allow the Company to use the authority of the federal state to advance its interests. The Northwest Territory included the present-day states of Ohio, Indiana, Illinois, Michigan, Wisconsin and the northeastern part of Minnesota.[85]

Privatization would not last. When the Northwest Territory advanced to

124

its second stage of government, the Ohio Company lost its monopoly over territorial politics. The second stage came with a new territorial legislature which was filled with non-proprietors who began to tax the Company's lands. Western agents found themselves unable to pay the taxes on the eastern proprietors' lands, which were seized.

Another gigantic venture for the proposed colony of Vandalia was intended to cover 20 million acres in what now comprises West Virginia and Kentucky. Parties to the enterprise at various times included Benjamin Franklin and two of George Washington's brothers. Unfortunately, Virginia claimed the land in question, as did Connecticut and Pennsylvania—each state having sold the land to settlers and investors—although by 1774 it was all, according to the British government, under the jurisdiction of Québec. This region, allegedly granted to different parties by conflicting royal charters, was heavily populated by a number of Indian Nations. The tangle of competing claims led to a full docket for the Kentucky courts. A request for Thomas Jefferson to render a title opinion is set forth below. He handled numerous Indian land title questions which resulted in his expertise on this subject.

### To President Thomas Jefferson from John George Jackson, 2 March 1805

> About ten Millions of acres of land in the district I represent, are claimed by the "Indiana Company" in virtue of a grant from the Indians with which you are acquainted; the importance of the stake has induced us to investigate the grounds of our title, as well as those of the Company...[86]

George Washington biographer Paul Johnson observed that Washington "was a soldier and statesman but, above all, he was a landed gentleman. This was what he wished to be; in a sense all he wished to be." Over the years his holdings increased until they totaled about ninety-six square miles. These lands were situated in New York, Pennsylvania, Maryland, Virginia, North Carolina, the District of Columbia, and the present states of West Virginia, Ohio and Kentucky.[87]

Once more, Marshall's proselytization that England's colonies failed to recognize Indian ownership of their land is laid bare for what it is—false.

Notes

1. Banner, Stuart. *How the Indians lost their land: Law and power on the frontier*. Harvard University Press, 2005:39. Reprinted at London, 1752. DAB; Lawrence C. Wroth, An American Bookshelf, 1755 (Phila., 1934), pp. 12–15, 118–26.

2. Wroth, Lawrence C. *An American Bookshelf, 1775*. University of Pennsylvania Press, 1934: 12–15, 118–26.

3. de Vattel, Emerich. *The Law of Nations or the Principles of Natural Law Applied to the Conduct and to the Affairs of Nations and of Sovereigns*. Carnegie Institution of Washington, 1916. Book I, Chap. XII, §210.

4. Banner, Stuart. *How the Indians lost their land: Law and power on the frontier*. Harvard University Press, 2005: 25.

5. Royce, Charles C. "Indian land cessions in the United States." *Eighteenth annual report of the Bureau of American Ethnology, 1896-1897* (1902): 563.

6. https://avalon.law.yale.edu/17th_century/va01.asp (accessed online November 7, 2020).

7. Hening's Statutes of Virginia, I, 57-66.

8. Royce, Charles C. "Indian land cessions in the United States." *Eighteenth annual report of the Bureau of American Ethnology, 1896-1897* (1902): 566.

9. "II. Depositions concerning Claims to Lands under Purchases from the Indians, [April 1777–October 1778]," *Founders Online*, National Archives, https://founders.archives.gov/documents/ Jefferson/01-02-02-0033-0003. [Original source: *The Papers of Thomas Jefferson*, vol. 2, *1777–18 June 1779*, ed. Julian P. Boyd.

Princeton: Princeton University Press, 1950, pp. 68–111.] (accessed online November 7, 2020).

10. https://avalon.law.yale.edu/17th_century/mass01.asp (accessed online November 5, 2020).

11. https://avalon.law.yale.edu/17th_century/mass02.asp (accessed online November 5, 2020).

12. https://avalon.law.yale.edu/17th_century/mass03.asp (accessed online November 5, 2020).

13. The Treaty That Saved Plymouth Colony, March 22, 2017, Nathan Dorn. https://blogs.loc.gov/law/2017/03/the-treaty-that-made-thanksgiving/ asp (accessed online November 5, 2020).

14. Royce, Charles C. "Indian land cessions in the United States." *Eighteenth annual report of the Bureau of American Ethnology, 1896-1897* (1902): 601.

15. Massachusetts Historical Society. "Collections of the Massachusetts Historical Society." 1871. Vol. IX, first series: 159-160.

16. Banner, Stuart. *How the Indians lost their land: Law and power on the frontier*. Harvard University Press, 2005: 21.

17. Ibid., p. 22.

18. Royce, Charles C. "Indian land cessions in the United States." *Eighteenth annual report of the Bureau of American Ethnology, 1896-1897* (1902): 602.

19. Ibid, p. 603.

20. https://avalon.law.yale.edu/17th_century/charter_003.asp (accessed online November 5, 2020).

21. https://avalon.law.yale.edu/17th_century/ma01.asp (accessed online November 5, 2020).

22. Bozman, John. *The History of Maryland: From Its First Settlement, in 1633, to the Restoration, in 1660*. Applewood Books, 2010.

23. https://avalon.law.yale.edu/17th_century/ct03.asp (accessed online November 5, 2020).

24. Trumbull, Benjamin. A Complete History of Connecticut, Civil and Ecclesiastical, from the Emigration of its First Planters from England, in MDCXXX to MDCCXIII, Vol. 1, Hudson and Goodwin, Hartford, 1797: 98-99.

25. https://avalon.law.yale.edu/17th_century/ri04.asp (accessed online November 5, 2020).

26. Royce, Charles C. "Indian land cessions in the United States." *Eighteenth annual report of the Bureau of American Ethnology, 1896-1897* (1902): 619.

27. Watson, Blake A. "John Marshall and Indian Land Rights: A Historical Rejoinder to the Claim of Universal Recognition of the Doctrine of Discovery." *Seton Hall L. Rev.* 36 (2005): 482-483.

28. Ibid., p. 498.

29. Royce, Charles C. "Indian land cessions in the United States." *Eighteenth annual report of the Bureau of American Ethnology, 1896-1897* (1902): 623.

30. https://avalon.law.yale.edu/17th_century/nc01.asp (accessed online November 5, 2020).

31. Clark, Walter, William Laurence Saunders, and Stephen Beauregard Weeks, eds. *The State Records of North Carolina*. Vol. 1. PM Hale, 1909: 20-33.

32. Royce, Charles C. "Indian land cessions in the United States." *Eighteenth annual report of the Bureau of American Ethnology, 1896-1897* (1902): 626.

33. Mooney, James. *The Siouan tribes of the East*. No. 22. US Government Printing Office, 1894: 6.

34. Banner, Stuart. *How the Indians lost their land: Law and power on the frontier*. Harvard University Press, 2005: 24.

35. O'Callaghan, Edmund Bailey. *Documents relative to the colonial*

*history of the State of New-York*. Vol. IV. Weed, Parsons, printers, 1861: 345-346.

36. Banner, Stuart. *How the Indians lost their land: Law and power on the frontier*. Harvard University Press, 2005: 42.

37. Ibid., pp. 24-25.

38. Royce, Charles C. "Indian land cessions in the United States." *Eighteenth annual report of the Bureau of American Ethnology, 1896-1897* (1902): 580.

39. Macauley, James. *The natural, statistical, and civil history of the State of New-York*. Vol. II. Gould & Banks, 1829: 260.

40. Banner, Stuart. *How the Indians lost their land: Law and power on the frontier*. Harvard University Press, 2005: 25.

41. Ibid.

42. The Concession and Agreement of the Lords Proprietors of the Province of New Caesarea, or New Jersey, to and With All and Every the Adventurers and All Such as Shall Settle or Plant There – 1664, https://avalon.law.yale.edu/17th_century/nj02.asp (accessed online November 5, 2020).

43. Banner, Stuart. *How the Indians lost their land: Law and power on the frontier*. Harvard University Press, 2005: 25.

44. Royce, Charles C. "Indian land cessions in the United States." *Eighteenth annual report of the Bureau of American Ethnology, 1896-1897* (1902): 589.

45. https://avalon.law.yale.edu/17th_century/pa01.asp (accessed online November 5, 2020).

46. "Remarks on Thomas Penn's Estimate of the Province, 29 May 1759," *Founders Online*, National Archives, https://founders.archives. gov/documents/Franklin/01-08-02-0096. [Original source: *The Papers of Benjamin Franklin*, vol. 8, *April 1, 1758, through December 31, 1759*, ed. Leonard W. Labaree. New Haven and London: Yale University Press, 1965, pp. 360–379.] (accessed online November 7, 2020).

47. https://avalon.law.yale.edu/18th_century/de01.asp (accessed online November 5, 2020).

48. Royce, Charles C. "Indian land cessions in the United States." *Eighteenth annual report of the Bureau of American Ethnology, 1896-1897* (1902): 597.

49. Ibid., p. 631.

50. Ibid., p. 634.

51. https://avalon.law.yale.edu/18th_century/ga01.asp (accessed online November 5, 2020).

52. Royce, Charles C. "Indian land cessions in the United States." *Eighteenth annual report of the Bureau of American Ethnology, 1896-1897* (1902): 637.

53. Ibid., p. 636.

54. Banner, Stuart. *How the Indians lost their land: Law and power on the frontier*. Harvard University Press, 2005: 26-27.

55. Hoadly, Charles Jeremy, ed. *Records of the Colony and Plantation of New-Haven, from 1638 to 1649*. Appendix: 508. Case, Tiffany, 1857.

56. Banner, Stuart. *How the Indians lost their land: Law and power on the frontier*. Harvard University Press, 2005: 16.

57. Ibid., p. 23.

58. Ibid., p. 23.

59. Ibid., p. 16.

60. Watson, Blake A. "John Marshall and Indian Land Rights: A Historical Rejoinder to the Claim of Universal Recognition of the Doctrine of Discovery." *Seton Hall L. Rev.* 36 (2005): 493.

61. Banner, Stuart. *How the Indians lost their land: Law and power on the frontier*. Harvard University Press, 2005: 14.

62. Ibid., p. 22.

63. Ibid., p. 14.

64. Ibid., p. 41.

65. Purchas, Samuel. "Hakluytus Posthumus or Purchas his pilgrimes." (London 1625), 4:1814.

66. Watson, Blake A. "John Marshall and Indian Land Rights: A Historical Rejoinder to the Claim of Universal Recognition of the Doctrine of Discovery." *Seton Hall L. Rev.* 36 (2005): 494.

67. Ibid., p. 489.

68. Reprinted at Arneil, Barbara. *John Locke and America: the defence of English colonialism.* Oxford University Press, 1996: 58.

69. Watson, Blake A. "John Marshall and Indian Land Rights: A Historical Rejoinder to the Claim of Universal Recognition of the Doctrine of Discovery." *Seton Hall L. Rev.* 36 (2005): 489.

70. Banner, Stuart. *How the Indians lost their land: Law and power on the frontier.* Harvard University Press, 2005: 31.

71. "John Adams to Philip Mazzei, 26 Jun. 1786," *Founders Online,* National Archives, https://founders.archives.gov/documents/ Adams/99-01-02-0692. (accessed online November 7, 2020).

72. Purchas, Samuel. "Hakluytus Posthumus or Purchas his pilgrimes." (London 1625): 222.

73. God's promise to his plantations; [Three lines from Samuel] / As it was delivered in a sermon by John Cotton, B.D. and preacher of God's word in Boston [Seven lines from Psalms] Cotton, John, 1584-1652, J. H. [Boston]: London, printed by William Jones for John Bellamy and are to be sold at the three Golden Lyons by the Royal Exchange, 1634. Reprinted at Boston in New-England, by Samuel Green and are to be sold by John Usher. Anno. 1686: 4.

74. Banner, Stuart. *How the Indians lost their land: Law and power on the frontier.* Harvard University Press, 2005: 16.

75. Ibid.

76. de Vitoria, Francisco. *Francisci de Victoria De Indis et De ivre belli relectiones.* Carnegie Institution of Washington, 1917, Part 2:7.

77. Gray, Robert. *A good speed to Virginia*. Vol. 2. No. 9. Felix Kyngston, 1970.

78. Banner, Stuart. *How the Indians lost their land: Law and power on the frontier*. Harvard University Press, 2005: 14.

79. Ibid., p. 19.

80. Ibid., p. 20.

81. Ibid., p. 34.

82. Ibid.

83. Anthony F. C. and Timothy B. Powell. "How to Buy a Continent: The Protocol of Indian Treaties as Developed by Benjamin Franklin and Other Members of the American Philosophical Society." *Proceedings of the American Philosophical Society* 159.3 (2015): 269.

84. "On Claims to the Soil of America, 16 March 1773," *Founders Online*, National Archives, https://founders.archives.gov/documents/ Franklin/01-20-02-0071. [Original source: *The Papers of Benjamin Franklin*, vol. *20, January 1 through December 31, 1773*, ed. William B. Willcox. New Haven and London: Yale University Press, 1976, pp. 115–122.] (accessed online November 7, 2020).

85. Carter, Clarence Edwin, and John Porter Bloom, eds. *The territorial papers of the United States*. Vol. 636. US Government Printing Office, 1940: 42-43; "To George Washington from the Ohio Company Committee, 13 June 1789," *Founders Online,* National Archives, https://founders.archives.gov/documents/ Washington/05-02-02-0353. [Original source: *The Papers of George Washington*, Presidential Series, vol. 2, *1 April 1789–15 June 1789*, ed. Dorothy Twohig. Charlottesville: University Press of Virginia, 1987, pp. 484–485.] (accessed online November 7, 2020).

86. "To Thomas Jefferson from John George Jackson, 2 March 1805," *Founders Online,* National Archives, https://founders.archives.gov/ documents/Jefferson/99-01-02-1275 (accessed online November 7, 2020).

87. Johnson, Paul. *George Washington: The Founding Father*. Harper Collins, 2009: 11.

# 8

# EUROPEAN COLONIAL WARS

## European Wars over Competing Claims to 'Discovered' Land in 'New World'

European wars, over competing claims to 'discovered' land in the 'New World,' simmered year after year after year. Small engagements were fought, with none of them decisive enough to put an end to the squabbling. They did succeed in reducing the Indian population base, as the European countries jostled to secure Indian allies to increase their military size. If the doctrine of discovery was adhered to by the European countries' discoveries, why were there so many wars over who discovered what?

## King William's War, 1689–1697

King William's War took place in 1689–1697 between New France and the British colonies in New York and New England. In Europe, France and Britain were locked into yet another struggle over control of the League of Augsburg. The colonies were, therefore, left to fend for themselves. The English allied with the Iroquois Confederacy. The French allied with the Wabanaki Confederacy. There were continuous, numerous and intermittent skirmishes, retaliatory raids and military expeditions to Acadia, Quebec, Montreal and within New England. English settlers had moved into Acadia, which the French claimed. Also, the Iroquois dominated the Great Lakes fur trade which led to continuing conflict with New France.

The English settlers outnumbered the French 12 to 1. However, their division into multiple colonies diminished the advantage. Also, the

French had a higher number of trained soldiers and a strong relationship with the Wabanaki Confederacy. They nurtured their Indian alliance because they understood its importance to their survival.

The War ended with the 1697 Treaty of Ryswick which restored the status quo ante bellum (the situation as it existed before the war) between New France and the British. British expansionism would continue to threaten New France, fostering lingering resentments. The needless squabbling over territory simply would not end. Indian Nations were depleted of warriors and supplies as they remained engulfed in supporting allies with whom their interests were not aligned.

## Queen Anne's War, 1702–1713

Conflict in Europe between England, Spain, Portugal, Savoy and France in 1700 over who was to succeed to the Spanish throne after the death of the heirless King Charles II, a member of the Hapsburg dynasty, again spread to North America. Again, the Iroquois Confederacy as an ally of the British and the Wabanaki Confederacy allied with France, were drawn into a war over political rivalries in Europe. England feared that Spain and France would join forces to challenge her colonial dominancy. None of the countries gave any credence to who had 'discovered' what.

Acadia, Nova Scotia, Newfoundland and New England, along with Florida, would bear the brunt of fighting. In an attack on Deerfield, Massachusetts, on February 29, 1704, fifty French soldiers and 200 Abenaki killed 53 British settlers and took 111 prisoners. Regardless of the doctrine of discovery and Spain's claim to Florida, the British never ceased their efforts to undermine Spain's occupation. In November 1702, British soldiers from the Province of Carolina attacked and captured the Spanish town of St. Augustine, Florida. In 1704, Carolina colonial forces raided and destroyed a network of Spanish missions and villages, killing and capturing Spanish colonial settlers. In retaliation in September of 1706, the Charleston Expedition took place, during which unified French and Spanish forces tried to capture the capitol of the English Province of Carolina. Local militia successfully prevented its takeover.

Britain came to the aid of New England in the fall of 1709 by sending five warships with 400 marines. Combining this military force with the New England militia, enabled the capture of Port Royal. In response, France and its Abenaki allies successfully ambushed British and New England soldiers near the Annapolis River. In August of 1711, a British and New England effort to conquer French Quebec failed when seven British warships wrecked en route to Quebec.

The political War of the Spanish Succession ended in victory for Britain, except a Bourbon King retained the throne of Spain. France, Spain and the Dutch Republic signed the Treaty of Utrecht, which was a series of individual peace treaties between the various European countries. France ceded certain of its 'claimed' land in North America to Britain, including Newfoundland, Acadia and the Hudson Bay region of northeastern Canada. Spain kept Florida, relinquishing the islands of Minorca and Gibraltar to Britain. Furthermore, Britain was awarded the Asiento contract under which it gained exclusive rights to supply Spain's American colonies with black slaves, at the rate of 4,800 a year, for 30 years.

Despite the Treaty of Utrecht, the fighting between the French, English and Indians continued in North America for a number of years after the Treaty was signed. Lingering resentment between the British and the French would result in King George's War in 1744.

### Dummer's War, 1722–1725

In another testament to the failure of the doctrine of discovery to determine boundaries between France and England, the two countries fought over Maine. New France established three Catholic missions among the Wabanaki Indians to secure their control of the area; one on the Kennebec River, one on the Penobscot River and one on the St. John River. Again, the Indians suffered in New France's defeat to New England and they fled to Quebec.

## King George's War, 1744–1748

In 1744, the French and British were at war in Europe again, this time over the royal succession to Austria. Prussia, France, Bavaria, Spain and Saxony allied against Austria. England allied with Austria to prevent France's power grab. King George's War (1744–48) was the name given to its French and British theatre in New England and Nova Scotia. Again, the Iroquois Confederacy as an ally of the British and the Wabanaki Confederacy allied with France fought in colonial settlements in Massachusetts, New York, New Hampshire and New France over a war in Europe about who should sit on the throne of Austria.

In a repeat of Queen Anne's War, the French and British captured and recaptured disputed areas, abandoning ground fought over. The War ended in a stalemate and the signing of the Treaty of Aix-la-Chapelle in 1748. All land and property seized during the War by either side was to be returned to the other. Again, notwithstanding the 'doctrine of discovery,' the Treaty left the boundaries between the French and English colonies unsettled. Not long after the Treaty signing, France and England began to quarrel about the boundaries of the British colony of Acadia. France claimed Acadia was limited to the area of Nova Scotia, while England claimed it occupied a much larger region. Further, arguing over who 'discovered' what in the Ohio River Valley resulted in conflict, squatting by colonial settlers without regard to Indian land claims and escalating violence. Peace did not last long and war broke out between England and France again in 1754 with the Seven Years War (aka in the American theater, the French and Indian War).

# 9

# INDIAN WARS

The numerous wars fought by Indians to protect their lands unquestionably documents their belief in ownership of their lands. They were under-armed and under-populated, at times, yet they willingly put their lives and liberty at risk. Certain of the colonies created Articles of Confederation combining their forces on the grounds that "hostile Native American tribes to the west" posed an urgent, common threat to its members. If England claimed ownership of the land 'discovered,' the Indians continuing their habitation of the 'discovered' land was a direct contradiction. Marshall was fully aware of these wars as he chronicled them in his biography of Washington published in 1804. Also, he noted, in the *Johnson* case, that Kentucky was "a country, every acre of which was then claimed and possessed by Indians, who maintained their title with as much persevering courage as was ever manifested by any people."[1]

## Powhatan War, 1622–1624

About 350 English colonial settlers were killed by Powhatan Indians in 1622 at Jamestown. The English retaliated with a mock peace conference which was planned and carried out as an attack on the Powhatan. Skirmishes continued for the next several years. Chief Powhatan died in 1618. His brother, Opechancanough, formed the Powhatan Confederacy and continued the attacks. The English used a scorched earth policy by burning their crops. The Powhatan and English negotiated the Treaty of 1646 to end hostilities. The Indians vastly outnumbered the colonists and it is unknown why they did not engage in any sustained military action. The Indians came under the control of the King of England who guaranteed them protection, though it was uncertain what this meant. It also imposed numerous restrictions: confining the Indians to land north of the York River, the return of all hostages and guns and requiring "as an acknowledgmt & tribute for such protection, the said Necotowance & his Successors are to pay unto the King's Governor the Number of twenty beaver skin's att the goeing away of Geese yearely."[2]

Christopher Brooke, member of the Council for Virginia, lawyer and investor in the Virginia Company, wrote the poem below on the Late Massacre in Virginia in 1622. His poem was to encourage "All men of knowledge I now prompt thee to revenge the blood late shed / An expiable warre unto the dead" to join in the war.[3]

## Christopher Brooke, Late Massacre in Virginia in 1622

(I cannot call them men) no Character
Of God in them : Souls drown'd in flesh and blood;
Rooted in Evill, and oppos'd in Good;
Errors of Nature, of inhumane birth,
The very dregs, garbage, and spawne of Earth
Who ne're (I think) were mention'd with those creatures
Adam gave names to in their several natures
[...]

If these (I say) be but consider'd well,
(Father'd by Sathan, and the sonnes of hell,
What feare or pittie were it, or what sin,
To quite their Slaughter, leaving not a creature.

## Pequot War, 1637

Conflicts between New England colonial settlers encroaching on Pequot lands and settlers resenting Indian interference with their trade with the Dutch ended up erupting when two colonists were killed by allies of the Pequot. The Pequot were already warring with neighboring Indian

Nations which led the Mohegan and Narragansett Nations to ally with the New England Confederacy (Plymouth, Massachusetts Bay, New Haven and Connecticut Colonies) in the war. At Mystic, the New England Confederacy set fire to the Pequot village; any escapees were ordered to be shot. Seven hundred Indians were killed in this massacre. Pequot fugitives were sold as slaves in the Caribbean. Most of the Pequot Nation was destroyed. Narragansetts and British soldiers circled the village and set it to fire.

## Iroquois French Wars (aka Beaver Wars), 1638–1698

This was a war over the very valuable control of the fur trade—not only what European country would get it, but which Indian Nations would be reaping the riches of that European trade. The Iroquois dominated the economically important Great Lakes fur trade and had been in conflict with New France since 1680. Guns were supplied to the Iroquois by the Dutch making hunting easier. This resulted in the decimation of the beaver population on Iroquois Confederacy lands in New York. The Dutch allied with the Iroquois Confederacy and the French with the Huron and Algonquins.

The Dutch then encouraged the Iroquois to expand their hunting grounds into the Great Lakes region—Huron Territory. The Iroquois attempted to disrupt the French-Huron beaver trade alliance, but the French refused to trade with them. It was a bloody, vicious war, coinciding with the European Dutch-French War with Louis XIV trying to defeat and conquer The Netherlands.

The Iroquois-Huron War of 1650 essentially destroyed the Huron. Their conflict was terminated by the Peace Treaty of Montreal in 1698. In Europe, the French were victorious by 1696 over the Dutch. The Dutch forfeited New Netherland/New Amsterdam to the British in 1664. The Iroquois Confederacy continued their uneasy alliance with the British.

# Dutch Indian Wars, 1655–1664

The Dutch-Indian Wars were a series of three wars between the Dutch colony of New Netherland and neighboring Indian Nations, mostly Algonquin, over Dutch encroachments on Algonquin lands. Also, the Dutch West India Company traded with the Iroquois Confederacy, enemies of the Algonquin. More than 1,600 Indian were killed at a time when the European population of New Amsterdam was 250.

In 1641, the Algonquin attacked the Dutch on Manhattan and Long Island (Algonquin (Kieft) War). In 1642, the War resumed when the Mohawks attacked the Algonquins living on the Lower Hudson River. The Dutch intervened on the side of the Mohawks, subsequently killing 80 Algonquins at Pavonia. This outrage united eleven Algonquin Nations against the Dutch, who devastated New Netherland, except for New Amsterdam and Fort Orange (Albany). In 1644 the Dutch fortified New Amsterdam with a stone wall—present-day Wall Street—and brought in reinforcements from Dutch colonies in Brazil and the West Indies. Additionally, the Dutch engaged British Captain John Underhill, who had participated in the Pequot War. *In March 1644, 150 Dutch soldiers attacked an Algonquin village. Of 700 Indian warriors, only eight escaped; the Anglo-Dutch force lost only 15 men*. This destroyed the Algonquin alliance and they accepted peace in August 1645.

The Peach Tree War of 1655 resulted from a Dutch farmer killing an Indian woman who was allegedly stealing peaches. Approximately 2,000 Indians raided Manhattan, killing one hundred settlers, capturing one hundred fifty colonists and destroying three hundred homes.

The Esopus Wars (1658–64) resulted again from Algonquin resistance to Dutch encroachments on their lands in the Esopus Valley. The Dutch, supported by the Mohawk, defeated the Algonquins. Resentment over the peace terms led to the resumption of hostilities in June 1663. By a treaty concluded in May 1664, the Algonquin relinquished most of their lands and the Dutch regained control over the Esopus Valley.

The effective ending of these Wars coincided with the English-Dutch War of 1664, and the Dutch loss of New Netherland/New Amsterdam to the British.

## King Philip's War, 1670–1675

The Wampanoag Chief Metacomet (aka King Philip) formed and led a confederation of Indian Nations against British colonial settlers who sought to defeat each Nation individually. Fifty-two colonial settlements were attacked; twelve were destroyed. A Bounty on King Philip and His Subjects was proclaimed. The Wamponoag tried to extend their confederacy by allying with the Narragansetts. Even though they decided to remain neutral, the British, led by Colonel Benjamin Church, attacked them. Connecticut, Plymouth and Massachusetts united to defeat the Narragansetts in the bloodiest battle per capita in the Great Swamp Fight (1675). On July 15, 1675, King Philip surrendered (King Philip's Surrender Treaty). He was killed; his family enslaved. His head was put on a pike and displayed at Plymouth for two decades.

Chief Justice Marshall described King Philip's War as follows:

> Hostilities commenced in 1670 and went on through 1675. The war was carried on with great vigour and various success: the savages, led by an intrepid chief, who believed that the fate of his country depended on the entire destruction of the English, made exertions of which they had not been thought capable. Several battles were fought; and all that barbarous fury which distinguishes Indian warfare, was displayed in its full extent. Wherever the Indians marched, their route was marked with murder, fire, and desolation. Massachusetts, New Hampshire, and Plymouth, were the greatest sufferers. ... Though the warriors of the nation of which Philip was prince, were estimated at only five hundred men, he had, by alliances, increased his force to three thousand.[4]

## Tuscarora War, 1711–1713

Carolina backcountry colonists' encroached on Indian lands, capturing and enslaving Tuscarora children. The Tuscarora, part of the Iroquois, were defeated by the British with the help of their Indian allies. They were forced to move north into New York to join the other five Iroquois nations. This just led more Carolina colonists to squat on Indian lands, expanding their settlements westward.

## Yamasee War, 1715–1716

By 1715, increasing land encroachment on Indian lands by colonial settlers acted again as a catalyst for war. The Yamasee depended on game for subsistence and trading and as the settlers increased their rice farming it led to the depletion of the game necessary to generate income for the Indians. They became indebted to the trading posts. To recover these debts, the traders enslaved Yamasee women and children. The flashpoint was the 'Pocataligo Massacre' of a colonial deputation sent to negotiate. Neighboring Indian Nations joined in the uprising. The Yamasee attacked Port Royal, while the Catawba moved on Charles Town. However, the colonists rallied, and their militias defeated the Catawba at the Battle of the Ponds and the Yamasee at Salkehatchie. Again using Indian to fight Indian, the colonists enlisted the Cherokee as allies. By the war's end (1717), the Yamasee sought refuge in Spanish Florida.

Again and again, local governments were simply unable to prevent colonist squatters. Aware of the threat to peace they presented, it was still not enough to contain them.

Marshall wrote the following about the Yamassee War:

> The Yamassees, a powerful tribe of Indians on the north east of the Savanna, instigated by the Spaniards at St. Augustine, secretly prepared a general combination of all the southern Indians, against the province. Having massacred the traders settled among them, they advanced in great force against the southern frontier, spreading desolation and slaughter on their route.[5]

## Abanaki Wars

French Jesuit influence allegedly induced the Abanaki Indians to resist English encroachment into Maine. The British staunchly believed that the French used the Indians to create hostilities. Later, it would be the Americans who believed the British did the same thing against them. The United States also believed that the Spanish used the Seminoles and other Indians to threaten settlers in the south.

## Cherokee War, 1760–1762

This War was again due to the continued Carolina expansion west and colonial settler encroachments. Cherokees were pushed into Georgia and the future Tennessee, opening up more Carolina backcountry for non-Indian settlement.

Marshall noted the following about the Cherokee War: Hostilities commenced in 1759 after Governor Lyttleton took hostage thirty-two Cherokee chiefs en route to Charleston to complain about the Governor's military force entering Cherokee land. They were imprisoned together in a single hut. The Governor refused to release the prisoners until an equal number of Indians who had killed settlers were turned over.

The Cherokees tried to rescue their chiefs but were unsuccessful. In return, the soldiers massacred all thirty-two Chiefs. According to Marshall, they "wreaked their fury on the inhabitants of the country in indiscriminate murder." A skirmish at New Echota was indecisive, but the Cherokee settlements were destroyed. The 'savages' then besieged Fort Laudoun and the four hundred militia were compelled to surrender due to famine. In May 1862, a stronger force under Colonel Grant defeated the Cherokees at New Echota. Again, their homes, crops and countryside were destroyed. The Cherokees were forced to sue for peace.[6]

## Pontiac's War, 1763–1766

To prevent the incursion of settlers after the Seven Years War (aka French and Indian War), Pontiac, Chief of the Ottawas, who had sided with the French, united a coalition of Indian Nations to resist British rule in the Great Lakes region and Ohio River Valley. Between 1774 and 1794, Indian villages in New York, Pennsylvania, Indiana and Ohio were constantly attacked by the British and colonial militias. The Shawnee, Delaware, Iroquois, Miami, Odawa, Wyandot and Mingo saw unspeakable violence committed against their villages during this time period. Over 100 Indian villages were burned and destroyed, leaving an unknown number of Indian casualties. The most notorious frontier massacre occurred on March 8, 1782 on the Upper Sandusky River in Ohio, at a village known as Gnadenhutten. Over 90 Delaware Indians, the majority of whom were women and children, were returning to their village to gather food supplies. These Delaware, known as the Moraviantown Indians, were Christian and pacifists. Upon reaching their village, the Delaware were rounded up by Colonel David Williamson and the Pennsylvania militia. Two out-buildings served as slaughter houses where the Indians were led, two at a time, to their execution.

Notes

1. *Johnson v. M'Intosh*, 21 U.S. 543, 586 (1823).

2. Treaty between the English and the Powhatan Indians, October 1646

https://edu.lva.virginia.gov/online_classroom/shaping_the_
constitution/doc/treaty

(accessed online November 6, 2020).

3. Christopher Brooke, Late Massacre in Virginia in 1622.

4. Marshall, John. *The Life of George Washington-Volume 1*. Chap. VI, 1807: 166-167.

5. Ibid., 242-245.

6. Ibid., 354-357.

# 10

# FRAUD

Notwithstanding the purchases of Indian lands, there were unscrupulous parties creating havoc due to fraud. If the doctrine of discovery did not exist, this fraud would not have existed. Fraud is a broad term, which includes false representations, dishonesty and deceit. Blackstone, in his Commentaries, states that fraud will vitiate a deed. Specifically, he stated:

> [A] deed must be founded upon good and sufficient consideration. Not upon a usurious contract; nor upon fraud or collusion, either to deceive purchasers bona fide, or just and lawful creditors; any of which bad considerations will vacate the deed.[1]

In 1751, Archibald Kennedy, a Member of N.Y. Governor Clinton's Council affirmed that fraud occurred:

> ... those poor Indians have for many Years been under the Direction of the People of Albany, whose Interest it was to deceive and defraud them, and that they have been deceived and defrauded accordingly, is notorious...[2]

Examples of the fraud engaged in are detailed by Peter Wraxall, commissioner of Indian Affairs for New York:

> "An unaccountable thirst for large Tracts of Land," Wraxall explained, "hath prevailed over the Inhabitants of this and the neighbouring Provinces with a singular rage." Settlers increasingly seemed to be buying land from Indians with no right to sell it, making Indians drunk in order to get them to sign contracts, applying to colonial governments for patents stretching far beyond

146

the limits of the land actually purchased, or even forging Indians' signatures on purchase documents.[3]

### Conference with Indians, Easton, November 13, 1756, William Denny, Lieutenant-Governor, Pennsylvania and Six Nations, Delaware Indians, Shawanese and Mohiccons

At the Easton Conference, Teedyuscung, known as the King of the Delawares, complained of the fraud prevailing in Indian land transactions and provided examples:

> Teedyuscung: When one man had formerly liberty to purchase Lands, and he took the Deed from the Indians for it, and then dies; after his Death the Children forge a Deed like the true One, with the same Indian Names to it, and thereby take Lands from the Indians which they never sold—*this is Fraud*. Also, when one King has Land beyond the River, and another King has Land on this Side, both bounded by Rivers, Mountains and Springs, which cannot be moved, and the Proprietaries, greedy to purchase Lands, buy of one King what belongs to the other—*this likewise is Fraud*.[4] (Emphasis added.)

Pennsylvania's Lieutenant Governor Denny asked Teedyuscung whether he had experienced fraud:

> Yes; I have been served so in this province; all the land extending from Tohiccon, over the great mountain, to Wioming, has been taken from me by fraud; for when I had agreed to sell land to the old Proprietary, by the course of the river, the young Proprietaries came, and got it run by a strait course, by the compass, and by that means, took in double the quantity, intended to be sold.[5]

Other instances of fraud in colonial real estate transactions with Indians were consistently reported. This is most evident in the admission contained in King George's Royal Proclamation of 1763: *"Great Frauds and Abuses have been committed in purchasing Lands of the Indians."*[6]

147

In his Commentaries, Chancellor Kent noted the acts of fraud and violence:

> ...there were, at times, acts of fraud and violence committed by individuals among the colonists, prompted by cupidity, and a consciousness of superior skill and power, as well as springing from a very blunt sense of the rights of savages.[7]

Fraud could take many shapes. In several cases English purchasers told the Indians they wished to buy parcels of a given size but then, without alerting the Indians, inserted in the deeds descriptions of parcels much larger. As one duped seller complained, "when a Small parcel of Land is bought of us a Large Quantity is taken instead." Devious purchasers could also slip misdescriptions of the land past Indian sellers, Colden explained, by drafting deeds to express boundaries not in terms of natural landmarks but "by points or Degrees of the Compass & by English Measures which are absolutely unknown to the Indians." This led two colonies, New York and Virginia, to require that prior to the private purchase of land from an Indian, the exact territory be surveyed by a government-hired surveyor, with the seller or his representative present at the time of the survey.[8]

Mr. Madison observed that misunderstandings, quarrels and wars with the Indians had originated from the circumstance of persons having obtained, through fraud or other improper means, possession of the lands belonging to the Indians.

As noted by Professor Kades,

> In addition to bribery, the United States consciously engaged in ruse, subterfuge, circumvention, and outright fraud to achieve through chicanery, under the cloak of voluntary cooperation, a continued stream of land cessions. The Indians were, of course, aware of such tricks. ... The Americans were, the Shawnees argued, inevitably 'deceitful in their dealings with ... the Indians.'... Outright fraud, of course, cannot form the basis for enforceable contract rights under Anglo-American law.[9]

*For Indians, there were no legal protections against fraud, breaches of contract or other similar violations.*

## Bias/Racism

In addition to fraud was the documented bias against Indians. As a young man, after just one encounter with Indians, George Washington characterized them as "ignorant."[10]

Samuel Champlain observed: 'They have among them certaine Savages...which speak visibly with the Divell'. He concludes that, 'for the most part', Indians live like 'brute beasts'.[11] Samuel Purchas labeled them as "Barbarians, Borderers and Outlawes of Humanity."[12]

On June 15, 1756, in his Diary, future president John Adams exposed his bias as to the superiority of the colonists over the Indians:

> Consider, for one minute, the Changes produced in this Country, within the Space of 200 years. Then, the whole Continent was one continued dismall Wilderness, the haunt of Wolves and Bears and more savage men. Now, the Forests are removed, the Land coverd with fields of Corn, orchards bending with fruit, and the magnificent Habitations of rational and civilized People. ... The narrow Hutts of the Indians have been removed and in their room have arisen fair and lofty Edifices, large and well compacted Cities.[13]

In a letter to President Madison from an anonymous source, the author vented his racial fury: To James Madison from Americanus, 13 April 1816–

> Before an Indian can become a fit person for citizenship, he must learn our language, he must read our books, he must enter into our constitutional doctrines, he must become somewhat acquainted with our political characters, and our party politics. He must acquire notions of separate property, of regular industry. He must throw aside his propensity for ranging, for hunting, for war, for revenge. ... In a word, you must change the animal. ... Ameliorate their condition ... but you cannot make an Indian a white man ... Savages and forests go together. Destroy the forest, and the

savage retires. They have been tried often enough; they cannot bear civilization. I grant this is assertion, but you Sir, know it to be the assertion of matter of fact, now beyond dispute.[14]

Similarly, Daniel Webster, U.S. Senator and Secretary of State, in an Oration delivered at Plymouth, Massachusetts, December 22, 1820, proclaimed colonists' superiority:

> We have come to this Rock, to record here our homage for our Pilgrim Fathers ... they encountered the dangers of ... the violence of savages ... We feel that we are on the spot where ... Christianity, and civilization, and letters made their first lodgement, in a vast extent of country, covered with a wilderness, and peopled by roving barbarians.[15]

## Legal Capacity to Contract

Whether the Indians ever willingly or knowingly sold their lands to the European colonists and fully appreciated that they were permanently relinquishing their land is uncertain. By law, parties to a contract must have the 'legal capacity' to enter into that contract. They must also have the ability to do what the contract requires. Indian complaints that they did not understand the cession agreements that they had signed, or that the federal treaty commissioners had obtained their signatures by threat, or while intoxicated, or through outright fraud are all documented. Today, on many contract forms is written the following caveat:

> THIS FORM HAS IMPORTANT LEGAL CONSEQUENCES AND THE PARTIES SHOULD CONSULT LEGAL AND TAX OR OTHER COUNSEL BEFORE SIGNING.

This was not an option available to Indians. As explained earlier, colonists brought their knowledge of English law with them and there were competent practicing attorneys accessible to them for legal assistance. Historian John Bozman did not consider Indians capable of entering into contracts: "They stand by the laws of nations, when trafficking with the civilized part of mankind, in the situation of infants, incapable of entering into contracts, especially *for the sale of their country*."[16]

## Inability to Understand Contract

Mental capacity is defined as the ability to understand the full meaning and effects of the contract. If the person is not able to comprehend the rights and obligations imposed under the contract, there is a lack of legal capacity to enter it. Indians were taken advantage of because they did not speak or write English as a primary language and they had no formal or legal education. Cadwallader Colden, surveyor general of New York in the 1730s (and later governor), reported that such deception was possible because "the Indians have been perswaded to sign these Deeds without having them interpreted by persons sufficiently Skill'd in the English and Indian languages."[17]

## Inability to Perform Under Contract

A fee simple is the absolute ownership in land. A person with this estate in land may dispose of the land in any manner desired while living. For there to be a valid transfer of real property, there must be a competent grantor and a grantee capable of taking title and a corpus to be transferred. If Indians did not own their land or have the authority to sell the land, as alleged by parties seeking to merely steal their land, they lacked the legal competence to enter into the contract. Furthermore, if Indians only had a right of occupancy but were executing deeds transferring a fee simple absolute title, the deeds were invalid. Under English law, a grantor could not convey an interest he did not own (the nemo dat rule).

## Unconscionable Contracts

A contract may be found to be unconscionable based on three different factors:

**Undue Influence**: This is where one party exercises unreasonable pressure in order to get the other party to sign the contract (especially where one party takes advantage of the other in some way).

**Duress**: This is where one party uses threats in order to get the other to agree to the contract terms. This can take the form of

151

physical threats, or other types of threats (such as not releasing goods in the proper way until the other party signs).

**Unequal Bargaining Power**: This occurs where one party has an unreasonable advantage of the other.

**Unfair Surprise**: This is when the party who creates the contract includes a term in the contract without the other party's knowledge and it is not within the other parties expectations; for example, when a deed is drafted to express boundaries not in terms of natural landmarks but by points or degrees of the compass and by English measures which are absolutely unknown to the Indians.

The basic characteristic of most unconscionable contracts is that one party signed the contract under situations involving pressure, lack of information, or by being misled.

## Undue Influence

The unreasonable pressure imposed on Indians to sell their lands demonstrates the unconscionability of the colonists and government actions. One technique was bribery.

## Presidential Policy of Bribery

There were efforts made by the Spanish and the United States to give gifts to Alexander McGillivray, an influential Creek leader, as evidenced by the communication below:

**From George Washington to the Commissioners to the Southern Indians, 29 August 1789**

The presents [for Mr. McGillvery] will be regulated by your Judgement—The idea of military distinction arises from the information that Mr McGillvery possesses a commission of Colonel or Lieutant Colonel from the King of Spain. ... If he could be induced to resign that Commission by the offer of one, a grade higher the offer ought to be made and substantiated, on his taking a solemn Oath of Allegiance to the United States. ... Mr McGilivrey is stated to possess great abilities an[d] unlimited influence over the Creek nation and part of the Cherokees—It is an object worthy of considerable exertion to attach him warmly to the United States. ... In case you should be satisfyed of his compliance with your desires, you will deliver him the presents which are particularly designated for him, and also give him assurances of such pecuniary rewards from the United States as you may think reasonable, consequent on the evidence of his future favorable Conduct. ....[18]

The 1790 Treaty of New York with the Creeks, in which the United States purchased much of Georgia, included "Secret Articles" guaranteeing the Creek chief Alexander McGillivray a perpetual salary of twelve hundred dollars per year, and giving assorted lesser chiefs perpetual salaries of one hundred dollars per year.[19]

**To President George Washington from Secretary of War Henry Knox, 27 December 1790**

Showered with gifts and attention, the Seneca leader now expressed gratitude to the President and pledged the friendship of his people. In his instructions to Pickering, Knox expressed confidence in The Cornplanter's attachment and fidelity. Soon thereafter, more privately, he wrote: "The Cornplanter may be depended upon through all the changes of policy... [He] is our friend from the solid ties of interest, and we must rivet it by all ways and means in our power."[20]

**Duress**

Duress, in determining if a contract is unconscionable, can be seen where one party uses threats in order to get the other to agree to the contract terms. This can take the form of physical, economic or other types of threats.

## Violence

The technological advantages available to colonists were far beyond those of Indians, especially in regard to armaments. Christopher Columbus noted he could easily conquer the Indians with fifty men and govern them as he pleased. By dehumanizing Indians, a colonial settler policy of direct and indirect killing could be justified. Public and privatized violence resulted in massacres and loss of Indian lives thereby reducing the population and removing another barrier to westward expansion and settlement.

Chancellor James Kent notes the inequality of power between the colonists and the Indians:

> But the causes of wars with the Indians were inherent in the nature of the case. They arose from the fact of the presence and location of white people; and the Indians had the sagacity to perceive, what the subsequent history of this country has abundantly verified, that the destruction of their race must be the consequence of the settlements of the English colonists, and their extension over the country. *In all the wars of the whites with the Indians, the means and the power of the parties were extremely unequal, and the Indians were sure to come out of the contest with great loss of numbers and territory, if not with almost total extermination.*[21] (Emphasis added.)

Professor Kades' analysis of the threats of war are included here and his research in this area is specifically acknowledged.

Threats, of course, are antithetical to the voluntary exchange that supposedly legitimized American purchases of Indian lands. They undermine the essence of lawful negotiation: the right of both sides to simply leave the room, refuse to cut a deal, and retain whatever property rights they possessed ex ante. "The pressure [on Indians to cede lands] was such that it made a farce of the oft-repeated assertion that the Indians were equally free to sell or refuse to sell."[22]

One of the reasons given for a proposed military expedition against the Piankashaw and other Wabash tribes was "their refusing to treat with the United States when invited thereto." ... In negotiating with the Choctaws at Doak's Stand in 1820, Major General Andrew Jackson found the

Indians generally opposed either to ceding or exchanging any land. The few Choctaws who favored a treaty were compelled to be silent, and every chief threatened with death if he consented to sell or exchange an acre. ... [After long and tough negotiations] Major General Jackson resorted to threats. ... He warned them of the loss of American friendship; he promised to wage war against them and destroy the Nation; finally he shouted his determination to remove them whether they liked it or not.[23]

President Monroe agreed that "if the Indians did not voluntarily submit to the civilizing programs, compulsion would have to be resorted to." ... United States officials often couched their threats in polite, circumspect language. William Henry Harrison, for instance, adverted to "extinguishing the council fire" instead of a more direct threat to declare war. ... When the Creeks initially refused to permit the United States to build a road through their lands, Secretary of War Eustis stated his wish that the tribe would not "compel the Government to the use of means which it is desirous to avoid."[24]

## Colonists Commit Violence against Indians

In a 1623 letter from colonist Robert Bennett to his brother in London, we have documentation of the killing and poisoning of over 200 Indians in a fake colonial peace parley, as well as the killing and beheading of 50 more. Also, Mr. Bennett writes of a plan to cut down the corn and put to the sword neighboring Indians, God willing:

> Newse I have not anye worthe the wryting but onlye this. The 22nd of Maye Captin Tucker was sente with 12 men in to Potomacke Ryver to feche som of our Engleshe which the Indianes detayned, and withall in culler to conclude a pease with the great Kinge Apochanzion; soe the interpreter which was sente by lande with an Indian with hime to bringe the kinge to parle with Captain Tucker broughte them soe. After a manye fayned speches the pease was to be concluded in a helthe or tooe in sacke which was sente of porpose in the butte with Capten Tucker to poysen them. Soe Capten Tucker begane and our interpreter tasted before the kinge woulde tacke yt, but not of the same. Soe thene the kinge with the kinge of Cheskacke, [their] sonnes and all the great men

weare drun[torn] howe manye we canot wrtye of but yt is thought some tooe hundred weare poysned and thaye comyng backe killed som 50 more and brought hom parte of ther heades. From the text printed in the *American Historical Review*, XXVII, pp. 505-508.[25]

"A Governor of Virginia," Spotswood wrote, "has to steer between Scylla and Charybidis, either an Indian or a Civil War, for the famous Insurrection in the Colony called Bacon's Rebellion was occasion'd purely by the Governor and Councill refusing to let the People go out against the Indians."[26] In Greek mythology, Scylla is a monster who lives on one side of a narrow channel of water, opposite her counterpart, Charybdis. The two sides of the strait are within an arrow's range of each other—so close that sailors attempting to avoid Charybdis would pass dangerously close to Scylla and vice versa.

Bacon's Rebellion, which served as an example to colonial governments of citizen uprisings, made the prevention of colonists unlawful squatting on Indian lands almost impossible. In the early 1670s, settler encroachment into Indian territory on Virginia's western borders had created an escalating cycle of retaliation and reprisal. The colony's governor, William Berkeley, advocated containment by building a line of fortifications. The settlers, led by Nathaniel Bacon, saw this as a block to their westward expansion and an excuse for additional taxes. Despite some concessions by the governing House of Burgesses, in July 1676 discontent spiraled into open rebellion. At the head of a makeshift army comprised of settlers, indentured servants and slaves, Bacon marched on the colonial capital Jamestown and burned it to the ground. Shortly afterwards, Bacon died of dysentery, and a naval squadron quickly crushed the remainder of the rebellion. Berkeley was recalled to England shortly afterwards.

John Van Etten's Company, made up of colonial militia, gave the following instructions to its soldiers on January 12, 1756. You are to acquaint the Men, that if in their Ranging they meet with, or are at any Time attack'd by the Enemy, and kill any of them, Forty Dollars will be allow'd and paid by the Government for each Scalp of an Indian Enemy so killed, the same being produced with proper Attestations.[27]

Jack M. Sosin in his book, *The Revolutionary Frontier, 1763–1783*, explicitly described this violence:

> So brutal had been the relations between the races that it was difficult at times to tell who had been the more savage. Both the Indians and the frontiersmen had resorted to indiscriminate murders and retaliation in the decade preceding the Revolution. The greatest menace to the stability of the frontier was often the aggressive, undisciplined settler himself. He regarded the Indian as an animal to be exterminated without fear of punishment from law officials.[28]

In the spring of 1791, President Washington received "truly alarming" news of the killing of supposedly friendly Indians in western Pennsylvania by a party of Virginians. He feared, as did Secretary of State Jefferson, that this would defeat peaceful measures and expand the war.[29]

President Washington's Address to the United States Senate and House of Representatives on November 6, 1792, pointed out the need for aid to protect Indians from frontier settler violence.

> I cannot dismiss the subject of Indian Affairs, without again recommending to your consideration the expediency of more adequate provision for giving energy to the laws throughout our interior frontier; and for restraining the commission of outrages upon the Indians; without which all pacific plans must prove nugatory.[30]

## Paxton Boys—Conestoga Massacre

The Paxton Boys were frontiersman of Scottish Ulster Protestants and had settled along the Susquehanna River in central Pennsylvania. To retaliate against the local Indians after the Seven Years War (aka French and Indian War) and Pontiac's War, many of whom were not even involved, they formed a vigilante group. They are widely known for murdering Susquehannock Indians in a series of events collectively referred to as the Conestoga Massacre. They also presented their grievances to the Pennsylvania legislature. Many of the Indians attacked were Christians and had lived peacefully with the colonist settlers for decades. The colonial government held an inquest and determined that the killings were murder. None of the murderers was ever identified or prosecuted for their illegal actions, even though a reward was offered.

A contemporary shocking report reads as follows:

> O what a horrid sight presented itself to my view!- Near the back door of the prison, lay an old Indian and his women, particularly well known and esteemed by the people of the town, on account of his placid and friendly conduct. His name was Will Sock; across him and his Native women lay two children, of about the age of three years, whose heads were split with the tomahawk, and their scalps all taken off. Towards the middle of the gaol yard, along the west side of the wall, lay a stout Indian, whom I particularly noticed to have been shot in the breast, his legs were chopped with the tomahawk, his hands cut off, and finally a rifle ball discharged in his mouth; so that his head was blown to atoms, and the brains were splashed against, and yet hanging to the wall, for three or four feet around. This man's hands and feet had also been chopped off with a tomahawk. In this manner lay the whole of them, men, women and children, spread about the prison yard: shot-scalped-hacked-and cut to pieces. William Henry of Lancaster[31]

## Federal Government Repeatedly Threatens Extinction of Indians

Threatened Indian extinction was pronounced at the highest levels of government. In 1786 the United States implied it would attack the Shawnees if they refused to the proffered terms, despite the Secretary of War's later admission that the nation was "utterly unable to maintain an Indian war with any dignity or prospect of success" (quoting statement of Henry Knox, Secretary of War).[32]

Also, President Jefferson wrote in a private letter to William Henry Harrison in February 1803, the following which Harrison was not to disclose:

> ...[W]e presume that our strength & their weakness is now so visible that they must see *we have only to shut our hand to crush them* ... should any tribe be fool-hardy enough to take up the

hatchet at any time, the seizing the whole country of that tribe & driving them across the Missisipi, as the only condition of peace, would be an example to others, and a furtherance of our final consolidation.[33] (Emphasis added.)

He included the threat in his second inaugural address in 1805—Indian leaders who "clung tenaciously to tribal mores and insisted on inculcating reverence for the custom of their ancestors" must be ruthlessly expunged.[34] Consistently, the federal government used its superior military force to demonstrate to Indian Nations that it was futile to counter their authority.

## Financial Duress

Professor Kades notes that "All the time that "the United States had been refusing to pay the Indians more than two cents an acre for even the best land ... the government charged its own western settlers two dollars an acre."[35]

## Devaluing Currency

The Netherlands acquired mass quantities of clams from which shell wampum is made, flooding the market. Beads are cut from the white and purple parts of the shell; the pieces are rounded, sanded and drilled to make a bead. Belts made from wampum woven together referenced particular events, such as treaties and declarations of war. As this was the currency of the Six Nations, the Netherlands depreciated the value of their currency and caused them significant financial hardship.

In Massachusetts, William Pynchon used "[t]remendous amounts of wampum" to acquire a monopoly on the fur trade in the region: he extended credits to fellow townsmen for manufacturing wampum, or stringing together the beads, and sought to acquire the currency for local trade, but primarily to develop trade with the local natives.[36] To acquire the land for Springfield, he paid the local Agawam Indians 18 fathoms of wampum, 18 coats, and a quantity of hoes, hatchets, and knives.[37] The conversions in Pynchon's account books show that, in contrast to the prices Pynchon charged his colonial sub-traders in the region, he imposed a 56% mark-up for coats, a 66% mark-up for shirts, a 71-100% increase in the cost of "Bilboe rug" and a 37% increase for shag cotton in his Indian trade.[38]

In twenty-two transactions between February 13, 1659 and September 14, 1660, William Pynchon allowed the Norwottock Sachem Umpanchela to take a variety of goods on credit, including numerous coats, wampum, "shag" cotton and breeches. In July, to settle his outstanding debt of £75, Umpanchela executed a deed for land. Pynchon then assigned this land to the inhabitants of Hadley as West Hadley, now Hatfield.

## Loss of Land Equals Corresponding Loss of Income

In the state of Ohio alone, the loss of lands is inconceivable. The value of lands in the state of Ohio is immeasurable.

| MAIN TREATIES CEDING INDIAN LANDS IN OHIO | | | | |
|------|------|-------|------------|-----------------|
| NO. | DATE | PLACE | ACRES CEDED | TRIBES CONCERNED |
| 1. | Aug. 3, 1795 | Greenville, Ohio | 16,930,417 | Eleven northwestern tribes |
| 2. | July 4, 1805 | Fort Industry, Ohio | 2,726,812 | Ottawas, Wyandots,Chippewas, Pottawatamies, Shawnees, Delawares |
| 3. | Nov. 17, 1807 | Detroit, Michigan | 345,600 | Chippewas, Ottawas, Wyandots, Pottawatamies |
| 4. | Nov. 25, 1808 | Brownstown, Michigan | Two Roads | Same tribes as at Detroit |
| 5. | Sept. 29, 1817 | Fort Meigs (Maumee Rapids) | 4,554,459 | Ottawas, Shawnees, Wyandots, Senecas |
| 6. | Sept. 17, 1818 | St. Marys, Ohio | | Ottawas, Wyandots, and Shawnees, Senecas |
| 7. | Oct. 2, 1818 | St. Marys, Ohio | | Weas |
| 8. | Oct. 6, 1818 | St. Marys, Ohio | 297,600 | Miamis |

The U.S. specifically used land acquisition for agriculture to not only obtain land cessions but to reduce the Indians value of their land and make it more likely for them to agree to dispose of it. General Schuyler advised Congress to avoid expensive wars and to instead wait for nature to take its course.

[A]s our settlements approach their country, they must, from the scarcity of game, which that approach will induce to, retire farther back, and dispose of their lands, unless they dwindle comparatively to nothing, as all savages have done, who gain their sustenance by the chase, when compelled to live in the vicinity of civilized people, and thus leave us the country without the expence of a purchase, trifling as that will probably be.[39]

Washington whole-heartedly concurred, emphasizing the economy of letting settlers instead of soldiers dislodge the Indians:

> [T]he Indians as has been observed in Genl Schuylers Letter will ever retreat as our Settlements advance upon them and they will be as ready to sell, as we are to buy;

> That it is the cheapest as well as the least distressing way of dealing with them, none who are acquainted with the Nature of Indian warfare, and has ever been at the trouble of estimating the expence of one, and comparing it with the cost of purchasing their Lands, will hesitate to acknowledge.[40]

## Loss of Game Equals Corresponding Loss of Income

Ecologically and economically, the sustainability of subsistence hunting was necessary to provide for the basic needs of Indians and to assist in wildlife protection for thinning and culling of herds. Most Indians depended almost entirely on subsistence hunting and gathering to obtain essential protein and cash income and to supplement their livelihood. They were aware of the spectrum of species, the need for water and nutrients and the recovery necessary for species to recover from draught or other circumstances. There was also a ritual and spiritual component. To avoid depleting animal reserves, traditional rules regulated the category of animals allowed for killing, when and how much to hunt for, the population availability of particular game, population turn over in individual game species and the response of game populations to hunting.

The importance of hunting for subsistence is evident in this Ohio price schedule, as is the inventory of goods available for purchase: February

8, 1806, the average prices for furs and peltries by the trader at Fort Wayne, Indiana were: Raccoons = 37½ to 40 cents each Foxes, Cats, and Fishers = 50 to 67 cents each Minks = 50 cents each Musk Rats (grown ones) = 25 cents each Otters = 4 to 5 dills each Bears (grown ones) = 4 to 5 dills each Beavers = 125 cents each Buck Skins (always) = 100 cents each Doe Skins = 67 to 75 cents each 77 Drefsd, Does Skins, Bucks & Does = 75 cents each 5 Indian Mats = 112 Com. Moccasins = 25 cents each 13 Fine Ditto = 50 cents each.[41]

Over-exploitation and the destruction of natural habitats by the settler colonists meant that game became a dwindling resource. Indian hunters were unable to depend on the predictability of availability and were required to travel further afield and spend more time on hunting. Eventually, Indians were rendered dependent on the introduced economy.

Chief Justice Marshall adverted to the most important harmful effect of such colonial settlement in the *Johnson* opinion itself: "As the white population advanced, that of the Indians necessarily receded. The country in the immediate neighborhood of agriculturists became unfit for them. The game fled into thicker and more unbroken forests, and the Indians followed ..."[42]

Miantonomo, a Narragansett Chief, in trying to create a confederacy to fight against their losses of land, described the thinning of game they had experienced and why:

> [O]ur fathers had plenty of deer and skins, our plains were full of deer, as also our woods, and of turkies, and our coves full of fish and fowl. But these English having gotten our land, they with scythes cut down the grass, and with axes fell the trees; their cows and horses eat the grass, and their hogs spoil our clam banks, and we shall all be starved.[43]

The Mohegan Indians, in a 1789 petition for charity from the Connecticut legislature, described their past and present:

> For in times past, our Fore-Fathers lived in Peace, Love and great harmony; and had everything in great plenty. When they wanted meat, they would just run into the bush a little ways with their weapons and would soon bring home good venison, raccoon, bear and fowl, if they choose to have fish, they would only go to the

river or along the sea shore, and they would presently fill their canoes with variety of fish, both scaled and shell fish, and they had abundance of nuts, wild fruit, ground nuts, and ground beans, and they planted but little corn and beans and they kept no cattle or horses for they needed none. ... And they had no contention about their lands, it lay in common to them all, and they had but one large dish, and they could all eat together in Peace and Love.

But, the petition says, "it is not so now, all our fishing, hunting and fowling is entirely gone. And we have now begun to work on our land, keep cattle, horses, and hogs; and we build houses, and fence in lots. And now we plainly see, that one dish and one fire will not do any longer for us."[44]

Chancellor Kent also forecast the result of the settlers' systematic clearing of Indian game habitats:

[T]he Indians of this continent appear to be destined, at no very distant period of time, to disappear with those vast forests which once covered the country, and the existence of which seems essential to their own.[45]

## Loss of Homes, Crops and Orchards Leads to Starvation

The effect of the devastating loss of homes, crops and orchards can be seen after General Washington's campaign to 'chastise and intimidate' the Six Nations. The Indians were forced to flee to Canada and seek aid from the British who could not help them due to their overwhelming numbers.

## Loss of Lives from Disease

Professor Kades notes that, to obtain Indian lands "at bargain prices," the United States government was not required, in most instances, "to resort to violence or even threats to lower the price of Indian lands. Its most powerful alternative was breath-takingly simple: settlement on the frontier. Settlers killed relatively few Indians in raids, massacres, skirmishes and the like. They killed many more by spreading endemic diseases like smallpox."[46]

163

European diseases like tuberculosis, cholera, smallpox, measles, malaria, respiratory viruses, typhoid, typhus, dysentery and venereal diseases decimated indigenous communities. The epidemic that spread across Southern New England in 1616 might have been the bubonic plague or chicken pox. It left so many dead that when colonists arrived a few years later, they found heaps of bleached bones and skulls, leading Thomas Morton to describe the scene as "a new found Golgotha"[47] Smallpox destroyed half of the people of the Huron and Iroquois confederations during the 1630s and 40s, half the Cherokee in 1738, nearly half the Catawbas in 1759, half the Piegan tribe during the Revolutionary War, two-thirds of the Omahas and about half the population between the Missouri River and New Mexico shortly before the Louisiana Purchase, and revisited the people of the plains in 1837 to kill half of those who remained.[48]

Indians feared these diseases and believed that the colonists and government could use them to reduce their numbers, a form of biological warfare. William Bradford, the future governor of the Plymouth colony, allegedly wrote that Squanto, a New England Indian who cooperated with the settlers, convinced his fellow Indians that the colonists "kept the plague buried in the ground, and could send it amongst whom they would, which did much terrify the Indians."[49] The Wabash tribes in 1800 worried "that the United States intended to destroy them by means of the small pox, which was to be communicated to them by the goods which they received from [the Europeans]."[50] The depopulation through epidemics caused massive political and economic chaos creating even more difficulties for Indian Nations competing against a unified federal, state and settler citizenry whose interest was acquiring as much of their land as cheaply as possible.


## Debt Policies

### President Jefferson's Indian Policy of Pushing Indians into Debt

In a private letter from President Thomas Jefferson to William Henry Harrison on February 27, 1803, he proposes:

> ...we shall push our trading houses, and be glad to see the good & influential individuals among them run in debt, because we

observe that when these debts get beyond what the individuals can pay, they become willing to lop th[em off] by a cession of lands...[51]

To entice them into becoming consumers, we see the following excerpt on changing their tradition value systems:

The "Savages" aren't ashamed of their bodies and wear no clothes, and Carleill believes that this naïve worldview can easily be corrected: [The Savages] shall have wonderful great use of our said English clothes, after they shall come once to know the commodity thereof. The like will be also of many other things, over many to be reckoned, which are made here by our artificers and laboring people...[52]

## Consolidation of Debt

Panton, Leslie & Company (founding partners—William Panton, Thomas Forbes, John Leslie, William Alexander and Charles McLatchy) and Robert Mitchel & Associates, purchased debts incurred by Indians from traders and with the aggregated value it made it worthwhile to pursue collection against Indian Nations and to enlist the government's assistance. At a treaty negotiation, with the federal government's support, the debt amount would be used as an offset against the amount due to the Indian Nation. Panton's lobbying assured that the debt he aggregated would not be forfeited.[53]

Article 4 of the Treaty of Augusta (1773) with the Creek Indians defines that the ceded area between the Little and Tugeloo Rivers was to pay for debts owed to English fur traders. The Treaty of New York (1790) had a similar clause.

## Indian Nation Liable for Individual Member Debts

As Indian Nations were held liable for individual member debts, this could result in appalling circumstances. The Narragansetts repeatedly petitioned the Rhode Island legislature to ban their sachem from selling any more of the Nation's land to pay off his personal debts. If he "goes on selling Land," they despaired, "the Tribe will soon have none left."

But the legislature did nothing.[54]

Similarly, in a January 8-9, 1756, Meeting for Treaty between New-Jersey and Indians at Croswicks, the following exchange is noted:

> Ohiockechoque: As it is the Misfortune of some of us to be in Debt...We think we have still some Peices of Land, for which we have received no Consideration, if it should prove so, and we could get the Money for them...[55]

Also, President Jefferson's willingness to accept Indian land for the payment of debts in shown in the following Indian Address, To the Brothers of the Choctaw Nation, December 17, 1803 (Choctaws Had to Make Large Land Cession to Pay Debts):

> You say you owe a great debt to your merchants, that you have nothing to pay it with but lands, and you pray us to take lands, and pay your debt. The sum you have occasion for, brothers, is a very great one. ... we are willing to purchase as much as you will spare.[56]

## Annuities Promised under Treaties Used as Economic Sanctions

In a flurry of treaty councils from 1803 to 1805, President Harrison purchased millions of acres in what would become Indiana, Illinois and Wisconsin. He repeatedly threatened to withhold the annuities due under the Treaty of Greenville until chiefs agreed to meet with him to discuss land sales. Claims for damages to settlers' property as a result of Indian depredations could also be deducted from the annuities of accused Indian Nations. They created a perfect vehicle for fraud.

## Economic Sanctions Imposed against Osage results in Cession of Lands

Through economic sanctions, the federal government was able to secure land cessions. A letter to President Jefferson from Meriwether Lewis, December 15, 1808, details the withholding of goods as intimidation to require land cessions:

In consequence of the measures which were taken last spring in relation to the Osage nations they were reduced in the course of a few months to a state of perfect submission without bloodshed; this has in my opinion very fairly proven the superiority which the *policy of withholding merchandize* from the Indians has over the chastizement of the sword, when their local situations are such as will enable us to practice it. (Emphasis added.) *It extinguishes their title to a country nearly equal in extent to the state of Virginia and much more fertile.*[57] (Emphasis added.)

## Unfair Trade Practices

The United States employed a version of "divide and conquer" within tribes as well as among them. Professor Kades found that "Congress counseled Indian agents to "deal with each Indian tribe or nation as separately as possible," and insisted that "the tribes were6+ to be kept separated so that negotiations would be easier."[58]

Also, the U.S. willingly preyed on the animosities between Indian Nations. For example, in a letter from General St. Clair to President Washington, he evidences this tactic. St. Clair had been appointed by Congress to negotiate treaties with northern Indian Nations.

The Reason why the Treaties were made separately with the six Nations and the Wyandots & more westerly Tribes was a Jealousy that subsisted between them, which I was not willing to lessen ... I am persuaded their general Confederacy is entirely broken: indeed it would not be very difficult, if Circumstances required it to set them at deadly variance.[59]

During Governor Harrison's September 1809 negotiations in Indiana, one tribe, the Miami, initially adamantly refused to sell any land, declaring that the U.S. must end the settler encroachments and vowed to sell only for the price that it sells amongst yourselves. After five days of negotiation, Governor Harrison replied with a veiled threat: he would "extinguish the council fire" if the Miami would not agree to the substance of his terms.[60]

Another usual tactic was to get Indians inebriated complained of by

Indian leaders. In an October 3, 1753, meeting at Carlisle between colonial Commissioners and Ohio Indians, Scarrooyady, substantiated this practice:

> Traders come, They bring thirty or forty kegs and put them down before us, and make us drink, and get all the Skins that should go to pay the debts we have contracted for goods bought of the Fair Traders; and by this means, we not only ruin ourselves but them too.[61]

The Commissioners replying to Scarrooyady spoke as follows:

> THUS, may it please the Governor, we have given a full and just Account of all our Proceedings ... we cannot close our Report, without taking Notice, That the *Quantities of strong Liquors sold to these Indians in the Places of their Residence, and during their Hunting Season, from all Parts of the Counties over Sasquehannah, have encreased of late to an inconceivable Degree, so as to keep these poor Indians continually under the Force of Liquor*, that they are hereby become dissolute, enfeebled and indolent when sober, and untractable and mischevious in their Liquor, always quarreling, and often murdering one another:

RICHARD PETERS, ISAAC NORRIS, BENJ. FRANKLIN.[62] (Emphasis added.)

> Franklin included under "Indian Trade" the need for a regulation of the destructive commerce in whiskey, which "through the bad conduct of traders who cheat the Indians after making them drunk" cost the existing colonies "great expence ... in blood and treasure." In his Autobiography, he wrote: "If it be the design of Providence to extirpate these savages in order to make room for cultivators of the soil, it seems not improbable that rum may be the appointed means."[63]

## Unequal Bargaining Power

Unequal bargaining power exists when one party has an unreasonable advantage over the other. As divulged by Professor Kades, through being the first European to sight a given territory, as a discoverer it acquired the right, on behalf of the sovereign and vis-a`-vis other Europeans who came after it, to buy land from the Indians. This right, known as pre-emption, gave the 'discovering' power a monopsony over land transactions with the Indians, who were prevented from disposing of their land to any other European power. A lack of competition resulted in lower values for Indian lands. "Thus, the M'Intosh rule facilitated low-cost acquisition of Indian lands by stifling bidding by Americans for Indian land and making the United States a monopsonistic buyer."[64] With the lack of information regarding capital markets which were well developed in all the major cities in Europe, Indians had no way to comprehend investment and financial risk strategies or to raise capital through land speculative companies.

The government, in its dual capacity as regulator of and participant in the Indian land market itself, could also exclude competing purchasers based on its access to information. If the government was not interested, the right to purchase Indian land was given not to the highest bidder but to the first person to apply for a license. This lack of competition among purchasers forced land prices down.

The colonial, and later federal, governments were aware of the need and uses for such lands, and enhanced value they would bring, due to forecasted immigration from Europe. The Indians did not have this insider information.

Worst of all, the English controlled the government and legal systems within which these transactions were enforced. Some Indians, if dissatisfied with a sale to the English, had to get the approval of English authorities before they could get any redress. Settlers seeking to enforce Indian sales, on the other hand, had no equivalent need to petition the Indians. Whether appointed from England or chosen locally, colonial government officials considered themselves accountable to the English colonists first and foremost, rather than as equally accountable to the Indians.

The Mohawk sachem Hendrick was painfully aware, while assenting to the sale of much of the Mohawks's land in 1754, that: "After We have sold our Land We in a little time have nothing to Shew for it; but it is not so with You, Your Grandchildren will get something from it as long as the World stands; our Grandchildren will have no advantage from it;

They will say We were Fools for selling so much Land for so small a matter, and curse Us."[65]

Lewis Cass confirmed this in his letter to the Acting Secretary of War, George Graham, on April 17, 1817, advising him not to quibble too much about the details of land cessions from the Indians, since "[u]nder any circumstances, [the consideration we pay] will fall infinitely short of the pecuniary and political value of the country obtained."[66]

The collective action problem was most tragic when sachems were willing to accept payment for land the rest of the Indian Nation did not wish to sell. As an exasperated delegation of Mohegans explained during the course of their prolonged litigation against Connecticut over the validity of grants made by successive Mohegan sachems, "they had of late years been much dissatisfied & disgusted with their Sachems; for that they had betrayed the Tribe & sold or endeavoured to sell all their Lands to the Government and they were determined to have no Sachem at all." Philip Cortlandt and Daniel Horsmanden to Council of Trade and Plantations, November 1738.[67]

In some cases, Indian leaders were willing to sell land in order to distribute the proceeds among members to solidify their own position within the Nation, a position that depended in part on the ability to give gifts. Thus, the interests of a Nation and its leadership were not always in alignment. In addition to collective action problems within Nations, land sales also presented collective action problems between Nations. When more than one Nation had a claim to an area arguing its conquest, the incentive facing each of the Nations was to sell the land to the English before any other Nation did. At times, tribes would cede lands, not for cash, but for protection against strong enemy neighbors or common owners. This political fragmentation among the Indians drove land prices down. The joinder of political clout, business expertise, wealth and the colonial British judiciary system was no match for the Indians.

Professor Kades exposed the federal government's process by which it managed to expropriate Indian lands very cheaply based on its advantages:

> Step (1): exploiting its more united front, its military superiority, its negotiating advantages, its superior ability to rein in troublemakers, and the trade dependency of the tribes, the United

States buys Indian borderlands for pennies on the dollar;

Step (2): the nation then moves settlements into the lands purchased from the Indians, and spurs migration with subsidized land transfers;

Step (3): these settlers kill Indians by spreading diseases and thin game by clearing land and hunting-both making land less valuable to the Indians;

Step (4): go to Step (1) and repeat the process.[68]

## Unfair Surprise

When a party who creates a contract includes a term in the contract without the other party's knowledge, that is not within the other party's expectations, this is ripe ground for claiming 'unfair surprise.' The Walking Purchase was an example of this.

## January 29, 1757, Walking Purchase Fraudulent, Ben Franklin, Extract from Minutes of House of Representatives of Pennsylvania

With the Walking Purchase of 1737, Pennsylvania officials defrauded the Delaware Indians in the Delaware and Lehigh Valleys. John Penn (1700–1746) and Thomas Penn (1702–1775), the sons of William Penn (1644–1718), with James Logan (1674–1751), the provincial secretary of Pennsylvania, devised the land grab by using an unsigned draft of a 1686 deed which they said had not been fulfilled. The draft deed purported that the Delawares had agreed to relinquishing as much land as a man could walk in a day and a half, allegedly describing the area.

The Delawares, wishing to maintain favorable relations with the Penns, especially based on that they had with William Penn in the past, agreed. The Penns planned ahead, selecting seasoned runners, promising that the one who covered the most territory would win 500 acres, and clearing a trail covering the land they wanted. They surprised the Indians by going northwestward away from the Delaware River rather than parallel to it. In eighteen hours of travel, sixty-five miles were covered, which took in some 1,200 square miles (three-quarters of a million acres). The

171

Delawares soon learned that even this large piece of land (1200 square miles) did not satisfy the Penns' demands. Thomas Penn "keeps begging & plagueing us to Give Him some Land," they complained in 1740; "he Wearies us Out of Our Lives."[69]

By Royal Order in Council in 1759, Sir William Johnson, British Superintendent of Indian Affairs for the Northern District, a position he held from 1756 until his death in 1774, was instructed to examine the complaints of the Delaware Indians regarding the fraud surrounding the 'Walking Purchase.' At the Council of the Six Nations held in 1762 at Easton to formally settle Delaware complaints about the Walking Purchase, Johnson read the lengthy English defense of the legality of the Walking Purchase. At the close of the four-hour reading that was not translated into the Delaware language, Teedyuscung, without being asked, said that he "very well understood the purport, or meaning of what had been read."[70]

When Johnson asked Teedyuscung to prepare a written response, he replied:

> Brother, I desire you'll let me have the Writings which were read yesterday, that I may have time to Consider of them, as We did not understand what was read. I told you another Thing, which was, to let me have a Clerk, to write down what I have to say.[71]

Teedyuscung decided the forces against him were too powerful, and he declared: "I did not come to have a Difference, but to Settle matters upon a good Footing. I did not come to put my hand into your Purse, or to get Cloathing. I give up the Land to you, and the white People."[72]

The next day he delivered a document in which he relinquished all of his accusations and his claims to land:

> ...as to the Walk, the Proprietary-Commissioners insist that it was reasonably performed; but We think otherwise ... being desirous of living in peace and Friendship with our Brothers the Proprietaries, and the good People of Pennsylvania, We bury under Ground all Controversies about Land; and are ready, such of us as are hear, to Sign a Release for all the Lands in Dispute.[73]

Benjamin Franklin, reported that the "Transaction of that Walk was at Easton universally given up as fraudulent and not to be defended."[74]

## Intoxication

One trade item used to incur substantial debt was the sale of rum. Several leaders specifically pleaded to stop such sales due to the deleterious impact on their people and the debt burden incurred by a particular Nation.

## Persons Under the Influence

Individuals who are under the influence of alcohol or drugs are normally not considered to have the capacity to enter contracts. According to Peter Wraxall, Britain's Secretary of Indian Affairs, "Some unknowable but probably large quantity of land was acquired by this scandalous & irregular Method of purchasing Lands from Young Indians by making them drunk." Numerous Indian leaders informed the government officials overseeing Conferences or Treaty negotiations of the problem.[75]

## Cotton Mather—English Ruine the Indians by Selling them Strong Drink

Cotton Mather, a colonial minister, detailed the disastrous impact of alcohol on the Indians.

> That which now gives inexpressible pain to all *Good Men* among us, is, That there are some *Ill Men* among the *English* in all corners of the Land, who to obtain a little bit of *Money* do fit this [...]icious, drunken, so [...]tish Humour of the *Indians*, [...]nd Sell them the *Drink*, by which they cannot [...]ut think the Salvages will make themselves *Drunk*; and sometimes they take Advantage of the Humour which the Salvages are in, to *Scrue* them into Bargains full of cruel *Oppression* and *Ex [...]Jortion*, which afterwards throw them into the extreamest Inconveniencies. I dare not Relate, how many *Tuns of Strong Drink*, I am credibly informed, have been brought and spent among the *Indians*, within a few months even in *One Little Island*.[76]

## A Gallon of Rum for a Span of Land

Banner reveals additional sources on this topic:

> In 1717, Sir Bibye Lake petitioned the Crown for a grant to a parcel of land that Lake's grandfather had allegedly purchased from the Indians in a series of transactions between 1639 and 1654. Lake's petition drew quick opposition from Thomas Coram ... The purchases made by Lake's grandfather, Coram argued, "cannot be of any value," because *"Indians, when drunk would for a bottle of strong Liquor sign any paper presented to them."* (Emphasis added.)
>
> *The settlers "practised so with the Indian Natives," Coram alleged, "that debauching them with strong Liquors, they drew in the Indians to execute Deeds for Large Quantities of Land, whether their own or his Majesty's, without any valuable consideration for the same."* (Emphasis added.)
>
> Another English resident of Maine in the early eighteenth century recalled the "old *Indian grants when a span of land was got for a Gallon of Rum.*" How much land was a span? "Extend your hand as open as possible, then bring the hand close to the eye looking upon the Horizon and so far as the little finger and thumb extend from each other from the top of them, on that Horizon is called a span which perhaps is 20 miles."[77] (Emphasis added.)

In a January 8-9, 1756, Croswicks meeting to negotiate a treaty between New-Jersey and certain Indians, this 'evil' is again brought to the attention of colonial negotiators:

> Ohiockechoque: But a worse evil than that has come to us, which is the Use of strong Liquor, to which the Indians are too much addicted, and by which they are made Weak, Idle, and Quarrelsome, and for strong Drink often sell those Skins, and other Things, which would provide themselves and Families with Cloaths and Bread, and for this some of the English are too much to blame. ... We have to complain to our Brethren, that ill minded Persons are apt to take Advantage of the Indians when they are Drunk, and buy their Lands for a trifle, and often from the Indians who does not own it. ... As some bad People have got a long Lease from a Drunken Indian for the Indian Lands at Wepink, and for

which they pay mostly, or all in strong Drink, we beg that they may be removed from that Land, and we hope care will be taken that no loose People settle on our Lands, without buying them.[78]

Again, on August 19, 1762, in a conference with Northern Indians at Lancaster, Pennsylvania, Sympoyaffee, an Indian spokesperson, demands this insidious practice cease:

...no rum to be sold to the Indians in the woods, Selling rum there a pernicious practice because the young people there got drunk, and disposed of their skins for that commodity, and so were rendered unable to pay their debts to the traders in the nation, which frequently occasioned quarrels and mischief among them.[79]

In a letter from Major-General William Henry Harrison to Secretary of War Henry Dearborn, dated July 15, 1801, the extent of this dehumanizing practice is laid bare:

They say that their people have been killed—their lands settled on—their game wontonly destroyed—& their young men made drunk & cheated of the peltries which formerly procured them necessary articles of Cloathing, arms and amunition to hunt with. Of the truth of all these charges I am well convinced.

"I do not believe there are more than six hundred warriors upon the [Wabash]," Harrison stated, and yet the quantity of whiskey brought here [by whites] annually for their use is said to amount to at least six thousand gallons.... The Chiefs of the Kickapoos, Sacks, & Patawatimies, who lately visited me are sensible of the progress of these measures, and their Views amongst themselves—which they are convinced will lead to utter exterpation—and earnestly desire that the introduction of such large quantities of Whiskey amongst them may be prevented.[80]

Further, President Jefferson's speech to the Senate and the House of Representatives on January 27, 1802, forthrightly declares the Indians desire to stop the abuse of alcohol used to debilitate them:

These people are becoming very sensible of the baneful effects produced on their morals, their health & existence by the abuse of ardent spirits: and some of them earnestly desire a prohibition of that article from being carried among them.[81]

Notes

1. The British Constitution, Or an Epitome of Blackstone's Commentaries on the Laws of England for the Use of Schools, William Blackstone, Vincent Wanostrocht, London: Printed for Longman, Hurst, Rees, Orme, and Brown, Paternoster, Row, 1823: 292.

2. Archibald, Kennedy, The Importance of Gaining and Preserving the Friendship of the Indians to the British Interest Considered (London: E. Cave, 1752): 10-11.

3. O'Callaghan, Edmund Bailey. *Documents relative to the colonial history of the State of New-York*. Vol. IV. Weed, Parsons, printers, 1861: 17.

4. Kalter, Susan, ed. *Benjamin Franklin, Pennsylvania, and the First Nations: The Treaties of 1736-62*. University of Illinois Press, 2010:157. See also report on Treaty Proceedings: "To Benjamin Franklin from Charles Thomson, 10 December 1758," *Founders Online*, National Archives, https://founders.archives.gov/documents/Franklin/01-08-02-0057. [Original source: *The Papers of Benjamin Franklin*, vol. 8, *April 1, 1758, through December 31, 1759,* ed. Leonard W. Labaree. New Haven and London: Yale University Press, 1965, pp. 199–211.] (accessed online November 5, 2020).

5. Ibid.

6. Clarence S. Brigham, ed., British Royal Proclamations Relating to America, Volume 12, Transactions and Collections of the American Antiquarian Society (Worcester, Massachusetts: American Antiquarian Society, 1911): 212-18.

7. Kent, James, and Charles M. Barnes. *Commentaries on American law, Lecture 50,* Of the Foundation of Title to Land. Vol. 1. Little, Brown, 1884.

8. Banner, Stuart. *How the Indians lost their land: Law and power on the frontier*. Harvard University Press, 2005:64.

9. Kades, Eric. "The Dark Side of Efficiency: *Johnson v. M'Intosh* and the Expropriation of American Indian Lands." *University of Pennsylvania Law Review* 148.4 (2000): 1124.

10. The Diaries of George Washington, ed. Donald Jackson and Dorothy Twohig (Charlottesville: University Press of Virginia, 1979), 1: 9-10.

11. Samuel Purchas, 'Virginia's Verger', Purchas Pilgrims, XIX: 199.

12. Ibid., p. 224.

13. "[June 1756]," *Founders Online*, National Archives, https://founders.archives.gov/documents/Adams/01-01-02-0002-0006. [Original source: *The Adams Papers, Diary and Autobiography of John Adams*, vol. 1, *1755–1770*, ed. L. H. Butterfield. Cambridge, MA: Harvard University Press, 1961, pp. 32–34.] (accessed online November 5, 2020).

14. "Madison and "Americanus", April-May (Editorial Note)," *Founders Online,* National Archives, https://founders.archives.gov/documents/Madison/03-10-02-0379. [Original source: *The Papers of James Madison*, Presidential Series, vol. 10, *13 October 1815–30 April 1816*, ed. Angela Kreider, J. C. A. Stagg, Mary Parke Johnson, Katharine E. Harbury, and Anne Mandeville Colony. Charlottesville: University of Virginia Press, 2019, pp. 358–364.] (accessed online November 6, 2020).

15. Plymouth Oration, December 22, 1820, Source: Shewmaker, 94-9

https://www.dartmouth.edu/~dwebster/speeches/plymouth-oration.html (accessed online November 5, 2020).

16. Bozman, John, History of Maryland (1837), Vol. II, p. 570.

17. Banner, Stuart. *How the Indians lost their land: Law and power on the frontier*. Harvard University Press, 2005:64.

18. "From George Washington to the Commissioners to the Southern Indians, 29 August 1789," *Founders Online*, National Archives, https://founders.archives.gov/documents/Washington/05-03-02-0326. [Original source: *The Papers of George Washington*, Presidential Series, vol. 3, *15 June 1789–5 September 1789*, ed. Dorothy Twohig. Charlottesville: University Press of Virginia, 1989, pp. 551–565.] (accessed online November 6, 2020).

19. "Proclamation, 14 August 1790," *Founders Online,* National Archives, https://founders.archives.gov/documents/Washington/05-06-02-0122. [Original source: *The Papers of George Washington*, Presidential Series, vol. 6, *1 July 1790–30 November 1790*, ed. Mark A. Mastromarino. Charlottesville: University Press of Virginia, 1996, pp. 248–254.] (accessed online November 6, 2020).

20. "To George Washington from Henry Knox, 27 December 1790," *Founders Online,* National Archives, https://founders.archives.gov/documents/Washington/05-07-02-0074. [Original source: *The Papers of George Washington*, Presidential Series, vol. 7, *1 December 1790–21 March 1791*, ed. Jack D. Warren, Jr. Charlottesville: University Press of Virginia, 1998, pp. 121–128.] (accessed online November 6, 2020).

21. Kent, James, and Charles M. Barnes. *Commentaries on American law, Lecture 50,* Of the Foundation of Title to Land. Vol. 1. Little, Brown, 1884.

22. Kades, Eric. "The Dark Side of Efficiency: *Johnson v. M'Intosh* and the Expropriation of American Indian Lands." *University of Pennsylvania Law Review* 148.4 (2000): 1126.

23. Remini, Robert V. *Andrew Jackson: The Course of American Empire, 1767-1821*. Vol. 1. JHU Press, 2013: 395.

24. Kades, Eric. "The Dark Side of Efficiency: *Johnson v. M'Intosh* and the Expropriation of American Indian Lands." *University of Pennsylvania Law Review* 148.4 (2000): 1127.

25. "Letter of Robert Bennett to Edward Bennett Describing Use by the English of Poison and Other Treachery in Negotiations with the Indians." (Online *Thomas Jefferson Papers*, American Memory

Collection of the Library of Congress) (Kingsbury IV, 220-22) (Robinson 50-51) (accessed online November 6, 2020).

26. Hazard, Samuel, ed. *Colonial Records of Pennsylvania*. Vol. 8. T. Fenn & Company, 1852: 89.

27. "The Organization of John Van Etten's Company, 12 January 1756," *Founders Online*, National Archives, https://founders.archives. gov/documents/Franklin/01-06-02-0142. [Original source: *The Papers of Benjamin Franklin*, vol. 6, *April 1, 1755 through September 30, 1756*, ed. Leonard W. Labaree. New Haven and London: Yale University Press, 1963, pp. 352–357.] (accessed online November 6, 2020).

28. Sosin, Jack M., THE REVOLUTIONARY FRONTIER, 1763-1783 (New York: Holt, Rinehart and Winston, 1967): 82-84.

29. "Editorial Note: Unofficial Diplomacy on Indian Affairs," *Founders Online*, National Archives, https://founders.archives.gov/ documents/Jefferson/01-20-02-0016-0001. [Original source: *The Papers of Thomas Jefferson*, vol. 20, *1 April–4 August 1791*, ed. Julian P. Boyd. Princeton: Princeton University Press, 1982, pp. 104–141.] (accessed online November 6, 2020).

30. "Address to the United States Senate and House of Representatives, 6 November 1792," *Founders Online*, National Archives, https://founders.archives.gov/documents/ Washington/05-11-02-0189. [Original source: *The Papers of George Washington*, Presidential Series, vol. 11, *16 August 1792–15 January 1793*, ed. Christine Sternberg Patrick. Charlottesville: University of Virginia Press, 2002, pp. 342–351.] (accessed online November 6, 2020).

31. Engels, Jeremy. "Equipped for Murder": The Paxton Boys and the Spirit of Killing all Indians" in Pennsylvania, 1763-1764." *Rhetoric and Public Affairs* (2005): 355-381.

32. Calloway, Colin G. *The Indian World of George Washington: The First President, the First Americans, and the Birth of the Nation*. Oxford University Press, 2018: 316.

33. "From Thomas Jefferson to William Henry Harrison, 27 February 1803," *Founders Online*, National Archives, https://founders.archives.

gov/documents/Jefferson/01-39-02-0500. [Original source: *The Papers of Thomas Jefferson*, vol. 39, *13 November 1802 - 3 March 1803*, ed. Barbara B. Oberg. Princeton: Princeton University Press, 2012, pp. 589–593.] (accessed online November 6, 2020).

34. Thomas Jefferson's Second Inaugural Address, March 4, 1805 as quoted in Ford, The Works of Thomas Jefferson, vol. VIII, 345.

35. Kades, Eric. "The Dark Side of Efficiency: *Johnson v. M'Intosh* and the Expropriation of American Indian Lands." *University of Pennsylvania Law Review* 148.4 (2000): 1187.

36. Thomas, Peter. 1979. In the Maelstrom of Change: The Indian Trade and Cultural Process in the Middle Connecticut River Valley, 1635-1665. New York: Garland Publishing, Inc.: 182.

37. https://www.massmoments.org/moment-details/william-pynchon-buys-land-for-springfield.html (accessed online November 18, 2020).

38. Thomas, Peter. 1979. In the Maelstrom of Change: The Indian Trade and Cultural Process in the Middle Connecticut River Valley, 1635-1665. New York: Garland Publishing, Inc.: 305.

39. Letter from General Schuyler to the committee on Indian affairs, July 29, 1783. National Archives, Records of the Continental and Confederation Congresses and the Constitutional Convention

http://recordsofrights.org/records/228/letter-to-the-continental-congress/ (accessed online November 21, 2020).

40. "From George Washington to James Duane, 7 September 1783," *Founders Online,* National Archives, https://founders.archives.gov/documents/Washington/99-01-02-11798 (accessed online November 21, 2020).

41. Ohio Historical Society www.ohiohistory.org (accessed online November 5, 2020).

42. *Johnson v. M'Intosh*, 21 U.S. 543, 590-591 (1823).

43. Herbert Milton Sylvester, Indian Wars of New England (Cleveland, 1910), I, 386.

44. Excerpt, Mohegan Petition to the General Assembly, May 14,

1789. State Archives, Connecticut State Library. Accessed at Yale Indian Papers Project, Yale Digital Collections (accessed on November 15, 2020).

45. Kent, James, and Charles M. Barnes. *Commentaries on American law,* Lecture LI, Vol. 3, Of Real Property, Of the Foundation of Title to Land. Little, Brown, 1884: 505.

46. Kades, Eric. "The Dark Side of Efficiency: *Johnson v. M'Intosh* and the Expropriation of American Indian Lands." *University of Pennsylvania Law Review* 148.4 (2000): 1105.

47.Cronon, William. "Changes in the Land: Indians, Colonists, and the Ecology of New England" (New York: Hill and Wang, 1983): 86-87.

48. Crosby, Alfred W. "Virgin soil epidemics as a factor in the aboriginal depopulation in America." *The William and Mary Quarterly: A Magazine of Early American History* (1976):

290-91.

49. Bradford, William, and William J. A. Bradford. *Of Plymouth Plantation, 1620-1647.* Rutgers University Press, 1952: 99.

50. Messages and Letters of William Henry Harrison, Vol. 1, p. 38.

51. "From Thomas Jefferson to William Henry Harrison, 27 February 1803," *Founders Online*, National Archives, https://founders.archives. gov/documents/Jefferson/01-39-02-0500. [Original source: *The Papers of Thomas Jefferson*, vol. 39, *13 November 1802–3 March 1803*, ed. Barbara B. Oberg. Princeton: Princeton University Press, 2012, pp. 589–593.] (accessed online November 6, 2020); "To John Adams from the Marquis of Carmarthen, 11 December 1786," *Founders Online,* National Archives, https://founders.archives.gov/documents/ Adams/06-18-02-0274. [Original source: *The Adams Papers*, Papers of John Adams, vol. 18, *December 1785–January 1787*, ed. Gregg L. Lint, Sara Martin, C. James Taylor, Sara Georgini, Hobson Woodward, Sara B. Sikes, Amanda M. Norton. Cambridge, MA: Harvard University Press, 2016, pp. 517–518.] (accessed online November 5, 2020).

52. Quinn, David B., ed. *Voyages and Colonising Enterprises of Sir*

*Humphrey Gilbert*. London, Hakluyt Society, 1940: 358.

53. "To Alexander Hamilton from James McHenry, 19 August 1797," *Founders Online,* National Archives, https://founders.archives.gov/documents/Hamilton/01-21-02-0136. [Original source: *The Papers of Alexander Hamilton*, vol. 21, *April 1797–July 1798*, ed. Harold C. Syrett. New York: Columbia University Press, 1974, pp. 213–214.] (accessed online November 5, 2020).

54. Banner, Stuart. *How the Indians lost their land: Law and power on the frontier*. Harvard University Press, 2005: 72.

55. Treaty of Croswicks, 1756, Province of New Jersey; http://gnadenhutten.tripod.com/bethelindiantown (accessed online November 5, 2020).

56. "To Thomas Jefferson from Meriwether Lewis, 15 December 1808," *Founders Online*, National Archives, https://founders.archives.gov/documents/Jefferson/99-01-02-9323 (accessed online November 5, 2020).

57. McClure, James P., and Thomas Jefferson. *The Papers of Thomas Jefferson, Volume 42: 16 November 1803 to 10 March 1804*. Princeton University Press, 2017: 128.

58. "To George Washington from Arthur St. Clair, 2 May 1789," *Founders Online,* National Archives, https://founders.archives.gov/documents/Washington/05-02-02-0142. [Original source: *The Papers of George Washington*, Presidential Series, vol. 2, *1 April 1789–15 June 1789*, ed. Dorothy Twohig. Charlottesville: University Press of Virginia, 1987, pp. 196–200.] (accessed November 14, 2020).

59. Kades, Eric. "The Dark Side of Efficiency: *Johnson v. M'Intosh* and the Expropriation of American Indian Lands." *University of Pennsylvania Law Review* 148.4 (2000): 1120.

60. Ibid., p. 1126.

61. "Treaty of Carlisle, 1 November 1753," *Founders Online*, National Archives, https://founders.archives.gov/documents/Franklin/01-05-02-0026. [Original source: *The Papers of Benjamin Franklin*, vol. 5, *July 1, 1753, through March 31, 1755*, ed. Leonard

W. Labaree. New Haven: Yale University Press, 1962, pp. 84–107.]
(accessed online November 6, 2020).

62. "Treaty of Carlisle, 1 November 1753," *Founders Online*,
National Archives, https://founders.archives.gov/documents/
Franklin/01-05-02-0026. [Original source: *The Papers of Benjamin
Franklin*, vol. 5, *July 1, 1753 through March 31, 1755*, ed. Leonard
W. Labaree. New Haven: Yale University Press, 1962, pp. 84–107.]
(accessed online November 6, 2020).

63. Wallace, Anthony F. C. and Powell, Timothy B., "How to Buy a
Continent: The Protocols of Indian Treaties as Developed by Benjamin
Franklin and Other Members of the American Philosophical Society."
(2015): 268.

64. Kades, Eric. "The Dark Side of Efficiency: *Johnson v. M'Intosh*
and the Expropriation of American Indian Lands." *University of
Pennsylvania Law Review* 148.4 (2000): 1105.

65. Banner, Stuart. *How the Indians lost their land: Law and power on
the frontier*. Harvard University Press, 2005:75.

66. American State Papers, Indian Affairs, No. 149, p. 136.

67. Philip Cortlandt and Daniel Horsmanden to Council of Trade and
Plantations, November 1738. *British History Online*

http://www.british-history.ac.uk/cal-state-papers/colonial/america-
west-indies/vol44/pp241-255 (accessed online November 5, 2020).

68. Kades, Eric. "The Dark Side of Efficiency: *Johnson v. M'Intosh*
and the Expropriation of American Indian Lands." *University of
Pennsylvania Law Review* 148.4 (2000): 1185.

69. The Taking of Indian Lands: Perspectives of Native Americans and
European Americans, 1707-1765

http://nationalhumanitiescenter.org/pds/becomingamer/growth/text7/
indianlands.ppd (accessed online November 5, 2020).

70. Wallace, Anthony F. C. *King of the Delawares: Teedyuscung,
1700-1763*. Syracuse University Press, 1990: 246.

71. Ibid., p. 247.

72. Ibid., p. 249.

73. Ibid.

74. Franklin, Benjamin. *The Autobiography of Benjamin Franklin: 1706-1757*. Vol. 1. Regnery Publishing, 2007.

75. Banner, Stuart. *How the Indians lost their land: Law and power on the frontier*. Harvard University Press, 2005: 63.

76. A monitory and hortatory letter to those English who debauch the Indians by selling strong drink unto them written at the desire of some Christians to whom the mischiefs arising from that vile trade are matters of much apprehension and lamentation. Mather, Cotton, 1663-1728. Boston, Printed in the year 1700.

77. Banner, Stuart. *How the Indians lost their land: Law and power on the frontier*. Harvard University Press, 2005: 63.

78. Treaty of Croswicks, 1756, Province of New Jersey http://gnadenhutten.tripod.com/bethelindiantown (accessed online November 5, 2020).

79. https://quod.lib.umich.edu/e/evans/N07375.0001.001/1:2.8?rgn=div2;view=fulltext (accessed online November 5, 2020).

80. Messages and Letters of William Henry Harrison, Vol. 1, p. 29.

81. "From Thomas Jefferson to the Senate and the House of Representatives, 27 January 1802," *Founders Online*, National Archives, https://founders.archives.gov/documents/Jefferson/01-36-02-0289. [Original source: *The Papers of Thomas Jefferson*, vol. 36, *1 December 1801–3 March 1802*, ed. Barbara B. Oberg. Princeton: Princeton University Press, 2009, pp. 440–443.] (accessed online November 21, 2020).

# 11

# SEVEN YEARS WAR

# (AKA FRENCH AND INDIAN WAR), 1756–1763

Britain and France's 'discovery' claims in the Ohio Valley overlapped. The region in dispute included the territory drained by the upper Mississippi River—present day Ohio, Illinois, Indiana, Kentucky and West Virginia. As many as five Indian Nations also claimed this land— the Wyandotte, Delaware, Mingo, Miami and Shawnee. The Forks of the Ohio, where the Monongahela and Allegheny Rivers join to form the Ohio River, was a strategic key to control of the Valley.

In 1753 Major George Washington visited the Forks of the Ohio while enroute to the French-held Fort Le Boeuf to order the French to leave the Ohio Valley. Washington endorsed the Forks as a strategic position, and in 1754 the English began to construct a fort there. The French seized it that same year, however, completed it, and named it Fort Duquesne. The resulting tensions between the two nations led to a conflict known as the French and Indian War in America and abroad as the Seven Years' War. In 1754, the French defeated Washington, who failed in his attempt to recapture the Duquesne area, at Fort Necessity. The following year Fort Duquesne was the objective of the ill-fated force under British General Edward Braddock that suffered a disastrous defeat a few miles east of the Forks.

After the French military defeat in the Seven Years War (aka French and Indian War), the European countries involved ceded various lands under the Treaty of 1763: France ceded to Britain all Nova Scotia, or Acadie, and Canada, with their dependencies; and it was agreed, that the middle of the Mississippi River would be a boundary. France also ceded its claims to lands north of the Ohio River to the English and transferred control over the Louisiana Territory to Spain. The English then used the Treaty of 1763 as the basis for their claim to the Northwest Territory, replacing their prior claim that the English controlled the land by the right of conquest over the Iroquois.

## Proclamation of 1763 (Remedy for Great Frauds and Abuses Committed against Indians)

In 1757, when asked why his Nation was inclined to ally themselves with the French, Seneca chief Silver Heels answered that the British "intended to dispossess them of all their Lands."[1] In November 1761, the Board of Trade proposed to King George III that he do something to prohibit what the Board called "a Measure of the most dangerous Tendency"—the settlement of land not yet purchased from the Indians. The Board reminded the king that the primary reason most Indian Nations had sided with France was "the Cruelty and Injustice with which they had been treated with respect to their Hunting Grounds, in open violation of those solemn Compacts by which they had yielded to us the Dominion *but not the Property of their Lands*."[2] (Emphasis added.)

In 1763, at the end of the Seven Years War (aka French and Indian War), Britain's government in London took control over the business of Indian land acquisition in its North American colonies. Pontiac's War evidenced the need for London to obtain peace on British America's western frontier. Colonial settlement had to be brought under control to avoid continual expensive Indian wars, impacting Britain's debt. The War had cost the British £135 million.

The Royal government's Proclamation of 1763 instituted several reforms intended to remedy the colonial fraud in Indian land acquisitions. It banned English colonists from settling west of a border drawn by the Crown—essentially a north-south line that ran from New York to Georgia across the top of the Appalachian Mountains. East of this boundary, private sales of land between Indians and colonial settlers were banned. To try to avoid the problem of unauthorized or inappropriate individuals attempting to sell Indian land, all purchases by the government had to be made "at some publick Meeting or Assembly" in the presence of the Indian sellers. The expectation was that the transparency of public transactions would lessen the potential for spurious transactions.

The Proclamation explained, "It is ... essential to Our Interest and the Security of Our Colonies," that the Indians "should not be molested or disturbed in the Possession of such Parts of Our Dominions and Territories as, not having been ceded to, or purchased by Us, are reserved to them."[3] In the colonies, Indian land was instead to be purchased only by colonial governors, on behalf of the Crown, thereby reducing private graft. Having Crown officials supervise Indian land purchases would also allow for a method of maintaining an effective recording system of such purchases. Indians relied on oral tradition to preserve a record of its transaction, which might also be recorded in the depiction on wampum belts.

It turned out to be difficult to get all colonial parties to agree on a boundary, even though it appeared from the Proclamation it was intended to be the Appalachian Mountains. As colonies pushed to reduce the region closed for private acquisition, the boundary kept moving westward. It first moved to the demarcated line for the Treaty of Hard Labor which meant the Indians ceded what is today the state of West Virginia. At the 1768 Treaty of Fort Stanwix, Sir William Johnson, the British Crown's Superintendent of Indian Affairs for the Northern Colonies, brokered another treaty in which the Indians ended up ceding even more land in western Pennsylvania, Kentucky, West Virginia and New York. After 1768 in the north, and by the early 1770s in most of the south, there was a boundary between the British colonies and the Indians defining the westernmost limits of colonial settlement, established at great cost to the Indians who forfeited vast tracts of land.

## Land Speculators Ignore Proclamation of 1763

While the Royal Proclamation of 1763 prohibited colonial governors from issuing land grants west of the established boundaries, colonial land speculators totally ignored the restriction. They grumbled that the King lacked the authority to issue the Proclamation, which required Parliament's approval. One example of forging ahead to select, survey and purchase western land, regardless of the restraint, was George Washington. In a letter to James Duane in September 1767, Washington wrote:

> I can never look upon the Proclamation in any other light (*but this I say between ourselves*) than as a temporary expedient to quiet the minds of the Indians. It must fall, of course, in a few years, especially when those Indians consent to our occupying those lands. Any person who neglects hunting out good lands, and in some measure marking and distinguishing them for his own, in order to keep others from settling them will never regain it.[4] (Emphasis added.)

Washington selected surveyor William Crawford to begin his land acquisition plan. Though Washington was wary of conflict with the Ohio Company, he directed Crawford to make inquiries "so we may know what to apprehend from them." He ordered Crawford to "... keep this whole matter a profound Secret ... because I might be censurd ... in respect to the Kings Proclamation."[5] Crawford "heartily embraced" the offer. He promised shortly to set out in search of lands. "This may be done," he said, "under a hunting scheme."[6]

In another letter evidencing his characterization of the 'New Empire' opened up by westward settlement, Washington wrote to the Marquis de Chastellux:

> I shall not rest contented till I have explored the western country, and traversed those lines (or a great part of them) which have given bounds to a New Empire. ... Land is the most permanent estate and the most likely to increase in value.[7]

In the fall of 1770, Washington, Crawford and a fellow veteran named Dr. James Craig set out from Fort Pitt (what is today Pittsburgh) to explore possible sites for acquisition, allegedly for military veterans who possessed warrants for land based on their military service and rank. Out of a total of 64,071 acres selected, 19,383, or approximately 30 percent, were patented in Washington's name. In a letter to Presley Neville, Washington said that these lands were "the cream of the Country."[8]

On August 20, 1773, less than three years after his exploration,

Washington posted an advertisement in the Maryland Journal and Baltimore Advertiser to lease these lands: "The subscriber having obtained patents for upwards of twenty thousand acres of land on the Ohio and Great Kanawha ... proposes to divide the same ... and lease them upon moderate ... terms."[9]

In buying land, George Washington did not risk being punished by the government; his only danger was that he might lose the purchase price if the government later granted the same land to someone else. The potential profits from reselling the land were large enough for Washington and other speculators to be willing to bear the risk.

Many early settlers who had taken up tracts of land for development and resale had become rich. On July 24, 1783, Silas Deane wrote from London to James Wilson:

> It clearly appears to me that the two great objects of America must be the settlement and cultivation of good lands and the establishment of manufactures. If we review the rise and progress of private fortunes in America, we shall find that a very small proportion of them has arisen or been acquired by commerce, compared with those made by prudent purchases and management of lands.[10]

With prominent men, in the same league as George Washington, willing to buy land illegally, the flood of westward movement could not be controlled. They wanted to encourage additional migration to enhance their economies and political power. Lacking manpower and funding, British officials were stymied to prevent this rush for Indian land.

From the Indian perspective, the Proclamation was not necessarily a victory. It certainly did not stop settlers from selecting and amassing choice land. It did make purchasing Indian land more difficult. The centralized government procedures designed for transparency caused dissension among colonists that led to a black market in land sales. Partisan political animosity led to hostility between the British government and the colonies. The settlers had no desire to see land reserved for Indians west of the Appalachian's even if it might not be permanent. For Virginia, it was particularly acute—the Proclamation line bisected the colony.

In 1766 the Earl of Shelburne, secretary of state, urged each colonial governor to stem the tide of settlers moving west and squatting on Indian land. He complained that "Settlements have been made on the Back of the Provinces, without proper authority and beyond the Limits prescribed by His Majesty's Royal Proclamation of 1763," and urging each governor to "apply yourself in the most earnest manner, to remedy and prevent those Evils."[11]

Governor Francis Fauquier warned squatters also in 1766 that they "must expect no protection or mercy from Government, and be exposed to the revenge of the exasperated Indians."[12] Imposing the responsibility to restrain squatters to the Indians would only result in frontier violence. The blame for the intermittent assault on settlers by Indians only fed the frenzied chaos west of the Appalachians. Not only would there be settlers threatening the Indian land base, land speculators were on the prowl as well. Local officials had no effective means to regulate the land fever in the Ohio Valley.

On September 30, 1773, Sir William Johnson informed British General Frederick Haldimand,

> ...[T]he Spirit of purchasing & pushing Settlements in to the back country, remote from the Influence of Government, and where they do as they please is ... prevalent... The Indians justly observe that we have not half settled the Country near the Sea and that those who go back are a Banditti who disregard our Laws, as much as they hate them.[13]

"I have learnt from experience," wrote Lord Dunmore, Colonial Governor of Virginia, to his chief, Lord Dartmouth, on December 24, 1774, "that the established authority of any government in America, and the policy at home, are both insufficient to restrain the Americans, and they do and will remove as their avidity and restlessness incite them."[14]

As the colonists lacked revenue to purchase Indian land, it was done by investors providing revenue to the colonial government in return for a patent. Land speculator Jellis Fonda declared that he and his partners were "willing and desirous at their own Expence to vest the Indian Right and Title to the said Lands in the Crown." Of course, Fonda's proposal was not to buy land for the Crown. When the purchase had been completed, Fonda would "pray for and obtain his Majesty's Letters patent for the said Lands."[15] The colonial government would be a mere intermediary, a conduit passing land in one direction and money in the other, wedged between the Indians and the British government. Without capital or credit, individual settlers were crowded out of the market.

When, and if, the Crown purchased Indian land, the patent or 'deed' the buyer received vesting title came from the Crown, not from an Indian Nation. The concept of Indian land ownership would subtly and indelibly be altered. As analyzed by Stuart Banner, after 1763 Indian land ownership was easier to perceive as a second-class property right, something less complete than the full ownership enjoyed with a fee simple.[16]

## Lord Dunmore's War, 1774

With the tension brewing between the colonies and Britain, the Virginians took advantage of the chaos, rushing to secure more land for their own westward expansion at the expense of other colonies who did not have a western front. The Virginians were willing to incite violence by the Indians to obtain a valuable revenue source for parceling out and selling smaller tracts of land to individual settlers, thereby making it possible for them to acquire land. This illegal onslaught against Indian lands led to Dummer's War in 1774, with the Shawnee and Mingo, for control of the Ohio Valley, in present-day West Virginia and Ohio.

Precursors to the War included widespread encroachment on Indian lands in what would become Kentucky. Daniel Boone explored central Kentucky, up to the Ohio River and the Northwest Territory. Colonel Richard Henderson and Thomas Nathaniel Hart, with Boone as a member, formed a company to purchase 20 million acres between the Kentucky and Cumberland Rivers. His Company advertised widely for settlers for the communities of Harrodsburg, Boonesborough, McClellan's Station, Bryan's Station and St. Asaph's Station. These communities were attacked by Shawnee, Cherokee, Delaware, Chippewa, Mingo, Miami, Ottawa and Wyandot Indian Nations who claimed the land. In 1773, Shawnees attacked and killed Boone's son and Henry Russell.

The Treaty of Lancaster (1744), Treaty of Logstown (1752) and Treaty of Fort Stanwix (1768) created resentment among the Ohio Valley Indians as to who had authority to cede Indian lands to the U.S. The hostilities impacted river traffic negatively affecting Virginia's economy. Gov. Henry Hamilton, the British Lt. Col. and Superintendent of Indian Affairs, paid Shawnees for Indian scalps, pitting Indians against Indians. He was known as the 'Hair-buyer General.'

Significantly, the Ohio Valley land was part of the Virginia-Pennsylvania Boundary Dispute. Dunmore had the opportunity to strengthen Virginia's claim to this land while Pennsylvania was distracted by all of the activity pertaining to the forthcoming Declaration of Independence.[17]

Mingo Chief Logan's sister, brother and other relatives were murdered at Baker's Bottom by settlers, including Daniel Greathouse. Logan vowed to retaliate. Dunmore had no trouble raising a local militia to subdue the Mingos. Colonel Adam Stephen led 1200 men and Colonel Andrew Lewis had 1300 men. The Shawnee formed the Shawnee Ohio Confederacy under the leadership of Cornstalk with 800-1000 warriors. After the bloody hand-to-hand combat at Pt. Pleasant, the Shawnee decided to withdraw from the War to avoid the further loss of lives. Dunmore's militia outnumbered the Confederacy by 3-1. The Indian Confederacy suffered casualties of 215 dead, 140 wounded, losing Chief Logan, Shawnee Chief Silver Heels and Delaware Chief Bald Eagle.

The Shawnee Confederacy agreed to cede land south of the Ohio River to Virginia (present day Kentucky and West Virginia) under the Treaty of Camp Charlotte. On his return, Lord Dunmore was chastised by Lord Dartmouth for his absence during the crucial planning by the colonists for revolution.

Notes

1. Banner, Stuart. *How the Indians lost their land: Law and power on the frontier*. Harvard University Press, 2005: 87.

2. Brodhead, John Romeyn. *Documents Relative to the Colonial History of the State of New-York: Procured in Holland, England, and France*. Vol. 11. Weed, Parsons, 1861: 478.

3. https://www.ushistory.org/us/9a.asp (accessed online November 21, 2020).

4. "From George Washington to James Duane, 7 September 1783," *Founders Online*, National Archives, https://founders.archives.gov/documents/Washington/99-01-02-11798 (accessed online November 15, 2020).

5. "From George Washington to William Crawford, 17 September 1767," *Founders Online*, National Archives, https://founders.archives.gov/documents/Washington/02-08-02-0020. [Original source: *The Papers of George Washington*, Colonial Series, vol. 8, *24 June 1767–25 December 1771*, ed. W. W. Abbot and Dorothy Twohig. Charlottesville: University Press of Virginia, 1993, pp. 26–32.] (accessed online November 15, 2020).

6. Sakolski, Aaron M. "The Great American Land Bubble: The Amazing Story of Land-Grabbing, Speculations, and Booms from Colonial Days to the Present Time." (1932): 8.

7. "From George Washington to François-Jean de Beauvoir, marquis de Chastellux, 12 October 1783," *Founders Online*, National Archives, https://founders.archives.gov/documents/Washington/99-01-02-11929. (accessed online November 15, 2020).

8. "From George Washington to Presley Nevill, 16 June 1794," *Founders Online*, National Archives, https://founders.archives.

gov/documents/Washington/05-16-02-0192. [Original source: *The Papers of George Washington,* Presidential Series, vol. 16, *1 May–30 September 1794*, ed. David R. Hoth and Carol S. Ebel. Charlottesville: University of Virginia Press, 2011, pp. 236–240.] (accessed online November 15, 2020).

9. "Enclosure: Advertisement: Ohio Lands, 10 March 1784," *Founders Online*, National Archives, https://founders.archives.gov/documents/Washington/04-01-02-0149-0002. [Original source: *The Papers of George Washington,* Confederation Series, vol. 1, *1 January 1784–17 July 1784*, ed. W. W. Abbot. Charlottesville: University Press of Virginia, 1992, pp. 201–204.] (accessed online November 15, 2020).

10. Sakolski, Aaron M. "The Great American Land Bubble: The Amazing Story of Land-Grabbing, Speculations, and Booms from Colonial Days to the Present Time." (1932): 29-30.

11. Order of the King in Council on a Report of the Lords of Trade, November 23, 1761, in O'Callaghan, Edmund Bailey. *Documents relative to the colonial history of the State of New-York*. Vol. III. Weed, Parsons, printers, 1861: 472.

12. Banner, Stuart. *How the Indians lost their land: Law and power on the frontier*. Harvard University Press, 2005: 98.

13. Johnson, William. The Papers of Sir William Johnson. Albany: The University of the State of New York, 1922; Rasmussen, Barbara. "Anarchy and Enterprise on the Imperial Frontier: Washington, Dunmore, Logan, and Land in the Eighteenth-Century Ohio Valley." Ohio Valley History, vol. 6, no. 4, 2006, p. 1-26.

14. Dunmore to Dartmouth, official report of "Affairs in Virginia; The Indian Expedition" Williamsburg 24 December 1774, *Documentary History of Dunmore's War*, edited by Reuben Gold Thwaites and Louise Phelps Kellogg (Madison: Wisconsin Historical Society, 1905), p. 368-96.

15. Banner, Stuart. *How the Indians lost their land: Law and power on the frontier*. Harvard University Press, 2005: 105.

16. Ibid., pp. 108-109.

17. Greene, George E. (1911), History of Old Vincennes and Knox County, Indiana, Volume 1. S.J. Clarke Publishing Company: 182.

## 12

# DECLARATION OF INDEPENDENCE

Benjamin Franklin in a letter to James Parker, dated March 20, 1751, recognized the need for a strong colonial alliance. He criticized the colonies' inability to do what 'ignorant savages' had accomplished:

> A voluntary Union entered into by the Colonies themselves, I think, would be preferable to one impos'd by Parliament; for it would be perhaps not much more difficult to procure, and more easy to alter and improve, as Circumstances should require, and Experience direct. It would be a very strange Thing, if six Nations of ignorant Savages should be capable of forming a Scheme for such an Union, and be able to execute it in such a Manner, as that it has subsisted Ages, and appears indissoluble; and yet that a like Union should be impracticable for ten or a Dozen English Colonies, to whom it is more necessary...[1]

Advisors to King George III warned that the colonies were becoming overly populated and independent-minded and might consider creating an alliance among themselves. The Proclamation of 1763 had added fuel to the fire. When the colonists decided to revolt against England, one of their complaints against the King was the Proclamation:

> He has endeavoured to prevent the population of these States; for that purpose obstructing the Laws for Naturalization of Foreigners; refusing to pass others to encourage their migrations hither, and raising the conditions of new Appropriations of Lands.[2]

The last cause of a list of 27 grievances against the King denigrated Indians in a hostile manner, as "merciless savages," which would foment colonial and governmental rampages resulting in the utter devastation and destruction of villages and crops.

> He has excited domestic insurrections amongst us, and has endeavored to bring on the inhabitants of our frontiers, the merciless Indian savages whose known rule of warfare, is an undistinguished destruction of all ages, sexes, and conditions.[3]

The dehumanizing stereotype of Indians in such a formal colonial document made it possible to commit atrocities against Indians.

### Outbreak of American Revolution (1776) Resulted in Colonists Arguing that Crown Had No Legal Authority to Convey Indian Lands through Crown Charters; Indians Were Owners of Soil

Prior to the outbreak of the American Revolution, the colonists needed an argument to refute the British allegation that they were 'stealing' the King's lands. The American Revolutionaries countered this argument by claiming that the Indians owned the land, not the Crown. This came about not out of a moral concern toward Indians but because of the political rhetoric used to legitimize the Revolution itself. Loyalists claimed one reason the revolution was illegal was that the colonists had been given land through royal charters issued by the Crown. It was imperative that the colonists about to engage in a revolution against their home country undermine the title to American soil as being under English control. They did this by publicly scorning the idea that England had title to land based on royal charters from English monarchs.

In his pamphlet, On Claims to the Soil of America, March 16, 1773, Benjamin Franklin referred to the alleged royal grants as "chimerical Rights," which were only "an Exclusion of other Englishmen from the respective Boundaries of each Grant. The Grantees, to obtain some Title, were obliged to purchase of the Indians, or conquer them at their own Charges. And if they had insisted that the Crown should put them in Possession of what it granted, the Grant would probably never have been made."[4]

While reading Matthew Wheelock's defense of Parliament's supreme authority in North America, premised on the assumption that the earliest colonists had acquired their land from the Crown, Franklin noted in the margin: *"The British Nation had no original Property in the Country of America. It was purchas'd by the first Colonists of the Natives, the only Owners."* In the margins of another pamphlet making a similar argument, Franklin scrawled: "False! The Lands did not belong to the Crown but to the Indians."[5] (Emphasis added.)

"How, in common sense," asked future president John Adams in 1774, "came the dominions of King Philip, King Massachusetts, and twenty other sovereigns, independent princes here, to be within the allegiance of the Kings of England, James and Charles?" According to John Adams, *Royal charters "could give no title to the England King, by common law, or by the law of nature, to the lands, tenements and hereditaments of the native Indians here."* (Emphasis added.) Adams' opinion reflected the position of the northeastern colonies who predominantly secured native land by purchase: "Our ancestors were sensible of this, and therefore, honestly purchased their lands of the natives."[6]

Although Adams and Franklin agreed on who owned indigenous land in America, mere settlement without purchase occurred, not because the colonial settlers believed that Indians did not own the land, but because this usurpation was tolerated by the government and there was no official government will to prevent it.

The colonial government, consisting of a confederacy of the thirteen colonies during the Revolutionary War, did not hesitate to seek Indian alliances, active assistance or at a minimum their neutrality. This is evidenced in a letter from General George Washington to the Commissioners of Indian Affairs, dated March 13, 1778:

> You will percieve by the inclosed Copy of a Resolve of Congress that I am empowered to employ a Body of four hundred Indians if they can be procured upon proper Terms —Divesting them of the Savage Customs exercised in their Wars against each other, I think they may be made of excellent Use as Sevnts and light Troops mixed with our other parties.[7]

Close to fifty Indian warriors would be sent to Valley Forge. On May 15, 1778, they arrived at the encampment. On May 18, they were directed to participate in a reconnaissance for a force numbering 2,200 troops under the command of Marquis de Lafayette to an area called Barren Hill. It is thought that six Oneidas were killed during this engagement. In the middle of June, thirty-four of the original fifty returned home due to British and their Indian allies threats to their families and homes.

Notes

1. "From Benjamin Franklin to James Parker, 20 March 1751," *Founders Online,* National Archives, https://founders.archives.gov/documents/Franklin/01-04-02-0037. [Original source: *The Papers of Benjamin Franklin,* vol. 4, *July 1, 1750 through June 30, 1753*, ed. Leonard W. Labaree. New Haven: Yale University Press, 1961, pp. 117–121.] (accessed online November 14, 2020).

2. "V. The Declaration of Independence as Adopted by Congress, 11 June–4 July 1776," *Founders Online*, National Archives, https://founders.archives.gov/documents/Jefferson/01-01-02-0176-0006. [Original source: *The Papers of Thomas Jefferson*, vol. 1, *1760–1776*, ed. Julian P. Boyd. Princeton: Princeton University Press, 1950, pp. 429–433.] (accessed online November 14, 2020).

3. Ibid.

4. "On Claims to the Soil of America, 16 March 1773," *Founders Online*, National Archives, https://founders.archives.gov/documents/Franklin/01-20-02-0071. [Original source: *The Papers of Benjamin Franklin*, vol. 20, *January 1 through December 31, 1773*, ed. William B. Willcox. New Haven and London: Yale University Press, 1976, pp. 115–122.] (accessed online November 14, 2020).

5. Banner, Stuart. *How the Indians lost their land: Law and power on the frontier*. Harvard University Press, 2005: 116.

6. "VIII. To the Inhabitants of the Colony of Massachusetts-Bay, 13 March 1775," *Founders Online*, National Archives, https://founders.archives.gov/documents/Adams/06-02-02-0072-0009. [Original source: *The Adams Papers, Papers of John Adams*, vol. 2, *December 1773–April 1775*, ed. Robert J. Taylor. Cambridge, MA: Harvard

University Press, 1977, pp. 327–337.] (accessed online November 14, 2020).

7. "From George Washington to the Commissioners of Indian Affairs, 13 March 1778," *Founders Online*, National Archives, https://founders.archives.gov/documents/Washington/03-14-02-0133. [Original source: *The Papers of George Washington,* Revolutionary War Series, vol. 14, *1 March 1778–30 April 1778*, ed. David R. Hoth. Charlottesville: University of Virginia Press, 2004, pp. 167–168.] (accessed online November 14, 2020).

# 13

# CONTINENTAL CONGRESS (1774)

# AND U.S. CONSTITUTION RATIFIED (1788)

Between 1776 and 1789, the United States did not have a strong national government. The threat of British military power and the 'firm league of friendship' created by the Articles of Confederation held the thirteen independent states together. Many leaders clearly recognized that the United States needed to establish a truly national government. As Alexander Hamilton phrased it, Americans needed to learn to think 'continentally.'[1]

The individual states faced the difficult problems of rebuilding after the war, paying off war debts, providing for defense and improving transportation. Furthermore, by 1784 inflation had made Continental currency almost worthless. The Confederacy had no uniform currency, and Continental paper, state paper, bills of exchange and foreign coins circulated freely. The weaknesses of the Continental Congress were real—particularly in foreign affairs, national defense, mediation of interstate disputes and fiscal matters. Of significance, especially given the near bankruptcy of the Confederation, was its inability to impose taxes. This made land sales critical as the only major source of revenue. The leading defect of the Confederation was an utter want of all coercive authority to carry into effect its own constitutional measures. Congress possessed only the power of recommendation.

As to Indians, the Articles of Confederation gave the Confederacy only "the sole and exclusive right and power of ... regulating the trade and managing all affairs with the Indians not members of any of the states; *provided that the legislative right of any State within its own limits be not infringed or violated.*"[2] (Emphasis added.)

The states retained their authority over interactions with the Indian Nations located within the state, including matters of land acquisition. In 1783, the Congress prohibited unauthorized settlement on or purchase of Indian land outside "the limits or jurisdiction of any particular State." In 1784, in an ordinance providing for the eventual division of western land into new states, Congress recognized that the only land that could be incorporated into new states was land that had been "already purchased, or shall be purchased, of the Indian inhabitants."[3]

## Western Lands Claimed by Thirteen Colonies

In 1763, the Royal Proclamation had forbidden American colonists to settle west of the Appalachian Mountains. The Treaty of Paris (1783), concluding the American Revolutionary War, granted the new states additional territory from the Appalachians to the Mississippi. This led to a chaotic scramble from the original colonies for this added land. Again, no regard was given to Indian land rights. They would be a mere afterthought to be dealt with as needed.

The first step in the process was to untangle the snarl of conflicting state claims to the western lands, which were based on overlapping, outdated and unrealistic colonial charters, serving as a potential source of national disunion. Massachusetts, Connecticut, Virginia, North Carolina, South Carolina and Georgia claimed that their 'from sea to sea' charters gave them lands between the Appalachian mountains and the Mississippi River (or South Sea). New York claimed that they had purchased the Indian title to land in the Ohio River Valley.

Rhode Island, Delaware, New Jersey, Maryland, Pennsylvania and New Hampshire had no such claims. These 'landless' states feared that the 'landed' states would sell their western lands to pay off their own state's war debts or, worse, develop the lands and grow so large and powerful that they would threaten the independence of their neighbors.

In Debates in the Continental Congress, James Wilson argued that Virginia's claims were "extravagant" and founded on misconceptions:

> Every Gentleman has heard much of claims to the South Sea. They are extravagant. The grants were made upon mistakes. They were ignorant of the Geography. They thought the South Sea within one hundred miles of the Atlantic Ocean. It was not conceived that they extended three thousand miles.[4]

The landless states advocated that the landed states surrender their western claims to Congress to administer for the benefit of the union. State land claims would not be completely settled until 1802. By 1786, however, New York, Virginia, Massachusetts and Connecticut had surrendered sufficient lands north of the Ohio to give the Continental Congress clear title and allow it to begin the organization of western settlement.

## U.S. Constitution (Signed 1787, Ratified 1788)

Many leaders clearly recognized that the United States needed to form a national government. Federalists supported a strong national government. Anti-Federalists were wary of a potentially tyrannical national government. After the American Revolution, the U.S. Constitution, through its Commerce and Treaty Clauses, vested the federal government, and the federal government alone (not private citizens, not states, not foreign governments), with the power to enter into commerce and make treaties with the Indian nations. This was codified and reaffirmed through the Trade and Intercourse Acts, 25 U.S.C. §177.

Indians are only mentioned twice in the U.S. Constitution:

> Article I, Section 2, Clause 3: Representatives and direct Taxes shall be apportioned among the several States which may be included within this Union ... excluding Indians not taxed.

> Article I, Section 8 states that "The Congress shall have power to regulate Commerce with foreign Nations, and among the several States, and with the Indian Tribes ..."[5]

# Notes

1. "From Alexander Hamilton to George Washington, [8 April 1783]," *Founders Online*, National Archives, https://founders.archives.gov/documents/Hamilton/01-03-02-0204. [Original source: *The Papers of Alexander Hamilton*, vol. 3, *1782–1786*, ed. Harold C. Syrett. New York: Columbia University Press, 1962, pp. 317–321.] (accessed online November 12, 2020).

2. https://avalon.law.yale.edu/18th_century/artconf.asp (accessed online November 12, 2020).

3. Banner, Stuart. *How the Indians lost their land: Law and power on the frontier*. Harvard University Press, 2005: 119.

4. "John Adams, Notes on Debates in the Continental Congress (July 25, 1776)." *Founders Online*, National Archives, https://founders.archives.gov/documents/Adams/01-02-02-0006-0008-0001. [Original source: *The Adams Papers, Diary and Autobiography of John Adams*, vol. 2, *1771–1781*, ed. L. H. Butterfield. Cambridge, MA: Harvard University Press, 1961, pp. 241–243.] (accessed online November 12, 2020).

5. U.S. CONST. art. I, § 8. https://avalon.law.yale.edu/18th_century/art1.asp (accessed online November 12, 2020).

## 14

# AFTER AMERICAN REVOLUTION, RETRIBUTION LED TO OUTRIGHT CONFISCATION OF INDIAN LAND WITHOUT COMPENSATION

With the British defeated, the colonial war mentality came to bear fully against the Indians after the Revolutionary War. Rawlins Lowndes reported in the summer of 1778 that for residents of Charleston, South Carolina, the prospect "of Sharing the Indian Lands renders a War with those People a desireable Object not considering or Caring what expence is incured or by what means it is defrayed."[1] In Georgia, George Galphin urged an attack on the Creeks. "It will be an Exepense of warr," he counseled, "but there may be Lands got from them to pay a great part of it."[2]

The widely felt desire to exact retribution against the Indians coincided with strong political pressures to acquire land quickly and cheaply to be sold to raise revenue for a government burdened with a huge war debt. The result was a dramatic change in the method of obtaining Indian land. As a result, in the first few years after the end of the Revolution, between 1784 and 1793, the Continental Congress, and shortly thereafter the U.S. acting under its Constitution, abandoned the English policy of purchasing Indian land. They claimed by defeating the British, they defeated their Indian allies. By conquest, they won the unquestionable right to expropriate Indian lands. The years of war had created a revolution in Indian land policy.

In a series of "treaties" dictated to the Indians in the mid-1780s, the government confiscated what they considered conquered Indian lands without paying any compensation. American officials no longer believed themselves bound to negotiate with the Indians for their land or to offer the Indians any compensation.

The first of the forced treaties was signed at Fort Stanwix, New York, in 1784. After admonishing the Six Nations for allying with the defeated British, the officials haughtily proclaimed that the British conquest constituted a triumph over their Indian allies. The American confederated states now claimed the Indian British allies' land as a war bounty: "We shall now, therefore declare to you the condition, on which alone you can be received into the peace and protection of the United States. The conditions are these." Section 2 permitted the Oneidas and Tuscaroras, the two tribes that had sided with the colonists, to remain on their land. Under Section 3, the Senecas, Mohawks, Onondagas and Cayugas, for fighting alongside the British, forfeited much of western New York. The Confederacy paid them no compensation.[3]

Most of the Indian Nations in North America had fought on the losing side, the side of Britain, based on long-standing allegiances. They also feared the colonial drive to take their lands. Now, explained General Philip John Schuyler, Indian Nations would be considered as defeated enemies, and their land would be commandeered. "As we are the Conquerors," Schuyler declared, "we claim the lands and property of all the white people as well as the Indians who have left and fought against us. ... We enquired of the King what he intended to do for the Indians ... as we expected that he would have been very particular about them. He being the person that should have considered their situation; but the King answered, *What can I do? Nothing! You have conquered me therefore do with them what you please.*"[4]

In 1785, Richard Butler, George Rogers Clark and Arthur Lee, appointed by the committee of the Continental Congress responsible for supervising relations with the Indians, ordered the leaders of the Wyandot, Delaware, Chippewa and Ottawa Indian Nations to appear at Fort McIntosh. They continued the charade that they defeated the Indian allies of the British and, as a result, won their lands, without any recourse by the Indians. The chiefs of those Nations "held out an idea to the Continental Commissioners that they still looked upon the lands which the United States held by the treaty with Great Britain as their own," Josiah Harmar related, "but the Commissioners have answered them in a high tone, the purport of which was, that, as they had adhered during the war to the king of Great Britain, they were considered by us as a conquered people and had therefore nothing to expect from the United States, but must depend altogether upon their lenity and generosity."[5] As the commissioners dictated what land these Indian Nations would surrender, and after some of the Indians delegates had become drunk on alcohol provided by the Americans, the assembled delegates signed the Treaty of Fort McIntosh on January 21, 1785.

The confederated states captured much of present-day Ohio, again confiscated without compensation. The Treaty defined not the land ceded by the Indians, but rather the land the Continental Congress 'allotted' to them. The officials drubbed it in that the only reason Indians were left any land at all was a result of American mercy, not a result of any Indian property rights.

At Fort Finney in 1786, the Continental commissioners, Richard Butler and Samuel Holden Parsons, dictated a similar treaty to the Shawnees. "You joined the British King against us, and followed his fortunes ... We have overcome him, he has cast you off, and given us your country; and Congress, in bounty and mercy, offer you country and peace. We have told you the terms on which you shall have it; these terms we will not alter, they are liberal, they are just, and we will not depart from them." The commissioners warned the Shawnees that if they refused to agree, "we shall consider ourselves freed from all the ties of protection to you, and you may depend the U.S. will take the most effectual measures to protect their citizens, and to distress your obstinate nation."[6] Shawnee leaders, fearing the power of the American military, agreed to the Treaty of Fort Finney on January 31, 1786, relinquishing all claims to their land in southwestern Ohio and southern Indiana. This had been a bluff on the part of the U.S. commissioners. In 1787, the Secretary of War would report to the Confederation Congress that the nation was "utterly unable to maintain an Indian war with any dignity or prospect of success."[7]

The treaties with the southern Indian Nations followed the same pattern. The commissioners were to inform the Indians that they "are now in our power and at our mercy."[8] The United States accordingly confiscated land from the Cherokees, Choctaws and Chickasaws at the 1785 and 1786 Treaties of Hopewell.

While in France in 1786, serving as the American Minister, Thomas Jefferson advised that "not a foot of land will ever be taken from the Indians without their own consent. The sacredness of their right is felt by all thinking persons in America as much as in Europe."[9] It is unknown whether his statement was due to a lack of information regarding the American Indian land confiscation policy or to keep French opinion favorable to the United States.

This constant tension in what policies the U.S. would follow destroyed the possibility of a just relationship between the two polities. The U.S.' power to create such uncertainty and dread in the lives of an entire indigenous population only served to further decimate Indian peoples through terror and despair.

## Indian Leaders Refuse to Accept that Treaty of Paris Is Binding on Them

Alexander McGillivray refused to accept that the Treaty of Paris could alter Creek sovereignty. In a letter dated September 5, 1785, he wrote to federal Indian commissioners:

> We [Creeks] know our own limits and the extent of our hunting grounds; and, as a free nation ... we shall pay no regard to any limits that may prejudice our claims, that were drawn by an American, and confirmed by a British negotiator. ... We want our hunting grounds preserved from encroachments. They have been ours from the beginning of time.[10]

In three subsequent letters dated April 8, 1787, January 4, 1789 and February 26, 1789, he detailed the several, continuing efforts of Georgians to fraudulently obtain Creek land cessions by bribing two Creek Nation members and employing other devious methods.

## Corn Tassel (Cherokee, 1785) (*Cherokee Nation Claimed Rightful Ownership of Their Land, Disavowing Any Other Owner*)

> Again, were we to inquire by what law or authority you set up a claim [to our land], I answer, none! Your laws extend not into our

country, nor ever did. You talk of the law of nature and the law of nations, and they are both against you.[11]

## President Washington Recognizes Expediency of Purchasing Indian Lands

President Washington recognized the expediency of purchasing Indian lands. His rationale for choosing to purchase Indian lands may be discerned from his 'private letter' to his friend, James Duane. He knew the new republic was overwhelmed by its Revolutionary War debt and completely lacked the financial and military resources for an Indian war. According to him, conquest failed to get rid of the Indians permanently anyway. They would return as the 'beasts of prey' they are.

## Letter from George Washington to James Duane, September 7, 1783

...policy and economy point very strongly to the expediency of being upon good terms with the Indians, and the propriety of purchasing their Lands in preference to attempting to drive them by force of arms out of their Country; which as we have already experienced is like driving the Wild Beasts of the Forest which will return as soon as the pursuit is at an end and fall perhaps on those that are left there; when the gradual extension of our Settlements will as certainly cause the Savage as the Wolf to retire; both being beasts of prey tho' they differ in shape. In a word there is nothing to be obtained by an Indian War but the Soil they live on and this can be had by purchase at less expence...[12]

In 1786, a committee of the Continental Congress warned that the "Shawanese, Puteotamies, Chippewas, Tawas, and Twightees" were gathering for war, and seeking other Indian Nations to join them in the coming battles. Henry Knox, then commander of the Continental Army, calculated it would take an army of 2,500 to 3,000 men fighting for two years to overcome the Indian army, at a cost of two million dollars. Knox estimated that for a mere $20,000 the Government could buy their land and recommended that Congress do so.

As President Washington's Secretary of War, Knox urged that Congress return to the British practice of respecting Indian property rights and purchasing the Indians' land, as a way of saving money and lives: "The practice of the British government ... previously to the late war, of purchasing the right of the soil of the Indians, and receiving a deed of sale and conveyance of the same, is the only mode of alienating their lands that would be acceptable to the tribes," Knox reported to Congress in 1789. To dispossess the Indians by any means other than purchase "would be a gross violation of the fundamental laws of nature, and of the distributive justice which is the glory of a nation."

*"The doctrine of conquest is so repugnant to their feelings, that rather than submit thereto, they would prefer continual war."* **But a war so expensive, "and with an exhausted treasury, would be an event pregnant with unlimited evil." If such a war was to be fought without adequate resources, there was a good chance the Indians would win, particularly because they could expect the assistance of the British troops who still occupied Canada and the northwest.**[13] (Emphasis added.)

## Costs of American Revolution

The policy of confiscation had its detractors when it was initiated, but the spiraling American war costs totaled approximately £165 million in 1783 values. The new national government was bankrupt. Its notes, 'scrip,' 'certificates,' 'indents' and other forms of floating indebtedness were overdue and unpaid. Selling the land confiscated from the Indians was proposed as a means of debt liquidation. Thomas Jefferson in 1782 estimated that 5,000,000 acres could readily be sold at a dollar per-acre in government debt certificates and the whole national debt soon erased.

Paying off the newly formed government's debt provided the incentive needed to confiscate Indian lands outright, without payment, to sell them and thereby raise money to pay off their war debts, along with having badly needed collateral to secure loans from creditors. Everyone hoped that the sale of public land would become a source of substantial income for the treasury, but Treasury Secretary Alexander Hamilton quashed this solution when he included, in his 1790 Report on Vacant Lands, an admission that the lands concerned were not really vacant. "No Indian land shall be sold," he insisted, "except such, in respect to which the titles of the Indian tribes shall have been previously extinguished."[14]

## Senecas Desperate Plea to George Washington after Treaty of Fort Stanwix, 1790

In a letter to George Washington from the Seneca Chiefs, dated December 1, 1790, the suffering of the Senecas after the Fort Stanwix Treaty, is openly displayed. Their land had been confiscated, without compensation.

> We mean to open our hearts before you, and we earnestly desire, that you will let us clearly understand, what you resolve to do. When our chiefs returned from the treaty of fort Stanwix, and laid before our Council what had been done there our Nation was surprized to hear, how great a Country you had compelled them to give up, to you, without paying us any thing for it. Every one said your hearts were yet swelled with resentment against us for what had happened during the war: but that one day you would reconsider it with more kindness. We asked each other what we had done to deserve such severe chastisement.

> You have said we were in your hand, and that by closing it, you could crush us to nothing. Are you determined to crush us? If you are, tell us so that those of our nation who have become your children & are determined to die so, may know what to do: In this case one chief has said, he would ask you to put him out of pain: Another, who will not think of dying by the hand of his father, has said he will retire to the Chataughque, eat of the faral root, and sleep with his fathers in peace.[15]

President Washington replied summarily that he could not disannul treaties formed before his administration.

> You say your nation complain that you were compelled to give up too much of your lands. That you confess your nation is bound by what was there done, and acknowledging the power of the United States, that you have now appealed to ourselves against that treaty,

as made while we were angry against you, and that the said treaty was therefore unreasonable and unjust. ... I cannot disannull treaties formed by the United States before my administration, especially as the boundaries mentioned therein have been twice confirmed by yourselves.[16]

President Washington utterly refused to assume any responsibility for a people forced to suicide, whose humiliating shame can be palpably felt, whose lives had no meaning to him or to the United States. It is a clear message that Indian lives were superfluous.

## Indian Nations Sound Rallying Cry to Go to War

The Indians sounded the rallying cry for war and formed confederacies to avoid the government decimating them one-by-one. The Americans realized that if the United States wished to treat Indian Nations as conquered, they would have to actually conquer them.

## Sandusky Conference

At the Sandusky Conference, in the spring of 1793, delegates from 35 Indian Nations informed the U.S. Commissioners appointed to negotiate with them that they were previously provided with misleading information, which resulted in cessions of their land:

BROTHERS; You tell us that after you had made peace with the King our Father, about ten years ago, it remained to make peace between the U. States, and the Indian Nations who had taken part with the King, for this purpose Commissioners were appointed who sent messages to all those Indian Nations, inviting them to come and make peace and after reciting the periods at which you say Treaties were held at Fort Stanwix, Fort McIntosh, and Miami, all which Treaties according to your own acknowledgement, were for the sole purpose of making peace; ... those few, who attended these treaties. [said] that they went to meet your Commissioners to make peace, but through fear were obliged to sign any paper that was laid before them, and it has since appeared that deeds of cession were signed by them instead of Treaties of peace....[17]

## President Washington, Fearing an Indian War, Opens Negotiations with Indians and Reverses U.S. Confiscation Policy

President Washington, fearing an outright Indian war, with the British allying with the Indians, reversed the U.S. confiscation policy. A new government heavily in debt could ill afford a war with the confederated Indian Nations. Certainly, the British would ally with them to try and re-take the new republic. President Washington knew that the U.S. might easily lose such a war.

In 1793, when President Washington's Secretary of War gave instructions to Commissioners Benjamin Lincoln, Beverly Randolph and Timothy Pickering, appointed to negotiate with the northwestern Indian Nations, he informed them of the President's new policy. Secretary of War Knox ordered the Commissioners to make it crystal clear to the Indians that "the Government considers the Six Nations ... and other Western Indians, who were the actual occupants of the lands, **as the proper owners** thereof; that they had a right to convey the said lands to the United States ... with their free consent and full understanding."[18] (Emphasis added.)

The U.S., pursuant to President Washington's order, would no longer confiscate Indian lands.

## Negotiations between Western Indian Confederacy & U.S. Commissioners on Issue of Ohio River as Boundary of Indian Lands, July 1793

The negotiations between the Western Indian Confederacy and the appointed U.S. Commissioners are critical in understanding the position of the U.S. regarding Indian land ownership following the Revolutionary War.

The following Indian Nations attended the negotiations as the General Council of the Western Indian Confederacy: Wyandotís, Seven Nations of Canada, Delawareís, Shawanoeís, Miamiís, Ottawaís, Chippawaís, Senecaís of the Glaize, Potowatamieís, Connoyís, Munseyís, Nanticokeís, Mohikenís, Messasagaís, Creekís and Cherokeeís.

The U.S. commissioners were Benjamin Lincoln, Beverly Randolph and Timothy Pickering.

The negotiations were held at the Foot of the Miamis Rapids in July 1793. Over 1000 Indians and their leaders attended. They were ready to go to war with the U.S. over its confiscation of their lands.

During the course of the negotiations, the U.S. retreated from its former position of outright confiscation of Indian lands of British allies, publicly and clearly announcing its "error," to the **1000 Indians and their leaders** present at the negotiations. The U.S. conceded the "right of soil" of the Indians to their lands; the property was in the Indians. The U.S. only claimed the right to pre-emption, or the right of purchasing of the Indian Nations disposed to sell their lands.

The commissioners made it crystal clear to the **1000 Indians and their leaders** that the United States erred, was wrong, in challenging the Indians ownership of their lands and that the United States had not acquired ownership of the Ohio River Valley by the 1783 Treaty with Britain.

> Brothers: The Commissioners of the United States have formerly set up a claim to your whole country, southward of the great lakes, as the property of the United States, grounding this claim on the treaty of peace with your father, the King of Great Britain, who declared, as we have before mentioned, the middle of these lakes, and the waters which unite them, to be the boundaries of the United States.
>
> Brothers: We, therefore, frankly tell you, that we think that the Commissioners put an erroneous construction on that part of our treaty with the King ... *We now concede this great point; We by the express authority of the President of the United States, acknowledge the property or right of soil, of the great Country above described, to be in the Indian Nations so long as they desire, to occupy the same.* We only claim ... the right to pre-emption, or the right of purchasing of the Indian Nations disposed to sell their lands, to the exclusion of all other White People whatever.[19] (Emphasis added).

After fifteen years of hardship, suffering, bitterness, mistrust and war, during which the United States confiscated Indian lands, the U.S. reverted to the position that what had been transferred as a result of their victory in the Revolutionary War was not the fee title to Indian territory, but merely the exclusive right to acquire their land by solemn treaty with them. The Indians proved they would fight for their land, even though they knew it meant their death. The number of warriors available for combat had dwindled, due to war and disease. They, also, lacked the advanced technology and the armaments of the Americans. Yet, 1000 of them honored their ownership of their land and put their lives on the line – placing themselves in harm's way, willing to lose their lives, to achieve a guaranty of their ownership of their land. Had the United States conceded to the reality and truth of Indian land ownership earlier, a decade of Indian land dispossession and inhumane suffering and death might have been avoided.

## Future Treaties To Be Structured as Purchases, Not Forced Cessions of Indian Lands

Treaties between the U.S. and Indian Nations to acquire Indian land would be structured as purchases, not forced cessions of land. In dispatching Brigadier General Rufus Putnam to negotiate with the Wabash and the Illinois Indians in 1792, Secretary of War Knox ordered Putnam, in the only italicized portion of his lengthy instructions, to *"make it clearly understood, that we want not a foot of their land, and that it is theirs, and theirs only; that they have the right to sell, and the right to refuse to sell, and that the United States will guaranty to them their said just right."*[20]

In the treaty Putnam signed with the Wabash and the Illinois, he duly included an article stating exactly that: "The United States solemnly guaranty to the Wabash, and the Illinois nations, or tribes of Indians, all the lands to which they have a just claim; and no part shall ever be taken from them, but by a fair purchase, and to their satisfaction. **That the lands originally belonged to the Indians; it is theirs, and theirs only**. That they have a right to sell, and a right to refuse to sell. And that the United States will protect them in their said just rights."[21] (Emphasis added.)

215

Timothy Pickering, Secretary of State, sent in the 1790s to negotiate with the Six Nations, reported to President Washington that, "Indians have so often been deceived by White people, that White Man is among them, but another name for Liar."22

## Notes

1. Banner, Stuart. *How the Indians lost their land: Law and power on the frontier*. Harvard University Press, 2005: 121.

2. Taylor, James Wickes. *History of the State of Ohio... First Period, 1650-1787*. Cincinnati, Sandusky: HW Derby & Company, CL Derby & Company, 1854: 435.

3. Banner, Stuart. *How the Indians lost their land: Law and power on the frontier*. Harvard University Press, 2005: 127.

4. Ibid., p. 113.

5. Ibid., pp. 128; https://ohiohistorycentral.org/w/Treaty_of_Fort_McIntosh_(1785) (accessed online November 21, 2020).

6. Ibid., pp. 128-129; https://ohiohistorycentral.org/w/Treaty_of_Fort_Finney_(1786) (accessed online November 21, 2020).

7. 33 JOURNALS OF THE CONTINENTAL CONGRESS, 1774–1789, at 388 (Roscoe R. Hill ed., 1936).

8. Report of Committee on Southern Indian Affairs, March 4, 1785, in *Journals of the Continental Congress, 1774-1789*, ed. Worthington C. Ford, 34 vols. (Washington, DC., 1904-37) 28:119; Banner, Stuart. *How the Indians lost their land: Law and power on the frontier*. Harvard University Press, 2005: 129.

9. The Writings of Thomas Jefferson: 1784-1787, G.P. Putnam's Sons, 1894: 166; "IV. Jefferson's Observations on DéMeunier's Manuscript,

22 June 1786," *Founders Online,* National Archives, https://founders. archives.gov/documents/Jefferson/01-10-02-0001-0005. [Original source: *The Papers of Thomas Jefferson*, vol. 10, *22 June–31 December 1786*, ed. Julian P. Boyd. Princeton: Princeton University Press, 1954, pp. 30–61.] (accessed online November 5, 2020).

10. Letter from Alexander McGillivray to Andrew Pickens (Sept. 5, 1785), Walter Lowrie et al., eds. *American State Papers. Documents, Legislative and Executive, of the Congress of the United States*. 38 vols. Washington, D.C., Gales and Seaton, 1832–61: 1:17–20.

11. *Tatham's Characters Among the North American Indians, 7 Tenn. Hist. Mag.* 174, 177 (Sam'l C. Williams ed., 1921).

12. "From George Washington to James Duane, 7 September 1783," *Founders Online*, National Archives, https://founders.archives.gov/ documents/Washington/99-01-02-11798. (accessed online November 14, 2020).

13. Banner, Stuart. *How the Indians lost their land: Law and power on the frontier*. Harvard University Press, 2005: 131-132.

14. "Report on Vacant Lands, 20 July 1790,"*Founders Online*, National Archives, https://founders.archives.gov/documents/ Hamilton/01-06-02-0408. [Original source: *The Papers of Alexander Hamilton*, vol. 6, *December 1789–August 1790*, ed. Harold C. Syrett. New York: Columbia University Press, 1962, pp. 502–506.] (accessed online November 14, 2020).

15. "To George Washington from the Seneca Chiefs, 1 December 1790," *Founders Online,* National Archives, https://founders.archives. gov/documents/Washington/05-07-02-0005. [Original source: *The Papers of George Washington*, Presidential Series, vol. 7, *1 December 1790–21 March 1791*, ed. Jack D. Warren, Jr. Charlottesville: University Press of Virginia, 1998, pp. 7–16.] (accessed online November 14, 2020).

16. "From George Washington to the Seneca Chiefs, 19 January 1791," *Founders Online*, National Archives, https://founders.archives. gov/documents/Washington/05-07-02-0138. [Original source: *The Papers of George Washington,* Presidential Series, vol. 7, *1 December*

*1790–21 March 1791*, ed. Jack D. Warren, Jr. Charlottesville: University Press of Virginia, 1998, pp. 252–254.] (accessed online November 14, 2020).

17. "To John Adams from Benjamin Lincoln, 11 September 1793," *Founders Online,* National Archives, https://founders.archives.gov/documents/Adams/99-02-02-1472 (accessed online November 14, 2020).

18. Storrs, Henry Randolph. Speech of Mr. Storrs, of New-York, in Committee of the Whole House: On the Bill for the Removal of the Indians West of the Mississippi. United States, Northway & Porter, 1830: 38.

19. Storrs, Henry Randolph. Speech of Mr. Storrs, of New-York, in Committee of the Whole House: On the Bill for the Removal of the Indians West of the Mississippi. United States, Northway & Porter, 1830: 116.

20. Blodget, Joslin D., and Enos Thompson Throop. *American State Papers: Documents, Legislative and Executive, of the Congress of the United States...* Vol. 3. Gales and Seaton, 1834: 234.

21. Banner, Stuart. *How the Indians lost their land: Law and power on the frontier*. Harvard University Press, 2005: 135.

22. "To George Washington from Timothy Pickering, 21 March 1792," Founders Online, National Archives, https://founders.archives.gov/documents/Washington/05-10-02-0084.: University of Virginia Press, 2002, pp. 141–143.] (accessed online November 14, 2020).

# 15

# SQUATTERS

**As Population of European Colonists Increased Opposition Grows to Indian Nations Right to Land**

|        | 1650 | 1700 | 1750  | 1770  |
|--------|------|------|-------|-------|
| White  | 53   | 234  | 964   | 1,816 |
| Black  | 2    | 31   | 242   | 467   |
| Total  | 55   | 265  | 1,206 | 2,283 |

Population of Colonies, John J. McCusker, "The Rum Trade and the Balance of Payments of the Thirteen Continental Colonies, 1650-1775" (Ph.D. diss., University of Pittsburgh, 1970, appendix B, 548-552).

As the English population grew, however, and as the demand for land increased, settlers bordering on uncultivated Indian land were often unconvinced of the legitimacy of Indian property rights. The most blatant frontier problem that refused to go away, and would continue to linger, was squatters who simply occupied Indian land, without any authority whatsoever.

General, and later President, George Washington recognized this problem several times in his correspondence.

To Major-General Knox From General George Washington, September 23, 1783

> ...while the United States and the State of Virginia are disputing about the right, or the terms of the Cession, *Land jobbers and*

*a lawless Banditti*, who would bid defiance to the authority of either, and more than probably involve this Country in an Indian War, *would spread themselves over the whole of it (Virginia's western lands)*, to the great injury to the Officers, &c., of the Army, who are patiently waiting the decision of Congress to settle in a legal manner and under a proper form of Government.[1] (Emphasis added.)

In August 1787, a congressional committee blamed the southern states for encroaching on Indian lands and threatening the outbreak of a major Indian war. These problems arose primarily from an "avaricious disposition in some of our people to acquire large tracts of land and often by unfair means."[2]

The new national government would inherit the problem of squatters - the problem of settlers encroaching on Indian land refused to go away. President Washington knew that land speculation would continue to lead to Indian hostilities, as can be seen in his letter to David Humphreys on July 20, 1791. Humphreys had served as a Revolutionary War colonel and aide de camp to General Washington. He would be appointed to several diplomatic positions by Presidents Washington, Adams and Jefferson. President Washington shared his concerns with land speculation and frontier settlers with Humphreys:

> For some time past the western frontiers have been alarmed by depredations committed by some hostile tribes of Indians ... Though I must confess I cannot see much prospect of living in tranquillity with them, so long as a spirit of landjobbing prevails, and our frontier settlers entertain the opinion, that there is not the same crime (or indeed no crime at all) in killing an Indian, as in killing a white man.[3]

President Washington was faced with the inability of the new republic to prevent the land speculation in Indian lands, theft of Indian lands by squatters and outright murder of Indians.

In a letter to Edmund Pendleton on January 22, 1795, President Washington shared his concerns about settler encroachment on Indian lands and acknowledged that Indians had justifiable complaints. He confirmed his impotency in preventing their unlawful acts. Pendleton was an elder Virginia statesman and friend to President Washington. They shared a long history as fellow farmers and politicians. Pendleton served in the Virginia legislature before and during the Revolutionary War, rising to the position of Speaker. As one of Virginia's delegates alongside George Washington, Pendleton attended the First Continental Congress. He served as Virginia's Chief Justice from 1788–1803.

> I accord ... that the plan of annual presents is not the best mode of treating ignorant savages, from whose hostile conduct we experience much distress; but it is not to be forgotten, that they in turn are not without serious causes of complaint, from the encroachments which are made on their lands by our people, who are not to be restrained by any law now in being, or likely to be enacted. They, poor wretches, have no press through which their grievances are related; and it is well known, that, when one side only of a story is heard and often repeated, the human mind becomes impressed with it insensibly.[4]

Thomas Jefferson, then Governor of Virginia, issued a Proclamation Requiring Settlers Northwest of the Ohio to Vacate (January 24, 1780):

> ...no person so removing to, settling on the said lands (Ohio Valley), should be entitled to or allowed any right of preemption or other benefit whatever from such settlement or occupancy, and authorized the Governor, with the advice of the Council of State to remove with armed force all such settlers and occupants.[5]

Nonetheless, the squatters would be removed and return as soon as the military threat was gone.

The squatters begin to organize, as Congress refused to secure to them the land they had stolen. National leaders considered them a nuisance. Delegates from Virginia referred to these squatters as "lawless banditti" who "must necessarily have involv'd us in continued Indian wars" and would eventually "prove destructive" to "our Republican Constitutions."[6] The commissioners of Indian Affairs sent instructions to Colonel Josiah Harmar, commander of the United States Army, to "employ such force as he may judge necessary in driving off persons attempting to settle on the Lands of the United States."[7]

Thomas Worthington, an Ohio leader in the squatter movement, leveraged his appointment as the register of the Chillicothe land office, a position that gave him immense influence over the interpretation of the law, to increase his political base and power. The Land Act of 1800 which opened four land offices in the territory, reduced the size of available tracts, and extended federal credit to all purchasers. Worthington negotiated with squatters and would-be speculators alike, determining what lands to sell and to whom. These negotiations allowed Worthington to build his own network of patronage made up of former squatters.

New laws allowed for squatters to negotiate with federal officials over the lands they wanted. Taking advantage of changing attitudes, Worthington travelled to Washington to meet with President Jefferson in order to affect a more egalitarian land policy that was inclusive of the squatters. By utilizing federal power, he was able to bring squatters into the formal political process, thereby creating a personal network of politically active voting supporters affiliated with President Jefferson. This network became crucial for securing Ohio's statehood, as it formed Worthington's political base in the territory and his primary bargaining chip for securing Republican support at the national level. By linking his local Ohio constituency to national politics, particularly the administration of President Jefferson, Worthington was able to effectively secure statehood for Ohio through partisanship and personal networks. A former illegal squatter on Indian lands, he ended up holding several state offices, including that of Ohio's Governor.[8]

Notes

1. "From George Washington to Henry Knox, 23 September 1783," *Founders Online,* National Archives, https://founders.archives.gov/documents/Washington/99-01-02-11847 (accessed online November 21, 2020).

2. Committee Report of the Southern Department, August 3, 1787, Prucha, Francis Paul, ed. *Documents of United States Indian Policy*. 3rd ed. Lincoln: U of Nebraska P, 2000: 10.

3. "From George Washington to David Humphreys, 20 July 1791," *Founders Online,* National Archives, https://founders.archives.gov/documents/Washington/05-08-02-0251. [Original source: *The Papers of George Washington*, Presidential Series, vol. 8, *22 March 1791–22 September 1791*, ed. Mark A. Mastromarino. Charlottesville: University Press of Virginia, 1999, pp. 358–361.] (accessed online November 21, 2020).

4. "From George Washington to Edmund Pendleton, 22 January 1795," *Founders Online,* National Archives, https://founders.archives.gov/documents/Washington/05-17-02-0282. [Original source: *The Papers of George Washington*, Presidential Series, vol. 17, *1 October 1794–31 March 1795*, ed. David R. Hoth and Carol S. Ebel. Charlottesville: University of Virginia Press, 2013, pp. 424–428.] (accessed online November 21, 2020).

5. "Proclamation Requiring Settlers Northwest of the Ohio to Vacate, 24 January 1780," *Founders Online,* National Archives, https://founders.archives.gov/documents/Jefferson/01-03-02-0302. [Original source: *The Papers of Thomas Jefferson*, vol. 3, *18 June 1779–30 September 1780*, ed. Julian P. Boyd. Princeton: Princeton University

Press, 1951, pp. 266–267.] (accessed online November 12, 2020).

6. "Editorial Note: Threat of Disunion in the West," *Founders Online*, National Archives, https://founders.archives.gov/documents/Jefferson/01-19-02-0119-0001. [Original source: *The Papers of Thomas Jefferson*, vol. 19, 24 *January–31 March 1791*, ed. Julian P. Boyd. Princeton: Princeton University Press, 1974, pp. 429–518.] Richard Henry Lee (accessed online November 21, 2020).

7. Banner, Stuart. *How the Indians lost their land: Law and power on the frontier.* Harvard University Press, 2005: 128; https://ohiohistorycentral.org/w/Treaty_of_Fort_McIntosh_(1785) (accessed online November 21, 2020).

8. Thomas Worthington, Sixth Governor of Ohio https://en.wikipedia.org/wiki/Thomas_Worthington_(governor) (accessed online November 21, 2020).

that would be used to characterize America as vacuum domicilium, or

## 16

# "SEMANTIC WORLD CREATED
# BY ONE GROUP TO RULE ANOTHER"

In reviewing the writings of monarchs, lawyers, judges, colonists, businessmen, leaders, philosophers and theologians, one will see that there was no uniformity regarding the postulate that indigenous lands 'discovered' could be lawfully possessed and colonized without the indigenous owners' consent. There were those though who used specious arguments allowing for the lawful dispossession of indigenous peoples' lands. Peter d'Errico characterized this so artfully as a "semantic world created by one group to rule another."[1]

Change was needed with the discovery in the colonies of tobacco and cotton's value as trade commodities. Whereas the fur trade required Indian trappers and hunters, tobacco and cotton could be produced by the colonists themselves, with the use of slaves. Millions of slaves were imported into the southern colonies, vastly outnumbering the colonist population. Indians hindered the new plantation gentry, blocking access to land that could be used for this large-scale profitable agriculture.

Thus, Indians became an obstacle in America and with the need to attract both investment and settlers, questions and debates began regarding the Indian's natural right to property and under what conditions Europeans could occupy and settle it. As the English settlers were not dominant enough to engage in warfare to secure Indian lands, they turned to theories such as 'vacuum domicilium' or natural law as paradigms for dispossessing Indians of their land.

## European Philosophers Opinions Used to Justify New Claim that Indians Do Not Own Land

A survey of all the published American political writing in the founding era, the period from 1760 to 1805, finds that Montesquieu and Blackstone were by far the most commonly cited sources, but the next common were Locke and Hume.[2] It was ideas by these supposed learned writers that would be used to characterize America as 'vacuum domicilium' or vacant land, open to all for appropriation. Also, the blatant racism of some of them was notoriously obvious.

## Law of Nations regarding Indian Land—Vattel (1797)

The Law of Nations is alleged to be based on certain axioms adopted by different nations which they considered obligatory among them. In reality, as to indigenous lands in the Western hemisphere, it is a set of principles developed by three European countries, which they modified as they chose to best suit their needs at a particular time. They were not immutable, even though Emerich de Vattel in The Law of Nations, states this as a premise from which the mutual consent of the parties is derived. The doctrine of discovery was honored in the breach, which under Vattel's analysis was anathema.

In Section 26, Preliminaries, Vattel confirms that the countries of a certain continent may determine obligatory laws between those consenting, such as Europe.

> § 26. When a custom or usage is generally established, either between all the civilized nations in the world, or *only __between those of a certain continent, as of Europe__* ... it becomes obligatory on all the nations in question, who are considered as having giving their consent to it, and are *__bound to observe it towards each other__*, as long as they have not expressly declared their resolution of not observing it in future.[3] (Emphasis added).

Also in Section 9, Preliminaries, he acknowledges the alleged immutability of the Law of Nations as follows:

§ 9. Whence, as this law is immutable, and the obligations that arise from it necessary and indispensable, nations can neither make any changes in it by their conventions, dispense with it in their own conduct, nor reciprocally release each other from the observance of it.[4]

In Vattel's mind, there was no need to pay attention to claims based upon a papal decree, unless they had been followed up by occupation of the territory concerned. Also, acts of symbolic possession, such as planting of a flag or marking landmarks were devoid of any effect.

'But it is questioned whether a Nation can thus appropriate, by the mere act of taking possession, lands which it does not really occupy, and which are more extensive than it can inhabit or cultivate. It is not difficult to decide that such a claim would be absolutely contrary to the natural law. Hence the Law of Nations will only recognise the ownership and sovereignty of a Nation over unoccupied lands when the Nation is in actual occupation of them, when it forms a settlement upon them, or makes some actual use of them. In fact, when explorers have discovered uninhabited lands through which the explorers of other Nations had passed, leaving some sign of their having taken possession, they have no more troubled themselves over such empty forms than over the regulations of Popes, who divided a large part of the world between the crowns of Castile and Portugal.[5]

Vattel's foundation of immutability and the need and indispensability of conforming to the obligations under the law of nations were simply not followed. This is clearly evidenced by the continuous wars between Spain, France and England over disputed land in America.

To ascertain the uncertainty surrounding the Law of Nations, Johann Wolfgang Textor, in 1680 in his Synopsis of the Law of Nations, queried when a practice became a part of the Law of Nations as follows:

Here a difficult question emerges, namely, what amount of time and usage is needed in order to beget a Law of Nations out of the usage of Kings and peoples. My view ... is that if all or most peoples, even once only, have adopted a given course of conduct, any period or interval of time is enough for the introduction of a Law.[6]

Thus, if all or most peoples, followed a given course of conduct once, it could be embraced within the principles of the Law of Nations. There was no enforceability to the Law of Nations. They sounded principled, but had no 'teeth.'

During the establishment of the United States' government after the American Revolution, Vattel's version of the Law of Nations was widely disseminated and studied. President George Washington's copy, borrowed from the New York Library, wasn't returned until 221 years after his death.

Benjamin Franklin received three French copies from Swiss editor Charles W.F. Dumas. Franklin donated one copy to the Library Company of Philadelphia. On December 9, 1775, Franklin thanked Dumas: "It came to us in good season, when the circumstances of a rising State make it necessary to frequently consult the Law of Nations." Franklin also informed Mr. Dumas that Vattel's book "has been continually in the hands of the members of our Congress now sitting."[7]

The immutability of the Law of Nations was not immutable when it came to the maxims applicable to Indian land. For example, Section 15, Preliminaries and Section 4, Chapter I, Of Nations or Sovereign States, provides that:

> § 15. Nations being free and independent of each other ... each nation should be left in the peaceable enjoyment of that liberty which she inherits from nature.[8]
>
> § 4. Every nation that governs itself, under what form soever, without dependence on any foreign power, is a Sovereign State.[9]

Vattel's carved out exception regarding the rights of indigenous peoples to their land, which permitted disregarding them, provided as follows:

> § 81 Those who still pursue this idle mode of life [hunting], usurp more extensive territories than, with a reasonable share of labour, they would have occasion for, and have therefore no reason to complain, if other nations, more industrious, and too closely confined, come to take possession of a part of those lands. Thus, though the conquest of the civilised empires of Peru and Mexico was a notorious usurpation, the establishment of many colonies

on the continent of North America might, on their confining themselves within just bounds, be extremely lawful. The people of those extensive tracts rather ranged through than inhabited them.[10]

Thus, this ethnocentric version of what constitutes the Law of Nations permitted the stealth and colonization of allegedly 'discovered' indigenous lands, without any input by indigenous peoples. Countries unquestionably failed to adhere to the doctrine of discovery resulting in colonial skirmishes and wars, drawing Indians in as allies to multiply their forces to fight against Indians. The doctrine of discovery was simply of no effect, as countries scrambled in their land hungry fever to grab as much land as they could.

## Montesquieu's View of Indian Land Title (1748)

Baron de Montesquieu, a French judge and political philosopher, was the principal source of the theory of separation of powers. This concept was incorporated into the U.S. Constitution. He did not write on Indian land ownership but his theory that "[shepherds and hunters] are not possessed of landed property" supported the view that Indians did not own land.[11]

## Locke's View of Indian Land Title

John Locke, a British philosopher, who served as secretary to both the Lords Proprietors of Carolina and the Council of Trade and Plantations, was immersed in shaping colonial policy. A new definition of property, which would allow the English to supersede the rights of Indian Nations to their land was needed. Locke provided the answer.

> As much Land as a Man Tills, Plants, Improves, Cultivates and can use the Product of, so much is his Property. He by his Labour does, as it were, inclose it from the Common.[12]

Locke not only argued that labour begins the concept of property, but 'makes the far greatest part of the value' of it, and 'a fruitful Soil, apt to produce in abundance...for want of improving it by labour' will have no real value. To him, Indians neglected their land due to the absence of industriousness, leaving it nothing more than waste and available for appropriation through the labour of others....He that...subdued, tilled and sowed any part of it...another had no Title to, nor could without injury take from him. The vast majority of land in America could thus be taken without injury from that which was used by the Indians in America, but not from the Englishmen, once settled.[13]

Once Indian land was farmed by these settlers, Indians could not lay claim thereafter to the land. His opinion was adopted by various colonists. The law of nature, explained the Connecticut minister John Bulkley, "makes and allows the Land a Man Tills & Subdues to be his Peculiar Property." The Indians had none of the "Essentials of a state of Civil Policy," Bulkley concluded, so they lacked property rights in their uncultivated land.[14]

Thus, Locke approved the title of colonist settlers to Indian lands based on their private farming and enclosure of their lands thereby identifying them as appropriated. He failed to consider the value of Indians engaging in agricultural activities as a collective unit, rather than as individuals within enclosed ground, denying their right to their property.

Moreover, as John Locke never tired of pointing out, agriculture supports a larger population than non-sedentary modes of production. In settler—colonial terms, this enables a population to be expanded by continuing immigration at the expense of native lands and livelihoods. He explicitly stated:

> Sec. 50. ... a man may fairly possess more land than he himself can use the product of, by receiving in exchange for the overplus gold and silver, which may be hoarded up without injury to any one.[15]

Locke's prejudicial view of Indians prevented him from acknowledging them as agrarian societies, even though this was public knowledge from the beginning of the settlement of British colonies.

> Natural men or native Americans are inferior to Englishmen, according to Locke, primarily because his reason has not yet developed to the same extent, comparing the gap in understanding to that between children and adults. In An Essay Concerning Human Understanding, Locke draws a parallel between native Americans, idiots and children, asserting that all have a diminished

sense of understanding and responsibility before the law.[16]

Also, notwithstanding the freedom of religion concept that would dominate the lives of the settler colonists, it did not translate to Indians. In his Essay Concerning Human Understanding, Locke asks: "What true or tolerable Notion of a Deity, could they have, who acknowledged, and worshipped hundreds?"[17]

The reality of Locke's impact on our government is undoubted. Justice M'Lean cites Locke's view of Indian land title in *Worcester* in 1832:

> The abstract right of every section of the human race to a reasonable portion of the soil, by which to acquire the means of subsistence, cannot be controverted. And it is equally clear that the range of nations or tribes who exist in the hunter state may be restricted within reasonable limits. They shall not be permitted to roam, in the pursuit of game, over an extensive and rich country whilst, in other parts, human beings are crowded so closely together as to render the means of subsistence precarious. The law of nature, which is paramount to all other laws, gives the right to every nation to the enjoyment of a reasonable extent of country, so as to derive the means of subsistence from the soil.[18]

But not everyone agreed about the property rights of peoples under the law of nature. John Cowell's 1651 treatise affirmed that any occupation of land, including hunting, fishing, and fowling, gave rise to property rights under the law of nature.

## Hume's View of Non-White Peoples (1758)

David Hume in a footnote in "Of National Characters," in his Essays, Moral, Political and Literary, explicitly wrote that there were human races and that non-whites were inferior to 'whites.'

> I am apt to suspect the negroes, *and in general all the other species of men (for there are four or five different kinds)* to be naturally inferior to the whites. There never was a civilized nation of any other complexion than white, nor even any individual eminent either in action or speculation. No ingenious manufactures amongst them, no arts, no sciences. On the other hand, the most

rude and barbarous of the whites, such as the ancient GERMANS, the present TARTARS, have still something eminent about them, in their valour, form of government, or some other particular.[19] (Emphasis added.)

To avoid public controversy, Hume later revised it by applying it only to Negroes and changed 'never' to 'scarcely ever.'

## Hobbes' View of Indians in America

Hobbes wrote that civil war and the brute situation of uncivilized man could be avoided only by a strong, undivided government. Man's greatest fear—of a violent death—must be used to institute government. This fear would form the basis of control over Indian Nations as they were continually threatened by the United States of being 'crushed' or extinguished.

> Whatsoever therefore is consequent to a time of war ... the life of man, solitary, poor, nasty, brutish, and short. ... For the savage people in many places of America, except the government of small families, the concord whereof dependeth on natural lust, have no government at all, and live at this day in that brutish manner, as I said before.[20]

## Pufendorf's View of Indian Land Title

Samuel von Pufendorf, a German jurist and historian, wrote The Law of Nature and of Nations in 1672, in which he makes clear that he believes the inhabitants of the Americas are members of nations who must be treated with the same respect as those of European states. The manner, intensity and extent of use of the land was completely in the determination of the polity. Land could be held individually or in common.

## For Some, Whether Indians Were Living in 'State of Nature' Also Determined Their Land Title

For some American writers it was crucial to know whether the Indians "were a People in the *State of Nature*, and so had only what the *Law of*

232

*Nature* gave them, or had quitted that State, entred into *Communities*, and ... had fixed the *Bounds* of each Community respectively and Settled or Determin'd the matter of Property in Land."[21]

Blackstone described the state of nature as "a state of primeval simplicity: as may be collected from the manners of many American nations when first 'discovered' by Europeans; and from the antient method of living among the first Europeans themselves."[22]

## Adam Smith's View of Indian Land Title (1776)

Adam Smith was a Scottish economist, philosopher and author. His capitalist economic theories published in 1776 influenced many contemporary colonial Americans. He theorized that societies progressed through four stages: hunting, pasturage, farming and commerce. Each stage corresponded to a particular set of political and economic institutions, including the institution of property. According to Smith, hunters knew no property. This was incorrect. Indians did in fact have designated hunting grounds and as settler colonists progressed in claiming Indian lands, they damaged the ecological conditions necessary for the hunting and gathering lands claimed by Indians.

Smith wrote that pastoralists needed, and thus developed, property in their animals. Farmers developed property in their land. Similarly, William Blackstone, legal author, wrote "the art of agriculture introduced and established the idea of a more permanent property in the soil."[23] The idea that in the mind of an educated Englishman, property in land went along with agriculture is not necessarily uniformly the case given the extensive manorial land holdings for fox hunting and other purposes. When the House of Representatives was debating the bill that would become the Trade and Intercourse Act of 1796, Representative Sedgwick queried the following:

> Where was the difference between this and saying to a man who had a million acres of land, because you do not improve your land as well as it is capable of being improved, we will take it from you.[24]

Again, when describing Indians, it was easier to dispossess their lands if they were roaming hordes or fierce savages, rather than agrarian as were the Six Nations, Cherokee, Mandans and other Indian Nations.

Commerce, according to Smith, required more complex property arrangements to suit financial needs. Yet, Smith completely ignores the extensive commerce that existed among the Indian Nations, prior to the arrival of Europeans. Transition zones between primarily agricultural and hunting populations would feature the trade of crops for meat. Rare minerals were highly prized: turquoise mined in New Mexico was traded for cacao and macaws from Mexico; copper from Lake Superior reached the Plains Indians via Mandan and Arikara middlemen. The Northwestern peoples traded dried salmon, oolichan (an oily fish used for lighting as well as food) and dentalium shells (of wide decorative and ritual use) for bison hides, chert and obsidian.

Trading entrepots existed across the continent: the Mandan/Hidatsa Center, the Arikara Center, the Dakota Rendezvous, the Shoshone Rendezvous, the Dalles Rendezvous and the massive southwestern networks.

Notes

1. d'Errico, Peter. "American Indian sovereignty: Now you see it, now you don't." *Decolonising Indigenous Rights*. Routledge, 2008. 115-131. https://people.umass.edu/derrico/nowyouseeit.html (accessed online November 4, 2020).

2. Wilson, Douglas L. "Jefferson vs. Hume." *The William and Mary Quarterly,* vol. 46, no. 1, 1989, pp. 49, 63.

3. de Vattel, Emerich, *The Law of Nations or the Principles of Natural Law*, 1797, trans. Charles G. Fenwick (New York: Oceana Publications for the Carnegie Institute, 1964), §26.

4. Ibid., §9.

5. de Vattel, Emerich, *The Law of Nations or the Principles of Natural Law*, 1797, trans. Charles G. Fenwick (New York: Oceana Publications for the Carnegie Institute, 1964), Chap. XVIII, Occupation of a Territory by a Nation, §208.

6. Green, Leslie C. *The law of nations and the new world.* University of Nebraska Press, 1989: 59.

7. "From Benjamin Franklin to Charles-Guillaume-Frédéric Dumas, 9 December 1775," *Founders Online*, National Archives, https://founders.archives.gov/documents/Franklin/01-22-02-0172. [Original source: *The Papers of Benjamin Franklin*, vol. 22, *March 23, 1775, through October 27, 1776*, ed. William B. Willcox. New Haven and London: Yale University Press, 1982, pp. 287–291.] (accessed online November 12, 2020).

8 de Vattel, Emerich, *The Law of Nations or the Principles of Natural Law*, 1797, trans. Charles G. Fenwick (New York: Oceana Publications for the Carnegie Institute, 1964), Chap. I, Preliminaries, § 15.

9. Ibid, §4.

10. Ibid, §81.

11. Montesquiedeu, Charles Secondat. "The spirit of the laws." Chap. XII: Of the Law of Nations among People who do not cultivate the Earth (Thomas Nugent trans., The Colonial Press 1900) (1650).

12. Locke, John. Second Treatise on Civil Government, Of Property, 1690, Chap. V, §32.

13. Ibid., Chap. V, §41.

14. Banner, Stuart. *How the Indians lost their land: Law and power on the frontier*. Harvard University Press, 2005: 33-34.

15. Locke, John. Second Treatise on Civil Government, Of Property, 1690, Chap. V, §50.

16. Locke, John. *An essay concerning human understanding*, Peter Nidditch, ed., Oxford, 1975, Book I, chapter II, §27.

17. Locke, John. *An essay concerning human understanding*, Peter Nidditch, ed., Oxford, 1975, Book I, chapter III, §15.

18. *Worcester v. Georgia*, 31 U.S. 515, 579 (1832).

19. Hume, David. *Essays: Moral, political, and literary*. Vol. 1. Longmans, Green, and Company, 1907: 252.

20. Hobbes, Thomas. "Chapter XIII of the natural condition of mankind as concerning their felicity and misery." *Leviathan* (2008): 113.

21. Banner, Stuart. *How the Indians lost their land: Law and power on the frontier*. Harvard University Press, 2005: 33.

22. Morrison, Wayne. *Blackstone's Commentaries on the Laws of England, Book the Second, Chapter the First, Of Property in General*, Routledge, 2013: 3.

23. Ibid., 7.

24. Annals of the Congress of the United States, Vol. 5, United States Congress, Gales and Seaton, 1849: 900.

# 17

# PRESIDENTIAL INDIAN POLICIES

This country's Founding Fathers attitudes and policies about Indians Nations and peoples and the drive for a continental empire shaped our formative history.

## General George Washington: Sullivan Campaign of 1779—Chastise and Intimidate

In 1779, General George Washington planned an expedition of destruction and devastation of the Six Nations. Generals John Sullivan, James Clinton and Horatio Gates were to "chastise and intimidate" the Haudenosaunee. The fact that four brigades of Continental troops totaling around 4,469 men were earmarked for this expedition underlines just how important General Washington considered this enterprise. Hundreds of U.S. troops marched north to "extirpate those hell-hounds off the face of the Earth."[1] This government sanctioned persecution, imprisonment and extermination of the Haudenosaunee was not only to affect them, but to neutralize other Indians from challenging U.S. authority.

General Washington's instructions to General Sullivan were as follows:

> The Expedition is undertaken to Destroy those Indian Nations & to Convince others that we have it in our power to Carry the war into their Country whenever they Commence hostilities.[2]

Further instructions followed a month later:

From George Washington to Major General John Sullivan, 31 May 1779

The expedition you are appointed to command is to be directed against the hostile tribes of the six nations of Indians, with their associates and adherents. ***The immediate objects are the total destruction and devastation of their settlements and the capture of as many prisoners of every age and sex as possible. It will be essential to ruin their crops now in the ground and prevent their planting more.***

I would recommend that some post in the center of the Indian Country should be occupied with all expedition, with a sufficient quantity of provision, whence parties should be detached to lay waste all the settlements around with instructions to do it in the most effectual manner, ***that the country may not be merely overrun but destroyed.*** But you will not by any means listen to (any) overture of peace before the total ruin of their settlements is effected...[3] (Emphasis added.)

Major General Sullivan's report to Washington specifically identifies the number of houses destroyed, indicators of the permanent settlement of the Six Nations. Also, he recounts the number of corn fields, vegetables and orchards of every kind proving the extensive agriculture practiced.

At Kanasedagea, town consisted of 50 Houses and was very pleasantly situated with a large amount of Corn and fruit trees which we destroyed. At Kanandaique we found 23 very elegant Houses, mostly framed, and in general very large. We also found very extensive feilds of Corn, which having destroyed we marched to Honyaye, a small town of ten Houses which we also destroyed. At Kanegsaus we destroyed 25 Houses and some large Corn fields.

The Army moved in that day to the Castle last mentioned and which consist(ed) of 25 Houses, and had very extensive feilds of Corn, which being destroyed we moved on the next day to the Chenessee Town. At Chenessee we found some large Corn fields and 128 Houses mostly very large and elegant. The town is beautifully situated—almost incircled with a clear flat, which extends for a number of Miles, on which were the most extensive feilds of Corn, and every kind of Vegetable, that can be conceived. The whole Army was immediately engaged in destroying the Crops—The Corn was gathered and burnt in Houses and in Kilns, that the Enemy might not reap the least advantage from it, which method we have pursued in every other place.

Col. Butler destroyed in the Cayuga Country five principal Towns and a number of scattering Towns, the whole making about 100 in number exceedingly large & well built—He also destroyed 200 Acres of excellent corn with a number of orchards one of which had in it 1500 fruit Trees—another Indian settlement was discovered near new Town (by a party) consisting of 39 new houses which was also destroyed. The number of Towns destroyed by this army amounts to 40 besides scattering houses—the quantity of Corn destroyed at a moderate computation must amount to 160,000 Bushls with a vast quantity of vegetables of every kind—

Col. Dearborne burnt in his route six Towns including one which had been before partly destroyed by a small party—destroying at the same time large quantity's of Corn. Cortland was then detached with 500 Men up the Tioga branch to seek for settlements in that quarter and in the space of two days destroyed several fields of corn & burnt several houses. Col. Butler destroyed in the Cayuga Country five principal Towns and a number of scattering Towns, the whole making about 100 in number exceedingly large & well built—He also destroyed 200 Acres of excellent corn with a number of orchards one of which had in it 1500 fruit Trees— another Indian settlement was discovered near new Town (by a party) consisting of 39 new houses which was also destroyed. The number of Towns destroyed by this army amounts to 40 besides scattering houses—the quantity of Corn destroyed at a moderate computation must amount to 160,000 Bushls with a vast quantity of vegetables of every kind—Every creek & river has been traced and the whole Country explored in search of Indian settlements, *& I am persuaded except one Town situated near the allegany about 57 Miles from Chenessee—there is not a single Town left in the Country of the five nations—*

*I flatter myself, that the orders with which your Excellency was*
*pleased to honor me, are fully executed...*[4] (Emphasis added.)

At the very best, it was hoped this expedition would force the Six Nations to sue for peace with the Americans which did not occur. At the very least, it was hoped that the Six Nation's ability to remain on the attack would be permanently crippled. Noticeably missing however, was the presence of any Indian captives, one of the main goals of the expedition. For the remainder of the War, the Indians would be almost wholly dependent upon the British for food, clothing and equipment which strained the British resources.

## General George Washington: Americans' Sole Lords and Proprietors, Revolutionary War Victory Foundation of Empire

Prior to becoming President at the end of the Revolutionary War, General George Washington referred to Americans as "the sole Lords and Proprietors of a vast Tract of Continent" and believed the success of the Revolutionary struggle was nothing less than the "foundation of our Empire[.]"[5]

## Future President John Adams: Civilization and Conversion of Indians to Christianity Failing

In a letter to William Tudor, future president John Adams expressed his views regarding the 'aversion' of Indians to civilization and Christianity. Tudor, a lawyer and holder of various civic offices, studied law under Adams:

> What infinite pains have been taken and expenses incurred in treaties, presents, and stipulated sums of money, instruments of agriculture, education...to convert these poor savages to Christianity! And, alas! with how little success! The Indians are as bigoted to their religion as the Mohametans [sic] are to their Koran, the Hindoos are to their Shaster, the Chinese to Confucius, the Romans to the Saints and angels, or the Jews to Moses and the Prophets. It is a principle of religion, at bottom, which inspires the Indian with such invincible aversion both to Civilization

and Christianity. The same principle has excited their perpetual hostilities against the colonists and the independent Americans.[6]

## President John Adams: Strongest Obligation to His Distressed White Children who Had Illegally Squatted on Cherokee Nation Lands

When elected as the country's second President, John Adams, in an effort to defuse a conflict between the Cherokee Nation and the Tennessee legislature sided with the state. The Legislature informed the President that the Indians were mere 'tenants at will' and the state would not remove colonial squatters encroaching on the Cherokee's land guaranteed them in a 1791 Treaty. In a letter to the Cherokee Nation, dated August 27, 1798, President Adams asked the Cherokee to consider the "sincere friendship of the United States," but said his "strongest obligations" were to "hear the complaints, and relieve, as far as in my power, the distresses of my white children, citizens of the United States."[7] The result was the 1798 Treaty of Tellico in which the Cherokee ceded more of their homelands in eastern Tennessee. President Adams characterized many of these colonial squatters as "deserving people" who had made "valuable improvements" and were "worthy and well-intentioned."[8]

## President Thomas Jefferson: Remove Eastern Indians West of Mississippi

The country's third President, Thomas Jefferson, planned to remove eastern Indians west of the Mississippi after the Louisiana Purchase. Offices to sell land on the western bank of the Mississippi were to be opened, laying off a range of states.

## From President Thomas Jefferson to John Breckinridge (U.S. Attorney General), 12 August 1803

...the best use we can make of the country for some time will be to give establishments in it to the Indians on the East side of the Mispi in exchange for their present country, and open land offices in the last, & thus make this acquisition the means of filling up the Eastern side instead of drawing off it's population. *When we shall be full on this side, we may lay off a range of states on the Western bank from the head to the mouth, & so range after range, advancing compactly as we multiply.*[9] (Emphasis added.)

## Thomas Jefferson: Empire of Liberty

Thomas Jefferson used the phrase "Empire of Liberty" in 1780, while the American Revolution was still being fought. In his instructions to George Rogers Clark to take Fort Detroit he envisioned a future of commerce and expansion:

> We shall divert through our own Country a branch of commerce which the European States have thought worthy of the most important struggles and sacrifices and ... shall form to the American union a barrier against the dangerous extension of the British Province of Canada and add to the Empire of Liberty an extensive and fertile Country...[10]

This false narrative of spreading liberty across the continent was used to justify removing Indians who were seen as obstacles to progress.

## From Secretary of State Thomas Jefferson to Charles Carroll, April 15, 1791

In a letter dated April 15, 1791 from Secretary of State Thomas Jefferson to Charles Carroll, he repeated his bribery policy: "The most economical as well as most humane conduct towards them is to bribe them into peace, and to retain them in peace by eternal bribes."[11]

Also, President Jefferson wrote in 1801,

> It is impossible not to look forward to distant times, when our rapid multiplication will...cover the whole northern, if not the whole southern continent, with a people speaking the same language, governed in similar forms, and by similar laws; nor can we contemplate with satisfaction either blot or mixture on that surface.[12]

242

Later, in a letter from former President Thomas Jefferson to James Madison, April 27, 1809, Jefferson advocated for expansion, including Canada:

> ...we should have such an *empire for liberty* as she has never surveyed since the creation: & I am persuaded no constitution was ever before so well calculated as ours for extensive empire & self government...[13] (Emphasis added.)

Former President Jefferson's concept of westward expansion was brought to life in a John Gast landscape painting, "American Progress." He had described this expansion in a letter to William Ludlow which Gast replicated:

> ...let a philosophic observer commence a journey from the savages of the Rocky mountains, Eastwardly towards our seacoast. these he would observe in the earliest stage of association living under no law but that of nature, subsisting and covering themselves with the flesh and skins of wild beasts. he would next find those on our frontiers in the pastoral state, raising domestic animals to supply the defects of hunting. then succeed our own semibarbarous citizens, the pioneers of the advance of civilisation, and so in his progress he would meet the gradual shades of improving man until he would reach his, as yet, most improved state in our seaport towns this in fact is equivalent to a survey, in time of the progress of man from the infancy of nation to the present day. ... I have observed this march of civilisation advancing from the sea coast, passing over us like a cloud of light, increasing our knolege and improving our condition insomuch as that we are at this time more advanced in civilisation here than the seaports were when I was a boy. and where this progress will stop no one can say. barbarism has in the mean time been receding before the steady step of amelioration; and will in time I trust disappear from the earth.[14]

The lighting in Gast's painting represents the expansion of light (civilization) from the east to the west. A large, luminous, angelic, feminine figure of "American Progress" with the "star of the empire" on her forehead leads settlers and miners from east to west. As she advances, she suspends telegraph cable. She holds the excess wire in her right hand where she also carries a schoolbook, an emblem of education. Two farmers are shown plowing a field, their permanent, fenced homestead in the background. Technological advances are depicted in the various methods of transportation: horseback, covered wagon, wagon trains, carriage, steam engine (trains) and ships.

In the west, wild bison, deer and a bear retreat into the darkness. Indians dancing near their teepees are being overrun. Several Indians are shown fleeing to the west from the onslaught of America's western progression. A bare-chested male raises a tomahawk and another carries a bow and arrow.

A horse led by a bare-breasted Indian woman draws a travois carrying a mother and a child. The miners and settlers are quickly and inevitably advancing upon the Indians who are soon be overtaken.

The tracks for the trains only go so far leading one to surmise that this is an open invitation for the further development of transportation. President Jefferson came to realize that publicly financed transportation infrastructure was a core foundation of America's economic, political, military and strategic progress. It would be infrastructure that would enable 2.5 million Americans, huddled along the Atlantic coastline in the late 18th century, to fill up a continent.

## Secretary of State Thomas Jefferson: 'Drub' and 'Bribe' Them

He also proclaimed his policy of drubbing the Indians and repeated his policy of bribery since it was cheaper than war.

From Secretary of State Thomas Jefferson to James Monroe, 17 April 1791

I hope we shall *drub the Indians well this summer and then change our plan from war to bribery.* We must do as the Spaniards and English do, keep them in peace by liberal and constant presents. They find it the cheapest plan, and so shall we. The expence of this summers expedition would have served for presents for half a century. ...Every rag of an Indian depredation will otherwise serve as a ground to raise troops...[15] (Emphasis added.)

Concerned about the prospect of war with the Shawnees, in 1807, President Jefferson wrote to Secretary of War Dearborn referencing Tecumseh:

> If ever we are constrained to lift the hatchet against any tribe we will never lay it down til that tribe is exterminated, or driven beyond the Mississippi ... in war they will kill some of us; but we will destroy all of them. Adjuring them, therefore, if they wish to remain on the land which covers the bones of their fathers, to keep the peace with a people who ask friendship without needing it, who wish to avoid war without fearing it. In war, they will kill some of us; we shall destroy all of them.[16]

## President Thomas Jefferson: Settler Colonists Grown Out of America, Equivalent to Indians

In President Jefferson's Speech to a Delegation of Indian Chiefs on January 4, 1806, he described the relationship of the United States to Indians in the following manner:

> My friends & children. We are descended from the old nations which live beyond the great water: but we & our forefathers have been so long here that we *seem like you to have grown out of this land ... We are become as numerous as the leaves of the trees, and, tho' we do not boast, we do not fear any nation. We are now your fathers; and you shall not lose by the change.*[17] (Emphasis added.)

In describing the settler colonists in equivalent terms to the indigenous inhabitants—"we ... have grown out of this land," President Jefferson justifies dispossession of Indian lands as the settlers are considered 'native' inhabitants and become entitled to Indian lands.

## President James Madison: Purchase Their Favorable Lands for Our Own Best Interest, Allot Their Land and Assimilate Them

Our fourth President, James Madison, planned to complete the work of transitioning the Indians from the "habits of the savage to the arts and comforts of social life" and divide up their land in a terrifying precursor to future allotment. This is a settler colonial strategy to justify dispossession of Indian lands as there is no need for a separate land base for peoples assimilated into the general society. It is also a management policy of the restricted containment and exclusion of a people. By the political administration of Indians in reduced areas, land and natural resource expropriation and exploitation would be easier.

> The Indian tribes within our limits appear also disposed to remain at peace. From several of them purchases of lands have been made particularly favorable to the wishes and security of our frontier settlements, as well as to the general interests of the nation. In some instances the titles, though not supported by due proof, and clashing those of one tribe with the claims of another, have been extinguished by double purchases, the benevolent policy of the United States preferring the augmented expense to the hazard of doing injustice or to the enforcement of justice against a *feeble and untutored people* by means involving or threatening an effusion of blood. ... the facility is increasing for *extending that divided and individual ownership, which exists now in movable property only, to the soil itself*, and of thus establishing in the culture and improvement of it the true foundation for a transit from the habits of the savage to the arts and comforts of social life.[18] (Emphasis added.)

President Madison also supported continental expansion. On December 5, 1815, delivering his State of the Union message to Congress, President Madison asserted: Among the means of advancing the public interest the occasion is a proper one for recalling the attention of Congress to the great importance of establishing throughout our country the roads and canals which can best be executed under the national authority.[19]

### President James Monroe: Extinguishment of Indian Title Inevitable; Removal of Indians Paramount; Assimilation Policy Defunct

In March of 1824, President James Monroe established the Office of Indian Affairs in the Department of War to oversee and carry out the Federal government's trade and treaty relations with the tribes. In

1849, the Office of Indian Affairs ("OIA") was transferred to the newly created U.S. Department of the Interior to implement policies designed to subjugate and assimilate Indians.

President, James Monroe, in his First Annual Message to Congress proclaimed his success in extinguishing Indian title in seven states, Ohio, Michigan, Indiana, Georgia, North Carolina, Tennessee and Alabama and pursuing his goal of individual Indian ownership of land:

> From several of the Indian tribes inhabiting the country bordering on Lake Erie purchases have been made of lands on conditions very favorable to the United States, and, as it is presumed, not less so to the tribes themselves.

> In this progress, which the rights of nature demand and nothing can prevent, marking a growth rapid and gigantic, it is our duty to make new efforts for the preservation, improvement, and civilization of the native inhabitants. The hunter state can exist only in the vast uncultivated desert. It yields to the more dense and compact form and thus was given to mankind to support the greatest number of which it is capable, and no tribe or people have a right to withhold from the wants of others more than is necessary for their own support and comfort.

> It is gratifying to know that the reservations of land made by the treaties with the tribes on Lake Erie were *made with a view to individual ownership among them* and to the cultivation of the soil by all, and that an annual stipend has been pledged to supply their other wants. (Emphasis added.) A considerable and rapid augmentation in the value of all the public lands, proceeding from these and other obvious cases, may henceforth be expected.[20]

## Second Inaugural Address of President James Monroe, March 5, 1821

President Monroe's Second Inaugural address was a scathing attack of Indian sovereignty. He planned to use his authority to deny recognition of their nationhood and terminate their communal land holdings.

The care of the Indian tribes ... has not been executed in a manner to accomplish all the objects intended by it. We have treated them as independent nations, without their having any substantial pretensions to that rank. The distinction has flattered their pride, retarded their improvement, and in many instances paved the way to their destruction. The progress of our settlements westward, supported as they are by a dense population, has constantly driven them back, with almost the total sacrifice of the lands which they have been compelled to abandon. Their sovereignty over vast territories should cease, in lieu of which the right of soil should be secured to each individual and his posterity in competent portions.[21]

Five weeks before President Monroe left office, he declared that the removal of the Indians was of paramount importance to the United States. The concept of assimilation was officially defunct. In 1825, ominously, he acknowledged that without protection, they were doomed to extermination.

"Experience has clearly demonstrated that in their present state it is impossible to incorporate them in such masses, in any form whatsoever, into our system," Monroe stated. "It has also demonstrated with equal certainty that without a timely anticipation of and provision against the dangers to which they are exposed, under causes which it will be difficult, if not impossible, to control, their degradation and extermination will be inevitable."[22]

The Monroe presidential administration would eventually conclude a total of forty-one treaties with twenty-nine different Indian Nations. All but eight involved a cession of Indian lands to the United States.

Of the eight remaining treaties, in accord with Secretary of War Calhoun's policies, six placed the signatory Indian Nations under the protection, and de facto sovereignty, of the United States. For Calhoun, anything short of "a complete extension of the laws and authority of the U.S. over the Indians was unacceptable."[23] Any Indian authority was to be choked off.

In proclaiming the Monroe Doctrine of 1823, President Monroe adopted an isolationist policy, which advocates minimal participation of a country in the internal affairs of another nation, and, an interventionist policy, which believed that certain forms of intervention or involvement are necessary to protect economic and political national interests. Thus, anyone seeking to colonize the Americas would face the utmost resistance. The doctrine proposed the following key elements: The American continents should not be considered for future colonization by the European powers; any attempt by European countries to impose their system on any nation in the western hemisphere would be considered by the U.S to be a threat to their own peace and safety; and the United States in turn would not interfere in European affairs. President Monroe knew that building empires involves not just acquiring new land or territories, but also exercising political, economic and military control over other nations.

## President John Quincy Adams: Indian Right of Possession Questionable

Our sixth President, John Quincy Adams, proudly delivered his position regarding westward expansion:

> The United States would dominate the Americas, President Adams said, and assert its hemispheric hegemony without challenge. He wrote, "We have it; we constitute the whole of it."[24]

On Indian land title, in his oration at the Jubilee of the Constitution, delivered at New York, April 30, 1839, before the New York Historical Society, he questioned the right of Indians to possess lands:

> *The Indian right of possession itself stands, with regard to the greatest part of the country, upon a questionable foundation.*

> Their cultivated fields, their constructed habitations, a space of ample sufficiency for their subsistence, and whatever they had annexed to themselves by personal labor, was undoubtedly by the laws of nature theirs.

> But what is the right of a huntsman to the forest of a thousand miles over which he has accidentally ranged in quest of prey? ...

Shall the lordly savage not only disdain the virtues and enjoyments of civilization himself, but shall he control the civilization of a world?[25] (Emphasis added.)

Henry Clay, Secretary of State under President John Quincy Adams, claimed that "it was impossible to civilize Indians; that there never was a full-blooded Indian who took to civilization. It was not in their nature."

President Adams recorded the moment:

> He [Clay] believed they were destined to extinction, and, although he would never use or countenance inhumanity towards them, he did not think them, as a race, worth preserving. He considered them as essentially inferior to the Anglo-Saxon race, which were now taking their place on this continent. They were not an improvable breed, and their disappearance from the human family will be no great loss to the world. In point of fact they were rapidly disappearing, and he did not believe that in fifty years from this time there would be any of them left.[26]

By portraying Indians as unimportant and destined to become extinct, Henry Clay employed a perception of Indians which made it easier to justify dispossession of their lands and extermination of them as a people.

## President Andrew Jackson: Kill and Lay Captive Their Women and Children

Our seventh President's (Andrew Jackson) despotic policy toward indigenous peoples is unquestioned. While a General in our armed forces, he appealed to the Tennessee legislature and implored them to approve and fund a military invasion of the Creek territory. In correspondence with Governor Blount, President Jackson made it clear that he intended to invade the Creek Nation even without the authorization of the legislature "and think myself Justifiable, in laying waste their villages, burning their houses, killing their warriors and leading into Captivity their wives and children..." He would carry this attitude into the presidential office.[27]

President Jackson's impotency is revealed by Representative John Test in his a

> He tells the poor savage, I cannot protect you—you must submit to the laws of the States, or you must march to the wilderness; you must seek in the desert that repose which is denied you here. Georgia is a sovereign State—I cannot undertake to control her: she must do as she pleases with you. If I were to attempt to control her, she might do something injurious to us, and ruinous to you.[28]

## Theodore Roosevelt: We Are Indebted to the Fierce Settler who Drives the Savage from the Land

The bias against Indians was still prevalent in 1889 when Theodore Roosevelt wrote The Winning of the West, a decade before he would be elected President:

> The most ultimately righteous of all wars is a war with savages, though it is apt to be also the most terrible and inhuman. The rude, fierce settler who drives the savage from the land lays all civilized mankind under a debt to him. American and Indian, Boer and Zulu, Cossack and Tartar, New Zealander and Maori,—in each case the victor, horrible though many of his deeds are, has laid deep the foundations for the future greatness of a mighty people. ... It is of incalculable importance that America, Australia, and Siberia should pass out of the hands of their red, black, and yellow aboriginal owners, and become the heritage of the dominant world races.[29]

## Notes

1. Mann, Barbara Alice. "Extirpate Those Hell-Hounds from off the Face of the Earth: The Sullivan-Clinton Campaign, 9 August – 30 September 1779" in *George Washington's War on Native America*. Lincoln: University of Nebraska Press, 2009, pp. 51-110.

2. "To George Washington from Major General John Sullivan, 16 April 1779," *Founders Online*, National Archives, https://founders.archives. gov/documents/Washington/03-20-02-0089. [Original source: *The Papers of George Washington,* Revolutionary War Series, vol. 20, *8 April–31 May 1779*, ed. Edward G. Lengel. Charlottesville: University of Virginia Press, 2010, pp. 90–96.] (accessed online November 13, 2020).

3. "From George Washington to Major General John Sullivan, 31 May 1779," *Founders Online*, National Archives, https://founders.archives. gov/documents/Washington/03-20-02-0661. [Original source: *The Papers of George Washington*, Revolutionary War Series, vol. 20, *8 April–31 May 1779*, ed. Edward G. Lengel. Charlottesville: University of Virginia Press, 2010, pp. 716–719.] (accessed online November 13, 2020).

4. "To George Washington from Major General John Sullivan, 28 September 1779," *Founders Online*, National Archives, https:// founders.archives.gov/documents/Washington/03-22-02-0450. [Original source: *The Papers of George Washington,* Revolutionary War Series, vol. 22, *1 August–21 October 1779*, ed. Benjamin L. Huggins. Charlottesville: University of Virginia Press, 2013, pp. 528–541.] (accessed online November 13, 2020).

5. "From George Washington to The States, 8 June 1783," *Founders*

*Online,* National Archives, https://founders.archives.gov/documents/ Washington/99-01-02-11404 (accessed online November 13, 2020).

6. "From John Adams to William Tudor, Sr., 23 September 1818," *Founders Online*, National Archives, https://founders.archives.gov/ documents/Adams/99-02-02-6993. (accessed online November 13, 2020).

7. "From John Adams to Cherokee Nation, 27 August 1798," *Founders Online*, National Archives, https://founders.archives.gov/documents/ Adams/99-02-02-2892 (accessed online November 13, 2020).

8. Ibid.

9. "From Thomas Jefferson to John Breckinridge, 12 August 1803," *Founders Online,* National Archives, https://founders.archives.gov/ documents/Jefferson/01-41-02-0139. [Original source: *The Papers of Thomas Jefferson*, vol. 41, *11 July–15 November 1803*, ed. Barbara B. Oberg. Princeton: Princeton University Press, 2014, pp. 184–186.] .] (accessed online November 13, 2020).

10. "From Thomas Jefferson to George Rogers Clark, 25 December 1780," *Founders Online*, National Archives, https://founders.archives. gov/documents/Jefferson/01-04-02-0295. [Original source: *The Papers of Thomas Jefferson*, vol. 4, *1 October 1780–24 February 1781*, ed. Julian P. Boyd. Princeton: Princeton University Press, 1951, pp. 233–238.] (accessed online November 13, 2020).

11. "From Thomas Jefferson to Charles Carroll, 15 April 1791," *Founders Online,* National Archives, https://founders.archives.gov/ documents/Jefferson/01-20-02-0046. [Original source: *The Papers of Thomas Jefferson*, vol. 20, *1 April–4 August 1791*, ed. Julian P. Boyd. Princeton: Princeton University Press, 1982, pp. 214–215.] (accessed online November 19, 2020).

12. "From Thomas Jefferson to James Monroe, 24 November 1801," *Founders Online*, National Archives, https://founders.archives.gov/ documents/Jefferson/01-35-02-0550. [Original source: *The Papers of Thomas Jefferson*, vol. 35, *1 August–30 November 1801*, ed. Barbara B. Oberg. Princeton: Princeton University Press, 2008, pp. 718–722.] (accessed online November 13, 2020).

13. "Thomas Jefferson to James Madison, 27 April 1809," *Founders Online*, National Archives, https://founders.archives.gov/documents/Jefferson/03-01-02-0140. [Original source: *The Papers of Thomas Jefferson, Retirement Series,* vol. 1, *4 March 1809 to 15 November 1809*, ed. J. Jefferson Looney. Princeton: Princeton University Press, 2004, pp. 168–170.] (accessed online November 13, 2020).

14. "From Thomas Jefferson to William Ludlow, 6 September 1824," *Founders Online*, National Archives, https://founders.archives.gov/documents/Jefferson/98-01-02-4523 (accessed online November 13, 2020).

15. "From Thomas Jefferson to James Monroe, 17 April 1791," *Founders Online*, National Archives, https://founders.archives.gov/documents/Jefferson/01-20-02-0051. [Original source: *The Papers of Thomas Jefferson*, vol. 20, *1 April–4 August 1791*, ed. Julian P. Boyd. Princeton: Princeton University Press, 1982, pp. 234–236.] (accessed online November 13, 2020).

16. "From Thomas Jefferson to Henry Dearborn, 28 August 1807," *Founders Online*, National Archives, https://founders.archives.gov/documents/Jefferson/99-01-02-6267 (accessed online November 19, 2020).

17. https://millercenter.org/the-presidency/presidential-speeches/january-10-1806-address-chiefs-cherokee-nation (accessed online November 13, 2020).

18. "From James Madison to United States Congress, 3 December 1816," *Founders Online*, National Archives, https://founders.archives.gov/documents/Madison/99-01-02-5598 (accessed online November 4, 2020).

19. James Madison Presidency, December 5, 1815: Seventh Annual Message

https://millercenter.org/the-presidency/presidential-speeches/december-5-1815-seventh-annual-message (accessed online November 13, 2020).

20. James Monroe, First Annual Message Online by Gerhard Peters and John T. Woolley, The American Presidency Project https://www.

presidency.ucsb.edu/node/205560 (accessed online November 4, 2020).

21. Second Inaugural Address of James Monroe, March 5, 1821

https://avalon.law.yale.edu/19th_century/monroe2.asp (accessed online November 14, 2020).

22. President James Monroe, in an 1825 message to Congress in Native American Voices: A History and Anthology, ed. Steven Mintz (St. James, New York: Brandywine P, 1995), pp. 111-112.

23. John C. Calhoun to James Monroe, February 8, 1822, ASP: Indian Affairs, 2: 275-6.

24. Adams, John Quincy. *Memoirs of John Quincy Adams: comprising portions of his diary from 1795 to 1848*. JB Lippincott & Company, 1874, 5:176.

25. Orations, John Quincy Adams, "The Jubilee of the Constitution, delivered at New York, April 30, 1839, before the New York Historical Society." https://www.gutenberg.org/files/896/896-h/896-h.htm (accessed online December 12, 2020).

26. Adams, John Quincy. *Memoirs of John Quincy Adams: comprising portions of his diary from 1795 to 1848*. JB Lippincott & Company, 1874, 7:89.

27. Rogin, Michael P. *Fathers and Children: Andrew Jackson and the Subjugation of the American Indian*, 1975:147.

28. Speeches on the Passage of the Bill for the Removal of the Indians, Delivered in the Congress of the United States, April and May, 1830, Perkins and Marvin. 1830, p. 302.

29. Roosevelt, Theodore. *Winning of the west*, Vol. 4., Putnam, 1889: 56.

# 18

# WESTERN SETTLEMENT

The Presidents from Washington to Jackson recognized that Western settlement was intimately related to the country's future wealth and power. In 1783, 2 percent of colonists lived west of the Alleghenies; by 1830 the figure was 28 percent. R. Kent Newmyer wrote:

> It would be difficult to overemphasize the importance of land greed in American history...Land was America's most abundant and most sought-after resource. For the better part of two centuries, the vision of cheap land was the magnet that attracted millions of immigrants. It was billed as 'free,' but it never was. First, it had to be wrested from the Native Americans; from the Spanish and French, who sold out; and from the Mexicans, who were forced out. It was fought over by the rich and powerful to see who could get the most and the best. It was fought for by the poor, who wanted a little piece of the action and who, unlike the large buyers and sellers, were willing to put their lives on the line to get it.[1]

## Northwest Ordinance—Pattern for Western Settlement

In the Ordinance of 1785, Thomas Jefferson proposed that the vast new territories acquired under the Treaty of Paris should be incorporated into the new union as separate (rather than expanded) states: the mechanism for new state creation would be further clarified in the Northwest Ordinance of 1787. The Northwest Ordinance was adopted as a means of facilitating disposal of the federal territorial lands. Its importance in settling the west efficiently cannot be overstated.

Professor Kades in his analysis also recognizes the significance of this Ordinance:

> The lynchpin of this orderly advance was the rectangular survey system. By refusing to sell land, and later refusing to recognize preemption (squatter) rights, before an area had been surveyed, the United States government exercised significant control over when settlers went to the frontier and where they went. Controlled, contiguous, concentrated land rushes into predesignated areas conferred a number of advantages in expropriating Indian lands at least cost.[2]

Under the direction of the Surveyor General new land would be divided into townships 6 miles square, forming 36 plots of a square mile each, of which the revenues from the 16th square would be reserved for funding public education. An appointed Governor and three judges would rule a Territory until the population reached 5,000. At that time, the citizens could elect a legislature, and, when the population numbered 60,000, the Territory could apply for admission to the Union as a State on a basis of full equality with the original thirteen states. The Ordinance would govern settlement of millions of square miles of the American continent, until superseded by the 1862 Homestead Act. Northwest Ordinance, Act of Aug. 7, 1789, ch. 8, 1 Stat. 50, 52.

Thomas Jefferson wrote to William Carmichael on August 18, 1785, that Congress had purchased the Indian rights to fifty million acres under the Land Ordinance of 1785 and that the sale of the land will pay all the domestic debt.[3]

Consonant with the purchasing policy in 1787 following the blatant confiscation of Indian lands, Congress declared that, in the newly formed Northwest Territory "The utmost good faith shall always be observed toward the Indians; their lands and properties shall never be taken away from them without their consent."[4] In 1788, Congress appropriated $6,000 to begin buying their land. This declaration of good faith was not out of benevolence. As eloquently phrased by Professor Kades: Indian wars were expensive, risky, and unrewarding even in victory. The costs were high—human lives, labor that could have been used more productively, misspent capital, reduced productive capacity and destroyed property—deadweight losses.[5]

The Northwest Ordinance, while seemingly innocuous, was a key linchpin in westward expansion as state after state was laid out, populated and inaugurated into the union. The terms of sale under various land acts are detailed below.

| TERMS OF SALE UNDER VARIOUS U.S. LAND ACTS 1785–1862 | | | |
|---|---|---|---|
| 1800–1862 Initial Sale by Public Auction | | | |
| Year | Minimum Price | Terms | Minimum Purchase |
| 1785 | $1.00 per acre | Specie, loan-office or debt certificates | 640 Acres |
| 1796 | $2.00 per acre | One-half down, one half due in one year | 640 Acres |
| 1800 | $2.00 per acre | One-quarter cash, remainder to be paid in three annual installments | 320 Acres |
| 1804 | $2.00 per acre | One-quarter cash, remainder to be paid in three annual installments | 160 acres |
| 1820 | $1.25 per acre | Cash | 80 Acres |
| 1830 | | Land Scrip acceptable in lieu of cash | |
| 1832 | $1.25 per acre | Cash, Land Scrip | 40 Acres |
| 1841 | $1.25 per acre | Squatters who built homes and improved land could purchase one-quarter section before it was offered for public sale | 160 Acres |
| 1855 | $1.00 per acre | Land not sold for 10 years to be offered at $1.00 per acre; if not sold for 30 years, land could be disposed of at 12.5¢ per acre | 40-320 Acres |
| 1862 | $10 (filing fee) | Title could be obtained after 5 years residence under Homestead Act | 160 Acres |

Terms of Sale under Various U.S. Land Acts 1785-1862, Ohio Lands Book

The object of the Land Acts was to encourage settlement of the Ohio River Valley and the Great Lakes region to thwart incursions by the British. Detroit and Pittsburgh were prime areas to control as they provided ready access from Canada into the U.S. The presence of Indians was secondary to controlling this vital geographic area.

## Indian Nations Living in Ohio at Risk

The Ohio River Valley also presented unique questions regarding land titles. The local government's failure to administer a purchasing policy with adequate documentation procedures resulted in a mass of conflicting titles.

From George Washington to the Commissioners to the Southern
Indians, 29 August 1789

The tangle of Illinois country land claims that Winthrop Sargent
and other federal and territorial officials attempted to unravel in
the spring and summer of 1790 resulted from frontier conditions,
careless record keeping, and the multiplicity of governments that
had administered the area.[6]

Winthrop Sargent was a politician, writer and a member of the Federalist
party.

In another case in 1796, the House of Representatives tried a matter
involving two speculators claiming 20-30 million acres of land, even
though Congress had no legal authority. The problem of land jobbers
would not go away. James Madison was concerned the House had acted
precipitously.

### From James Madison to Thomas Jefferson, 10 January 1796

The House of Representatives have been latterly occupied with a
pretty curious affair. Certain Traders and others, of Detroit, entered
into a contract with certain individuals of the United States, for
obtaining the peninsula formed by Lakes Huron and Michigan,
and containing 20 or 30 million of acres of valuable land. *The
traders, by means of their influence over the Indians, were to
extinguish the Indian Title; and the other party, by means of
their influence, and that of their connexions, with Congress, to
extinguish the title of the United States*. ... There cannot be the
least doubt, either of the turpitude of the charge, or the guilt of the
accused...[7] (Emphasis added.)

The partners had offered to reserve twenty-four shares for legislators
who would support their scheme in Congress and who might wish
to join it later; and, it was claimed, they had won over thirty to forty
members of the House.

While the federal government tried to maintain order over the
'uninformed, and perhaps licentious people' who tended to migrate
west, they simply lacked the military might to do so. The feeble military

presence in the Northwest Territory rendered them impotent. At the same time, government representatives followed the government's expansion interests under Secretary of War Knox's directive: "you will not neglect any opportunity that may offer of extinguishing the Indian rights to the westward as far as the river Mississippi."[8]

In 1786, under the Second Treaty of Fort Stanwix, the once powerful Iroquois ceded their claims to Ohio lands. The Treaty created serious conflicts between the Six Nations and the Shawnee who claimed that they, not the Six Nations who ceded the land in present-day West Virginia and Kentucky, had dominion over the land. The Ohio Indian Nations realized that the rapid expansion of the American population into the west presented a dire threat to their continued autonomy. They refused to subscribe to the Treaty and resolved to drive the Americans back to the Ohio River. They formed the Western Confederacy comprising the Miami, Shawnee, Delaware and Lenape Indian Nations.

After the Treaty of Fort Stanwix, settlers poured into the area. President Washington could foresee the possibility of war. Also, concerned with the British using the Indians to populate a buffer state between the U.S. and Canada, President Washington sent a force in 1790, under Gen. Josiah Harmar, to build a post at Miami Town. The Western Confederacy, led by Little Turtle, a Miami Chief, attacked and defeated Harmar's force at the Battle of the Wabash, and the following year, along with Blue Jacket, a Shawnee, defeated a follow-up expedition under General Arthur St. Clair in present Ohio. St. Clair's defeat in 1791 saw the American army incur heavy losses—632 soldiers of 932 killed, 264 wounded, a 97% casualty rate.

In 1793, the Legion of the U.S. Army moved against the Indians once again, this time under General 'Mad Anthony' Wayne. Wayne's forces met and soundly defeated an Indian army at the Battle of Fallen Timbers. The battle crippled the Indian's ability to continue their fight for their lands. Their British allies had not helped them. The following year, in the Treaty of Greenville (1795), the Indians ceded to the United States most of the present State of Ohio. Ratification of Jay's Treaty (November 1794) that same year dealt them a further blow. By its terms, the British would withdraw from their northwestern posts by 1796 and leave the Indians to fend for themselves.

One of the terms of the Treaty of Greenville was the promise, by the U.S. to the Indians, of annual annuities, usually food and clothing. This ended up being a disaster to Indians. The U.S. would use the threat of withholding annuities to force additional land cessions. The food was not healthy and led to the introduction of diseases, such as diabetes.

The purchase of Indian land in the Northwest Territory left a troubled legacy. The effect of that legacy would lead to the loss of more Indian land in a pattern described by politician George Mason.

George Mason to James Monroe (February 9, 1792)

> When our Ancestors first setled on the American Shores, they purchased, or obtained by Treaty (in some few Instances by force) from the Indian Nations, a small Tract of Country: the Settlement of this was the Means of destroying, or driving away the wild Game, and rendering the adjacent Country unfit for the savage Life. The Indians removed further back for the Convenience of hunting; and sold, upon easy terms, the Lands, which were no longer of much Use to them. And thus, by making Purchase after Purchase, our Settlements gradually advanced; and the Indian Natives, following the wild Game, gradually retired; so imperceptibly, that we are now at a Loss to know, what became of the numerous Tribes of Indians, who once inhabited Virginia; very few of them, comparatively speaking, having been destroyed by Wars with us.
>
> Had we continued to pursue this safe and easy Plan, we shou'd have saved a great deal of Money, and prevented many horid Scenes, with the Effusion of much Blood. But unfortunately, the Avidity of Individuals to engross large Tracts of Land, and the vain Expectation of raising a Fund, from the Sale of the Western Lands, for the Extinction of the public Debt, extended our Views to the Indian Country over the Ohio, before we had setled the adjacent Lands. Our people begun to settle upon the Indian hunting Grounds, yet full of Game. ... It was shewing the Indians (to use a Phrase of their own) that we were preparing to drive them from the Face of the Earth; and it is no Wonder, that it has created a general Confederacy of the Indian Tribes against us.[9]

## Example of Dispossession of Land in Ohio—No Indians Left Residing in Ohio

President Jefferson's policy in his Memorandum for Henry Dearborn on Indian Policy, dated December 29, 1802, confirms the ongoing threat to Indian lands in the Ohio Valley based on the government's specific interest in lands between the Mississippi and Illinois and the Ohio and Wabash Rivers.

> Hints on the subject of Indian boundaries, suggested for consideration:
>
> "... establishment of a strong front on our Western boundary leaving the extinguishment of [Indian] title to fall ... The Indians being once closed in ... will, for want of game, be forced to agriculture ... and will [part with land] for money to buy stock, utensils & necessaries for their farms & families." The country between the Missisipi & Illinois on one side, & the Ohio & Wabash on the other, is also peculiarly desirable to us...[10]

President Jefferson would get his wish.

In Ohio, Indians were completely divested of their lands and there were no remaining Indian Nations in the state.

**State of Ohio**—Indian land divided up even while Indians still lived there.

**Ohio River Valley**—Fought over due to confluence of Monongahela, Allegheny and Ohio Rivers with access to Miss. River—French and British and Indians.

**Michigan Survey**—land disputed between Ohio and Michigan—per U.S. Supreme Court, went to Ohio.

**Congress Lands**—public domain, opened for purchase, western lands US acquired by treaty with Great Britain or by cession from the states "shall be disposed of for the common benefit of the United States." Congress sold large acreage packages so as to bring money into the federal treasury faster than the sale of many small amounts to a large number of individual purchasers. Sold by 640 acres lots for $1 an acre, after 1796 $2 per acre.

**Connecticut Reserve**, except the Firelands, sold by Connecticut Land

Company to 35 investors. Connecticut's western land claims were based on several royal Charters, the most determining of which was the royal charter of 1662 issued by King Charles II of England.

**Virginia Military District**—for VA veterans who served in Amer. Rev. & Virginia Militia—Ultimately some **25 individuals** controlled about 1,035,408 acres within the Virginia Military District.

**U.S. Military District**—for veterans in Continental Army. Many veterans sold their warrants to speculators. Of the 1,043,460 acres claimed by land warrant, 569,542 acres were patented to just **22 persons**.

**Ohio Company Lands**—sold to investors led by General Rufus Putnam. Original sale of 1,500,000 acres was cut in half due to Putnam's inability to pay for all of it —even so, it was paid for in severely depreciated Continental securities—the price was actually about twelve and a half cents per acre.

**Judge John Cleves Symmes Purchase**, a member of Congress, persuaded Congress to sell him 1,000,000 acres. Congress later restricted his purchase to 311,682 acres, due to mishandling. Paid about two-thirds of a dollar per acre.

**Firelands**—to 1,866 Connecticut residents whose property had been damaged by British coastal raiders during the American Revolution.

**Refugee Lands**—for Canadians who supported U.S. in American Revolution.

**The Donation Tract**—100,000 acres, to create a buffer zone sheltering Ohio Company lands from Indian incursions. To this end, a **free 100-acre** lot would be given to any male, eighteen or older, who would actually settle on the land at the time the deed was conveyed.

**Other Misc. Grants** for university (OU, OSU, Miami U.), schools, churches, etc.[11]

## Great Lakes Region Still at Stake—Odawa Indian Nation in Michigan

The only remaining significant Indian populations east of the Mississippi River lived in Michigan and Wisconsin. The Odawa knew they had to enter into a treaty in order to secure lands in Michigan or they would be removed to Kansas or Oklahoma. On multiple occasions, the Odawa petitioned the federal government to hold councils regarding treaties. They also held councils amongst themselves and the Ojibway. In 1835, a delegation of Odawa leaders from Little Traverse departed on an uncertain trip to Washington D.C. in the hopes of creating a home for future generations of Odawa in northern Michigan.

On December 5, 1835, Augustin Hamlin, Odawa head man and interpreter for treaty negotiations, wrote this impassioned letter to Lewis Cass, then Secretary of War under President Jackson:

> The principal objects of our visit here, are these: we would make some arrangements with the government remaining in the Territory of Michigan in the quiet possession of our lands, and to transmit the same safely to our posterity. We do not wish to sell all the lands claimed by us and consequently not to remove to the west of the Mississippi...
>
> It is a heart-rending thought to our simple feelings to think of leaving our native country forever, and which has been bought with the price of, their native blood, and which has been thus safely transmitted to us. It is, we say, a heart-rending thought to us to think so; there are many local endearments which make the soul shrink with horror at the idea of rejecting our country forever—the mortal remains of our deceased parents, relations and friends, cry out to us as it were, for our compassion, our sympathy and our love.[12]

The result of that fateful trip and a subsequent return visit was the Washington Treaty of 1836. Nearly 16 million acres of land in the Upper and Lower Peninsula were ceded to the United States. It was the best the Odawa could do with tremendous odds against them.

## Black Hawk's War

Five years later, the Sauk and Fox contested the validity of the Treaty of St. Louis (1804) in which four unauthorized Indian members had ceded all of their territory east of the Mississippi River. Black Hawk and his band contended that they had never signed away their lands in Illinois. The U.S. Army quickly mobilized the Illinois militia, U.S. troops and Indian allies to repel and quench an 'invasion' by several hundred Sauk men, women, and children seeking to re-occupy a village on the Rock River in Illinois that they believed still belonged to them. The Sauk and Fox unsuccessfully tried to form a confederacy with other Indians in the Great Lakes region and to seek British help. Battles were fought at Stillman's Run and the Wisconsin Heights. The Americans pursued the Sauk and Fox for months, and one hundred fifty Indians were killed during the Battle of Bad Axe, as Black Hawk's band attempted to cross from Wisconsin back to the other side of the Mississippi. The U.S. reported casualties of 5 killed, 19 injured. Black Hawk was captured, put in chains and imprisoned at Jefferson Barracks, outside St. Louis. The author Washington Irving visited him there and found "an old man, upward of seventy, emaciated & enfeebled by the sufferings he has experienced and a touch of cholera."[13]

Although the treaties of cession were ostensibly conducted according to protocol, they were often defective. Some treaties were held under coercion, leaders representing Indian Nations were, in certain instances such as the Treaty of New Echota with the Cherokees, not legitimate authorized representatives, Indian Nations sold each other's land, land changed occupants over the years resulting in duplicate purchases of the same tracts, boundaries were vaguely described before being surveyed, financial details were misrepresented and the language of crucial articles was often ambiguous and subject to differing interpretations.

## Letter To George Washington from Henry Knox, Secretary of War, February 22, 1791 concerning Frontier Operations

Secretary of War Knox submitted his plan for frontier operations to President Washington on February 22, 1791, which focused on convincing the Indians of the futility of resistance:

> The Secretary for the department of war, submits the following report to the President of the United States, upon the operations to be adopted for the ensuing year upon the frontiers. ... The first and most pressing demand on the government is, the restoration of peace, and the effectual protection of the frontier inhabitants, lying along the Ohio river, against the depredations of the Indians North west of the said river. ... The great object of the campaign

will be, to convince the Indians of the futility of resistance, and of the absolute necessity of submitting to the justice and mercy of the United States. ... That for this purpose, besides destroying their towns, and provisions, defeating their force, and capturing as many of them as possible, particularly their women and children, it will be necessary to establish a post at the Miami village, or, some other place in its vicinity which might be proper.[14]

Knox was also concerned with the potential for the Yazoo sales to disrupt relations with the southern Indians, as the treaties were being threatened with violation "by the measures pursuing by the three companies or associations of men, who have purchased the pre-emption of the greater part of the lands of the Choctaws, Chickasaws, and Cherokees, of the State of Georgia."[15]

## William Clark's Betrayal as Trusted Indian Agent

For 30 years after the U.S. Military Expedition, William Clark ranked as the leading federal official in the west, the point man for six Presidents, from Jefferson to Van Buren, who trusted him with protecting American interests on territory, bitterly contested by Britain and Spain under the doctrine of discovery. At the same time, Clark was also the one government agent that Indians thought they could trust. Along with overseeing Indians living on the Missouri and the Upper Mississippi Rivers, Clark negotiated treaties with the leaders of these 100,000 indigenous inhabitants. The alleged purpose was to keep peace between them and settler colonists on the borderlands. One of the first was with the Osage, the dominant Indian Nation on the Lower Missouri.

Clark regretted his participation in the Osage Treaty—the Osage never fought a war with the U.S. Yet in 1808 Clark forced on them a treaty that all but destroyed their culture.

In return for ceding 50,000 square miles of their prized hunting grounds—almost all of Missouri—thereby ruining their fur-based economy, the Osage were given $1,400 in gifts, an $1,800 annuity, the services of a blacksmith, some farm tools and the use of a gristmill. Osage land purchased by the government for 10 cents per square mile was later resold for $1 to $2 per acre. Even Clark came to regret the terms of the treaty. Ethan Allen Hitchcock said Clark told him "it was the hardest treaty on the Indians that he ever made, and that *if he was damned hereafter, it would be for making that treaty.*"[16] (Emphasis added.)

In 1831, Clark advocated for the removal of all the Indians in the State of Illinois to the west of the Mississippi. He argued for duplicity to be used to encourage removal, as follows:

> If they were informed that the State had the power from the General Government, or otherwise, to remove them, they would, in my opinion, go off, of their own accord, in peace.

The record is clear that under his direction Indian rights to millions of acres were extinguished on either side of the Mississippi resulting in the forced relocation of tens of thousands of Indians from their homes in the east and south to lands in Oklahoma and Kansas.

## Treaties with Huge Land Cessions

It was the destruction of Indian forces by Anthony Wayne in the Battle of Fallen Timbers of 1794, for example, that led to a treaty transferring, for a fee, most of Ohio and Indiana to the federal government. After the Creek War of 1814, Major General Andrew Jackson imposed a treaty on the defeated Creeks that ceded much of Georgia and Alabama, opening the door for the expansion of slave plantations in the Deep South. Discussing the removal of the Cherokees to Oklahoma from lands in the east, Stuart Banner remarks: The Seminoles would follow soon after—an inadequate description of a war that lasted from 1835 to 1842, in which some 1500 American soldiers and a similar number of Seminoles perished. James Gadsden wrote to the Secretary of War of the 1823 treaty with the Seminoles that "[i] t is not necessary to disguise the fact that the treaty effected was in a degree a treaty of imposition-The Indians would never have voluntarily assented to the terms had they not believed that we had both the power & disposition to compel obedience."[17]

Banner is quite correct to note that even after decisive military victories, Americans went through the charade of signing treaties that made the land transfers appear to be mutually agreed transactions. Between 1783–1814, millions of acres of Indian Nation lands were ceded in Georgia, the Mississippi Territory, Tennessee, Ohio and the Michigan Territory.

## Revenue from Public Land Sales

In 1825, receipts from public land sales amounted to but $1,216,090. They rose to $2,329,356 in 1830, then continued as follows:

| YEARS | ACRES SOLD | RECEIPTS |
|---|---|---|
| 1831 | 2,777,857 | $3,557,024 |
| 1832 | 2,462,342 | $3,115,376 |
| 1833 | 3,856,227 | $4,972,285 |
| 1834 | 4,658,219 | $6,099,981 |
| 1835 | 15,999,804 | $12,564,479 |
| 1836 | 25,167,833 | $20,074,871 |
| 1837 | 5,601,003 | $7,007,523 |

Thus, the big bulge occurred in 1835 and 1836. The land was paid for in "rag money," i.e., in bank notes that were in many cases irredeemable and worthless.[18]

## New York State Revenues from Indian Land Sales, 1790-95

New York asserted a monopsony power to purchase Indian lands. State leaders claimed their goal was to protect Indians from fraudulent purchases. In reality, the state became fiscally dependent on the profits made by procuring and selling Indian land. The state legislators and commissioners minimized what they paid to the Indians and maximized the lands extracted from them. *In 1834, the state's surveyor general, Simeon DeWitt, conceded that the state's pre-1829 Indian treaties "were conducted with a view to the benefit of the treasury."* In addition to the revenue generated by selling Indian lands, the state annually collected taxes on the farms and other properties established within the cessions.[19] (Emphasis added.)

The state's fiscal benefit peaked during the early to mid-1790s, when the state sold the Oneida lands procured by the 1788 Treaty of Fort Schuyler. From 1790 to 1795, nearly half the state's revenue came from selling land recently obtained from the Indians.

| | LAND SALES | PERCENTAGE | ALL OTHER REVENUE | PERCENTAGE |
|---|---|---|---|---|
| 1790 | $3,164 | 2.5% | $124,484 | 97.5% |
| 1791 | $123,878 | 48.3% | $132,552 | 51.7% |
| 1792 | $325,677 | 58.2% | $233,823 | 41.8% |
| 1793 | $224,172 | 56.7% | $170,877 | 43.3% |
| 1794 | $203,994 | 60.7% | $190,334 | 39.3% |
| 1795 | $142,849 | 46.8% | $162,169 | 30.3% |
| TOTALS | $1,113,734 | 52.3% | $1,014,239 | 47.7% |

During the six-year period, the state took in $13.94 in land revenue for every $1.00 it spent on surveys and Indian affairs (including purchases and annuities) combined, making for a net surplus of $1,040,447.

# Notes

1. Newmyer, R. Kent. *John Marshall and the Heroic Age of the Supreme Court*. LSU Press, 2007.

2. Kades, Eric. "The Dark Side of Efficiency: *Johnson v. M'Intosh* and the Expropriation of American Indian Lands." *University of Pennsylvania Law Review* 148.4 (2000): 1157.

3. "From Thomas Jefferson to William Carmichael, 18 August 1785," *Founders Online,* National Archives, https://founders.archives.gov/documents/Jefferson/01-08-02-0316. [Original source: *The Papers of Thomas Jefferson,* vol. 8, *25 February–31 October 1785*, ed. Julian P. Boyd. Princeton: Princeton University Press, 1953, pp. 401–402.] (accessed online December 10, 2020).

4. Northwest Ordinance, Act of Aug. 7, 1789, ch. 8, 1 Stat. 50, 52. https://avalon.law.yale.edu/18th_century/nworder.asp (accessed online December 10, 2020).

5. Kades, Eric. "The Dark Side of Efficiency: *Johnson v. M'Intosh* and the Expropriation of American Indian Lands." *University of Pennsylvania Law Review* 148.4 (2000): 1132.

6. "From George Washington to the Commissioners to the Southern Indians, 29 August 1789," *Founders Online,* National Archives, https://founders.archives.gov/documents/Washington/05-03-02-0326. [Original source: *The Papers of George Washington*, Presidential Series, vol. 3, *15 June 1789–5 September 1789*, ed. Dorothy Twohig. Charlottesville: University Press of Virginia, 1989, pp. 551–565.] (accessed online November 10, 2020).

7. "From James Madison to Thomas Jefferson, 10 January 1796,"

*Founders Online*, National Archives, https://founders.archives.gov/ documents/Madison/01-16-02-0103. [Original source: *The Papers of James Madison*, vol. 16, *27 April 1795–27 March 1797*, ed. J. C. A. Stagg, Thomas A. Mason, and Jeanne K. Sisson. Charlottesville: University Press of Virginia, 1989, pp. 180–183.] (accessed online November 10, 2020).

8. Banner, Stuart. *How the Indians lost their land: Law and power on the frontier*. Harvard University Press, 2005: 132.

9. The Papers of George Mason, https://www.consource.org/document/ george-mason-to-james-monroe-1792-2-9/ (accessed online November 21, 2020).

10. "Memorandum for Henry Dearborn on Indian Policy, 29 December 1802," *Founders Online*, National Archives, https://founders.archives. gov/documents/Jefferson/01-39-02-0208. [Original source: *The Papers of Thomas Jefferson*, vol. 39, *13 November 1802–3 March 1803*, ed. Barbara B. Oberg. Princeton: Princeton University Press, 2012, pp. 231–234.] (accessed online November 21, 2020).

11. Knepper, George W. *The official Ohio lands book*. Auditor of State, 2002.

12. https://studylib.net/doc/8080846/the-war-of-1812-from-the-native-american-perspective, p.18 (accessed online November 21, 2020).

13. Iron Will, Landon Y. Jones, Smithsonian Magazine, August 2002

https://www.smithsonianmag.com/history/iron-will-67312615/ (accessed online November 21, 2020).

14. "To George Washington from Henry Knox, 22 February 1791," *Founders Online*, National Archives, https://founders.archives.gov/ documents/Washington/05-07-02-0237. [Original source: *The Papers of George Washington,* Presidential Series, vol. 7, *1 December 1790–21 March 1791*, ed. Jack D. Warren, Jr. Charlottesville: University Press of Virginia, 1998, pp. 402–415.] (accessed online November 6, 2020).

15. Ibid.

16. Iron Will, Landon Y. Jones, Smithsonian Magazine, August 2002.

https://www.smithsonianmag.com/history/iron-will-67312615/ (accessed online November 21, 2020).

17. Letter from James Gadsden to the Secretary of War (Sept. 29, 1823).

18. Sakolski, Aaron M. "The Great American Land Bubble: The Amazing Story of Land-Grabbing, Speculations, and Booms from Colonial Days to the Present Time." (1932): 235.

19. Taylor, Alan. *The divided ground: Indians, settlers, and the northern borderland of the American Revolution.* Vintage, 2007: 201.

# 19

# LAND SPECULATION

Before a strong centralized government could be established, land speculators seized on the opportunity to grab more western lands. Historian Forrest McDonald wrote of the delegates to the Constitutional Convention in 1787:

> only eight can be identified as speculators on a grand scale. These were Washington, who owned scores of thousands of acres in all parts of the country; Robert Morris, who had begun the speculations that would see titles to several million acres pass through his hands before he would go bankrupt; Thomas Fitzsimons, who was to be Morris's partner in several ventures; Nathaniel Gorham, who in 1787 was negotiating a contract to buy, with a partner, a million acres of the land that Massachusetts owned in western New York; Jonathan Dayton of New Jersey, who had begun land operations that would ultimately run into hundreds of thousands of acres; Wilson, who operated on a somewhat smaller scale in Pennsylvania; Mason, who had acquired fifteen thousand acres in the upper Potomac region and another sixty thousand in Kentucky; and William Blount of North Carolina, who was in process of acquiring scores of thousands of acres in Tennessee."[1]

In a 1790 report to Congress, Alexander Hamilton highlighted the ongoing land speculation—the real estate investments of "[m]onied individuals and companies, who will buy to sell again," was "the major get-rich-quick activity" of the period, in which virtually all of the founders were engaged.[2]

The President was kept informed of purchases of Indian lands by large speculators.

> To George Washington from Secretary of State Thomas Jefferson, 27 March 1791:
>
> You knew of mister R. Morris's purchase of Gorham and Phelps of 1,300,000 acres of land of the state of Massachusets, at 5d. an acre, it is said that he has sold 1,200,000. acres of these in Europe...[3]

"Such is the rage for speculating in, and forestalling of Lands on the No. West side of the Ohio," George Washington complained in 1784, "that scarce a valuable spot within any tolerable distance of it, is left without a claimant. Men in these times, talk with as much facility of fifty, a hundred, and even 500,000 Acres as a Gentleman formerly would do of 100 acres."[4] This was land still occupied by the Indians. The only way to avoid war, Washington advised, was for the federal government to keep up with the settlers, and to "purchase, if possible, as much Land of them immediately back [i.e., west] of us, as would make one or two States."[5]

Even those in federal service under President Washington were drawn to land speculation on grand scales. Historian Jerry W. Markham wrote that Secretary of War Knox and William Duer "formed an association called the Eastern Land Associates to purchase large tracts of land. Knox and Duer acquired rights to some four million acres in Maine in 1791. Those holdings constituted most of the arable land there that was not already being farmed."[6]

American land syndicates knew the value European investors could add to their portfolios so many of them had 'ambassadors' in England and France seeking funding.

Historian Bernard Bailyn describes the frenetic activity:

> Everyone with any ambition and capacity, it seems, on both sides of the Atlantic, sought some profit from what promised to be the greatest land boom in history. Plans were drawn up, revised, expanded, abandoned; companies formed overnight, sometimes quickly disappeared, sometimes grew into syndicates; and connections between American and British groups were universal, conceived of as a requirement for ultimate success.[7]

In 1793, James Madison, then serving in the Second Continental Congress, revealed the intensity of this land speculation and related shady legislation to the Attorney General Edmund Randolph:

> In 1775 Virginia General Assembly passed legislation "for adjusting and settling the titles of claimers to unpatented lands under the present and former government" and for opening a land office. That office was empowered to issue assignable warrants for land to many varieties of past and future "claimers," including ... squatters who had gained or should gain pre-emption rights by living on and improving public land unencumbered by earlier private titles. ... By 1780 the patents, and especially the warrants issued by the Virginia land office, had become a source of constant speculation...[8]

Squatters were being rewarded by legislating granting them preemption rights for living on and improving public land.

## Federal Government's Effort to Understand its Right to Purchase Indian Lands: Right of Preemption

Given the pervasive land speculation, the new republic bandied about its understanding of Indian land rights and the state and federal government's right to purchase Indian land in official correspondence between the President, the Secretary of State, the Secretary of War and the Attorney General.

In a letter from Secretary of State Jefferson to Henry Knox, dated August 26, 1790, Jefferson first recognized the Cherokee's right to occupation of the lands guaranteed to them by treaty. Second, the state of North Carolina had a right sell to these lands to its citizens, subject to the U.S. obtaining the right of occupation from the Indians. The citizens right to the lands was inchoate and a fee simple title would not result until and unless the federal government secured the Indians right of occupation.

> The Cherokees were entitled to the sole occupation of the lands within the limits guaranteed to them. The state of N. Carolina, according to the jus gentium established for America by universal usage, had only a right of preemption of these lands against all

other nations. It could convey then to it's citizens only this right of preemption, and the right of occupation could not be united to it till obtained by the U.S. from the Cherokees.[9]

There were those concerned with private speculation on lands still claimed by Indians, but they were powerless to do anything about it, other than lament the affront to justice. Secretary of State Jefferson warned of possible Indian aggression in his letter to President Washington, dated April 1, 1791:

> It will be fortunate for the American public if private Speculations in the lands, still claimed by the Aborigines, do not aggravate those differences, which policy, humanity, and justice concur to deprecate.[10]

### Georgia Wants Indian Lands

An impoverished Georgia (founded by Britain as a penal colony) wanted to raise needed revenues by (1) encouraging immigration, promising land grants; (2) holding state lotteries for land grants; (3) controlling the gold mines in the state; (4) encouraging cotton production; and (5) settling ongoing disputes over prior corrupt land grants by the state. To accomplish what was already done, they needed land and the only way to get this land was to get rid of Indians living in Georgia.

As early as 1791, President Washington wrote in his Diary that Georgia settler colonists were willing to go to war on their own against the Indians:

> Was informed by Mr. Jno. Lewis, who had, not long since been in Richmond, that Mr. Patrick Henry had avowed his interest in the Yazoo company; and made him a tender of admission into it whh. he declined—but asking, if the Company did not expect the Settlement of the lands would be disagreeable to the Indians was answered by Mr. Henry that the Co. intended to apply to Congress for protection—which, if not granted they would have recourse to their own means to protect the settlement—That General Scott had a certain quantity of Land (I think 40,000 acres in the Company's grant, & was to have the command of the force which was to make

276

the establishment—and moreover that General Muhlenberg had offered £1000 for a certain part of the grant—the quantity I do not recollect if it was mentioned to me.[11]

Georgia's assertion that the Cherokees refusal to sell their land was the problem was decidedly opposed by Benjamin Hawkins, the federal government's emissary to the southern Indians, in a letter to George Washington, dated November 4, 1798:

> The Cherokees are no longer to be called Savages, they are a decent orderly set of people, who possess unbounded confidence in the Justice of our government, and are worthy of its continued attention.[12]

On the Georgia frontier, complained Benjamin Hawkins, "the doctrine" among settlers "was, let us kill the Indians, bring on a war, and we shall get land."[13] Timothy Pickering, Secretary of State, characterized the southern settlers as "the least worthy subjects in the United States ... They are little less savage than their tawny neighbors [Indians]."[14]

Under the Compact of 1802, the United States had paid Georgia $1.25 million for its western lands and agreed to extinguish as quickly as possible remaining Indian land claims within the state, when that could be done "peaceably" and "on reasonable terms:" The stipulation in their cession explains the purpose of the ceded claims to serve as a common fund for the country:

> § 33. ... all the lands in the ceded territory, not reserved, should be considered as a common fund, for the use and benefit of such of the United States as have become, or shall become, members of the confederation,' etc. 'according to their usual respective proportions in the general charge and expenditure, and shall be faithfully and bona fide disposed of for that purpose, and for no other use or purpose whatsoever.'[15]

Federal officials proved either unwilling or unable to extinguish these claims quickly enough for land-hungry Georgians. Angered over the delay in fulfilling the terms of the Compact, Georgia's leaders regularly prodded the federal government to complete the process of Indian removal. President Jefferson's Compact of 1802 directly contradicted the Washington era 1791 Treaty of Holston under which the United

States guaranteed the Cherokee Nation all of their lands not thereby ceded.

## The "Yazoo" Land

Georgia, following the Revolution, laid claim to the immense territory lying immediately to its west. The name "Yazoo" originally for the Yazoo River was applied to the whole territory, which comprised the entire areas of present-day Alabama and Mississippi. South Carolina, the federal government and Spain asserted competing claims. Spain claimed a part of the Yazoo lands as part of her 'discovery.' This resulted in continual sparring with the United States which served the U.S. military agenda of inculcating uncertainty and undermining Spain's presence in Florida.

The Chickasaws, Choctaws, Cherokees and Creeks inhabited the area as well. The United States had established a protectorate over them and forbade Georgia or any other state from dealing with them directly or taking any action to dispossess them. In view of these difficulties and uncertainty of title, the impoverished state was willing to accept any financial consideration for her doubtful claim and sought to dispose of these lands when a favorable opportunity presented itself.

In 1785, John Wood, one of the Yazoo land sales promoters, succeeded in 'purchasing' from the Choctaws a tract of two or three million acres lying near the mouth of the Yazoo River. The 'South Carolina Yazoo Company,' was formed to oversee the investment opportunities from this purchase. Among the shareholders was Alexander McGillivray, a famous chief of the Creek Nation. Three other companies presented petitions to the State to purchase it also. These were 'the Virginia Yazoo Company,' in which Patrick Henry is reputed to have been a participant; the 'Tennessee Yazoo Company' and the 'Georgia Yazoo Company.' Without much opposition or debate, an act was passed by the Georgia Legislature, with the sanction of the governor, on December 21, 1789, approving the grant. However, it later fell through.

278

## The Georgia Yazoo Land Sales (1795)

Another land scheme though was promptly promoted. On January 7, 1795, the Georgia state legislature passed a bill authorizing the sale of approximately 35 million acres of land in present-day Alabama and Mississippi to four land syndicates in the so-called "Great Yazoo Lands Sale" for $500,000. The largest transaction in this "Great Yazoo Lands Sale" was made with the Georgia Land Company, a land syndicate led by United States Senator James Dunn. Associate Justice Wilson was the largest single shareholder in this Company, having invested $25,000 in exchange for a claim to 750,000 acres. In August 1795, Wilson appears to have purchased the rights to another 1,000,000 acres of Yazoo land. The Yazoo land companies were also owned and controlled by many prominent Americans, including two U.S. Senators (James Gunn of Georgia and Robert Morris of Pennsylvania).[16] *Thus, approximately 30,000,000 acres, comprising the bulk of the States of Alabama and Mississippi, were sold for $500,000 or about a cent and a half an acre.*

Georgia did not guarantee title against other claimants, and disclaimed responsibility for the acts or the claims of the Indians. The Indian title was to be extinguished in each instance by the purchasers, with the approval of the federal government. The purchasers subsequently sold the land to third parties.

The Yazoo Land Sales generated controversy almost immediately. Edmund Randolph sent President Washington a copy of a letter from José de Jaudenes, Spanish commissioner to the United States, dated July 8, 1795. Jaudenes called the Yazoo purchase of lands in Georgia an illegal action concerning territory that belonged to the king of Spain and the Indians under Spanish protection.[17]

Critics maintained that the deal was characterized by bribery, corruption, and fraud—allegations that did not leave Justice Wilson unscathed. At least one journalist writing in the Philadelphia Aurora called for him to be impeached.

Writing to James Monroe from Philadelphia on March 27, 1795, James Madison informed him that Justice Wilson was reprobated by all parties:

> You will see from the proceedings in Georgia what a scene is opened there by a landjobbing Legislature. Wilson & Pendleton the fedl. Judges, tho' not named in the law are known adventurers.

The former is reprobated here by all parties. The two Senators Gun & Jackson are now pitted agst. each other, and the whole State is in convulsions. It is not improbable that attempts may be made to set aside the law, either as having some flaw, or by the paramount authority of a Convention wch. is to meet in the course of the summer.[18]

When James Madison was accused of being one of the speculators, he vehemently denied it in the following letter to his father:

The Report in Georgia relating to me is as absolute a falsehood as ever was propagated. So far am I from being concerned in the Yazoo transaction, that from the nature of it, as it has been understood by me, I have invariably considered it as one of the most disgraceful events that have appeared in our public Councils, and such is the opinion which I have ever expressed of it.[19]

## George McIntosh Troup—Strong Opponent of Yazoo Land Scandal

George McIntosh Troup served in the Georgia General Assembly, U.S. House of Representatives and U.S. Senate before becoming the 32nd Governor of Georgia and then returning to the U.S. Senate. Following the Yazoo land sale, he denounced it:

**Do not believe, sir, that the corruption in which this transaction was engendered, was a corruption of any ordinary character; it was a corruption without example in history; may it never find a parallel! Not merely were the corrupted corrupted by the corrupters—the corrupters cheated the corrupted-the corrupters cheated one another, and the corrupters, as they say, cheated these claimants. The members of the Legislature were bribed with land and money...[20]** (Emphasis added.)

## President Washington's Major Concern with Yazoo Sales— Possibility of Indian War

President Washington's major concern with the Yazoo sales was the possibility of an Indian war. Georgia was willing to go to war, with or without the United States, to get rid of the Indians in her state. Georgia felt the United States had failed to live up to its bargain to remove the Indians, promised in the Compact of 1802. While the United States removed Indians from neighboring states, Georgia thought it taunted its authority over Georgia in refusing to accomplish its bargain. President Washington hoped that the Yazoo sales would fall through to avoid being pulled into a dispute between state and federal authority in his newly formed administration.

> In Georgia, the dissatisfied part of them at the late treaty with the Ck. Indians were evidently Land Jobbers, who maugre every principle of Justice to the Indians, and policy to their Country, would, for their own immediate emolument, strip the Indns. of all their territory if they could obtain the least countenance to the measure; but it is to be hoped the good sense of the State will set its face agains such diabolical attempts. And it is also to be wished and by many it was said it might be expected-that the sales by the State to what are called the Yazoo Companies will fall through.[21]

The Confederation Congress issued a Proclamation on September 1, 1788, forbidding intrusions onto Cherokee lands guaranteed them under the Treaty of Hopewell. It also required settlers to depart from these lands. It had no effect whatsoever as the encroachments continued.[22]

On August 11, 1790, President Washington advised the Senate of this violation.[23] On August 26, 1790, he issued another Proclamation ordering the over 500 settler families living on Choctaw and Chicasaw (sic) lands to move.[24] Local newspapers reporting on the Proclamation also included Cherokee lands.

Reproaching the Georgians for ignoring the Creeks sovereignty and continuing to intrude on their lands, the English-speaking Creek leader John Galphin challenged their actions:

> You well know that no sovereignty was ceded to you ... We are now, as we always have been, an independent and free people;

knowing this ... we view with astonishment the steps taken by the United States to rob us of our rights.[25]

James Seagrove's reputation, as President Washington's ambassador to the Creek Nation, was blatantly attacked by land speculators in the Georgia legislature due to his opposition to the Yazoo sales. He wrote to President Washington in January 1795 that settlers were moving into the area and the General Agent of the South Carolina Yazoo Company, James O'Fallon, was threatening to use force to remove the Indians, regardless of President Washington's proclamation to citizens to abide by the Hopewell Treaty made with the Cherokees and Chickasaws.

> ...the "sanction of government ... was immaterial" to plans to settle the Yazoo lands because "many of the Gentlemen of Congress were concerned in the business. ... certain persons claiming under the said Companies are raising troops for the purpose of establishing, by force, one or more settlements on the lands belonging to the aforesaid indian nations."[26]

Congress needed to be informed of O'Fallon's actions and that Georgia's statutes in 1794 and 1795 purported to appropriate Indian lands to which Indian title had never been extinguished. **On February 17, 1795, President Washington sent a dire message to Congress regarding Georgia's statutes raising the specter of an Indian war or the possibility of a civil war if Georgia defied federal law.[27]**

President Washington also issued the following Proclamation on March 19, 1791:

> Whereas it hath been represented to me that James O'Fallon is levying an armed force in that part of the State of Virginia which is called Kentucky, disturbs the public peace, and sets at defiance the treaties of the United States with the Indian tribes ... it is my earnest desire that those who have incautiously associated themselves with the said James O'Fallon may be warned of their danger, I have therefore thought fit to publish this proclamation, hereby declaring that all persons violating the treaties and act aforesaid shall be prosecuted with the utmost rigor of the law.[28]

## Georgia's Right to Make Preemptive Right Sales

Thomas Jefferson, the Secretary of State, who was outspoken in his denunciation of land grabbing, was firm in his opinion to President Washington that Georgia could make preemptive sales, but could not grant the right to the purchasers to extinguish Indian title.

V.- Opinion upon the validity of a grant made by the State of Georgia to certain companies of individuals, of a tract of country whereof the Indian right had never been extinguished, with power to such individuals to extinguish the Indian right. May 3d, 1790.

The State of Georgia, having granted to certain individuals a tract of country, within their chartered limits, whereof the Indian right has never yet been acquired; *with a proviso in the grants, which implies that those individuals may take measures for extinguishing the Indian rights under the authority of that Government, it becomes a question how far this grant is good ? ... If the country, instead of being altogether vacant, is thinly occupied by another nation, the right of the native forms an exception to that of the new comers; that is to say, these will only have a right against all other nations except the natives. Consequently, they have the exclusive privilege of acquiring the native right by purchase or other just means. This is called the right of preemption,* and is become a principle of the law of nations, fundamental with respect to America. There are but two means of acquiring the native title. First, war; for even war may, sometimes, give a just title. Second, contracts or treaty. *The States of America before their present union possessed completely, each within its own limits, the exclusive right to use these two means of acquiring the native title, and, by their act of union, they have as completely ceded both to the general government. ... She could convey to them the exclusive right to acquire; but she could not convey what she had not herself, that is, the means of acquiring. ... Perhaps it might not be superfluous to send some person to the Indians interested, to explain to them the views of government, and to watch with their aid the territory in question.*[29] (Emphasis added.)

**While President Washington was concerned about the Yazoo sales and his authority to take action against the purchasers, Attorney General Edmund Randolph, advised him in an opinion dated September 12, 1791, that he had no statutory authority to do anything**. This legal analysis also applied to the state of New York and other states which were still making purchases of Indian lands on their own authority, without federal approval and without regard to the preemptive right of the federal government. Such purchases were void, but the President could not punish the speculators as it suffered no harm.

> The question is, whether any punishment can be inflicted on persons, treating with the Indian tribes, within the limits of the United States, for lands, lying within those limits; the preemption of which is vested in the United States?
>
> The constitution is the basis of federal power. This power, so far as the subject of Indians is concerned, relates:
>
> 1. To the regulation of commerce with the Indian tribes.
>
> 2. To the exclusive right of making treaties.
>
> 3. To the right of preemption in lands.
>
> It may be indecent and impertinent for a citizen thus to behave. But where no law is, no crime is.
>
> As to the right of preemption. No man has a right to purchase my land from my tenant. But if he does purchase, I cannot sue him on the supposition of damages, arising from the mere act of purchase. Nor could the United States sue the purchaser of the right of preemption, since the purchase itself is void, and their interest cannot be prejudiced by any purchase, which an individual can make. Far less would the purchaser be indictable.
>
> ...It may perhaps be proper, if the testimony be strong, to warn all persons by proclamation, that the rights of government will be inforced; and possibly a monitory message to the Indians might have a good effect.[30]

Congress corrected the oversight in the Trade and Intercourse Act by making the unauthorized purchase of Indian land a misdemeanor punishable by up to a year in prison.

## Georgia Legislature Rescinded Yazoo Land Sales in 1796

The Georgia legislature subsequently rescinded the Yazoo land sales in 1796 on the basis of fraud, an act which itself triggered controversy and, eventually, multiple lawsuits. "Yazoo" and its perceived culture of corruption continued to be a hotly contested political issue until 1810, when the matter was brought before the U.S. Supreme Court.

Notes

1. The Founders and the Pursuit of Land. https://lehrmaninstitute.org/history/founders-land.html (accessed online November 10, 2020).

2. "From Alexander Hamilton to George Washington, [8 July 1790]," *Founders Online,* National Archives, https://founders.archives.gov/documents/Hamilton/01-06-02-0388. [Original source: *The Papers of Alexander Hamilton*, vol. 6, *December 1789–August 1790*, ed. Harold C. Syrett. New York: Columbia University Press, 1962, pp. 484–486.] (accessed online November 10, 2020).

3. "To George Washington from Thomas Jefferson, 27 March 1791," *Founders Online*, National Archives, https://founders.archives.gov/documents/Washington/05-08-02-0009. [Original source: *The Papers of George Washington,* Presidential Series, vol. 8, *22 March 1791–22 September 1791*, ed. Mark A. Mastromarino. Charlottesville: University Press of Virginia, 1999, pp. 12–14.] (accessed online November 10, 2020).

4. "From George Washington to Jacob Read, 3 November 1784," *Founders Online*, National Archives, https://founders.archives.gov/documents/Washington/04-02-02-0105. [Original source: *The Papers of George Washington,* Confederation Series, vol. 2, *18 July 1784–18 May 1785*, ed. W. W. Abbot. Charlottesville: University Press of Virginia, 1992, pp. 118–123.] (accessed online November 10, 2020).

5. Ibid.

6. Markham, Jerry W. *A Financial History of the United States: From*

*Christopher Columbus to the Robber Barons (1492-1900)*. Vol. 1. ME Sharpe, 2002: 103.

7. Bailyn, Bernard. *Voyagers to the West: A Passage in the Peopling of America on the Eve of the Revolution*. Vintage, 2011: 23.

8. "From James Madison to Edmund Randolph, 8 September 1783," *Founders Online*, National Archives, https://founders.archives.gov/ documents/Madison/01-07-02-0172. [Original source: *The Papers of James Madison*, vol. 7, 3 *May 1783–20 February 1784*, ed. William T. Hutchinson and William M. E. Rachal. Chicago: The University of University of Chicago Press, 1971, pp. 307–310.] (accessed online November 10, 2020).

9. "From Thomas Jefferson to Henry Knox, 26 August 1790," *Founders Online,* National Archives, https://founders.archives.gov/ documents/Jefferson/01-17-02-0125. [Original source: *The Papers of Thomas Jefferson*, vol. 17, *6 July–3 November 1790*, ed. Julian P. Boyd. Princeton: Princeton University Press, 1965, pp. 430–431.] (accessed online November 21, 2020).

10. "From George Washington to Thomas Jefferson, 1 April 1791," *Founders Online,* National Archives, https://founders.archives. gov/documents/Washington/05-08-02-0025. [Original source: *The Papers of George Washington*, Presidential Series, vol. 8, *22 March 1791–22 September 1791*, ed. Mark A. Mastromarino. Charlottesville: University Press of Virginia, 1999, pp. 35–36.] (accessed online November 10, 2020).

11. "[Diary entry: 9 April 1791]," *Founders Online*, National Archives, https://founders.archives.gov/documents/ Washington/01-06-02-0002-0003-0003. [Original source: *The Diaries of George Washington*, vol. 6, *1 January 1790–13 December 1799*, ed. Donald Jackson and Dorothy Twohig. Charlottesville: University Press of Virginia, 1979, pp. 107–108.] (accessed online November 10, 2020).

12. "To George Washington from Benjamin Hawkins, 4 November 1798," *Founders Online*, National Archives, https://founders.archives. gov/documents/Washington/06-03-02-0125. [Original source: *The Papers of George Washington, Retirement Series,* vol. 3, *16 September*

*1798–19 April 1799*, ed. W. W. Abbot and Edward G. Lengel. Charlottesville: University Press of Virginia, 1999, pp. 177–178.] (accessed online November 10, 2020).

13. Hawkins, Benjamin. *Letters of Benjamin Hawkins, 1796-1806*. Vol. 9. Georgia Historical Society, 1916.

14. "To George Washington from Timothy Pickering, 19 May 1778," *Founders Online*, National Archives, https://founders.archives.gov/documents/Washington/03-15-02-0162. [Original source: *The Papers of George Washington*, Revolutionary War Series, vol. 15, *May–June 1778*, ed. Edward G. Lengel. Charlottesville: University of Virginia Press, 2006, pp. 163–166.] (accessed online November 10, 2020).

15. Story, Joseph. *Commentaries on the Constitution of the United States*. 1873, Vol. 1, Chapter 1, § 33.

16. Mikhail, John. "James Wilson, Early American Land Companies, and the Original Meaning of Ex Post Facto Law." *Geo. JL & Pub. Pol'y* 17 (2019): 79, 127.

17. "To George Washington from Edmund Randolph, 10 July 1795," *Founders Online*, National Archives, https://founders.archives.gov/documents/Washington/05-18-02-0240. [Original source: *The Papers of George Washington*, Presidential Series, vol. 18, *1 April–30 September 1795*, ed. Carol S. Ebel. Charlottesville: University of Virginia Press, 2015, pp. 306–307.] (accessed online November 10, 2020).

18. "From James Madison to James Monroe, 27 March 1795," *Founders Online*, National Archives, https://founders.archives.gov/documents/Madison/01-15-02-0409 (accessed online November 10, 2020).

19. "From James Madison to James Madison, Sr., 2 July 1791," *Founders Online*, National Archives, https://founders.archives.gov/documents/Madison/01-14-02-0032. [Original source: *The Papers of James Madison*, vol. 14, *6 April 1791–16 March 1793*, ed. Robert A. Rutland and Thomas A. Mason. Charlottesville: University Press of Virginia, 1983, pp. 40–41.] (accessed online November 10, 2020).

20. Harden, Edward J. *The Life of George M. Troup*. 1859: 70.

21. "[June 1791]," *Founders Online,* National Archives, https://
founders.archives.gov/documents/Washington/01-06-02-0002-0005.
[Original source: *The Diaries of George Washington,* vol. 6, *1 January
1790–13 December 1799,* ed. Donald Jackson and Dorothy Twohig.
Charlottesville: University Press of Virginia, 1979, pp. 153–167.]
(accessed online December 10, 2020).

22. Worthington Chauncey Ford et al., eds. *Journals of the Continental
Congress, 1774-1789.* 34 vols. Washington, D.C., 1904–37: Vol 34:
476–78.

23. "From George Washington to the United States Senate, 11 August
1790," *Founders Online,* National Archives, https://founders.archives.
gov/documents/Washington/05-06-02-0114. [Original source: *The
Papers of George Washington,* Presidential Series, vol. 6, *1 July
1790–30 November 1790,* ed. Mark A. Mastromarino. Charlottesville:
University Press of Virginia, 1996, pp. 237–239.] (accessed online
November 10, 2020).

24. "Proclamation, 26 August 1790," *Founders Online,*
National Archives, https://founders.archives.gov/documents/
Washington/05-06-02-0159. [Original source: *The Papers of George
Washington,* Presidential Series, vol. 6, *1 July 1790–30 November
1790,* ed. Mark A. Mastromarino. Charlottesville: University Press of
Virginia, 1996, p. 342.] (accessed online November 10, 2020).

25. Ablavsky, Gregory. "Species of Sovereignty: Native Nationhood,
the United States, and International Law, 1783–1795." *Journal of
American History* 106.3 (2019): 591, 598.

26. "To George Washington from James Seagrove, 13 January 1795,"
*Founders Online,* National Archives, https://founders.archives.gov/
documents/Washington/05-17-02-0264. [Original source: *The Papers
of George Washington,* Presidential Series, vol. 17, *1 October 1794–31
March 1795,* ed. David R. Hoth and Carol S. Ebel. Charlottesville:
University of Virginia Press, 2013, pp. 391–402.] (accessed online
November 10, 2020).

27. "From George Washington to the U.S. Senate and House
of Representatives, 17 February 1795," *Founders Online,*
National Archives, https://founders.archives.gov/documents/

Washington/05-17-02-0361. [Original source: *The Papers of George Washington,* Presidential Series, vol. 17, *1 October 1794–31 March 1795,* ed. David R. Hoth and Carol S. Ebel. Charlottesville: University of Virginia Press, 2013, pp. 539–540.] (accessed online November 10, 2020).

28. "Proclamation, 19 March 1791," *Founders Online,* National Archives, https://founders.archives.gov/documents/ Washington/05-07-02-0343. [Original source: *The Papers of George Washington,* Presidential Series, vol. 7, *1 December 1790–21 March 1791,* ed. Jack D. Warren, Jr. Charlottesville: University Press of Virginia, 1998, pp. 605–606.] (accessed online November 10, 2020).

29. "To George Washington from Thomas Jefferson, 3 May 1790," *Founders Online,* National Archives, https://founders.archives. gov/documents/Washington/05-05-02-0241. [Original source: *The Papers of George Washington, Presidential Series,* vol. 5, *16 January 1790–30 June 1790,* ed. Dorothy Twohig, Mark A. Mastromarino, and Jack D. Warren. Charlottesville:University Press of Virginia, 1996, pp. 379–381.] (accessed online November 10, 2020).

30. "To George Washington from Edmund Randolph, 12 September 1791," *Founders Online,* National Archives, https://founders. archives.gov/documents/Washington/05-08-02-0367 (accessed online November 10, 2020).

# 20

# INDIAN LAND TENURE 1790, 1795 CONGRESSIONAL DEBATES

## U.S. House of Representatives Debate, 1790: Trade and Intercourse Act Raises Issue of Indian Land Tenure

When the House of Representatives was debating the bill that would become the Trade and Intercourse Act of 1790[1] the issue of Indian land ownership surfaced. The Act's purpose was to prohibit Indian Nations from trading or selling their lands to anyone other than the United States. The bill included a clause to enforce a ban on surveying Indian land not yet purchased from them, with a forfeiture of such land by any person holding a preemption right conducting a survey on such land. A vigorous debate ensued on the nature of Indian land tenure. Certain representatives introduced the idea that Indians did not hold fee simple title to their land.

According to Congressman James Hillhouse from Connecticut who took the traditional legal view of Indian property rights, *Indians held "the fee simple of the lands:"*

> Indeed, the right and title to the lands had been expressly recognised by the United States in the Treaties they had made with them. The God of Nature had given them the land. If the Indians were not the fee simple owners of their land, Hillhouse asked, then "who were the proprietors of this country previous to its being known to civilized nations (as they were called)? Were not those people?" And if the Indians had been the fee simple owners before European contact, "who gave us a right to call their title

in question, or forcibly to thrust them out?" They had, he said, suffered enough from the fraud and violence of those who, since the discovery of America, had been seeking to dispossess them of their lands. *The Indians, he concluded, must still own their land in fee simple. A preemption right is not a title, but a right only of becoming, in preference to all others, owners of the land, by some future grant or cession to be made by the Indians, who are the present proprietors.*[2] (Emphasis in original quote.)

Thus, Congressman Hillhouse challenged the occupancy theory of Indian land title based on (i) prior recognition of Indian land ownership by Indians based on U.S. treaties entered into with them for cession of lands; (ii) they were the first proprietors of the land; (iii) there was no legal basis for challenging their fee simple title; (iv) there was no law approving the use of force to remove them; and (v) the preemptive right to purchase their lands was an inchoate right.

Similarly, Representative William Cooper (NC), a merchant, land speculator and developer, observed that *"the idea advanced by the gentleman from North Carolina, that Indian nations could not hold the fee of the countries they possess, was new." Not only was it new, Cooper continued, it was "contrary to natural justice."*[3] (Emphasis added.)

Representative James Madison of Virginia addressed his concern that Indians not be able to cede their lands to foreigners. He did not think it necessary to inquire into Indian land tenure, other than to prevent sales of their lands to foreigners.

> Mr. Madison said it was not necessary to investigate the Indian mode of occupancy in opposition to that of civilized society. The natives are understood by the nations of Europe possessing territories on this continent, to have a qualified property only in the land. If they had an unqualified title they could not be prevented from ceding to foreigners their lands lying within the limits of the United States.[4]

**U.S. House of Representatives Supporters of European Sovereign Ownership of Indian Land as a Result of 'Discovery'**

Representative James Holland (North Carolina) argued that the Indians were not and never had been the fee simple owners of their land. "All titles to the soil were originally in the King," Representative Holland declared. "The savages of these Provinces, when under the British Government, were considered a conquered people, and tenants at will." *Tenants at will* was (and still is) the legal term for tenants who could be evicted by the land's owner at any time, without cause. The Indians held their land by "right of occupancy," Representative Holland continued; theirs was "not the dignity of a fee simple."[5]

According to Representative Holland, North Carolina had succeeded to the Crown's landholdings within the state's borders, with the victory of the confederated states in the American Revolution. It was thus the state, not the Indians, that held the fee simple to the Indian land in North Carolina. The Indians were merely 'tenants at will, and not tenants in possession of a fee simple estate.'[6] His purported legal basis was (i) title to the soil was originally in the King; (ii) the Indians were savages; and (iii) they had been conquered.

The debate on the floor of the House captures a frightening moment in a process of change, in which Indian land ownership would morph from a fee simple into a mere right of occupancy.

**Refuting Claim One: Title to Indian Land Was in the King**

In response to Representative Holland's first claim that title to the soil was in the King, the colonists did not uniformly agree that title to the soil was in the King. Some considered the idea as imaginary or delusionary.

John Burk, a historian, speaking of the London Company and the nature of its government, summarizes its dealings with the Indians as follows:

> At the coming of the English, the Indians naturally enjoyed the best and most convenient stations for fishing, and the most fertile lands: But in proportion as new settlers came in, they rapidly lost those advantages. In some cases the colonists claimed by the right of conquest, and the ***imaginary title conferred by the king's***

*charter*. In general however, they acted on better principles, and purchased from the heads of tribes, the right of soil, in a fair and (as far as was practicable) in a legal manner.[7] (Emphasis added.)

From available documentation, Indian land ownership in the colonial period evidences the transfer of fee simple title and references Indian Nations as "owners," or "proprietors," or "possessors" of their land.

## Refuting Claim Two: Indians Were Savages

With reference to Representative Holland's claim that Indians were savages and thereby may not be entitled to their land, William Crashaw, in a 1609 sermon, preached that the Virginia colonists must "take nothing from the Savages by power nor pillage, by craft nor violence, neither goods, lands nor libertie."[8]

## Refuting Claim Three: Indians Were Conquered

The U.S. did not act as a conqueror by abolishing their governments and subjugating them. Instead it ended hostilities by treaties. In a Senate Congressional debate, Senator Huntington distinguished between conquest and peace.

...if there ever was a right by conquest, it is very clear that it was surrendered by the crown, in the treaties which were made with them. In these compacts, the Indians were regarded as possessing the power to make them; they were treated as lawful and necessary parties to them; their claim to territory was acknowledged; boundaries were fixed; and pledges given that no interruption no interference with their respective territorial limits as settled by these treaties, should be allowed.[9]

Senator Frelinghuysen stated the following:

Here, again, we discover the same magnanimous policy of renouncing any pretended rights of a conqueror in our negotiations with the allies of our enemy. We invite them to peace; we engage to become their protectors...[10]

## Other Representatives Claim Indians Have Only Right of Occupancy

Representative John Milledge, who would later serve as Governor of Georgia, supported Representative Holland. As Governor, he created Georgia's first land lottery. He also reorganized the state militia and built a road from Georgia to Tennessee passing through Cherokee lands. Maryland's Representative Jeremiah Crabb of Maryland also sided with Representative Holland: Recipients of grants to Indian land "had nothing more than an unextinguished preemptive right,"[11] he urged, not a fee simple title. Representative William Lyman of Massachusetts also agreed with Representative Holland. "The Indians ought certainly to be treated with humanity," he suggested, but he "did not believe they had any real title to land." The land "was the property of the United States, which they were suffered to enjoy, but to which they had no real title."[12]

## Congressional Debate, 1795: Compensation to North Carolinian Purchasers of Indian Land on Parcels Subsequently Reserved to Indians

Indian land title came up in Congress again in January 1795. The House was debating whether to award compensation to North Carolinians who had purchased land from the State of North Carolina in the 1780s which was in an area that the federal government subsequently reserved to the Indians in the Treaty of Hopewell. Some North Carolinians had settled the land and begun farming, only to be evicted after the Treaty was signed.

Representative James Gillespie of North Carolina argued for compensating the citizens of his state:

> *"The Government of the United States has converted the property of the citizens of North Carolina to the uses of her Government"* and *"compensation ought to be made out of the public purse."*[13] (Emphasis added.)

Representative Elias Boudinot of New Jersey, though, objected to awarding compensation, on the ground that the claimants had not lost anything, because the state of North Carolina was never the owner of the land it had purported to grant them. "This claim of North Carolina to sell the lands was wrong," Representative Boudinot insisted.

"The Crown of Britain had never pretended to any right of this kind, nor ever thought it had a title to any lands till they were first purchased from the Indians. ... The Indian right of soil," he concluded, "had always been acknowledged." The Indians had been the land's owner all along.[14]

Members of Congress from North Carolina and from the other southern states voiced the occupancy view of Indian land rights predicated on the Indians inability to enjoy all of the land they held. "Much had been said about the Indian right" to their land, complained Representative John Nicholas of Virginia, but they had no such right. "It could never have been the design of nature that these people should be termed the possessors of land which they were incapable to enjoy."[15]

1. 1790 Nonintercourse Act, Trade and Intercourse Act of 1790, ch. 33, §4, 1 Stat. 137, 138 (codified as amended in part at 25 U.S.C . § 177 (2000)), asserted exclusive federal jurisdiction over Indian lands and prohibited state treaty-making to acquire Indian lands.

2. Annals of the Congress of the United States, Vol. 5, United States Congress, Gales and Seaton, 1849, p. 898.

3. Ibid., p. 897.

4. "Indian Intercourse Bill, [9 April] 1796," Founders Online, National Archives, https://founders.archives.gov/documents/ Madison/01-16-02-0200. [Original source: The Papers of James Madison, vol. 16, 27 April 1795–27 March 1797, ed. J. C. A. Stagg, Thomas A. Mason, and Jeanne K. Sisson. Charlottesville: University Press of Virginia, 1989, pp. 307–308.] (accessed online November 10, 2020).

5. Gales, Joseph. The Debates and Proceedings in the Congress of the United States: With an Appendix Containing Important State Papers and Public Documents, and All the Laws of a Public Nature. United States, Gales and Seaton, 1849, p. 895.

6. Ibid.

7. Burk, John Daly. "History of Virginia to Present Day." Petersburg, Va, Dickson and Pescud (1804), vol. I, p. 312 Appendix.

8. Banner, Stuart. How the Indians lost their land: Law and power on the frontier. Harvard University Press, 2005: 13.

9. Speeches of the Passage of the Bill for the Removal of the Indians,

Delivered in the Congress of the United States, April and May, 1830, Boston: Published by Perkins and Marvin. New York: Jonathan Leavitt. 1830, p. 192-193.

10. Speech of Mr. Frelinghuysen, of New Jersey, delivered in the Senate of the United States, April 6, 1830, on The Bill For An Exchange Of Lands With The Indians Residing In Any Of The States Or Territories And For Their Removal West Of The Mississippi, p. 11.

11. Annals of the Congress of the United States, Vol. 5, United States Congress, Gales and Seaton, 1849, p. 897.

12. Ibid., p. 900.

13. Ibid., p. 1150.

14. Ibid., p. 1152.

15. Ibid., p.1151.

# 21

# LOUISIANA PURCHASE (1803)

The Louisiana Purchase evidences the differences of opinion regarding 'discovery' and the extent of land related to same. Neither Spain, nor Britain, nor the United States agreed on the boundaries of the Louisiana Territory—what constituted the watershed of the Mississippi River and how far west it extended. Spain was too weak to go to war to defend its 'discovery' claim in the southwest.

When France sold Louisiana to the United States in 1803 it conveyed: "for ever and in full Sovereignty the said territory [Louisiana] with all its rights and appurtenances as fully and in the Same manner as they have been acquired by the French Republic in virtue of the above mentioned Treaty concluded with his Catholic Majesty."[1] (Treaty of San Ildefonso, 1800). France's Foreign Minister Talleyrand was deliberately vague and unhelpful about the boundaries: "You must take it as we received it."[2] Congress approved the purchase on October 31, 1803, and the U.S. took possession on December 20, 1803.

## President Jefferson's Draft on Amendment to the Constitution regarding Louisiana Purchase, 1803

Congress and President Jefferson, under whose presidency the Louisiana Purchase was completed, were unsure of the constitutionality of such a purchase. President Jefferson thought that it went beyond the constitutional powers of the government and required a constitutional amendment. He drafted two proposed amendments to clarify the constitutionality of the Purchase, but ultimately recognized that there was not enough time to implement a constitutional amendment given pressure by France for prompt action Accordingly, he fell back on political necessity to dispel his constitutional worries: "It will be desirable for Congress to do what is necessary in silence."[3]

President Jefferson's draft Amendment to the Constitution wasn't used, but it is critical to note the specific delineation of the 'rights of occupancy and self-government' proposed and the preemption authority as to Indian lands 'rightfully occupied by them' and other Indian policies contained in the Draft Amendment. Also, detailed are the vast assumptions of power by the United States.

## President Jefferson's Draft on an Amendment to the Constitution: 1803

II. Revised Amendment, [ca. 9 July 1803], Amendment to the Constitution to be added to Art. IV. section III.

> The Province of Louisiana is incorporated with the US. and made part thereof. the rights of occupancy in the soil, & of self-government, are confirmed to the Indian inhabitants, as they now exist. Preemption only of the portions rightfully occupied by them, and a succession to the occupancy of such as they may abandon, with the full rights of possession as well as of property & sovereignty in whatever is not rightfully occupied by them, or shall cease to be so, shall belong to the US.

> The legislature of the union shall have authority to exchange the right of occupancy in portions where the US. have full right, for lands possessed by Indians, within the US. on the East side of the Missisipi...[4]

After the Louisiana Purchase, President Jefferson examined everything that bore on the extent of Louisiana, its boundaries, the history of the various claims to it and the treaties relating to them. At the end of his study in 1802 he wrote a memorandum on 'An Examination into the Boundaries of Louisiana.' He wanted to assert a claim as far north as the 49th parallel so he was content to leave the extent of the northern boundary indefinite.[5]

President Jefferson sought input regarding the boundaries of the Louisiana Territory. There was limited geographical knowledge of North America, as well as confusion resulting from the competing territorial claims of the European powers.

From President Thomas Jefferson to Thomas Paine, Monticello, Aug. 10, 1803

The unquestioned extent of Louisania on the sea is from the Iberville to the Mexicana river, *or perhaps the high lands dividing that from the Missisipi.* it's original boundary however as determined by occupation of the French was Eastwardly to the river Perdido (between Mobile & Pensacola) & Westward to the Rio Norte or Bravo.[6]

In a similar effort in 1807, the Spanish viceroy in Mexico commissioned a scholar, Father Melchor Talamantes, "to compile a report on the boundaries" of Texas and Louisiana as they were before Louisiana was ceded to Spain in 1762. A Spanish manuscript map purported to describe the western borders of the Louisiana Territory.[7]

Nonetheless, President Jefferson would claim the Louisiana Territory encompassed New Orleans and the Gulf of Mexico northward through the plains into what is today part of Canada, and then from the Mississippi River west to the Rocky Mountains. This purchase more than doubled the area of the U.S., removed France entirely from North America and secured access to transport along the Mississippi River. It included what would later become all or part of 15 states and two Canadian provinces. As to the Indian Nations, he declared that the United States acquired the pre-emptive right to purchase their lands.

Due to the uncertainty of the Louisiana Territory's northern border, conflict between the United States and Canada flared into occasional violence from Maine to Oregon and along the Niagara Frontier. In addition, the uncertainty of land claims would create a morass of disputes as can be seen in a letter to President Jefferson from Isaac Briggs, September 8, 1803. President Jefferson had appointed Briggs as surveyor general of the Mississippi Territory in 1803.

It appears to me probable that not less than thirty millions of acres in the Territory of Louisiana will be hereafter claimed, under fraudulent, antedated Spanish Grants, issued since information has arrived here, of the cession of that Territory to the United States, and under privileges of pre-emption for surveys made since the knowledge of that event. ... Specifically, "a vast number of Adventurers" were surveying large quantities of land on the west side of the Mississippi River, which Spanish officers were claiming and disposing of at prices as low as ten cents per acre.[8]

The United States would challenge many of the Spanish land grants in the area. To do this, Congress appointed commissioners to determine the validity of Louisiana land titles. They required every holder of real estate allegedly obtained under Spanish and French dominion to prove ownership of their properties. Alexander Hamilton resigned from a Commission established to investigate these claims because it was so plagued with corruption. Corruption and fraud, threats and violence, suits and countersuits, characterized the proceedings throughout. It took over thirty years to complete. Of course, Indian land ownership was not discussed at all.

## Immediately After Louisiana Purchase, President Jefferson Commences Plan to Remove Eastern Indians to Land West of Mississippi River

President Jefferson's plans to remove Indians west of the Mississippi was discussed by him with many of his colleagues.

## To President Thomas Jefferson from Horatio Gates, 18 July 1803 (Gates–U.S. General)

*Your Idea of removing all the Indians on this, to the other side the Mississipi; is Excellent*: it will in great Measure prevent all Future Animosity with Them, restrict our own People to the East side, & add very considerably to the Furr Trade down the River.[9] (Emphasis added.)

Similarly, in another letter, he hoped the Louisiana Territory would offer the opportunity to get the Indians east of the Mississippi to cede their lands to the United States.

**From President Thomas Jefferson to Daniel D'Oyley, 14 August 1803** (From 1799 to 1804, D'Oyley served as state treasurer of the lower division of South Carolina).

> I particularly hope it will be made the means of inducing our Indians to cede their country on this side for an equivalent on the other.[10]

**From President Thomas Jefferson to John Milledge (Governor of Georgia, 1802-1806), November 22, 1803**

> ... the acquisition of Louisiana will it is hoped put in our power the means of inducing all the Indians on this side to transplant themselves to the other side the Missisipi, before many years get about.[11]

**To President Thomas Jefferson from James Jackson (Governor of Georgia in 1798), March 26, 1804**

> The Louisiana Government Bill authorized the president to exchange Indians' land east of the Mississippi River for western lands to be held under the protection of the United States. The law was to commence on 1 Oct. (U.S. Statutes at Large, 2:283-9; Vol. 42:34-5n).[12]

**To President Thomas Jefferson from William Henry Harrison, 12 May 1804**

> I observe by the law providing for the Government of Louisiana that it is in contemplation to exchange with the Indians lands in that province for their possessions to the east of the Mississippi—

If the measure is intended to be effected in the Course of this year I take the liberty to suggest that no time ought to be lost in commencing the negotiation. The Indians are remarkable for deliberation in all their Councils & they are still more so when ever the subject before them relates to their lands.[13]

## From President Jefferson to William C. C. Claiborne (Mississippi Territorial Governor), 7 July 1804

We are in hourly expectation of the arrival of some Osage chiefs, with whom we expect to make arrangements not only favorable to our peace and commerce on the West side of the Misipi, but also preparatory to the plan of inducing the Indians on this, to remove to the other side of that river.[14]

## Federal Government Failed to Consider Indians Already Living West of Mississippi

President Jefferson showed his correct understanding of preemption when he wrote the Senate in 1808 that it was now time for the United States to buy the lands west of the Mississippi River from the "native proprietors." He knew what the United States had bought from France—the right of preemption to Indian land.[15]

**Numerous Indian nations, including the Arapaho, Arikara, Assiniboine, Blackfoot, Cheyenne, Crow, Gros Ventre, Hidatsa, Iowa, Kansa, Mandan, Missouria, Omaha, Osage, Otoe, Pawnee, Ponca, and Sioux nations, inhabited the region as independent political entities.[16] The federal government failed to consider their rights or how the westward removal of eastern Indians would impact the balance of power and economies among the various Indian Nations.**

The ancestral home of the Osage was part of the immense Louisiana Purchase that the United States acquired in 1803. They ended up having to cede their lands in Missouri, Arkansas, Kansas and Oklahoma.

Though the circumstances of each Indian Nation's removal westward after the Louisiana Purchase would vary, those who inhabited its territory in the years from 1803 to 1835 found themselves not only living on coveted land, but on borrowed time as well. "The land we now live on belonged to our forefathers," said Heckaton, the Quapaws' leader. "The lands you wish us to go to belong to strangers. Have mercy -- send us not there."[17] The Quapaw were removed in 1826. They tried to return and were assigned lands along the Red River, which repeatedly flooded their crops. The territorial governor urged federal pity for the Quapaw. A treaty ratified in 1834 granted them land in what is now Oklahoma.

In a letter from William Clark to President Madison, the turmoil of moving west of the Mississippi for the Shawnees is detailed:

> They had been unable to find peace east of the Mississippi, and so they migrated west looking for answers, yet still hopeful that the U.S. government would fulfill promises that it had made previously to designate a specific territory west of the Mississippi for the Shawnee people where they could live unmolested. The chiefs lamented, "Where is the land we can say to our band, build your houses strong, make your fences high, and raise a plenty of cows & hogs, our great father, will protect us in our possessions? We know of no such land." They also spoke of their economic struggles, noting that the "Buffaloes & Elk is drove off to a great distance & Deer is getting scarce." ... The request was granted, and a few years later, Clark reported that about 1,300 Shawnees were living in three distinct towns in Missouri.[18]

Notes

1. https://www.archives.gov/exhibits/american_originals/louistxt.html (accessed online November 4, 2020).

2. https://lehrmaninstitute.org/history/louisiana-purchase.html (accessed online November 4, 2020).

3. "II. Revised Amendment, ca. 9 July 1803," *Founders Online*, National Archives, https://founders.archives.gov/documents/ Jefferson/01-40-02-0523-0003. [Original source: *The Papers of Thomas Jefferson*, vol. 40, *4 March–10 July 1803,* ed. Barbara B. Oberg. Princeton: Princeton University Press, 2013, pp. 686–688.] (accessed online November 9, 2020).

4. Ibid.

5. Jefferson, Thomas. "The Limits and Bounds of Louisiana", in Saul K. Padover, ed., The Complete Jefferson (1943, reprinted Freeport, NY, 1969), pp. 259-261.

6. "From Thomas Jefferson to Thomas Paine, 10 August 1803," *Founders Online*, National Archives, https://founders.archives.gov/ documents/Jefferson/01-41-02-0132. [Original source: *The Papers of Thomas Jefferson*, vol. 41, *11 July–15 November 1803*, ed. Barbara B. Oberg. Princeton: Princeton University Press, 2014, pp. 175–177.] (accessed online November 9, 2020).

7. https://blogs.loc.gov/maps/2016/02/rare-spanish-manuscript-map/ #:~:text=In%201807%2C%20the%20Spanish%20viceroy,ceded%20 to%20Spain%20in%201762 (accessed online November 4, 2020).

8. "To Thomas Jefferson from Isaac Briggs, 8 September 1803," *Founders Online*, National Archives, https://founders.archives.gov/

documents/Jefferson/01-41-02-0258. [Original source: *The Papers of Thomas Jefferson*, vol. 41, *11 July–15 November 1803*, ed. Barbara B. Oberg. Princeton: Princeton University Press, 2014, pp. 349–351.] (accessed online November 9, 2020).

9. "To Thomas Jefferson from Horatio Gates, 18 July 1803," *Founders Online*, National Archives, https://founders.archives.gov/documents/Jefferson/01-41-02-0057. [Original source: *The Papers of Thomas Jefferson*, vol. 41, *11 July–15 November 1803*, ed. Barbara B. Oberg. Princeton: Princeton University Press, 2014, pp. 87–88.] (accessed online November 9, 2020).

10. "From Thomas Jefferson to Daniel D'Oyley, 14 August 1803," *Founders Online*, National Archives, https://founders.archives.gov/documents/Jefferson/01-41-02-0151. [Original source: *The Papers of Thomas Jefferson*, vol. 41, *11 July–15 November 1803*, ed. Barbara B. Oberg. Princeton: Princeton University Press, 2014, pp. 199–200.] (accessed online November 9, 2020).

11. "From Thomas Jefferson to John Milledge, 22 November 1803," *Founders Online,* National Archives, https://founders.archives.gov/documents/Jefferson/01-42-02-0025. [Original source: *The Papers of Thomas Jefferson*, vol. 42, *16 November 1803–10 March 1804*, ed. James P. McClure. Princeton: Princeton University Press, 2016, pp. 29–30.] (accessed online November 9, 2020).

12. "To Thomas Jefferson from James Jackson, 26 March 1804," *Founders Online,* National Archives, https://founders.archives.gov/documents/Jefferson/01-43-02-0093. [Original source: *The Papers of Thomas Jefferson*, vol. 43, *11 March–30 June 1804*, ed. James P. McClure. Princeton: Princeton University Press, 2017, pp. 99–100.] (accessed online November 9, 2020).

13. "To Thomas Jefferson from William Henry Harrison, 28 May 1804," *Founders Online,* National Archives, https://founders.archives.gov/documents/Jefferson/01-43-02-0388. [Original source: *The Papers of Thomas Jefferson*, vol. 43, *11 March–30 June 1804*, ed. James P. McClure. Princeton: Princeton University Press, 2017, pp. 500–501.] (accessed online November 9, 2020).

14. "From Thomas Jefferson to William C. C. Claiborne, 7 July 1804,"

*Founders Online,* National Archives, https://founders.archives.gov/documents/Jefferson/99-01-02-0038 (accessed online November 9, 2020).

15. "From Thomas Jefferson to United States Senate, 15 January 1808," *Founders Online*, National Archives, https://founders.archives.gov/documents/Jefferson/99-01-02-7211 (accessed online November 9, 2020).

16. Carlson, Keith Thor. "Handbook of North American Indians, Volume 13, Plains, edited by Raymond J. DeMallie." *Canadian Journal of History* 37.2 (2002): 416-418.

17. 1803 Louisiana Purchase Sealed, Dismal Fate for Tribes in Arkansas, Jim Taylor, Arkansas Department of Parks and Tourism, https://www.arkansas.com/1803-louisiana-purchase-sealed-dismal-fate-tribes-arkansas (accessed online November 4, 2020).

18. Memorial of Chothe or Ohothe [aka James Rogers] and Noma [aka Fish], in Clark to Madison, April 1811, Letters Received by the Secretary of War Relating to Indian Affairs, Roll #1.

# 22

## U.S. MILITARY EXPEDITIONS

In spite of the doctrine of discovery, the boundary of the Louisiana Purchase on its southwestern side was vague in terms of where the Americans and where the Spaniards would draw a line between their respective imperial reaches. It was equally as vague as the boundary in the northwest between the British and the United States. Spain and the United States created a commission to determine the boundary between Louisiana and New Spain. Spanish administrators in Texas were already agitated about the boundary dispute.

Due to the lack of knowledge of the west, President Jefferson authorized exploratory military expeditions during his administration which included: Lewis and Clark to the Northwest Territory and California (1803–1806), Freeman and Custis to the Red River (1806), Hunter and Dunbar to the mouths of the Arkansas and Red Rivers (1804–1805), and Lt. Zebulon Pike to the Rockies (1805–1807). He used these expeditions to bolster 'discovery' claims to these areas and to conduct military reconnaissance regarding Indians.

### President Jefferson's concerns with Spanish Presence in West

President Jefferson resented Spanish interference with Indians in Florida and the west. He viewed it as a threat to the United States' military dominance and westward expansion. The Spanish treaties with the strong southeastern Indian Nations, most notably the Creek and Choctaw, impaired Indian negotiations with the U.S. In 1785, Spain's treaty with the Comanche, who controlled nearly one thousand miles of territory considered by the Spanish to be within their borderlands, aided the Comanche in sustaining their dominance over other Indians.

Following the Mexican Revolution in 1820, the new Mexican government immediately began making treaties with Indian Nations who resided primarily in the area later settled by the United States and continued to do so until the 1870s. The Texas Band of Comanches and Mexican government's Treaties of 1822, 1826 and 1834 played on settler fears living in Texas.

Spain was intent on maintaining a buffer between the United States and its most valuable colony, Mexico. The Spanish government was dependent on the production of Spanish silver mines in Mexico which accounted for half the export trade of the entire Spanish empire. Louisiana was that buffer and Spain did not plan to loosen its grip over its Indian allies.

President Jefferson inherited this fear of Spain's border presence from former President Washington who thought the western settlers could easily choose to be part of the southwest Spanish empire: "The Western settlers, (I speak now from my own observation) stand as it were upon a pivot—the touch of a feather, would turn them any way [toward the Spanish]."[1]

Spain's use of Indians to protect her colonial holdings is expressed in Edmond Charles Genet's correspondence. Genet was a French diplomat sent to the United States in 1792 during President Washington's first term as president. He created quite a political scandal while he was in the U.S.

**Enclosure: Papers on Spain Received from Edmond Charles Genet, I:**

> Montmorin adds 'that Spain is decided to make the savages a barrier between her possessions and those of the Americans, that it would oppose if necessary, other obstacles to their progress, and that his M.C.M. could not give to his Catholic Majesty a greater proof of his attachment, than in employing his influence in the US. to divert their views from the navigation of the Missisippi.'[2]

An example of the opposition to Spanish interference can be seen in Thomas Jefferson's letter to Spain's General Counsel, threatening to take Florida and exterminate or expatriate their Indian allies:

### Thomas Jefferson to Valentín de Foronda, 14 December 1813

...[T]he commanding officers in the Floridas have excited & armed the neighboring savages to war against us, and to murder & scalp many of our women and children as well as men, taken by surprise, poor creatures! they have paid for it with the loss of the flower of their strength, and have given us the right as we possess the power to exterminate, or to expatriate them beyond the Missisipi. this conduct of the Spanish officers will probably oblige us to take possession of the Floridas.[3]

Athanase de Mézières, governor of the Natchitoches Spanish district, an experienced Indian agent and diplomat, held conferences with the Comanches on the Red River and in 1771 made treaties with the Kichais, Tawakonis and Taovayas. The Spanish made a treaty with the Yamparikas (western Comanches) at the Taovaya village on the Red River (1774). In 1785, the Spaniards concluded a formal peace treaty with the Kosoteka and Penateka (southern Comanche) bands. In 1786 they made still another treaty with other western bands in order to permit travel through the vast Comanche plains.

To similarly flaunt their favorable relationships with southern Indian Nations, the Spanish also entered into a Treaty with the Creek Indians in 1784 (Treaty of Pensacola between Spain and the Creek Indians, June 1, 1784) and sent a Spanish agent to live among them. The U.S. complained about the appointment of a Spanish agent to Creek Indians living in territory claimed by the United States. In the Spanish response, they enclosed a copy of the Treaty to "serve to prevent the United States from entering into negotiations with the Indians in the future which might conflict with the Indians' agreements with us."[4]

They also sent a copy of the treaty concluded in 1792 with the Choctaw Nation and the Chickasaws (Treaty of Natchez between Spain and the Chickasaw and Choctaw Indians, May 14, 1792) , and stated: ... we flatter ourselves with the belief that the President of the United States, once informed of its contents, will avail himself of the most appropriate means conducive to keeping the United States from entering into accords with the aforementioned Indians that may conflict with those they have reached with us...[5]

Spain negotiated another Treaty to avoid any conflict with the Indians over the construction of Fort Nogales which was built to encumber the settlement plans of the Yazoo Company of South Carolina.[6]

## U.S. Military Expedition (1803–1806)

The Lewis and Clark U.S. Military Expedition must be considered as an element in the fiercely contested struggle for possession of the Oregon Territory. At the time of the U.S. Military Expedition to the Pacific Ocean, this vast domain was claimed based on 'discovery' by Spain, Russia and England, even though it was populated by a multitude of Indian Nations. The U.S. Military Expedition would encounter over seventy-two Indian Nations in the area visited. Searching for the coveted Northwest Passage to the Pacific Ocean, President Jefferson focused also on commerce. Sea-going vessels loaded with cargoes of furs journeyed to far-off China where they were traded for Asian commodities. President Jefferson's long range, geopolitical 'Empire of Liberty' view most certainly contemplated westward expansion to the Pacific, establishing a direct line of communication with Asian traders. The chart below itemizes by five year increments the value of furs exported by the British colonies to England.

| Colony | 1775 | 1770 | 1765 | 1760 |
|---|---|---|---|---|
| Continental Colonies | 53,709 | 47,758 | 49,293 | 19,985 |
| Canada | 34,486 | 28,433 | 24,512 | 1,930 |
| Hudson's Bay | 5,640 | 9,213 | 9,770 | 8,321 |

Value of Furs in Pounds Sterling Exported to England by British Continental Colonies: 1700-1775 (Extract), Colonial and Pre-Federal Statistics, Chapter Z, Series Z 418-431, p. 1188

# Excerpt from President Jefferson's Secret Message to Congress Regarding Lewis & Clark Expedition, January 18, 1803

*Part of this expedition would be to investigate the number, strength and capacity of Indians should the U.S. continue its westward expansion. It is extremely important to analyze President Jefferson's statement in regard to the unwillingness of Indian Nations to sell any more of their lands.*

> The Indian tribes residing within the limits of the United States, have, for a considerable time, been growing more and more uneasy at the constant diminution of the territory they occupy, although effected by their own voluntary sales: and the policy has long been gaining strength with them, of refusing absolutely all further sale, on any conditions; insomuch that, at this time, it hazards their friendship, and excites dangerous jealousies and perturbations in their minds to make any overture for the purchase of the smallest portions of their land.[7]

## Military Expedition's Goals

President Jefferson was eager to get Lewis and Clark underway because ownership of the Oregon Territory was still very much in question. The United States was relying on its 'discovery' claim to the entire Columbia River drainage basin, based on American sea captain Robert Gray's 'discovery' of the mouth of the River. Thus, the race was on between the U.S., Russia, Spain and England to turn their "claims" into actual and permanent possession. The U.S. Military Expedition would be a crucial part of President Jefferson's strategy to solidify America's Oregon Territory 'discovery' claim.

## Military Expedition's Team

The Military Expedition was a unit of the United States Army. President Jefferson officially named the expedition 'The Corps of Volunteers of North Western Discovery' (herein referred to as the "Military Expedition"). The Military Expedition was approved and funded by Congress. Supplies, provisions, and equipment were procured through the Army Quartermaster. President Jefferson chose his personal secretary, Meriwether Lewis, to lead the expedition. Lewis, a former army captain, selected Lieutenant William Clark, who he considered his co-captain. President Jefferson sent Lewis to Lancaster and Philadelphia where he received instructions in making scientific observations and in accumulating the instruments and medicines needed for the Military Expedition.

## Passports

The planned exploratory mission was communicated to the Ministers from France, Spain and England and through them to their governments. The participants (soldiers) would be traversing lands claimed by these countries en route to the Pacific and requested passports guaranteeing safe transport through the various countries' territories. The French government was willing to issue a passport which would ensure "protection with all it's subjects."[8] England's passport from the Minister of England entitled the explorers "to the friendly aid of any traders of that allegiance with whom you may happen to meet."

> The letter, issued by Edward Thornton, British diplomat in Washington City, stated, "... the bearer, Captain Merriwether [sic] Lewis, citizen of the United States of America, is sent (under the authority of the said United States) to explore the headwaters and shores of the Missoury [sic] and the western parts of the North American continent. I therefore pray all to whom these presents shall come, either his Majesty superintendents of Indian affairs or subjects of his Majesty who are engaged in trade with the said tribes, not only to permit the said Captain Lewis to pass without hindrance or impediment whatsoever, but also to rend him all the aid and all the protection which shall depend on them..."[9]

As for Spain, President Jefferson begin preparing the way in 1802 by broaching the subject with the Marques de Casa Yrujo, the Spanish Ambassador to the United States. This was before the negotiations leading to the Louisiana Purchase. Yrujo replied, "I persuaded myself that an expedition of this nature could not fail to give umbrage to our Government. ... President Jefferson returned to the subject again, however, and told Yrujo that Spain should have no fear as the purpose would not be other than 'to observe the territories' Which are found between 40 and 60 from the mouth of the Missouri to the Pacific Ocean, and unite the discoveries these men would make with those which the celebrated Mackensie made in 1793, and be sure if it were possible in that district to establish a continual communication, or little interrupted, by water as far as the South Sea."[10] Nonetheless, Spain adamantly opposed any American exploration of Spanish territory, threatening military reprisal for any trespass on their territory. They refused to grant Lewis a passport. Their mistrust of the U.S. is exemplified in the following letter:

> The President has been all his life a lover of letters, very speculative and a lover of glory, and it would be possible he might attempt to perpetuate the fame of his administration not only by measures of frugality and economy which characterize him, but also by discovering or at least attempting to discover the way by which the Americans may some day extend their population and their influence up to the coasts of the South Sea. Spanish Minister Marques de Casa Yrujo, December 2, 1802.[11]

President Jefferson did not let this deflect from his mission to learn more about the land constituting the Mississippi River drainage basin, along with the Columbia River drainage basis claimed by the 'discovery' of the mouth of the Columbia by Robert Gray. His 'empire of liberty' was on the cusp of fruition. Spain would send out four unsuccessful military expeditions trying to capture the Military Expedition team who they considered trespassers in Spanish territory.

## Diplomatic Gifts

President Jefferson knew that the expedition would encounter a multitude of Indian Nations which they planned to deal with in a diplomatic and friendly manner. They took U.S. flags and several President Jefferson Peace Medals of different sizes and President Washington 'Seasons' Medals to give to influential Native leaders. The 'Seasons' Medals focus on agriculture, husbandry and family supporting President Jefferson's goals of converting Indians to farmers.

**President Washington 'Seasons' Indian Peace Medals (1798)**

In October 1796, President Washington's third Secretary of War, James McHenry, ordered Seasons medals in silver and copper, as the first Indian peace medals struck for the United States. The U.S. minister to Great Britain, Rufus King, enlisted celebrated American artist John Trumbull to produce drawings for three designs (known today as The Shepherd, The Farmer and The Family) and a common reverse bearing the legend SECOND / PRESIDENCY / OF / GEO. WASHINGTON / MDCCXCVI surrounded by an olive branch representing peace and prosperity, with oak leaves symbolizing strength and loyalty.

> **The Shepherd Medal**: Trumbull described it as follows: "Alludes to the raising of cattle— a cow licking a young calf— sheep and a lamb suckling—a man in the character of a shepherd watching them—a small house and trees in the distance."[12]
>
> **The Farmer Medal**: The land cultivation and farming design— perhaps best known as The Sower—was intended by McHenry to be "emblematic of the progressive states of man from the savage to the earliest arts of civilized life." Trumbull hoped that the combination of the sower and the man plowing in the background would depict the first steps in agriculture, describing his medal as "a man sowing wheat—in the distance another person ploughing—a small house and enclosures—to characterize the first steps in agriculture."[13]
>
> **The Family**: The third medal extols the virtues of domestic tranquility and occupation by depicting women spinning, weaving and child rearing.

President Washington's Season Medals play a significant role in understanding his efforts to coerce a lifestyle change in Indians from hunters to farmers. As recognized by the early Presidents, this colonial strategy would lessen the land needed by Indians such that it would justify reducing their land base.

**Loyalty Certificates**

Lewis also took Certificates to give to Indians demonstrating their loyalty to the U.S.:

The Text of the Certificates reads as follows: THOMAS JEFFERSON, PRESIDENT OF THE UNITED STATES OF AMERICA.

> From the powers vested in us and ___ by the above authority: To all who shall see these presents, Greeting: KNOW YE, that from the special confidence reposed by us in the sincere and unalterable attachment of ____, chief of the ____ NATION to the UNITED STATES; as also from the abundant proofs given by him of his amicable disposition to cultivate peace, harmony, and good neighbourhood with the said States, and the citizens of the same; we do by the authority vested in us, require and charge, all citizens of the United States, all Indian Nations, in treaty with the same, and all other persons whomsoever, to receive, acknowledge, and treat the said ___ and his ___ in the most friendly manner, declaring him to be the friend and ally of the said States: the government of which will at all times be extended to their protection, so long as they do acknowledge the authority of the same. Having signed with our hands and affixed our seals this _ day of ___, 180_, M. Lewis, 1st U.S. Regt. [Infantry][wax seal].[14]

This covert action to have Indian Nations acknowledge the authority of the United States is reminiscent of the Requerimiento of the Spanish conquistadors. It is unlikely that Indian leaders presented with these Certificates would have understood the purported diminution of their sovereignty in accepting one and the unequal alliance forged with the U.S. government.

## Trade Gifts

The Military Expedition allocated $696 for trade goods for gift-giving. In Philadelphia, Lewis secured the services of Israel Whelan, purveyor of public supplies, and General William Irvine, superintendent of the Schuylkill Arsenal, to acquire a wide variety of goods, including: blue glass beads, common brass buttons, mirrors, ivory combs, red-handled knives used by fur traders, axes, hatches, awls, scissors, sewing needles, fish hooks and brass kettles which rounded out Lewis's catalog of high priorities. In addition to those items, Lewis listed substantial quantities of wampum, tobacco, military uniforms, ruffled shirts, coats, hats and textiles. Hawks bells, vermilion face paint, one hundred cheap rings with glass stones and brooches completed his stock. President Jefferson sent along two metal corn grinders: one for the Mandans because he was aware of their (i) extensive agriculture, (ii) importance as middle men in trading, and (iii) friendly manner.

## Armaments

With a letter written by Secretary of War Henry Dearborn in hand, Lewis arrived on March 16, 1803 in Harpers Ferry, Virginia. It was addressed to Joseph Perkins, the superintendent of the armory and said, "Sir: You will be pleased to make such arms & Iron work, as requested by the Bearer Captain Meriwether Lewis and to have them completed with the least possible delay."[15]

## President Jefferson's Message to Captain Lewis after Purchase of Louisiana

In January 1804, President Jefferson wrote another letter of instruction to Lewis explaining that he was to begin exercising America's newly acquired authority over the Louisiana Territory, which it took possession of on December 20, 1803. President Jefferson ceased to use the phrase "Friends and Brothers" in addressing Indians. Instead, he addressed them as "My Children" and himself as "Your Great Father."[16] This terminology is critical to understand in light of the sovereignty the federal government unilaterally assumed over the Louisiana Territory after purchasing it. As Children, Indians would be under the control and responsibility of the President.

## Lewis to Inform Indians of Sovereignty over Louisiana Territory

Lewis' new duties included informing the Indians that the United States was now sovereign over the Louisiana Territory and the Indians were now occupants. Lewis was directed to inform the Indian 'children' of the replacement of their late Spanish father with a new great father and awe the Indians with the U.S.'s military might.

*Being now become sovereigns of the country, without however any diminution of the Indian rights of occupancy* we are authorized to propose to them in direct terms the institution of commerce with them. It will now be proper you should inform those through whose country you will pass, or whom you may meet, that their late fathers the Spaniards have agreed to withdraw all their troops from all the waters and country of the Mississippi and Missouri, that they have surrendered to us all their subjects Spanish and French settled there, and all their posts and lands: that henceforward we become their fathers and friends, and that we shall endeavor that they shall have no cause to lament the change.[17] (Emphasis added.)

## Military Expedition Commences

The Military Expedition, accompanied by Captain Lewis' dog, Seaman, set out from Camp Wood River in Illinois on May 14, 1804. "We were now about to penetrate a country at least two thousand miles in width," wrote Lewis, "on which the foot of civilized man had never trodden... I could but esteem this moment of my departure as among the most happy of my life."[18]

Lewis wrote out a 2500-word speech for the expedition's first Indian Nation encounter on August 3–4, 1804, and he copied the speech into a letter that he sent to the Otoe chief Little Thief. He began with the grand announcement of American sovereignty over the newly purchased lands. The Otos and Missouris were told bluntly that their Spanish and French fathers had retreated beyond the eastern sea and would never return. In their place was a new Father, the "great chief of the Seventeen nations," and it was his will that all would "now form one common family with us."[19] Explaining the nature of the Military Expedition's mission proved a difficult task. Lewis declared that the explorers were on the river "to clear the road, remove every obstruction, and make it a road of peace."[20] Just who was to mark out that "road of peace" and where it might lead were matters Lewis addressed next.

Urging the Indians to "shut [their] ears to the councils of Bad birds," the Captain insisted that the new American father and his sons would bring peace and prosperity to the 'red children' on the troubled waters. Those 'red children' were required to make peace with their neighbors and trade with St. Louis merchants. If those words were heeded, advised Lewis, traders would come, a post would be built near the mouth of the Platte, and the Indians would "obtain goods on much better terms than ... before." But Lewis's words had the edge of threat as well. If river Indians ignored American orders and followed the 'bad birds,' trade would be cut off and there would be much suffering.[21]

## Hidatsa Indian Nation

Not all Indian Nations responded favorably to Captain Lewis' speech. The Hidatsas were worried by the sheer size of Fort Mandan built by the Military Expedition and its well-armed occupants. A number of chiefs were offended also at what they called "the high-sounding language the American captains bestowed upon themselves and their nation, wishing to impress the Indians with an idea that they were great warriors, and a powerful people, who, if exasperated, could crush all the nations of the earth." As Alexander Henry the Younger later explained, such saber rattling did not set well with the proud Hidatsas.[22]

## Lewis' Branding Iron

Lewis carried a heavy metal branding iron with the inscription "M. Lewis Capt. U.S. Army." The frame below Lewis' name contained a space for details such as numbers or letters. Private Joseph Whitehouse wrote in his journal that the captains "had several Trees branded, with their Names" on June 4, 1804, near the mouth of the Moreau River, about 140 miles up the Missouri.[23] Most likely, the branding activity was to import public notice of 'symbolic possession' under the 'Doctrine of Discovery.'

## Inscriptions

Similarly, Clark marked the pine tree on what is now the Long Beach Washington peninsula with this inscription, "William Clark December

3rd 1805. By Land from the U. States in 1804 & 1805."[24]

He, also, carved his name and the date on Pompey's Pillar which features an abundance of Indian petroglyphs. Clark wrote in his Journal that he climbed the sandstone pillar and "had a most extensive view in every direction on the Northerly Side of the river."[25]

## Military Expedition's Declaration at Fort Clapsop

Lewis and Clark posted a public document at Fort Clatsop as a memorial of their presence in the Pacific Northwest and gave copies to various Indian chiefs as they planned for their 'return' to the United States. They understood that the Pacific Northwest was not yet a part of the United States. The document explained plainly their presence and purpose of their *exploratory* journey:

> The Object of this list is, that through the medium of Some civilized person who may See the Same, it may be made known to the informed world, that the party consisting of the persons [whose] names are hereunto annexed, and who were Sent out by the Government of the United States in May 1804, to *explore the interior of the Continent of North America*, did penetrate the Same by way of the Missouri and Columbia Rivers, to the discharge of the latter into the Pacific Ocian. ... The captains drew a rough map of their route from St. Louis on the memorial and directed the chiefs to give their copies to any passing ship captains.[26] (Emphasis added.)

## Clark's Slave, York

Another image of Clark is seen in his relationship with his personal slave, York, who accompanied him on the expedition to the northwest. York returned to St. Louis with Clark in early 1809, but the two were not getting along. "He is here but of verry little Service to me," Clark wrote to his brother, Jonathan. "[York is] insolent and Sulky, I gave him a Severe trouncing the other Day and he has much mended Sence." York's inclination to mend his ways was temporary apparently, because on July 22, William informed Jonathan that he had "taken York out of the Cale boos and he has for two or three weeks been the finest Negrow I ever had." What trouble York had gotten into that merited him being jailed is not known. In writing Jonathan a month later, William stated that "Sence I confined York he has been a gadd fellow to work."[27]

The reason for the trouble—York and his wife had been separated. He was owned by Clark and taken to St. Louis. However, his wife was owned by someone else and remained behind in the Louisville area. York did not want to be separated from her and began agitating to return to Louisville. William wanted him in St. Louis and became irritated with York's attitude. By early November he had relented enough to allow York to visit his wife, but the rift between the two men is obvious. On November 9, William wrote Jonathan that he would:

> send York ... and promit him to Stay a flew weeks with his wife. he wishes to Stay there altogether and hire himself which I have refused. he prefers being Sold to return[ing] here, he is Serviceable to me at this place, and I am determined not to Sell him, to gratify him, and have derected him to return in John H. Clarks Boat if he Sends goods to this place, this fall. if any attempt is made by York to run off, or refuse to provonn his duty as a Slave, I wish him Sent to New Orleans and Sold, or hired out to Some Sevare Master untill he thinks better of Such Conduct.[28]

## President Jefferson's Plans to Reduce Indian Land Base

President Jefferson's interest in pursuing peace and having warring Indian Nations cease, was to make it easier to (1) reduce their land base which would make hunting impossible and eliminate this segment of their economy; (2) push the U.S. agrarian policies; (3) eliminate the matriarchal agricultural tradition; (4) establish trading houses to get them in debt by changing their consumption patterns so they would adopt American consumerism lifestyles and be forced to cede lands; (5) accelerate impoverishment; (6) depress the value of their lands by relentlessly encroaching on Indian settlements so the inhabitants would be compelled to either assimilate or relocate beyond the Mississippi River; (7) internalize a sense of weakness by continually demonstrating the U.S.'s military force's superiority so they would be unlikely to threaten colonizing settlers; and (8) confiscate their land, forcibly remove them and exterminate them if desired. His military expeditions were to have the U.S. Army reconnoiter and report back on potential Indian resistance to his ideology of westward expansion and an "empire of liberty."

## After Military Expedition Night Enters Our Future

Indians would later express their dismay at the arrival of the settler colonists. "We were happy when he [the white man] first came," explained the Flathead chief Charlot. "We first thought he came from the light; but he comes like the dusk of evening now, not like the dawn of morning. He comes like a day that has passed, and night enters our future with him."[29]

## Military Expedition II: 200 Years to the Future

To celebrate the Lewis and Clark Bicentennial, a "Military Expedition II" was officially dispatched by President George W. Bush on July 3, 2002. As noted in their publication:

> During the nineteenth century, the Military Expedition became an important cultural touchstone for European Americans, who associated the Military Expedition with U.S. expansionist success and a glorious frontier era... Americans used Lewis and Clark as cultural symbols, deploying them for a variety of purposes and transforming them into larger-than-life heroes. That transformation took place in three phases: (1) the publication of the journals and written narratives of the Lewis and Clark Expedition starting soon after the Corps returned, which made Lewis and Clark household names, (2) the use of the Military Expedition to make a legal claim to western lands in the mid-nineteenth century, and (3) the association of Lewis and Clark with nostalgia for the frontier era at the end of the nineteenth century.[30]

## American Indian Movement Protest against Bicentennial of Lewis and Clark Expedition

The American Indian Movement protested against the celebration of the Bicentennial of the Lewis and Clark Expedition.

> One of the most dramatic controversies during Corps II occurred when a group of about twenty-five American Indians, many from the Pine Ridge Reservation in South Dakota, attempted to block the Discovery Expedition of St. Charles reenactors as they traveled along the Missouri. The group—led by Alex White Plume (Oglala Sioux) and Carter and Vic Camp (Ponca)—consisted mostly of young people and American Indian Movement (AIM) members. They called themselves the "Stop Lewis and Clark Movement." Carter Camp told Indian Country Today, "Lewis and Clark did not come on an excursion to make friends with the tribes. ... They came on a trip of conquest." When the Discovery Expedition of St. Charles met the Stop Lewis and Clark Movement protestors on the Missouri River, Camp told the reenactors, What they [Lewis and Clark] wrote down was a blueprint for the genocide of my people. You are reenacting something ugly, evil and hateful. You are re-enacting the coming of death to our people. You are re-enacting genocide.[31]

## Freeman-Custis Red River Expedition (1806)

In early 1805, Congress appropriated five thousand dollars for another expedition into the Louisiana Territory, the 'Grand Excursion.' Capt. Richard Sparks of the U.S. Army was selected for overall command of the group. Thomas Freeman, a civil engineer and surveyor, and Peter Custis, a medical student and naturalist, were to map the Red River and travel as close to Santa Fe as possible. In total, there were 50 members of the expedition.

President Jefferson's instructions to Thomas Freeman convey his purpose for these expeditions:

> The government of the US. being desirous of informing itself of the extent of the Country lately ceded to them under the name of

324

Louisiana to have the same with its principal rivers geographically delineated, to learn the character of the soil climate productions & inhabitants.[32]

Spain, having been informed of the Grand Excursion, adamantly opposed any American exploration of their territory. Capt. Francisco Viana, commander of the garrison at Nacogdoches, was dispatched with 212 dragoons to stop the mission. From Santa Fe, the Spaniards ordered Lt. Fernando Malgares, commanding 600 soldiers, to also search for them. On July 28, 1806, Viana tracked down Freeman and Custis. He ordered them to leave. To avoid instigating an international incident, the Americans left.

## Hunter-Dunbar Expedition (1804–1805)

In order to understand the waterways within the Louisiana Territory, President Jefferson sent explorers up the waterways which would establish trade and transit routes for future settlement. Enlisting William Dunbar and Dr. George Hunter, a chemist, to travel to the sources of the Arkansas and the Red Rivers, Congress appropriated three thousand dollars for the expedition. The Marquis of Casa-Calvo was unwilling to grant permission for the 'merely scientific' expedition to travel through Spanish territory, even though President Jefferson offered for two Spaniards to accompany the expedition.

Just how important President Jefferson considered information about the Indians can be gleaned from the lengthy portion of the instructions regarding them. Hunter was to secure information regarding their names, numbers, relations with other Indian Nations, capacity for war and armaments and state of morality and religion. Similarly to Lewis and Clark, they were to communicate to the natives that the Spanish were gone and the President was their 'father,' in other words they were now purportedly under the sovereignty of the U.S.

Court an intercourse with the natives as intensively as you can, treat them on all occasions in the most friendly and conciliatory manner which their conduct will admit. allay all jealousies as to the object of your journey make them acquainted with the position extent, character, peaceable & commercial dispositions of the US.

inform them that their late fathers, the Spaniards, have agreed to withdraw all their troops from the Missisipi & missouri, and from all the countries watered by any rivers running into them; that they have delivered to us all their subjects, Spanish & French settled in those countries, together with their posts and territories in the same: that hence forward we become their fathers & friends; that our first wish will be to be neighborly, friendly & useful to them, and especially to carry on commerce with them on terms more reasonable & advantageous for them than any other nation ever did; confer with them on the points most convenient as mutual emporiums for them & us; say that we have sent you to enquire into the nature of the country & the nations inhabiting it, to know their wants, and the supplies they will wish to dispose of, and that after you shall have returned with the necessary information, we shall take measures with their consent for settling trading houses among them, at suitable places: that in the mean time, the same traders who reside among, or visit them, & who are now become our citizens, will continue to supply them as usual, and that they will find us in all things just & faithful friends & patrons.[33]

Further, President Jefferson instructed Hunter to confer with them on the subject of commerce, particularly with the Arcansas and Panis residing on the Red River, and do everything possible to "attach them to us affectionately. in the present state of things between Spain & us, we should spare nothing to secure the friendship of the Indians within reach of her."[34]

The Osage Indians though thwarted the President's scheme, and Dunbar suggested exploring the Ouachita River instead. For a month the expedition camped at what is today Hot Springs, Arkansas.

## Lieutenant Pike's Expedition (1805–1807)

In 1805, U.S. Army General James Wilkinson ordered Lieutenant Zebulon Pike to lead 20 soldiers on a reconnaissance of the upper Mississippi River. He traveled up the Mississippi and spent a hard winter near present-day Little Falls, Minnesota before returning in the spring of 1806. On a second expedition, Lieutenant Pike ultimately explored the west and southwest, including today's Kansas, Colorado, New Mexico, Texas and Louisiana. Most importantly, Lieutenant Pike was to ascertain what the Spanish were doing along the uncertain southwestern border of the Louisiana Territory. A letter between Lieutenant Pike and General Wilkinson, written on July 22, 1806, directed Lieutenant Pike to scout as close as possible to Santa Fe, allowing for the possibility that he might be captured by Spanish authorities. If discovered, he would use the cover story that he had become lost while en route to Natchitoches, Louisiana.

Lieutenant Pike set out on July 15, 1806. On February 26, 1807, a troop of Spanish soldiers rode up to his stockade and informed him that he was in Spanish territory. The Spanish patrol rounded up the frostbitten stragglers, escorting the entire party to Santa Fe. Lieutenant Pike's papers were confiscated, and he was sent south to Chihuahua. Neither Lieutenant Pike nor his men were mistreated; the majority were returned to U.S. territory at Natchitoches on June 30, 1807. The Spanish governor was reprimanded by the King for releasing Lieutenant Pike before receiving an apology from the U.S. Government for trespassing.

## Long Expedition (1819–1820)

Major Stephen Long's 1819–1820 expedition developed out of U.S. concerns over British interest in the northern Plains. His expedition eventually was redirected to map the central Plains to the Rocky Mountains. Major Long was the first Army explorer to include professional scientists on his survey team. He also was the first to use a steamboat for exploration purposes. Setting out from Council Bluffs, he crossed the plains to Colorado, explored the Front Range of Colorado, and then followed the Rocky Mountain Front down into New Mexico. His expedition provided a description of Indian customs and life as they existed among the Omaha, Otoes and Pawnees and characterized the land west of the Missouri River as a desert.

Notes

1. "From George Washington to Benjamin Harrison, 10 October 1784," *Founders Online,* National Archives, https://founders.archives.gov/documents/Washington/04-02-02-0082. [Original source: *The Papers of George Washington*, Confederation Series, vol. 2, *18 July 1784–18 May 1785*, ed. W. W. Abbot. Charlottesville: University Press of Virginia, 1992, pp. 86–98.] (accessed online November 16, 2020).

2. "Enclosure: Papers on Spain Received from Edmond Charles Genet, I, [2 July 1793]," *Founders Online,* National Archives, https://founders.archives.gov/documents/Jefferson/01-26-02-0421. [Original source: *The Papers of Thomas Jefferson*, vol. 26, *11 May–31 August 1793*, ed. John Catanzariti. Princeton: Princeton University Press, 1995, pp. 477–478.] (accessed online November 16, 2020).

3. "Thomas Jefferson to Valentín de Foronda, 14 December 1813," *Founders Online*, National Archives, https://founders.archives.gov/documents/Jefferson/03-07-02-0023. [Original source: *The Papers of Thomas Jefferson,* Retirement Series, vol. 7, *28 November 1813 to 30 September 1814*, ed. J. Jefferson Looney. Princeton: Princeton University Press, 2010, pp. 50–52.] (accessed online November 16, 2020).

4. "To Thomas Jefferson from Josef Ignacio de Viar and Josef de Jaudenes, 7 May 1793," *Founders Online*, National Archives, https://founders.archives.gov/documents/Jefferson/01-25-02-0618. [Original source: *The Papers of Thomas Jefferson*, vol. 25, *1 January–10 May 1793*, ed. John Catanzariti. Princeton: Princeton University Press, 1992, pp. 677–678.] (accessed online November 16, 2020).

5. "To Thomas Jefferson from Josef de Jaudenes and Josef Ignacio

de Viar, 12 May 1793," *Founders Online*, National Archives, https://founders.archives.gov/documents/Jefferson/01-26-02-0009. [Original source: *The Papers of Thomas Jefferson*, vol. 26, *11 May–31 August 1793*, ed. John Catanzariti. Princeton: Princeton University Press, 1995, pp. 9–10.] (accessed online November 16, 2020).

6. "From Thomas Jefferson to Josef Ignacio de Viar and Josef de Jaudenes, 21 May 1793," *Founders Online*, National Archives, https://founders.archives.gov/documents/Jefferson/01-26-02-0071. [Original source: *The Papers of Thomas Jefferson*, vol. 26, *11 May–31 August 1793*, ed. John Catanzariti. Princeton: Princeton University Press, 1995, pp. 78–79.] (accessed online November 16, 2020).

7. "From Thomas Jefferson to the Senate and the House of Representatives, 18 January 1803," *Founders Online,* National Archives, https://founders.archives.gov/documents/Jefferson/01-39-02-0303. [Original source: *The Papers of Thomas Jefferson*, vol. 39, *13 November 1802–3 March 1803*, ed. Barbara B. Oberg. Princeton: Princeton University Press, 2012, pp. 350–354.] (accessed online November 16, 2020).

8. Lewis Receives Passport from Great Britain

https://www.nps.gov/articles/lewis-receives-passport-from-great-britain.htm (accessed online November 16, 2020).

9. Ibid.

10. Carlos Martínez de Yrujo to Pedro Cevallos 2 December 1802

http://www.lewisandclarkexhibit.org/4_0_0/4_1_0_supportingdocs/4_1_8_2/read_L2_spanish_group.pdf (accessed online November 16, 2020).

11. Ibid.

12. https://nnp.wustl.edu/library/book/534388?page=62 all 3 (accessed online November 16, 2020).

13. https://coins.ha.com/itm/u.s.-mint-medals/-1798-washington-seasons-indian-peace-medal-the-farmer-tooled-ngc-details-au-baker-171-julian-ip-53a-musante-gw-/a/1252-4152.s (accessed online November 16, 2020).

14. Wm. Clark Capt on an Expedition for NW Discovery [wax seal] Courtesy Huntington Library, San Marino, California, http://www. lewis-clark.org/article/361#:~:text=Know%20ye%2C%20that%20 from%20the,good%20neighbourhood%20with%20the%20said (accessed online November 4, 2020).

15. Harpers Ferry. https://www.nps.gov/articles/harpers-ferry. htm#:~:text=On%20March%2016%2C%201803%2C%20 Lewis,with%20the%20least%20possible%20delay (accessed online November 4, 2020).

16. Ronda, James P. *Lewis and Clark among the Indians*. U of Nebraska Press, 2002. https://lewisandclarkjournals.unl.edu/item/ lc.jrn.1806-07-23#lc.jrn.1806-07-23.03

(accessed online November 4, 2020).

17. "From Thomas Jefferson to Meriwether Lewis, 22 January 1804," *Founders Online*, National Archives, https://founders.archives.gov/ documents/Jefferson/01-42-02-0285. [Original source: *The Papers of Thomas Jefferson*, vol. 42, *16 November 1803–10 March 1804*, ed. James P. McClure. Princeton: Princeton University Press, 2016, pp. 325–326.] (accessed online November 16, 2020).

18. Ronda, James P. *Lewis and Clark among the Indians*. U of Nebraska Press, 2002.

https://lewisandclarkjournals.unl.edu/item/lc.jrn.1805-04-07 (accessed online November 16, 2020).

19. Ronda, James P. *Lewis and Clark among the Indians*. U of Nebraska Press, 2002.

https://lewisandclarkjournals.unl.edu/item/lc.sup.ronda.01.01 (accessed online November 16, 2020).

20. Ibid.

21. Ibid.

22. Ronda, James P. *Lewis and Clark among the Indians*. U of Nebraska Press, 2002.

https://lewisandclarkjournals.unl.edu/item/lc.sup.ronda.01.04 (accessed online November 16, 2020).

23. Lewis's Branding Iron

https://www.lewis-clark.org/article/951 (accessed online November 4, 2020).

24. Ronda, James P. *Lewis and Clark among the Indians*. U of Nebraska Press, 2002

https://lewisandclarkjournals.unl.edu/item/lc.jrn.1805-12-03 (accessed online November 4, 2020).

25. https://www.nps.gov/places/pompeys-pillar-mt.htm (accessed online November 16, 2020).

26. https://nanopdf.com/download/doctrine-of-discovery-manifest-destiny-and-oregon_pdf (accessed online November 4, 2020).

27. Holmberg, James J. *" I Wish You to See & Know All": The Recently Discovered Letters of William Clark to Jonathan Clark*. 1992: 7-8.

28. Ibid.

29. Ronda, James P. *Lewis and Clark among the Indians*. U of Nebraska Press, 2002.

https://lewisandclarkjournals.unl.edu/item/lc.sup.ronda.01.afterword (accessed online November 4, 2020).

30. Commemoration and Collaboration: An Administrative History of the Lewis and Clark National History Trail, U.S. Department of the Interior, National Park Service, Midwest Regional Office, 2018

http://npshistory.com/publications/lecl/adhi.pdf (accessed online November 4, 2020).

31. Indian Country Today, Brenda Norell, May 17, 2005, Commemoration and Collaboration: An Administrative History of the Lewis and Clark National Historic Trail, National Park Service, 2018: 228.

32. Library of Congress Thomas Jefferson to Thomas Freeman, April

14, 1804, Partly Illegible; Recipient is Samuel or Thomas Freeman, from Thomas Jefferson and Early Western Explorers, Transcribed and Edited by Gerard W. Gawalt, Manuscript Division, Library of Congress http:// www.loc.gov/resource/mtj1.030_0377_0382 (accessed online November 4, 2020).

33. "From Thomas Jefferson to William Dunbar, 25 May 1805," *Founders Online*, National Archives, https://founders.archives.gov/documents/Jefferson/99-01-02-1777. (accessed online November 16, 2020).

34. Ibid.

# 23

# WAR OF 1812, PLAY FOR

# CANADA AND FLORIDA (1812–1815)

The War of 1812 resulted from a British blockade on the American coast, which undermined American commerce and cut sharply into government revenue. Also, to maintain adequate crews, the British stopped, searched and removed suspected British deserters from neutral ships, especially U.S. ships. This practice violated the sovereignty of the United States and inflamed public opinion against Great Britain. In 1807 the Royal Navy accosted the U.S. Frigate Chesapeake in U.S. territorial waters. When the surprised Chesapeake ignored the challenge, she received a deadly broadside. The British then boarded her and removed four crewmen, one of whom they later hanged as a deserter. President Jefferson tried embargos and economic sanctions, but they proved of negligible value, only infuriating the U.S. business and merchant shipping communities.

Britain's failure to evacuate military posts in the Northwest Territory required under the Treaty of Paris in 1783, the contested northern boundary of the Louisiana Territory based on Spain and France's contested 'discovery' claims and the territorial claims secured by George Rogers Clark's military victories in the Revolution were also sources of dispute leading to the War of 1812. In the midst of the American Revolution, Clark had been sent from Virginia to lead an expedition against the British in the Ohio Valley. Clark's success in capturing British forts in 1778 and 1779 allowed the Americans to claim territories that would eventually become the states of Ohio, Illinois, Indiana, Michigan and Wisconsin.

Britain argued that the United States violated the Treaty of Paris by failing to pay Loyalist claims for confiscated property. Congress could not solve the problem, lacking as it did the military power to drive the British out of the Canadian border region and the authority to force states to pay the Loyalist claims.

In August 1814, a U.S. peace commission began negotiations with the British at Ghent, in Belgium. The Commissioners were to demand an end to impressment, British adherence to international law in the enforcement of blockades and payment for the illegal seizure of U.S. ships. The British wanted territorial concessions from the United States, notably portions of New York and Maine, surrender of the U.S. control of the Great Lakes and an Indian-occupied buffer state in the west. They also demanded navigation rights on the Mississippi River and restrictions on American fishing rights. The negotiations proved unsuccessful.

In his request to Congress for a declaration of war, President Madison listed as justification the violation of the flag on the high seas, the impressment of U.S. seamen, trade restrictions against U.S. commerce and the frontiersmen's charge of British sponsorship of Indian attacks along the frontier. There were other factors. After 1811 a group of freshmen Congressmen from the south and west, all Democratic-Republicans, clamored for war against Britain. *These 'War Hawks' aimed to end Indian harassment of western settlements, to conquer Canada and the Floridas and to make the United States a fully independent power in North America.*[1]

Also, Britain failed to recognize the U.S. 'discovery' claims to portions of Georgia, Alabama and Mississippi and further disputed the location of the boundary between Florida and the United States, based on a 'discovery' claim dispute between Spain, England and the United States.

The conquest of most of Canada was expected to be "a mere matter of marching." The United States had a huge population advantage—7.7 million to 500,000—and many people living north of the border—the original French population and recent American immigrants who had moved to Canada to take advantage of free land and low taxes—were not expected to put up much of a fight. Many Republicans anticipated what antiwar critic John Randolph of Virginia called "a holiday campaign." With "no expense of blood, or treasure, on our part—Canada is to conquer herself—she is to be subdued by the principles of fraternity."[2] It also presented the opportunity to resolve a border war with the Indian Nations in the area which had simmered since 1810.

## Tecumseh Confederacy 1812–1813 (Battle of the Thames, 1813)

Tecumseh and his brother, the Prophet, Shawnee Indians, formed a confederacy of Indian Nations in the region, hoping to include others from the Great Lakes to the Gulf of Mexico. In 1810 Tecumseh visited William Henry Harrison, Governor of Indiana Territory, to protest the Treaty of Fort Wayne (1809), by which other Indian leaders had surrendered 3 million acres of land for less than 1 cent per acre. The protest fell on deaf ears. Tecumseh wanted to avoid all-out war, but the dispute flared into a northern frontier border war in the winter of 1810.[3]

In the summer of 1811, Tecumseh traveled south to meet with the Creek, Chickasaw and Choctaw people to enlist them to join his Confederacy. With Tecumseh away, Governor Harrison decided to take advantage. "His absence," Governor Harrison noted, "affords a most favorable opportunity for breaking up his Confederacy."[4] In November 1811, Governor Harrison's army marched to Prophetstown, the headquarters of the Confederacy. At the Battle of Tippecanoe, Governor Harrison's men drove the Indians off and destroyed 'Prophet's Town.' When Tecumseh returned, he concluded that any chance for peace with the settlers had vanished. With his remaining followers, he set out for Upper Canada where he negotiated an alliance with the British.[5]

General William Hull (territorial Governor of Michigan) proposed invading Canada from the west, using Fort Detroit as a base. He reached Fort Detroit and crossed into Canada proclaiming "I come to find enemies not to make them. I come to protect and not to injure you."[6] Initially, 500 Canadian militia deserted. British Major General Isaac Brock, though, bolstered Canadian morale and enlisted Indian allies. He successfully besieged General Hull at Fort Detroit using General Hull's fear of Indian warfare to the advantage of the allied British-Indian forces. Major General Brock paraded his Indian allies around Fort Detroit for psychological effect, demanding General Hull's surrender with this unnerving message: "It is far from my intention to join in a war of extermination, but ... the numerous body of Indians who have attached themselves ... will be beyond control the moment the contest commences."[7] On August 16, 1812, a terrified General Hull surrendered Fort Detroit, along with his 2,500 men. This victory closed the American's western invasion route into Canada. Unfortunately, Major General Brock died in combat on October 13, 1812, at the battle of Queenstown Heights.

On October 5, 1813, General William Henry Harrison led his army of 3,500 American troops against a combined force of eight hundred British soldiers and five hundred American Indian warriors at Moraviantown, along the Thames River in Ontario, Canada. Colonel Henry Procter commanded the British troops while Tecumseh commanded the Indian warriors. As soon as the American troops advanced, the British soldiers fled or surrendered. Tecumseh died on the battlefield. This loss led to the Treaty of Greenville in 1814 under which the Shawnee ceded their claims to Ohio. The U.S. could claim complete military and diplomatic hegemony over the Indians in the Ohio River Valley. The hopes of an Indian challenge to western expansion in Ohio died with Tecumseh.

In a letter from former President Thomas Jefferson to his friend, Alexander von Humboldt, a Prussian explorer, scientist, and geographer, dated December 6, 1813, he ominously acknowledged western expansion and the fate the British Indian allies would face—brutalization, if not extermination:

America has a hemisphere to itself: it must have it's separate system of interests, which must not be subordinated to those of Europe ... in 50 years more the US. alone will contain 50 millions of inhabitants ... for the happiness of the Aboriginal inhabitants in our vicinities. we spared nothing to keep them at peace with one another, to teach them agriculture and the rudiments of the most necessary arts, and to encourage industry by establishing among them separate property. in this way ... they would have mixed their blood with ours and been amalgamated and identified with us within no distant period of time ... England has seduced the greater part of the tribes, within our neighborhood, to take up the hatchet against us, and the cruel massacres they have committed ... will oblige us now to pursue them to extermination, or drive them to new seats beyond our reach ... we have cut off all possibility of intercourse and of mutual aid ... the confirmed brutalisation, if not the extermination of this race in our America is therefore to form an additional chapter in the English history of the same colored man in Asia, and of the brethren of their own colour in Ireland and wherever else Anglo-mercantile cupidity can find a two-penny interest in deluging the earth with human blood.—but let us turn from the loathsome contemplation of the degrading effects of commercial avarice.[8]

Similarly, in another letter, he repeated his recommendation of the extermination of Britain's Indian allies and removal of the Creek Indians to west of the Mississippi: Excerpt of a Letter from Thomas Jefferson to David Bailie Warden, American Consul at Paris, December 29, 1813:

[M]uch however has been effected by our insulating the British from their savage allies, to whom alone, and not at all to themselves they are indebted for every success they have obtained. this unfortunate race, whom we had been taking so much pains to save and to civilize, have by their unexpected desertion and ferocious barbarities justified extermination, and now await our decision on their fate. the Creeks too on our Southern border, for whom we had done more than for any other tribe, have acted the same part (tho' not the whole of them) and have already paid their defection with the flower of their warriors. they will probably submit on the condition of removing to such new settlements beyond the Missisipi as we shall assign them.[9]

## Creek War (1813–1814)

The Creek War was the result of the federal government's failure to fulfill obligations contained in the Treaty of New York of 1790. The Treaty guaranteed protection of Creek territory, but the U.S. government was unwilling or unable to prevent encroachment by settlers. In the January 30, 1794 Message below, President Washington informs Congress of the need for laws to protect Indians from the actions of "lawless white men."

Communications have been made to Congress, during the present Session, with the intention of affording a full view of the posture of affairs on the south western frontiers. By the information, which has lately been laid before Congress, it appeared, that the difficulties with the Creeks had been amicably and happily terminated. But it will be perceived, with regret, by the papers herewith transmitted, that the tranquility has unfortunately been of short duration, owing to the murder of several friendly Indians by some lawless white men.

The condition of things, in that quarter, requires the serious & immediate consideration of Congress; and the adoption of such wise and vigorous laws, as will be competent to the preservation of the national character, and of the peace, made under the authority of the United States, with the several Indian tribes. Experience demonstrates that the existing legal provisions are entirely inadequate to those great objects.[10]

McHenry, the Secretary of War, advised President Washington in a private letter, dated August 3, 1796, that the militia engaged in the Creek War were thirsty for Indian land and willing to plunder their property.

It strikes me, as among the first measures arising out of the proceedings of the Creek commissioners, that of a letter to the Governor of Georgia, somewhat in the stile of the inclosed—It would prove a considerable saving to the U.S. could the defence of the frontiers be carried on by regular troops without the aid of militia. *It would give more consistency to military operations there, and more certainty to their effects. It would besides lessen that thirst for Indian land & plunder which is kept up by militia incursions into their country.*[11] (Emphasis added.)

Commissioners were appointed to negotiate with the Creeks, but from their instructions for reconnaissance of the Creek, Cherokee, Choctaw, Chickasaw and Seminole Indians, it is obvious that President Washington was preparing for the inevitability of war. He instructed his Southern Commissioners for negotiating treaties to gather sixteen different categories of military reconnaissance information on the Creeks. *"The accurate knowledge of this subject is of considerable importance but the enquiries thereto should be circuitously conducted."*[12] (Emphasis added.)

The bitter controversy between the federal government and Georgia over the Indian lands cast a pall over any other outcome. Georgia was willing to take up the musket herself. Regardless of the lawless settlers encroaching on their land, Indians would suffer huge land losses. Though, the federal government knew of the rampant illegal squatting, the Indians lacked the political influence to mobilize their protection. Another deadly war loomed in the south.

In August 30, 1813, the Creek War began as Red Stick Creek Indians, resisting settler invasion of their traditional lands, attacked Fort Mims, Alabama. The Red Sticks, who derived their name from their red ceremonial war clubs, predominantly from the Upper Towns, rejected the relationship that the Lower Towns were fostering with the United States. In August of 1813, following a series of skirmishes with the Mississippi Territorial militia, the Red Sticks overwhelmed Fort Mims. Seven hundred Creek warriors attacked and overran a garrison of militiamen and civilians. The U.S. Army attachment assigned the task of burying the dead counted 246 corpses (including women, children and black slaves).[13]

At the Battle of Tallushatchee, Alabama, on November 3, 1813, the Red Stick Creek Indians were defeated by Major General Jackson and U.S. troops, including Indian allies. Again, on November 9, 1813, Major General Jackson's troops defeated the Red Stick Creeks at the Battle of Talladega, Alabama. Then, on March 27, 1814, Major General Jackson's army of 3,000 defeated the Red Stick Creeks at the Battle of Horseshoe Bend, Alabama, ending the Creek War. Around eight hundred Creeks were killed and five hundred women and children captured. Major General Jackson reported his losses as twenty-seven militia deaths and 106 wounded.

In celebrating his victory, Major General Jackson congratulated his soldiers for the Indians that had disappeared from the face of the earth as a result of the soldiers' fortitude.

> "They knew not what brave men could effect," Jackson declared, "when they came to chastise an insolent foe." He went on: "The fiends of the Tallapoosa will, no longer murder our women and children, or disturb the quiet of our borders. Their midnight flambeaux will no longer illuminate the council-house, or shine

upon the victims of their infernal orgies. They have disappeared from the face of the earth."[14]

The Creek Nation would never recover to resist the U.S. again and the prospect of removal was a foregone conclusion. On August 9, 1814, the Creeks signed the Treaty of Fort Jackson, ceding half of their lands, twenty million acres, including large sections of present-day Alabama and Georgia to the United States. Certain leaders were bribed. William McIntosh, also known as Tustunnuggee Hutke, one of the most prominent chiefs of the Creek Nation, was awarded one thousand acres surrounding the location of the negotiations, the Indian Spring, and 640 acres on the west bank of the Ocmulgee River. He had headed the group of warriors appointed by the Creek National Council known as "Law Menders." These warriors were responsible for apprehending and punishing by beatings, ear cropping, or execution those who had committed crimes against Americans. He served as a Major of a regiment of Creek Indians who fought alongside American forces against Red Stick Creeks, notably at Horseshoe Bend. He later fought with the United States during the First Seminole War. The Fort Jackson cession was, and remains, the largest single acquisition of Indian territory in United States history.[15]

When Major General Jackson's Creek allies pointed out that only a faction of the Creek Nation had attacked Americans, he replied that they were still responsible for their failure to prevent the Red Stick attacks. He justified the seizure of so much territory as payment for the expense of an "unprovoked, inhuman, and sanguinary" war.[16]

The majority of the land taken opened up a transportation artery between Tennessee and the Gulf Coast and secured land for American settlers. According to Article 1 of the Treaty, allied Creek headmen whose property lay within the cession were given the opportunity to apply for private reservations of one square mile. The Creek Nation, including a leader, Menawa, persisted in pressing for compensation for this southern territory for generations. The Treaty also required the Creeks to break off all communication with Spanish Florida and Great Britain, severing Creek claims to lands they had traditionally claimed in the Florida peninsula. It also gave the United States the right to establish military posts, trading houses and roads across Creek territory, guaranteeing free navigation of all rivers for American citizens. All Creeks who fought against the United States were to surrender, and the Creek leadership was to assist in restoring all property, including slaves and horses. In return, the United States promised to provide food rations to the displaced and starving population of the Upper Creek towns.

In an 1828 letter to his friend Justice Story, Chief Justice Marshall lamented the treatment which the Creek Indians had received: "I often think, with indignation, on our disreputable conduct (as I think it is) in the affair of the Creeks of Georgia."[17]

After the tragic defeat of Tecumseh and the Red Sticks, the impacts the War of 1812 had on Indian Nations were horrific. The United States, entrenched as the preeminent power in North America, used its power to diminish the Indian land base. With a dominant military force at its disposal and pressure for westward expansion by settlers, Indian Nations were compelled to accept the terms dictated by the United States for land cessions or face annihilation. The time of Indian confederacies was over; there would be no more forged alliances to challenge the voracious demand for Indian land. Indians in the eastern half of the United States ceased to be military threats and became obstacles to be removed.

## Using Indians to Fight Indians

The colonial and United States' policy of using Indians to fight Indians to divide and conquer can be seen in the following August 20, 1756 correspondence between Governor Dinwiddie and George Washington:

> Your Honor spoke of sending some Indians to our assistance, in which no time should be lost, nor means omitted to engage all the Catawbas and Cherokees, that can possibly be gathered together and immediately despatche.[18]

It was a successful policy for the federal government. Unable to see the consequences for the future, Indian Nations would ally with them against other Indian Nations with whom they had longstanding internecine conflicts.

## Enclosure II William Blount (agent for North Carolina) and Andrew Pickens (Indian commissioner) to Henry Knox, 1 August 1793

> Since it is certain the United States must be involved in a War with the Creeks if not the Cherokees no doubt can remain, but it is their true Interest to cherish and support the Chickasaws in the War against that Nation, and it certainly would be good Policy to use Savages against Savages.[19]

In 1793 for an unknown reason, Secretary of State Jefferson, who was an expert in securing Indian reconnaissance by using federal Indian agents, sought an opinion on this subject from his Cabinet. They were strongly opposed on moral grounds. It may have deterred him in this instance, but it was a strong ploy which he used to advantage.

## Cabinet Opinion on Sending an Agent to the Choctaws [Philadelphia June 1–5, 1793]

> That an Agent be sent to the Choctaw nation to endeavor secretly to engage them to support the Chickasaws in their present war with the Creeks, giving them for that purpose arms and ammunition sufficient: and that it be kept in view that if we settle our differences amicably with the Creeks, we at the same time mediate effectually the peace of the Chickasaws & Choctaws, so as to rescue the former from the difficulties in which they are engaged, and the latter from those into which we may have been instrumental in engaging them. Th: Jefferson, H. Knox

> Altho' I approve of the general policy of employing Indians against Indians; yet I doubt greatly, whether it ought to be exercised under the particular existing circumstances with Spain; who may hold herself bound to take the part of the Creeks, and criminate the U.S. for some degree of insincerity. Edm: Randolph.

Alexander Hamilton did not consider it honorable or moral to enlist the Choctaws in the portended war against the Creeks.

> My judgment ballanced a considerable time on the proposed measure; but it has at length decided against it, and very materially on the ground that I do not think the U. States can honorably or

morally or with good policy embark the Chocktaws in the War, without a determination to extricate them from the consequences even by force. Accordingly it is proposed that in settling our differences with the Creeks, "we mediate effectually the peace of the Chickesaws and Choctaws" which I understand to mean, that we are to insist with the Creeks on such terms of peace for them as shall appear to us equitable, and if refused will exert ourselves to procure them by arms. I am unwilling, all circumstances foreign and domestic considered, to embarrass the Government, with such an obligation. Alex. Hamilton[20]

## The End of the War of 1812

Americans had underestimated the logistical problems, the lack of readiness of an American army filled with amateur officers and untried enlisted men, and the lack of a dependable militia that had little discipline or training and even less taste for battle, especially outside the United States. The War ended in a stalemate. Future president John Quincy Adams, remained unconvinced that America had gained anything by fighting the War of 1812. Writing privately to his father in 1816, he grumbled that many Americans were "rather more proud than they have reason [to be]..."[21]

Many felt that the United States' entanglement with Britain and France's battle for control of the European continent was unwise. British diplomat Augustus Foster on February 1806, described the relationship among the three countries as follows.

> "The two greatest Commercial Nations in the Globe [England and France] cannot move in the same Spheres without jostling one another a little... we want Elbow room and these good Neutrals [U.S.] won't give it to us... they get a few side Pushes, which makes them grumble."[22]

Indian country was never the same following the War of 1812. Indian aspirations to maintain their land base and relative autonomy were forever lost. The undisputed hegemony of the U.S. over the Ohio Valley culminated in displacing the Indian Nations from their homelands, while over 300,000 colonial settlers traveled to the west, across Indian lands, in search of land and gold.

## Spanish Florida Invaded by Major General Andrew Jackson to Punish Seminole Indians

After the Battle of New Orleans, fought after the War of 1812 was over as news had not yet reached the Americans, Major General Jackson moved on to invade Spanish Florida and seize the port of Pensacola. He led a military force from Fort Scott, Georgia, into Spanish Florida to punish the Seminole Indians and runaway slaves for their continuing assaults on Georgia settlers. After making only minor contact with the Seminoles, Major General Jackson determined to exceed his orders. He led his army across northern Florida, during which time he executed several Seminoles and two British subjects. The high points of the expedition were the seizures of the Spanish forts at St. Marks and Pensacola. Major General Jackson "put a legal face on illegal actions" by alleging that the raids were the result of encouragement by British traders and the Spanish government's inability to control the region.[23] Specifically, Major General Jackson blamed Gonzalez Manrique, the Spanish governor of Pensacola, for the unrest. In communications with Manrique, Major General Jackson warned that retaliation would be "Eye for an Eye, Toothe for Toothe, and Scalp for Scalp."[24]

When the news of the exploit reached Washington D.C., Major General Jackson was again the hero of the hour. Although his violation of Spanish sovereignty was embarrassing to the United States, at the same time it strengthened future president Adams' hand in his negotiations with Spain's diplomat, Luis de Onís, for Florida and the Oregon Territory. Major General Jackson had demonstrated the weakness of Spain's grip. Its hold on its North American empire was so weak that it was only a matter of time before the various pieces of that empire—its claims to parts of Georgia, Alabama and Mississippi and to East and West Florida —fell like ripe fruit 'piece by piece' into American hands.

Under the 1819 Adams-Onis Treaty, Spain relinquished any remaining claims to territory north of the 42nd parallel to the United States. Thus, the U.S. received ownership of Spanish Florida (British East Florida and West Florida 1763–1783) and the Spanish also relinquished a boundary to the Louisiana Territory that followed the Sabine, Red, and Arkansas rivers to the Continental Divide and the 42nd parallel to the Pacific, thus abandoning Spain's claim to a huge area beyond the Rockies that had no connection at all with the Louisiana Purchase, including its claims to the Oregon Territory. The boundaries of the Louisiana Purchase were finally determined. The U.S. did not pay Spain for Florida, but instead agreed to pay the legal claims of American citizens against Spain, to a maximum of $5 million.

Notes

1. Founders and Frontiersmen: Historic Places Commemorating Early Nationhood and the Westward Movement, 1783-1828, Volume 7, p. 49, United States, National Park Service, Jan. 1968.

2. Annals of the Congress of the United States, Volume 1; Volume 23, December 1811, p. 447.

3. Berkin, Carol, et al. *Making America: a history of the United States*. Nelson Education, 2011: 212.

4. Summer 1811: Tecumseh attempts to negotiate with white American settlers. https://www.nps.gov/articles/tecumseh.htm#:~:text=With%20 Tecumseh%20away%20meeting%20with,the%20headquarters%20 of%20the%20Confederacy (accessed online November 20, 2020).

5. Barrett, Ryan, "The War of 1812: The End of an Uncommon Alliance" (2013). History Theses. Paper 21.

6. "I come to find enemies not to make them, I come to protect not to injure you." https://www.nps.gov/articles/american-proclamation.htm (accessed online November 20, 2020).

7. Isaac Brock, The Fall of Detroit, August 1812, Jonathon Riley. http://generalship.org/military-history-articles/fall-of-detroit.html (accessed online November 20, 2020).

8. "Thomas Jefferson to Alexander von Humboldt, 6 December 1813," *Founders Online*, National Archives, https://founders.archives.gov/ documents/Jefferson/03-07-02-0011. [Original source: *The Papers of Thomas Jefferson,* Retirement Series, vol. 7, *28 November 1813*

*to 30 September 1814*, ed. J. Jefferson Looney. Princeton: Princeton University Press, 2010, pp. 29–32.] (accessed online November 20, 2020).

9. "Thomas Jefferson to David Bailie Warden, 29 December 1813," *Founders Online*, National Archives, https://founders.archives.gov/documents/Jefferson/03-07-02-0046. [Original source: *The Papers of Thomas Jefferson*, Retirement Series, vol. 7, *28 November 1813 to 30 September 1814*, ed. J. Jefferson Looney. Princeton: Princeton University Press, 2010, pp. 90–93.] (accessed online November 20, 2020).

10. https://www.presidency.ucsb.edu/documents/special-message-1805 (accessed online November 20, 2020).

11. "To George Washington from James McHenry, 3 August 1796," *Founders Online*, National Archives, https://founders.archives.gov/documents/Washington/99-01-02-00813. (accessed online November 20, 2020).

12. "From George Washington to the Commissioners to the Southern Indians, 29 August 1789," *Founders Online*, National Archives, https://founders.archives.gov/documents/Washington/05-03-02-0326. [Original source: *The Papers of George Washington*, Presidential Series, vol. 3, *15 June 1789–5 September 1789*, ed. Dorothy Twohig. Charlottesville: University Press of Virginia, 1989, pp. 551–565.] (accessed online November 20, 2020).

13. Waselkov, Gregory A. *A conquering spirit: Fort Mims and the Redstick War of 1813–1814*. University of Alabama Press, 2009.

14. Martin, Joel W. *Sacred Revolt: The Muskogees' Struggle for a New World*. Beacon Press, 1991: 162-163.

15. https://www.nps.gov/articles/treaty-of-fort-jackson.htm (accessed online November 20, 2020).

16. Ibid.

17. John Marshall Letter to Justice Story, 1828.

18. "To George Washington from Robert Dinwiddie, 20 August 1756,"

*Founders Online*, National Archives, https://founders.archives.gov/
documents/Washington/02-03-02-0324. [Original source: *The Papers
of George Washington*, Colonial Series, vol. 3, *16 April 1756–9
November 1756*, ed. W. W. Abbot. Charlottesville: University Press of
Virginia, 1984, pp. 371–372.] (accessed online November 20, 2020).

19. "Enclosure II William Blount and Andrew Pickens to Henry Knox,
1 August 1793," *Founders Online*, National Archives, https://founders.
archives.gov/documents/Washington/05-13-02-0240-0003. [Original
source: *The Papers of George Washington*, Presidential Series,
vol. 13, *1 June–31 August 1793*, ed. Christine Sternberg Patrick.
Charlottesville: University of Virginia Press, 2007, pp. 359–362.]
(accessed online November 20, 2020).

20. "Cabinet Opinion on Sending an Agent to the Choctaws, 1–5
June 1793," *Founders Online*, National Archives, https://founders.
archives.gov/documents/Washington/05-13-02-0003. [Original source:
*The Papers of George Washington*, Presidential Series, vol. 13, *1
June–31 August 1793*, ed. Christine Sternberg Patrick. Charlottesville:
University of Virginia Press, 2007, pp. 3–5.] (accessed online
November 20, 2020).

21. Taylor, Alan. *The Civil War of 1812: American Citizens, British
Subjects, Irish Rebels, & Indian Allies*. Vintage, 2010: 439.

22. Ibid., p. 110.

23. Keeton, Robert Michael, ""To Preserve This Much-Injured Race":
Techniques of Neutralization and Indian Removal, 1829-1831." PhD
diss., University of Tennessee, 2012, 148. https://trace.tennessee.edu/
utk_graddiss/1587 (accessed online November 20, 2020).

24. Rogin, Michael P. *Fathers and Children: Andrew Jackson and the
Subjugation of the American Indian*, 1975: 160.

# 24

## STATE CASES REGARDING INDIAN LAND

## TITLE SPLIT; *FLETCHER* CASE

The first known case to address the legality of preemptive rights was *Marshall v. Clark*, 8 Va. 268, 273 (1791), decided by the Virginia Supreme Court. The lead plaintiff was Thomas Marshall, John Marshall's father, who challenged the validity of a grant Virginia had made to the war hero, George Rogers Clark. Marshall was acting on behalf of the state militia, which claimed the same land. One of Marshall's arguments was that the grant to Clark was void because, when it took effect, the land the state purported to grant had not yet been purchased from the Indians. The Virginia Supreme Court rejected the argument. "The Indian title did not impede ... the power of the legislature to grant the land," the court held. The grantee "must risque the event of the Indian claim, and yield to it, if finally established, or have the benefit of a former or future extinction thereof," the court reasoned, but these contingencies did not invalidate the grant.[1] If the government ever acquired the land from the Indians, it would become Clark's.

In *Marshall v. Clark*, the court considered the issue of how Indian land titles were extinguished and stated:

> The dormant title of the Indian tribes remained to be extinguished by government, either by purchase or conquest; and when that was done, it enured to the benefit of the citizen, who had previously acquired a title from the crown, and did not authorize a new grant of the lands...[2]

A few years later, the Pennsylvania and Tennessee Supreme Courts reached the same result. States had the power to grant land not yet purchased from the Indians.

In 1795, however, the Pennsylvania Supreme Court affirmed that both before and after the Revolution "the soil belonged to the aborigines" until they sold it.[3] The Indians held "title" to their land and they possessed the "right of soil"—in the earliest years of the United States. Judges and government officials used the same words to describe land ownership by Indians as they used to describe land ownership by colonist settlers who purchased land from the Indians.

In *Strother v. Cathey*, 5 N.C. 162 (N.C. 1807), decided by the North Carolina Supreme Court in 1807, two parties claimed the same land, one under a 1787 grant from the state, the other one also under a grant from the state, dated 1803, upon a 1791 entry. Under the Treaty of Holston, the United States had purchased the disputed land from the Cherokees. Cathey argued that North Carolina had no right to grant the land to Strother because after the Treaty of Holston the land was owned by the federal government. The North Carolina Supreme Court posited that while the United States could extinguish the Indians claim to the land, the state had title to the land that it had conveyed in fee to Strother. Judge David Stone, a future North Carolina governor and United States senator, explained the state's position more dogmatically. *The federal government could not have purchased the fee simple title from the Cherokees because they had only a possessory right:* "neither the European governments, nor the government of the United States, nor that of North Carolina, have considered the Indian title other than a mere possessory right."[4] The state could convey fee title even while the Indians occupied the lands.

New York would face this issue in *Jackson v. Hudson*, 3 Johns. Rep. 375 (1808). Again, one party claimed land by virtue of a 1731 patent from the colony of New York, at a time when the land was still occupied by the Mohawks. His opponent argued that the state could not convey a fee simple title before it purchased the land from the Mohawks. Chief Justice James Kent used the political question argument—that this is a matter within the domain of Congress, not the judiciary: "The policy, or the abstract right of granting lands in the possession of the native

Indians, without their previous consent, as original lords of the soil, is a political question with which we have at present nothing to do." Justice Kent was able to avoid deciding whether an Indian possession or title would hold sway over a state grant.[5]

*Van Gorden v. Jackson*, 5 Johns. Rep. 440 (N.Y. 1809), was another New York dispute over land in New York, where a prior Indian purchase was in the chain of title. Chancellor John Lansing held that "Though Indian deeds were obtained for the purpose of proving that the rights of the natives, were extinguished," they "were never admitted, as of themselves, to be a source of legal title." The procedure to acquire title to Indian land required an Indian purchase of the land, along with a patent from the colonial government. Chancellor Lansing went on, though, to state that an Indian deed was a mere inducement to the colonial government to extend a patent. According to Lansing, "the firm and unbending principle has uniformly been, that all titles must be derived, either mediately or immediately, actually or presumptively, from the crown."[6] Indian deeds had flipped from conveying title to serving as a mere administrative step required before title was conveyed by the Crown, who owned the land.

In 1813 the question of Indian ownership came before the Pennsylvania Supreme Court again. This time the result would be different:

> Chief Justice William Tilghman and Justice Hugh Henry Brackenridge declared. The Indians had never owned it. "From the first discovery of the continents or islands of America," Brackenridge explained, incorrectly, "these ***Aborigines were not considered as having any right, not being Christians, but mere heathens and unworthy of the earth.***" (Emphasis added.) But as a matter of Pennsylvania colonial law, the court reasoned, the colony's proprietors had established the policy (except in this instance, evidently) of granting no land before purchasing the Indian title. The 1773 grant was invalid, but the court nevertheless affirmed that unpurchased Indian land in Pennsylvania was owned by Pennsylvania rather than the Indians.[7]

### Fletcher v. Peck, 10 U.S. 87 (1810)

Chief Justice Marshall's first foray on the subject of preemptive rights occurred in *Fletcher v. Peck*, 10 U.S. 87 (1810), a case that had originated in 1807. It took twenty-five years to reach the Supreme Court. The case did not directly involve Indians. Rather, it had to do with Americans, arguing over who held title to land that Georgia had granted to one group in 1795 and another in 1796. Thomas Jefferson tried to arrange a compromise by having the federal government purchase the land from Georgia and compensate the New Yazooists, but it was defeated. As part of the legal proceedings, a question was raised whether the state legislature could give the land to anyone, since, inconveniently, the Indian land had never been ceded by treaty to the United States.

> The question, whether the vacant lands within the United States became a joint property, or belonged to the separate states, was a momentous question which, at one time, threatened to shake the American confederacy to its foundation."[8]

On March 16, 1810, the Court handed down its decision which voided Georgia's repeal of the purchase on the basis of the Constitution's Contract Clause. The Court's ruling held that the original sale of land constituted a contract with the purchasers, and the Contract Clause prohibits states from 'impairing the obligations of contracts.'

Chief Justice Marshall stated in obiter dicta ("something said in passing") that:

> The majority of the Court is of opinion that the nature of the Indian title, which is certainly to be respected by all Courts until it be legitimately extinguished, is not such as to be absolutely repugnant to seisin in fee on the part of the State.[9]

Chief Justice Marshall's assertions regarding "Indian title" did not go unquestioned. Justice Johnson, in his dissent, declared "Indian title" a legal absurdity. Either the Natives owned the land or they did not own it. Justice Johnson could not comprehend how the law could be understood to have some middle position. Reflecting the older legal understanding of the matter, Justice Johnson's minority opinion asserted that Indians owned the land, in the simplest sense of that idea and with all the related rights it implied.

[I]numerable treaties formed with [Indians] acknowledge them to be an independent people, and the uniform practice of acknowledging their right of soil, by purchasing from them, and restraining all persons from encroaching upon their territory, makes it unnecessary to insist upon their right of soil. And if the Indians owned the land, how could Georgia own it too? "Can, then," asked Johnson, "one nation be said to be seised of a fee-simple in lands, the right of soil of which is in another nation?"[10]

Britain had claimed only a right to purchase the Indians' land, to the exclusion of all competing purchasers, and upon American independence Georgia had succeeded to that right, but not to anything more.

It is awkward to apply the technical idea of a fee simple to the interests of a nation, but I must consider an absolute right of soil as an estate to them and their heirs. A fee simple estate may be held in reversion, but our law will not admit the idea of its being limited after a fee simple. In fact, if the Indian nations be the absolute proprietors of their soil, no other nation can be said to have the same interest in it. What, then, practically, is the interest of the States in the soil of the Indians within their boundaries? Unaffected by particular treaties, it is nothing more than what was assumed at the first settlement of the country, to-wit, a right of conquest or of purchase, exclusively of all competitors within certain defined limits. All the restrictions upon the right of soil in the Indians amount only to an exclusion of all competitors from their markets, and the limitation upon their sovereignty amounts to the right of governing every person within their limits except themselves. If the interest in Georgia was nothing more than a preemptive right, how could that be called a fee simple which was nothing more than a power to acquire a fee simple by purchase, when the proprietors should be pleased to sell? And if this ever was any thing more than a mere possibility, it certainly was reduced to that state when the State of Georgia ceded to the United States, by the Constitution, both the power of preemption and of conquest, retaining for itself only a resulting right dependent on a purchase or conquest to be made by the United States.[11]

Chancellor Kent, renowned jurist and author of a landmark treatise on American common law, concluded that Chief Justice Marshall's decision in *Fletcher* was "a mere naked declaration, without any discussion or reasoning by the court in support of it."[12]

In 1810, in *Jackson v. Wood*, 7 Johns. Rep. 290 (1810), Chief Justice Kent for the New York Supreme Court went out of his way to disagree with Chief Justice Marshall's ruling in *Fletcher*, writing that it was, "a fact too notorious to admit of discussion or to require proof, that the Oneida Indians still reside within this state, as a distinct and independent tribe, and upon lands which they have never alienated, but hold and enjoy as the original proprietors of the soil."[13]

Attorney General William Wirt, who served as the U.S. Attorney General in the Monroe and Adams presidential administrations, when asked about the matter in 1821, wrote: "So long as a tribe exists and remains in possession of its lands, its title and possession are sovereign and exclusive. We treat with them as separate sovereignties, and while an Indian nation continues to exist within its acknowledged limits, we have no more right to enter upon their territory than we have to enter upon the territory of a foreign prince." Wirt would go on to write Indian Nation governments, "do not hold [title] under the States, nor under the United States; their title is original." Wirt, however, was among the last federal officials to take this position.[14]

Chief Justice Marshall's dicta in *Fletcher* disintegrated the concept of Indian land ownership. An absolute title to land cannot exist, at the same time, in different persons, or in different governments. Colonists begin to push for Indian removal so that their vested fee simple title could be put to use by them.

# Notes

1. *Marshall v. Clark*, 8 Va. 268, 273 (1791).

2. Ibid.

3. *Thompson v. Johnston*, 6 Binn. 68, 75 (1813), Sept. 11, 1813, Supreme Court of Pennsylvania.

4. *Strother v. Cathey*, 5 N.C. 162, 168 (N.C. 1807).

5. *Jackson v. Hudson,* 3 Johns. Rep. 375 (1808).

6. *Van Gorden v. Jackson*, 5 Johns. Rep. 440 (N.Y. 1809).

7. Banner, Stuart. How the Indians lost their land: Law and power on the frontier. Harvard University Press, 2005: 176.

8. *Fletcher v. Peck*, 10 U.S. 87, 142 (1810).

9. Ibid., pp. 142-143.

10. Ibid., p. 147.

11. Ibid.

12. Kent, James, and Charles M. Barnes. *Commentaries on American law*. Lecture 51, Of the Law concerning Real Property. Vol. 3, Part VI, p. 378 n.d. Little, Brown, 1884.

13. *Jackson v. Wood*, 7 Johns. Rep. 290 (1810).

14. 1 OAG 465, 466-467 (1821); The United States Attorneys General and International Law, David R. Deener.

# 25

# ANDREW JACKSON'S INDIAN REMOVAL CAMPAIGN

Andrew Jackson's 1828 Presidential Campaign made American Indian Removal his goal—relocating eastern Indians west of the Mississippi River.

As cotton culture spread across Georgia, federal officials proved either unwilling or unable to extinguish quickly enough for land-hungry Georgians the claims of the Creeks and the Cherokees to lands within the state. Angered over the delay in fulfilling the terms of the Compact of 1802, Georgia's leaders, throughout the 1820s and 1830s, regularly prodded the President then in office to complete the process of Indian removal. In 1820, a congressman from Georgia bitterly complained that when the state gave up its claim to western lands to the federal government in 1802, everyone assumed they would quickly gain title to the land from Indians and open it to settlement. Many Georgians were concerned that many Indian Nations, particularly the Creek and the Cherokee, were not interested in selling their land, much less leaving. What the Georgians refused to acknowledge was that 90 percent of Indian land claims within the state had been extinguished, at enormous cost, instead accusing the federal government of bad faith and threatening armed conflict.

When the Creek informed the federal government that, "We deem it impolitic and contrary to the true interests of this nation to dispose of any more of our country," the commissioners sent by Washington, D.C., offered a chilling reply: "If you wish to quit the chase, to free yourself of barbarism, and settle down in the calm pursuits of civilization, and good morals, and to raise up a generation of Christians, you had better go." If you choose otherwise, "You must be sensible that it will be impossible for you to remain for any length of time in your present situation as a distinct Society or Nations, within the limits of Georgia. Such a community is incompatible with our System and must yield to it."[1]

## Conflict between Creeks and Georgia Leads to Federal Threat of War against the State

The rhetoric coming from Governor George Troup and the Georgians expressed the sentiment of many colonial settlers who wanted no proximity to Indians, regardless of their culture or modes of living. Secretary of War James Barbour's February 1826 plan for the Indians made it clear that, in the eyes of the government, the Indians must be removed—but not, as had often been promised in earlier years, for the benefit of being free from settler corruption and abuse, but to destroy their autonomy. This seeming federal support led the Georgians to vigorously pursue inclusion of Indian land under state hegemony.[2]

It put President John Quincy Adams in a quandary. In a message to Congress sent on February 5, 1827, which he termed "the most momentous," he informed Congress, that the Creeks had invoked the protection of the federal government to defend their rights as guaranteed by a ratified treaty. "Their forbearance and reliance on the good faith of the United States will, it is hoped, avert scenes of violence and blood, which there is otherwise too much cause to apprehend will result from these proceedings." The message then delineated the stipulations of the Trade and Intercourse Act of March 30, 1802, and the punishments prescribed for colonial settler intruders in Indian country. There was no previous instance in which the disagreement between state and federal authority "has been urged into a conflict of actual force"—if not civil war, at least a potential prelude to it.[3]

In the present instance President Adams presaged the possibility of civil war:

> ... it is my duty to say, that if the legislative and executive authorities of the State of Georgia shall persevere in acts of encroachment upon the territories secured by a solemn treaty to the Indians, and the

laws of the Union remain unaltered, a superadded obligation, even higher than that of human authority, will compel the Executive of the United States to enforce the laws, and fulfill the duties of the nation by all the force committed for that purpose to his charge.[4]

The Adams' presidential administration saber rattling to protect the rights of the Creeks and Georgia's governor action to prevent precisely that resulted in the status quo. President Adams was unwilling to risk civil war. A select Senate committee chaired by Missourian Thomas Hart Benton, "Old Bullion," requested the President to take every action possible to convince the Creeks to accept payment for their lands. Senator Benton included a dire warning:

> "The committee will not enlarge upon the frightful consequence of civil wars," he wrote. "They are known to be calamitous to single Governments, and fatal to confederacies. A contagious fury rages in such contests. No matter how small the beginning, or how insignificant the cause, the dissension spreads, until the whole confederacy is involved."[5]

Negotiations commenced that summer before Congress even approved funding for a cession of Creek lands which allowed for a cooling off period. In the autumn, the Creeks ceded the lands.

## President Jackson's Justification for Indian Removal

President Jackson justified Indian removal based on an understanding that the Indians were savages and had made no improvements to the U.S.:

> What good man would prefer a country covered with forests and ranged by a few thousand savages to our extensive Republic, studded with cities, towns, and prosperous farms, embellished with all the improvements which art can devise or industry execute, occupied by more than 12,000,000 happy people, and filled with all the blessings of liberty, civilization, and religion?[6]

He also refused to recognize them as sovereign nations. President Jackson declared, "I have long viewed treaties with the Indians an absurdity not to be reconciled to the principles of our Government." The

358

Indians, said President Jackson, were subjects of the United States, pure and simple, "inhabiting its territory and acknowledging its sovereignty." It was a fiction that the tribes were in fact separate and independent entities, and it was absurd to negotiate with them as such.[7]

## Tenor of Times—They May Begin to Dig Their Graves and Prepare to Die

Alfred Balch, President Jackson's Commissioner of Indian Treaties, echoed the tenor of the times: "[the] removal of Indians would be an act of seeming violence—But it will prove in the end an act of enlarged philanthropy. These untutored sons of the Forest, cannot exist in a state of Independence, in the vicinity of the white man. **If they will persist in remaining where they are, they may begin to dig their graves and prepare to die.**"[8] (Emphasis added.)

Hezekiah Niles, editor of the Niles Weekly Register newspaper, offered the starkest comment on removal: "The fate of the Indians within the present states and territories—is sealed." The eastern Indian Nations would remove or become extinct.[9]

Just nineteen days into his presidency, in a bold move, President Jackson stated his removal policy in a speech to the Creek Indians.

> Where you now are, you and my white children are too near to each other to live in harmony and peace. Your game is destroyed and many of your people will not work and till the Earth. Beyond the great river Mississippi, where part of your nation has gone, your father has provided a country large enough for all of you, and he advises you to remove to it. There your white brothers will not trouble you; they will have no claim to the land, and you can live upon it, you and your children, as long as the grass grows or the water runs, in peace and plenty. It will be yours forever.[10]

Balch's assurance to President Jackson that he would ramrod Indian removal legislation through Congress was underway. On February 24, 1830, John Bell and the Indian Affairs committee introduced a removal bill—officially, H.R. 287. The Senate version of the bill, submitted at the same time by Bell's counterpart on the Senate's Indian Affairs committee, Hugh Lawson White, was known as S. 102.[11] The House version of the bill was preceded by a report of over 15,000 words that was part opposition to removal, part history of United States Indian policy, especially the peculiarities of the treaty system, and part assertion of the southern Indians' rapid decline and, should they remain, certain extinction.

## Secretary of War Threatens Cherokees—They Will Be Left to Whims of Georgia

In 1824, Secretary of War John Calhoun threatened to leave the Cherokees "exposed to the discontent of Georgia and the pressure of her citizens" if they continued to refuse to exchange their land in Georgia for land west of the Mississippi. They responded: "Sir, to these remarks we beg leave to observe, and to remind you, that the Cherokees are not foreigners, but original inhabitants of America; and that they now inhabit and stand on the soil of their own territory; and that the limits of their territory are defined by the treaties which they have made with the Government of the United States."[12]

The Cherokees hoped the U.S. would intercede on their behalf:

> General Carroll, to the secretary of war, describing the difficulties he met with in inducing the Indians to emigrate, says, "The truth is, they rely with great confidence on a favorable report on the petition they have before Congress. If that is rejected, and the laws of the States are enforced, you will have no difficulty of procuring an exchange of lands with them."

> General Coffee, upon the same subject says, "They express a confident hope that Congress will interpose its power, and prevent the States from extending their laws over them. Should they be disappointed in this, I hazard little in saying that the government will have little difficulty in removing them west, of the Mississippi."[13]

Reports from Indians that had moved west, however, were dismal and they feared for their survival. General Clark, Superintendent of Indian Affairs, credits the southern Indians fear of moving with the dire stories of the Indians who had moved west. Senator Evans described it as follows:

The condition of many tribes west of the Mississippi is the most pitiable that can be imagined. During several seasons in every year, they are distressed by famine, in which many die for want of food, and during which the living child is often buried with the dead mother, because no one can spare it as much food as would sustain it through its helpless infancy.[14]

## Georgia Enacts Laws Abolishing Cherokee Indian Sovereignty, Self-Government and Right to Land

The State of Georgia seized on *Fletcher*, the feigned case regarding the fraudulent Yazoo land sales, where U.S. Supreme Court Chief Justice Marshall stated Georgia held fee title to Indian lands, as well as the *Johnson* case. They enacted laws abolishing the Cherokee's right to sovereignty, self-government and land. President Jackson and Congress refused the direct request of the Cherokee Nation for federal intervention to uphold their Hopewell Treaty (1785) rights against Georgia's legislative encroachments.

Georgia's first act was passed the 12th of December 1829, and is entitled:

An act to add the territory lying within the chartered limits of Georgia, and now in the occupancy of the Cherokee Indians, to the counties of Carroll, De Kalb, Gwinnett and Habersham, and to extend the laws of the State over the same, and to annul all laws made by the Cherokee Nation of Indians ... Resolved, Indians are tenants at her will, and that she may at any time she pleases, determine that tenancy, by taking possession of the premises.[15]

In Congressional debates on these Georgia statutes and Indian removal, Senator Frelinghuysen found the prohibition of the Indians' rights to be witnesses in cases extremely oppressive. This meant that "a gang of lawless white men may break into the Cherokee country, plunder their habitations, murder the mother with the children, and all in the sight of the wretched husband and father, and no law of Georgia will reach the atrocity." In his view, this "shut [the Cherokees] out of the protection of Georgia laws" and "stripped these people of the protection of their government."[16]

Representative Bates asked for proof of the right of Georgia's to enact the statutes robbing the Cherokees of their soverrignty:

> ...[T]here is not an act of Georgia ... that does not tend to establish the fact, that the Indians are the proprietors of the lands and hunting grounds they claim, subject only to the restriction upon their right of alienation. What, then, becomes of the tenancy at will—at sufferance, as asserted by Georgia? ... Sir, when were they otherwise. In what field were they conquered? Produce the proof.[17]

## Gold Discovered on Cherokee Lands—1829

When gold was discovered on Cherokee land, the State of Georgia passed another act, entitled An act to authorize the Governor to take possession of the gold, silver, and other mines lying and being in that section of the chartered limits of Georgia commonly called the Cherokee country, and those upon all other unappropriated lands of the State, and for punishing any person or persons who may hereafter be found trespassing upon the mines.

## 1828 War Department Annual Report Guardianship of Indians, Letter to President from P. B. Porter, Sec. of War, Nov. 24, 1829

Secretary of War P. B. Porter advised President Jackson that given the present reality, Indians would not be permitted to retain land in the midst of the onslaught of white settlers. Indians, to many whites, were considered "as mere tenants at will, subject, like the buffalo of the prairies, to be hunted from their country whenever it may suit our interest or convenience to take possession of it."

Secretary of War Porter declared that outright guardianship should be the policy of the federal government.

> In their present destitute and deplorable condition, and
> which is constantly growing more helpless, it would seem
> to be not only the right, but the duty of the Government,
> to take them under its paternal care; and to exercise, over

their persons and property, the salutary rights and duties of guardianship.

Under Porter's proposal, the federal government, as a legal guardian, would possess the right to make all legal and financial decisions on behalf of their wards, the Indians. Thus, the U.S. would be legally authorized to manage its ward's substantial personal and property interests.

President Jackson in his message to Congress of December 8, 1829, however, did not propose guardianship, only removal.

Notes

1. Green, Michael D. *The politics of Indian removal: Creek government and society in crisis.* U of Nebraska Press, 1982: 69-141; 7 Stat. 215 (1821); "Creek Indians," Niles' Weekly Register 22 (1824): 223; U.S. Commissioners to Creek Chiefs, 9 Dec. 1824, Document TCC008, SNA.

2. James Barbour to John Crowell, January 29, 1827; Barbour to Troup, January 29, 1827; Barbour to John H. Morel, January 30, 1827; Barbour to R. W. Habersham, January 30, 1827; Barbour to Lieutenant J. R. Vinton, January 30, 1827, ASP: Indian Affairs, 2: 864-5. James Barbour to John Crowell, January 31, 1827, M21 3: 349.

3. February 5, 1827: Message Regarding the Creek Indians

https://millercenter.org/the-presidency/presidential-speeches/february-5-1827-message-regarding-creek-indians (accessed online November 4, 2020).

4. Ibid.

5. Relinquishment of the Claims of the Creeks to the Lands in Georgia, American State Papers: Indian Affairs, 2: 871.

6. President Andrew Jackson's Message to Congress "On Indian Removal," December 6, 1830; Records of the United States Senate, 1789-1990; Record Group 46; National Archives.

7. Andrew Jackson to James Monroe, March 4, 1817, Jackson Papers, 4: 93-98.

8. Alfred Balch to Andrew Jackson, January 8, 1830; Andrew Jackson

Papers: Series 1, General Correspondence and Related Items, 1775-1885 (15,697).

9. Niles' Weekly Register, December 19, 1829.

10. President Jackson's Message to Congress "On Indian Removal", December 6, 1830; Records of the United States Senate, 1789-1990; Record Group 46, National Archives and Records Administration.

11. Bills and Resolutions, Senate, 21st Cong., 1st Sess., February 22, 1830.

12. Banner, Stuart. How the Indians lost their land: Law and power on the frontier. Harvard University Press, 2005: 199.

13. Letter from General John Coffee to Secretary of War Eaton, October 14, 1829.

14. *Speeches on the Passage of the Bill for the Removal of the Indians, Delivered in the Congress of the United States, April and May, 1830.* Perkins and Marvin, 1830: 172.

15. Foster, Arthur. *A Digest of the Laws of the State of Georgia: Containing All Statutes, and the Substance of All Resolutions of a General and Public Nature, and Now in Force, which Have Been Passed in Said State from the Year 1820 to the Year 1829 Inclusive: with Occasional Explanatory Notes and Connecting References, and a List of the Statutes Repealed Or Obsolete to which is Added an Appendix, Containing the Constitution of the State of Georgia, as Amended, Also References to Such Local Acts as Relate to Towns ....* Towar, J. & D.M. Hogan, 1831: 126-129.

16. Frelinghuysen, Theodore. *Speech of Mr. Frelinghuysen, of New Jersey, Delivered in the Senate of the United States, April 6, 1830: On the Bill for an Exchange of Lands with the Indians Residing in Any of the States Or Territories, and for Their Removal West of the Mississippi.* Vol. 23. No. 8. Printed and published at the Office of the National Journal [by George Watterston], 1830, p. 23.

17. Speeches on the Passage of the Bill for the Removal of the Indians, Delivered in the Congress of the United States, April and May 1830, Perkins and Marvin. 1830: 247.

# 26

# EXTERMINATE, ASSIMILATE, PROTECT
# OR REMOVE INDIANS

Four alternatives identified with regard to Indians included: exterminating them, assimilating them, protecting them or removing them. Exterminating them was not realistic. The United States Army in 1830 was small, with only seven infantry regiments responsible for manning forty-nine military posts and arsenals from Maine to Florida and from Louisiana to Michigan. War would be too costly in money and American lives. Assimilation was considered impractical. Affording meaningful protection was impossible, militarily and, even more importantly, politically. The government lacked the finances and the United States Army lacked the will to fend off the westward squatting colonists. Removal, sanctioned from President Jefferson to President Jackson, represented the only viable action, and, certainly with the defeat of such renowned Indian leaders as Pontiac, Tecumseh, Little Turtle, Blue Jacket, McGillivray, John Ross and Black Hawk, there remained no effective Indian resistance.

William Crawford, a former Secretary of War, and Secretary of the Treasury under President Monroe, advocated intermarriage to save the Indians:

> "The utter extinction of the Indian race must be abhorrent to the feelings of an enlightened and benevolent nation." If it came down to the Indians' survival, it would be best to let them and whites intermarry. This would preserve the Indian race but "with

the modifications" necessary to become productive and happy members of American society.[1]

The support of the New York Indian Board, long an advocate for Indians, agreed that removal was the only viable alternative:

>...the harmony of these United States, the preservation of the American Indians from total extinction, and consequently the cause of humanity, require some prompt and decisive measure calculated to carry into effect the only alternative left, namely, the final and speedy removal of the scattered remains of the Indian tribes from within the jurisdictional limits of the sovereign states.[2]

Speaking to a Baptist missionary who had spent time among the Indians, President John Quincy Adams expressed his sorrow for the situation of "that unfortunate race of hunters, who are themselves hunted by us like a partridge upon the mountains." He admitted the gross inconsistency of United States Indian policy, such as it was. "We have talked of benevolence and humanity, and preached them into civilization, but none of this benevolence is felt where the rights of the Indian come into conflict with the interest of the white man." President Adams thought the best thing to do with the American Indians would be to make them citizens, "as a part of our own people." He also knew it was a forlorn hope: "Even this the people of the States within which they are situated will not permit."[3]

## Indian Removal Bill Introduced in Congress

The introduction of the Indian Removal Bill led to lengthy debates in the public and in Congress. President Jackson emphasized that the emigration of the Indians "should be voluntary, for it would be cruel and unjust to compel the aborigines to abandon the graves of their fathers and seek home in a distant land."[4] In support of Georgia, those who remained would be subject to the authority of local and state law and jurisdiction.

Removal was also supported by many Eastern and Christian groups who regularly expressed sympathy for American Indians. Thus, in 1828, U.S. Indian Commissioner Thomas McKenney wrote, "What are humanity and justice in reference to this unfortunate race?"[5] The solution lay in geography—place Indians so far west that colonist settlement would not be a problem for a very long time, perhaps centuries. The Federal Government should create "a land of refuge, where this unhappy race may find rest and safety," wrote Lewis Cass, Territorial Governor of Michigan.[6] Further, Cass contributed an essay to the North American Review in 1830 arguing for the removal of the Indians. He wrote: "A barbarous people, depending for subsistence upon the scanty and precarious supplies furnished by the chase, cannot live in contact with a civilized community."[7]

## Congressional Senate Debates on Indian Removal Act Challenging Doctrine of Discovery and Occupancy Theory

The Congressional Senate debate on the Indian Removal Act lasted from April 6 to April 24, 1830. Of the 48 senators, only eight spoke for any length of time—four of whom voted for the removal bill, four against. Senator Theodore Frelinghuysen of New Jersey and his allies, Peleg Sprague of Maine and Asher Robbins of Rhode Island, intended to prove that the Act violated the higher authority of the United States as expressed in its treaties with the Indians. Opposing them were John Forsyth of Georgia, Hugh Lawson White of Tennessee, John McKinley of Alabama and Robert Adams of Mississippi.

## Georgia's Governor Lumpkin Eviscerates Treaties between U.S. and Indians

Georgia Governor Lumpkin averred on the Congressional floor that Indian treaties were meaningless:

> … treaties were expedients by which ignorant, intractable, and savage people were induced without bloodshed to yield up what civilized peoples had a right to possess by virtue of that command of the Creator delivered to man upon his formation-be fruitful, multiply, and replenish the earth, and subdue it.[7]

Also, he remarked "I will have my bond, I will have my pound of flesh," declaring that he would have the terms of the Compact of 1802 fulfilled to "the twentieth part of one poor scruple, and to the division of a hair."

## Speech of Senator Frelinghuysen of New Jersey

Senator Theodore Frelinghuysen from New Jersey, in his six-hour speech opposing the Indian Removal Act, asserted three fundamental and, as he saw it, undeniable precepts about the relationship of the Indians to the United States:

(1) [T]he Indians held the original and absolute title to their lands—*"I insist that, by immemorial possession, as the original tenants of the soil, they hold a title beyond and superior to the British Crown and her colonies, and to all adverse pretensions of our confederation and subsequent Union. ... Where is the decree or ordinance that has stripped these early and first lords of the soil? Sir, no record of such measure can be found."* (Emphasis added.)

(2) [T]he Indian tribes were sovereign political entities with their own governments—"Our ancestors found these people, far removed "from the commotions of Europe, exercising all the rights, and enjoying the privileges of free and independent sovereigns of this new world. *They were not a wild and lawless horde of banditti; but lived under the restraints of Government, patriarchal in its influence. They had chiefs, head men and councils."*[8] (Emphasis added.)

[T]he paradigm of the Indian treaty system, in conjunction with the Trade and Intercourse Acts, was the only established and recognized mode of interacting with the American Indians.

Importantly, Senator Frelinghuysen in debates in 1830 emphasized that grants to the King, Colony, State or Territory of Indian lands were made from the Indians, not from the governing authority to them:

No King, Colony, State or Territory, ever made, or attempted to make, a grant or title to the Indians, but universally and perpetually derived their titles from them. This one fact, that stands forth broadly on the page of Indian history-which neither kings nor colonies-neither lords, proprietors, nor diplomatic agents, have on any single occasion disputed, is alone sufficient to demolish the whole system of political pretensions, conjured up in modern times to drive the poor Indian from the last refuge of his hopes.[9]

He refused to concede that the citizens of the new republic would agree to the false front Georgia was using to take away the lands of the Cherokees. There were many who stood with him in speaking the truth, but unfortunately, not enough.

*The people of this country will never acquiesce in such violent constructions. They will read for themselves; and when they shall learn the history of all our intercourse with the Indians; when they shall perceive the guaranties so often renewed to them, and under what solemn sanctions, the American community will not seek the aids of artificial speculations on the requisite formalities to a technical treaty. No, Sir.*[10] (Emphasis added.)

He also condemned the 'most odious proposal' to divide, conquer and bribe Cherokee leaders and influential men. In the instructions of the Secretary of War to Generals Carroll and Coffee, is found the following language: "The best resort [to induce the Indians to emigrate] is believed to be that which is embraced in an appeal to the chiefs and influential men—*not together, but apart at their own houses ... whilst offers to them of extensive reservations in fee simple, and other rewards*, would it is hoped, result in obtaining their acquiescence. This had, their people, as a body, it is believed, would gladly go."[11]

Senator Frelinghuysen:

For, Sir, after the first day of June next, a gang of lawless white men may break into the Cherokee country, plunder their habitation, murder the mother, with the children, and all in sight of the wretched husband and father-and no law of Georgia will reach the atrocity. It is vain to tell us, Sir, that murder may be traced by circumstantial probabilities. The charge against this State is--you have by force and violence stripped these people of the protection of their government, and now refuse to cast over them the shield of your own. The outrage of the deed is, that you leave the poor Indian helpless and defenceless (sic), and in this cruel way hope to banish him from his home. Sir, if this law be enforced, I do religiously believe that it will awaken tones of feeling that will go up to God- and call down the thunders of his wrath.[12]

Justice M'Lean described this Georgia Act in *Worcester*:

This act annexes the territory of the Indians, within the limits of Georgia, to the counties named in the title, and extends the jurisdiction of the State over it. It annuls the laws, ordinances, orders and regulations of any kind made by the Cherokees, either in council or in any other way, and they are not permitted to be given in evidence in the Courts of the State. By this law, no Indian or the descendant of an Indian residing within the Creek or Cherokee Nation of Indians shall be deemed a competent witness in any Court of the State to which a white person may be a party, except such white person reside within the Nation.[13]

William Lloyd Garrison would later compose a poem honoring Senator Frelinghysen and assailing the motives of the Indian Removal Act's supporters.

TO THE HON. THEODORE FRELINGHUYSEN: ON READING HIS ELOQUENT SPEECH IN DEFENCE OF INDIAN RIGHTS, IN THE UNITED STATES SENATE

Fruitless thy mighty efforts—vain appealing

To grasping Avarice, that ne'er relents;

To Party Power, that shamelessly is stealing,

Banditti-like, whatever spoil it scents;

To base Intrigue, his cloven foot revealing,

That struts in Honesty's habiliments.[14]

## Speech of Senator Sprague of Maine

Senator Sprague of Maine focused on the fourteen treaties entered into with the Cherokees promising them protected, undisturbed possession of their lands. He vigorously contested Georgia's assertions that the treaties were informal, and hence malleable. As late as 1825, as everyone in Congress knew, Georgia had contended that the Treaty of Indian Springs was valid and must be enforced. Senator Sprague went on to enunciate the obligations under these treaties:

> By several of these treaties, we have unequivocally guarantied to them that they shall forever enjoy—
>
> 1st. Their separate existence as a political community;
>
> 2d. Undisturbed possession and full enjoyment of their lands, within certain boundaries, which are fully defined and fully described;
>
> 3d. The protection of the United States, against all interference with, or encroachments upon their rights by any people, state, or nation. For these promises, on our part, we received ample consideration. By the restoration and establishing of peace; By large cessions of territory; of other important stipulations.
>
> 1st. That the Cherokees shall continue to exist as a distinct political community, under the protection of the United States.
>
> 2d. That they shall enjoy the undisturbed possession of their lands.
>
> 3d. That the power to manage 'their affairs' shall be exercised for the benefit and comfort of the Indians; and for the prevention of injuries and oppressions.
>
> Did this give to the United States the right to drive them from all their lands?---Or to destroy the Cherokee Nation, to strike it out of existence; and instead of managing for their 'benefit' to annihilate 'their affairs' as a body politic? Or could we convey a greater right than we ourselves possessed?
>
> ... a treaty of peace, not a truce, not an armistice, not a temporary cession of hostilities-but a treaty of peace, is in its nature, a permanent, enduring contract, must bind each party to respect the

existence of the other, and never to assail or attempt its destruction-must obligate each also to permit the other to continue that existence upon its own territory without attack or violence. To attempt to expel them by force, or subjugate or destroy their separate being, is a violation of the compact of peace, and a renewal of the war.[15]

## Speech of Senator Robbins of Rhode Island

Mr. President: The whole argument in favor of this bill turns upon the question, whether the Indian nations within our territorial boundaries are competent to make treaties with the United States. I should think, to make gentlemen pause a little, and even fear the success of their own argument; for the consequence would be such that the whole body of the rights acquired by Indian treaties or held under them, would be torn from their foundations, and the resulting evils would be incalculably great. I have said that in that case these treaties would be nullities, and who can doubt it?

Besides this notorious fact, the right of pre-emption, claimed by discovery, is decisive to prove that the right of jurisdiction was not claimed. If the crown claimed these Indian nations as his subjects, why claim a preemptive right to their titles? Did any king claim a preemptive right to the land titles of his own subjects? Never. If discovery then is a good authority for what it claims it is food for what it disclaims; it disclaims the right of jurisdiction over and for the Indian nations.

I will say, that these Indians have been made the victims of power exerted against right; the victims of violated faith, the nation's faith; the victims of violated justice; yes, I call God to witness of his violated justice.

Ill fated Indians! barbarism, and attempts at civilization, are alike fate to your rights; but attempts at civilization the more fatal of the two. The jealous of their own rights are the contemners of yours; proud and chivalrous states do not think it beneath them to take advantage of your weakness. You have lands which they want or rather which they desire, for they do not want them; your rights stand in their way, and those proud and chivalrous states do not think it beneath them to destroy your rights by their legislation.- Proud and chivalrous states do not think it beneath them to present to your feeble and helpless condition, this alternative-either to abandon your homes, the habitations you have built, the fields you have planted, and all the comforts you have gathered around you; the homes of your fathers, and the sepulchers of their dead; and go far into the depths of an unknown wilderness; there to abide the destiny which may there await you; or to surrender your rights, and submit yourselves to their power, but to expect no participation in their rights.[16]

Georgia's legislation was yet another tactic of settler colonial policy— get Indians to voluntarily move, rather than endure living under the cloak of tyranny. Also, the various removals of different Indian Nations caused a dispersal of Indians and a weakening of their status as sovereigns.

## Other Senators

The exchange between Senators Forsyth and Webster was particularly acrimonious. After hours of argument between the two men, Senator Forsyth professed to want to see the entire matter settled by the judiciary.

> "That might," replied Webster, "have been a remarkably good argument to address to the State of Georgia before she took the remedy into her own hands." It is a new mode of settling a Constitutional question [Webster continued], to seize the lands in dispute, and send out the Hancock troop of horse to defend the possession of them. But, at this stage of the affair, that appeal to the Courts comes with rather an awkward grace. When a man advances a claim against the lands of his neighbor, he makes his appeal to the law; but, when he forcibly enters into possession of them, he makes his appeal to something different than the law.[17]

Senator Forsyth, in his anger and frustration, turned on Representative Robert Letcher of Kentucky when he expressed sympathy for the Georgians and their "peculiar situation." He noted that he felt a "strong sympathy for the Indians, and deeply regretted the controversy that had arisen between them and the state of Georgia."[18] At this Senator Forsyth stood and professed incredulity and disgust. "What, sir, a Representative from Kentucky neutral between Indians and White People—between his brothers and this miserable and dependent tribe of Indians, in whose name, for years, money has been filched from your Treasury?"[19]

## Congressional House of Representatives Debates on Indian Removal Act Challenging Doctrine of Discovery and Occupancy Theory

Other opponents of the Indian removal legislation in the House of Representatives similarly agreed with Senator Frelinghuysen, including Henry Storrs of New York, William Ellsworth and Jabez Huntington of Connecticut, George Evans of Maine, Isaac Bates and Edward Everett of Massachusetts, John Test of Indiana, Jensey Johns, Jr., of Delaware, David Crockett of Kentucky and Joseph Hemphill of Pennsylvania. They labelled removal plans as open and rank assaults on Indian sovereignty. Prominent members of Congress characterized the bill as designed to flout firm and binding treaty obligations, including the Treaty of Holston with the Cherokee. They also assailed the provisions of the removal bill itself, arguing that it was vague in its goals and unrealistic in its expectations.

## Speech of Representative Storrs

Representative Henry Storrs in his speech reveals the major problem at hand for Georgia—her citizens didn't have the money to pay taxes and her debt made her situation precarious. She needed 'every pound of flesh' to survive.

> I have been inclined to think, Sir, that under all the circumstances, some of the new states were admitted into the Union before they had acquired a sufficient population and strength to sustain their State governments with advantage and convenience to themselves. But their early admission into the Union imposed upon them the burthen of supporting independent governments when they were not yet well able to bear taxation, and while their resources were too much exhausted in payments for the public domain.

Representative Storrs in regard to the bribery proposed by President Jackson's Secretary of War Eaton:

> It is sheer, open bribery—a disreputable proposition to buy up the chiefs, and reward them for treason to their people. It is the first time, so far as my knowledge extends, that such a practice has been unblushingly avowed.

Representative Storrs was also opposed to portraying treaties as other than a negotiated agreement between sovereigns:

> The committee [on Indian Affairs] have suggested that we should not give much weight to 'the stately forms which Indian treaties have assumed, nor to the terms often employed in them,' but that we should rather consider them as 'mere names' and 'forms of intercourse.' ... Words no longer mean what words import, and things are not what they are.[20]

In justifying his position that the term 'treaty' was the proper nomenclature for the agreements between the government and Indian Nations, Representative Storrs described the types of understandings negotiated to document that they were the type customarily contained in a treaty:

> We have not only recognized them as possessed of attributes of sovereignty, but, in some of these treaties, we have defined what these attributes are. We have taken their lands as cessions—terms totally senseless if they are citizens or individuals. We have stipulated for the right of passage through their country, and for the use of their harbors, for the restoration of prisoners, for the surrender of fugitives from justice, servants, and slaves. ... If these acts of the Federal Government do not show them to be sovereign to some extent, you cannot show that you have ever acknowledged any nation to be so.[21]

In addition, he raised the critical question of conquest. If the U.S. was to argue it conquered the Indians, where were the attributes of conquest?

> But it is essential to title by conquest, that we should have exercised the right which the laws of war allow to the conqueror. *Have we taken away their lands, abolished their governments,*

*and put them in subjection to our laws*. If this has not been done, (and history shows that it has not,) it is too late now to say that there has been a time when we might have done it. So far from claiming to exercise this right, we have closed our hostilities by treaties ever since we became an independent government; and both parties were restored to their original condition, except on points which the treaties provided for. It must be considered, too, *that when we set up the title of conquest, we seem to feel that discovery alone would not have reached the rights of soil against the native inhabitants...*[22] (Emphasis added.)

## Speeches of Other Advocates for Indian Rights

Should the members of Congress sanction removal, said Representative Woods, "the blood of these People, reduced by us to the condition of wretchedness and horror, in which 'the living child is buried with the dead mother,' will be upon our heads."[23]

Representative Isaac Bates of Massachusetts accused President Jackson and his supporters of bad faith even more pointedly. **"You cooperate with Georgia—you give effect to her laws—you put the Indians aside and trample your treaties with them in the dust,"** Bates alleged. **"And it will be in vain you tell the world you did not set fire to the city, when you saw it burning, and would not put it out, though you were its hired patrol and watch."** (Emphasis added.)

> My positions are, that the Cherokees are not the tenants of Georgia, nor subject to her jurisdiction; but that they are the sole proprietors of the territory they occupy, whether as hunting grounds or otherwise, and are sovereign; and that the United States are pledged to defend their boundary, and to protect them in all their rights and privileges as a nation.[24]

He argued the bill and the administration's removal scheme were deceptive. Their true purpose was not to save the Indians or improve their condition but to sanction the bullying actions of the southern states, thus constituting a de facto program of forcible removal.

Representative Edward Everett, Massachusetts, decried it as follows:

> The evil, Sir, is enormous; the inevitable suffering incalculable.
> Do not stain the fair fame of the country.... Nations of dependent
> Indians, against their will, under color of law, are driven from
> their homes into the wilderness. You cannot explain it; you cannot
> reason it away.... Our friends will view this measure with sorrow,
> and our enemies alone with joy. And we ourselves, Sir, when the
> interests and passions of the day are past, shall look back upon it, I
> fear, with self-reproach, and a regret as bitter as unavailing.[25]

Representative David Crockett, Kentucky, represented more citizens
than any other representative. He voted with his conscience against
removal.

> He knew the Indians were unwilling to go and therefore he could
> not consent to place them in a situation where they would be
> obliged to go. ... He knew that he stood alone, having, perhaps,
> none of his colleagues from his state agreeing in sentiment. ... He
> knew that he should return to his home glad and light in heart, if
> he voted against the bill. If he should be the only member of that
> House who voted against the bill, and the only man in the United
> States who disapproved it, he would still vote against it; and it
> would be matter of rejoicing to him till the day he died, that he
> had given the vote. ... He had seen much to disgust him here, and
> he did not wish to represent his fellow citizens, unless he could be
> permitted to act conscientiously. ... He had never been six months
> at school in his life: he had raised himself by the labor of his hands.
> ... Humble as he was, he meant to exercise his privilege.[26]

Representative Jensey Johns, Jr. of Delaware refused to concede to the
disgrace of disregarding the rights of the Indians:

> If we should in an evil hour sully the lustre of the American name,
> and destroy the last hope of liberty I would rather share with the
> Cherokee the fate that awaits him, than encounter the infamy and
> disgrace which must be our portion. Sir, I cannot yield my assent.[27]

## The Memorial of the Cherokee Nation (April 14, 1830)

When the Cherokee Nation petitioned Congress to prohibit Georgia's incursion on its lands, they confirmed the government's recognition of their ownership of their land:

> It is evident from facts deducible from known history, that the Indians were found here by the white man, in the enjoyment of plenty and peace, and all the rights of soil and domain, inherited from their ancestors from time immemorial, well furnished with kings, chiefs, and warriors, the bulwarks of liberty, and the pride of their race. Great Britain established with them relationships of friendship and alliance, and at no time did she treat them as subjects, and as tenants at will, to her power. In war she fought them as a separate people, and they resisted her as a nation. In peace, she spoke the language of friendship, and they replied in the voice of independence, and frequently assisted her as allies, at their choice to fight her enemies in their own way and discipline, subject to the control of their own chiefs, and unaccountable to European officers and military law. Such was the connexion of this nation to Great Britain, to wit, that of friendship, and not allegiance, to the period of the declaration of Independence by the United States.[28]

## Impact of *Fletcher* and *Johnson* on Indian Removal Act

The U.S. Supreme Court, under *Johnson*, had determined that Indians had a right to occupy land, but they did not own it. Since Natives did not own the land, they became prey to an increasingly loud argument within the United States that Indian occupancy of land in close proximity to settlers inevitably led to trouble. To avoid the trouble, Indians should be moved away from the edges of western settlement.

Since under *Fletcher*, the states held fee title to all land within the state, it led the southern states to enact legislation incorporating Cherokee land into the counties of Georgia and totally abrogating their sovereignty. They would be citizens of Georgia and subject to its laws.

Senators John McKinley (ALA), Thomas F. Foster (GA) and Richard H. Wilde (GA) supported Senator John Forsyth of Georgia's assertion that the Indians possessed no inherent rights to the soil by invoking the well-known Supreme Court case of *Johnson* in which Chief Justice Marshall had affirmed that the United States held dominion over Indian lands by an established right of 'discovery' and conquest, inherited from the country's European predecessors. The Indians had a right of occupancy, but not a right to title. Furthermore, Congressman Henry Lamar from Alabama argued the Supreme Court case of *Fletcher* supported his position for the Indian Removal Act.

## The Indian Removal Act Passed

In 1830, Congress passed the act titled: "An Act to provide for an exchange of lands with the Indians residing in any of the states or territories, and for their removal west of the river Mississippi," commonly referred to as the Indian Removal Act of 1830, 4 Stat. 411. The *Fletcher* and *Johnson* decisions bolstered support for the Act in Congress. It passed the Senate by a vote of 28-19. It passed the House by a vote of 102-97. It was signed by President Jackson on May 28, 1830.

It included funds to pay for removal—$500,000 was appropriated to pay to move Indians west of the Mississippi River. The bill, conspicuously, contained no stipulation which allowed the Indian Nations to refuse relocation or even any indication they might not wish to do so, and nothing further was said of assimilation. It made no mention of the use of force.

## Typical Removal Treaty

A typical removal treaty provided for the costs of removal and one year of subsistence thereafter:

> The 6th article of the treaty concluded on September 3, 1839, with the Stockbridge-and Munsee Tribes of Indians provided "that, whenever those who are desirous of emigrating shall signify their wish to that effect, the United States will defray the expenses of their removal west of

the Mississippi, and furnish them with subsistence for one year after their arrival at their new homes.[30]

## 1837 Revised Regulations Concerning the Emigration of Indians

Revised Regulations in 1837 to govern the removal of Indians demonstrated the callousness of the federal government, which was even unwilling to pay for medicine chests.[31]

> Rule 26. Those who are too young, or too infirm to travel on foot, will be transported in wagons, or upon horses.
>
> Rule 44. Medicines will only be procured when actually required, or danger from sickness is apprehended. In no instance will full medicine chests or surgical instruments be purchased.

## Removal of Indian Nations Became Mandatory

Over 60 removal treaties were signed which resulted in the forced westward migration of approximately 80,000 American Indians. Although removal was supposed to be voluntary, relocation of Indian Nations became mandatory whenever the government decided. Many of the eastern Indian Nations were destroyed or decimated. Millions of acres of lands were opened to settlers moving west.

## 1840 War Department Annual Report, Commissioner of Indian Affairs T. Hartley Crawford – Tribes Requiring Removal

In 1840, the Commissioner of Indian Affairs detailed the tribes still to be removed:

> [T]here yet remain northeast of Missouri and east of the Mississippi rivers, who will soon require a western home, the Winnebagoes, the Sacs and Foxes of the Des Moines, the united band of Ottawas, Chippewas, and Pottawatomies, the Ottawas and Chippewas, several bands of Chippewas, the Menomonies, the New York Indians, the Miamies,

and the Wyandots. The day is probably not distant, either, when the Sioux and other tribes will be asked to cede their land.[32]

The New York Indians remained averse to relocation, yet the U.S. would only allow five years for them to remain at their homelands.

Unfortunately for the Kansas Indians, the federal government intended to purchase part of their land, whether they agreed or not. They had miscalculated on how much land they needed to settle the Indians they were removing from the east. Indian Nations west of the Mississippi River, such as the Kansas Indians, would be required to make up the shortfall.

## 1840 War Department Annual Report, Commissioner of Indian Affairs – Pottawatomies Removal Delayed

The Pottawatomies were under the control of General Brady. Whenever an Indian nation resisted removal, they were placed under military control. Their removal was delayed and their condition described by General Brady as follows:

> In the two or three or more years that they linger in idleness and debauchery, gazing listlessly upon the streams and hills they must soon leave, habits are strengthened – drinking. For five years and more they have been literally eating to-day without knowing where to-morrow's supplies were; uncertain of their own movements, with nothing stable for them but the heavens above and the earth below them, they were in that most wretched of all human conditions, in which there is no object or end but to appease hunger, without regard to the how, and to satisfy the animal passions of our nature, without reflection on the consequences, or commiseration for their victims.[33]

The delays in removing certain tribes who had agreed to removal was due to the federal government's indecision as to whether the removed tribes should all be confined to one territory or there would be a northern and a southern refuge. The extent of the country set aside as Indian territory and the country south of the Missouri were inadequate to locate all the tribes.

## 1840 War Department Annual Report, Commissioner of Indian Affairs – Wyandot Indian Nation Sub-Agency

As reported by Sub-Agent Jonathan Phillips in 1840, 100 Wyandot died due to fatigue from removal, change of climate, intemperance and living in low, unhealthy ground.[34]

## 1844 War Department Annual Report, Commissioner of Indian Affairs – Turkey Creek Sub-Agency

The Winnebagoes again faced perishing during the winter due to the lack of game and the use of their annuities for whiskey. Agent John Chambers warned that the existing system of trade and intercourse with the Indians is destroying them and stressed the dire need for Congressional corrective action.[35]

Agent James McGregor appealed to the U.S. for a revocation of all licenses and the admittance only of government agents to Indian country to quell the prodigious amount of liquor made available for sale to the Indians and the concomitant intemperance of the Indians. He also noted the unsuitable quality of the guns provided as part of their annuities – they burst, locks were damaged and they were unusable.[36]

Agent Benjamin Terrill stated that Indians were discouraged from building homes due to their possible future removal. He advised that their excessive drinking was understandable due to their continued "perplexity" and "anxiety."[37]

## 1844 War Department Annual Report, Commissioner of Indian Affairs – Green Bay

Agent D. Jones entreated the federal government to do something about the trade in liquor. Every Menominee adult—male and female—were addicted to alcohol. He also implored the government to do something about the traders who charged unbelievably exorbitant prices for goods.[38]

## 1844 War Department Annual Report, Commissioner of Indian Affairs – St. Louis

Superintendent Thomas H. Harvey visited the Kanzas, Ottawas, Weas, Chippewas, Piankeshaws, Peorias, Pottawatomies and Osages and found that the weather had ruined their substantial efforts in raising crops for subsistence. He cautioned that if they did not receive federal aid "suffering and death would be the result."[39]

## 1844 War Department Annual Report, Commissioner of Indian Affairs – Willow Creek, Pawnee Country

James and Carolan Mathers, farmers employed by the federal government to teach the Pawnees how to farm, reported the Indians suffered "great and general suffering" in the spring due to the scarcity of provisions.

> "It was painful to behold their meagre visages and emaciated frames, becoming every day more wan, which but too plainly revealed the fact, they were suffering severally for want of alimentary sustenance."[40]

## 1844 War Department Annual Report, Commissioner of Indian Affairs – Choctaw Agency

The Senecas, Shawnees and Quapaws were dying at a high rate due to imperceptible causes. They were expected to become extinct.[41]

Notes

1. William H. Crawford to John Gaillard, March 13, 1816, ASP: Indian Affairs, 2: 26-28.

2. Documents and Proceedings Relating to the Formation and Progress of a Board in the City of New York, for the Emigration, Preservation, and Improvement, of the Aborigines of North America. (New York: Vanderpool and Cole, 1829), pp. 21-22.

3. Adams, John Quincy. *Memoirs of John Quincy Adams: comprising portions of his diary from 1795 to 1848*. Vol. 2. JB Lippincott & Company, 1874: 410-411.

4. James D. Richardson, Messages and Papers of the Presidents, Vol. 2, 456-9.

5. Banner, Stuart. *How the Indians lost their land: Law and power on the frontier*. Harvard University Press, 2005: 208.

6. Ibid.

7. http://nativeamericannetroots.net/diary/1440

8. https://www.wcu.edu/library/DigitalCollections/CherokeePhoenix/ Vol3/no25/this-issue-of-the-phoenix-is-published-in-four-columns- only-page-1-column-1a-page-3-column-1a.html (accessed on December 13, 2020).

9. Speech of Mr. Frelinghuysen, of New Jersey, delivered in the Senate of the United States, April 6, 1830, on The Bill For An Exchange Of Lands With The Indians Residing In Any Of The States Or Territories And For Their Removal West Of The Mississippi: 5.

10. Ibid., p. 10.

11. Ibid., p. 22.

12. Ibid., p. 5.

13. Ibid., p. 24.

14. *Worcester v. Georgia,* 31 U.S. 515, 577 (1832).

15. TO THE HON. THEODORE FRELINGHUYSEN: ON READING HIS ELOQUENT SPEECH IN DEFENCE OF INDIAN RIGHTS, IN THE UNITED STATES SENATE, IN 1890.

16. Speech of Mr. Sprague, of Maine: Delivered in the Senate of the United States, 16th April, 1830, in Reply to Messrs. White, Mckinley, and Forsyth, upon the Subject of the Removal of the Indians. Published at the Office of the National Journal, Peter Force, 1830: 40.

17. United States. Congress. Speeches on the Passage of the Bill for the Removal of the Indians, Delivered in the Congress of the United States, April and May, 1830, Perkins and Marvin, 1830: 76.

18. Register of Debates, H. of R., 19th Cong., 2nd Sess., 1035.

19. Ibid., p. 1045.

20. Ibid. p. 1049.

21. Speeches on the passage of the Bill for the removal of the Indians, delivered in the Congress of the United States, April and May, 1830. United States, Perkins & Marvin, 1830: 112.

22. Storrs, Henry Randolph. Speech of Mr. Storrs, of New-York, in Committee of the Whole House: On the Bill for the Removal of the Indians West of the Mississippi. United States, Northway & Porter, 1830: 39.

23. Speeches on the passage of the Bill for the removal of the Indians, delivered in the Congress of the United States, April and May, 1830. United States, Perkins & Marvin, 1830: 119.

24. Rives, John Cook, et al. The Congressional Globe. United States, Blair & Rives: 1559.

25. United States. Congress. Speeches on the Passage of the Bill for

the Removal of the Indians, Delivered in the Congress of the United States, April and May, 1830, Perkins and Marvin, 1830: 232.

26. United States. Congress. Speeches of the Passage of the Bill for the Removal of the Indians, Delivered in the Congress of the United States, April and May, 1830, Perkins and Marvin, 1830: 299.

27. United States. Congress. Speeches on the Passage of the Bill for the Removal of the Indians, Delivered in the Congress of the United States, April and May, 1830, Perkins and Marvin, 1830: 253.

28. United States. Congress. Speeches on the Passage of the Bill for the Removal of the Indians, Delivered in the Congress of the United States, April and May, 1830, Perkins and Marvin, 1830: 228.

29. Lamar Marshall, Larry Smith, Michael Wren. Alabama Collection Camps, Forts, Emigrating Depots and Travel Routes Used During the Cherokee Removal of 1838-1839

https://www.nps.gov/trte/learn/historyculture/upload/Alabama-Collections-Camps-Forts-Depots-and-Routes-508.pdf (accessed online November 29, 2020).

30. 1837 War Department Annual Report, Commissioner of Indian Affairs T. Hartley Crawford, Washington: Government Printing Office, 1838.

31. 1837 War Department Annual Report - Commissioner of Indian Affairs C. A. Harris, Washington: Government Printing Office, 1838.

32. 1840 War Department Annual Report, Commissioner of Indian Affairs T. Hartley Crawford, Washington: Government Printing Office, 1841.

33. Ibid.

34. Ibid.

35. 1844 War Department Annual Report, Commissioner of Indian Affairs T. Hartley Crawford, Washington: Government Printing Office, 1845.

36. Ibid.

37. Ibid.

38. Ibid.

39. Ibid.

40. Ibid.

41. Ibid.

# 7

# 'FIVE CIVILIZED TRIBES' UNDER U.S. SOVEREIGNTY AND CONTROL

In 1830, the 'Five Civilized Tribes'—the Chickasaw, Choctaw, Creek, Seminole and Cherokee Indian Nations were still living east of the Mississippi River. Many of them had adopted various aspects of European-American culture, including Christianity. They were agriculturists so their cultivation of their lands could not be questioned. The Cherokees had their own written language, developed by Sequoyah, and published a newspaper in Cherokee and English. The majority of the Cherokees did not want to move—they refused to cede additional lands to the Indian commissioners led by James Wilkinson. In frustration, one of the federal commissioners wrote to Secretary of War Dearborn: "I leave the Red people to adjust their respective pretensions to the soil."[1]

## Cherokee Nation Constitution

The 1827 Cherokee Constitution claimed absolute sovereignty over its land, refusing to concede to Chief Justice Marshall's decision in *Johnson*.

> Article 1 THE BOUNDARIES of this nation ... guarantied and reserved forever to the Cherokee Nation by the Treaties concluded with the United States, are as follows ... and shall forever hereafter remain unalterably the same...[2]

Georgia leaped on this as a violation of Article IV, Section 3 of the U.S. Constitution which prohibited any new state from being formed within the jurisdiction of any other state, an 'imperio in imperium.' Rather than perceiving it as establishing a method of government, it was considered an illegal action.

Representative George Evans of Maine countered the imperio in imperium argument:

> It is said, however, that these Cherokees are forming a government, and are taking rapid strides to power. This position is equally untrue. They have not formed a government. They always had a government. They were ruled by councils, and by traditionary laws; and all they have done is to put that which was formerly oral only, into a written form. This may be improving their government, but it is not creating it, nor assuming any new power.[3]

## George "Corn" Tassels, Cherokee Indian Nation Citizen, Hung by State of Georgia on Christmas Eve

In state court, Georgia tried a Cherokee man (George "Corn" Tassels) for murdering another Cherokee within the boundaries of the Cherokee Nation.

A writ of error from the U.S. Supreme Court was obtained, and Georgia was ordered to appear before that tribunal and defend the judgment of the State Court. The order was signed by Chief Justice Marshall. Georgia's reply from the Legislature resolved that:

> "...[T]he interference by the chief justice of the supreme court of the U. States, in the administration of the criminal laws of this state, ... is a flagrant violation of her rights;" that the Governor "and every other officer of this state" be directed to disregard any and every mandate and process ... purporting to proceed from the chief justice or any associate justice of the supreme court of the United States; that the Governor be "authorised and required, with all the force and means ... at his command ... to resist and repel any and every invasion from whatever quarter, upon the administration of the criminal laws of this state"; that Georgia refuses to become a party to "the case sought to be made before the supreme court"; and that the Governor, "by express, direct the sheriff of Hall County to execute the law in the case of George Tassels."[4]

**Five days later, Tassels was hanged. The Supreme Court, powerless to vindicate its authority, defied and insulted by a 'sovereign' state, abandoned by the administration, was powerless to take any action.**

John Quincy Adams, then a member of Congress, wrote in his diary January 4, 1831 that:

> ...the resolutions of the legislature of Georgia setting at defiance the Supreme Court of the United States are published and approved in the Telegraph, the Administration newspaper at this place.... The Constitution, the laws and treaties of the United States are prostrate in the State of Georgia. Is there any remedy for this state of things? None. Because the Executive of the United States is in League with the State of Georgia.... This example ... will be imitated by other States, and with regard to other national interests—perhaps the tariff.... The Union is in the most imminent danger of dissolution.... The ship is about to founder.[5]

## Cherokees Turn to U.S. Supreme Court to Enforce Their Treaty Rights; *Cherokee Nation v. Georgia*, 30 U.S. 1 (1831)

As the executive and Congressional branches of the federal government refused to take action on behalf of the Cherokees, they filed suit in the U.S. Supreme Court—*Cherokee Nation v. Georgia*, 30 U.S. 1 (1831).

President Jackson expressed his unequivocal support for state authority over the Indians as individuals in his address to the Creeks. "My white children in Alabama have extended their law over your country," continued President Jackson. "If you remain in it, you must be subject to that law. If you remove across the Mississippi, you will be subject to your own laws, and the care of your father, the President."[6] The Creeks who chose to remain in the East would be provided a homestead in fee simple, but there was to be no Indian Nation identity, much less authority, east of the Mississippi River.

The question was whether the U.S. Supreme Court had jurisdiction over the case. Under the U.S. Constitution, the U.S. Supreme Court has *original jurisdiction* over disputes between states, and disputes between United States and a foreign state. Original jurisdiction means the case is tried before the Court, not on appeal. The Court, led by Chief Justice Marshall, had to determine whether an Indian Nation is a state or foreign nation or some other entity.

The Cherokee Nation represented by attorney William Wirt appeared as "a foreign state, not owing allegiance to the United States, nor to any state of this union."[7] It argued it was a foreign state because none of its members were U.S. citizens.

A narrow ruling was possible by relying on the Commerce Clause. The Constitution empowers Congress to "regulate commerce with foreign nations, and among the several States, and with the Indian tribes."[8] Thus, in the Constitution itself, tribes are distinguished from foreign nations and states, implying they are neither.

## Domestic Dependent Nations

Chief Justice Marshall though chose again to go beyond what was necessary to decide the case before him by characterizing what Indian Nations were in his opinion.

> **"They may, more correctly, perhaps, be denominated domestic dependent nations. They occupy a territory to which we assert a title independent of their will... Meanwhile they are in a state of pupilage. Their relation to the United States resembles that of a ward to his guardian."[9]** (Emphasis added.)

He described them as completely under the sovereignty and dominion of the United States.

> They look to our government for protection; rely upon its kindness and its power; appeal to it for relief to their wants; and address the President as their Great Father. They and their country are considered by foreign nations, as well as by ourselves, as being so **completely under the sovereignty and dominion of the United States** that any attempt to acquire their lands, or to form a political connexion with them, would be considered by all as an invasion of our territory and an act of hostility.[10] (Emphasis added.)

For Chief Justice Marshall, the question presented was not a proper subject for judicial inquiry or decision—it was a political question.

> The case requires us to control the Legislature of Georgia, and to restrain the exertion of its physical force.... It savours too much of the exercise of political power to be within the proper province of the judicial department.[11]

## Split Court

The Court's decision was a split of 2, 2 and 2. Two justices held that Indian Nations were not states at all; two justices held that Indian Nations were states but were not foreign; and two justices held that Indian Nations were states and were foreign. As there was no majority, the practical effect was that there was no government branch which would stop Georgia in its actions against Cherokees. The Court did leave an opening for an appropriate case to litigate the issue.

Justice William Johnson opined as follows regarding Indians:

> But I think it very clear that the Constitution neither speaks of them as States or foreign states, but as just what they were, Indian tribes, an anomaly unknown to the books that treat of States, and which the law of nations would regard as nothing more than wandering hordes, held together only by ties of blood and habit, and having neither laws or government beyond what is required in a savage state.[12]

Justice Joseph Story co-signed Justice Thompson's dissent to the majority opinion authored by Chief Justice Marshall in the *Cherokee Nation* case.

> Testing the character and condition of the Cherokee Indians by these rules, it is not perceived how it is possible to escape the conclusion that they form a sovereign state. They have always been dealt with as such by the Government of the United States, both before and since the adoption of the present Constitution. They have been admitted and treated as a people governed solely and exclusively by their own laws, usages, and customs within their own territory, claiming and exercising exclusive dominion

over the same, yielding up by treaty, from time to time, portions of their land, but still claiming absolute sovereignty and self-government over what remained unsold.[13]

It is a rule which has been repeatedly sanctioned by this Court that the judicial department is to consider as sovereign and independent States or nations those powers that are recognized as such by the executive and legislative departments of the government, they being more particularly entrusted with our foreign relations.[14]

Although the U.S. had promised in a compact with Georgia to extinguish the aboriginal title, it had not done so yet, and thus: "[T]he state has not even a reversionary interest in the soil. ... [U]ntil this is done, the state can have no claim to the lands. ... If the U.S. never extinguished the title, Thompson opined, Georgia could not force the U.S. to specifically perform the compact.[15]

Some measure of Story's regret regarding the government's treatment of the Cherokees can be seen in this excerpt from a January 13, 1832, letter to his wife:

At Philadelphia, I was introduced to two of the chiefs of the Cherokee Nation so sadly dealt with by the State of Georgia. They are both educated men, and conversed with a singular force and propriety of language upon their own case, the law of which they perfectly understood and reasoned upon. I never in my whole life was more affected by the consideration that they and all their race are destined to destruction. And I feel, as an American, disgraced by our gross violation of the public faith towards them. I fear, and greatly fear, that in the course of Providence there will be dealt to us a heavy retributive justice.[16]

## Other Southern States Follow Georgia's Lead

The states of Alabama (Creek Indian Nation), Mississippi (Chickasaws and Choctaws Indian Nations) and Tennessee (Cherokee Indian Nation) also enacted laws that abolished the Indian Nations rights to sovereignty and land.[17]

# Notes

1. James Wilkinson to Henry Dearborn, September 8, 1801, M-271, reel 1, #0113.

2. Cherokee Phoenix, February 21 and 28, March 6, 1828.

3. Speeches on the Passage of the Bill for the Removal of the Indians, Delivered in the Congress of the United States, April and May 1830, Perkins and Marvin. 1830: 160.

4. Beveridge, Albert J. *The Life of John Marshall: Volume 4: 543.*

5. John Quincy Adams Diary 38, 1 October 1830 - 24 March 1832: 77-78; https://www.masshist.org/jqadiaries/php/doc?id=jqad38_77 (accessed online November 4, 2020); https://www.masshist.org/jqadiaries/php/doc?id=jqad38_78 (accessed online November 4, 2020).

6. President Andrew Jackson Inaugural Speech.

https://millercenter.org/the-presidency/presidential-speeches/march-4-1829-first-inaugural-address (accessed online November 4, 2020).

7. *Cherokee Nation v. Georgia*, 30 U.S. 1, 3 (1831).

8. Ibid., p. 18.

9. Ibid., p. 17.

10. Ibid., pp. 17-18.

11. Ibid., p. 20.

12. Ibid., p. 27.

13. Ibid., p. 53.

14. Ibid., p. 59.

15. Ibid., p. 76.

16. Justice Story Letter to His Wife, January 13, 1832, Lubbers, Klaus. *Born for the Shade: Stereotypes of the Native American in United States Literature and the Visual Arts, 1776-1894*. Vol. 3. Rodopi, 1994: 65.

17. Corntassel, Jeff, and Richard C. Witmer. *Forced federalism: Contemporary challenges to indigenous nationhood*. Vol. 3., University of Oklahoma Press, 2008.

https://www.digitalhistory.uh.edu/active_learning/explorations/indian_removal/cartoon1.cfm (accessed online November 4, 2020).

# 28

# *WORCESTER V. GEORGIA*—DOCTRINE OF DISCOVERY

Samuel A. Worcester and Eliza Butler, missionaries, were condemned to hard labor for four years under a Georgia statute requiring all 'white' persons residing within the limits of the Cherokee Nation to have a license or permit from the Georgia Governor and to swear an oath to comply with Georgian law. They refused to comply with the statute. Worcester was also the U.S. Postmaster at New Echota. He sued the State of Georgia, seeking to overturn his sentence. The case, *Worcester v. Georgia*, 31 U.S. 515 (1832), was heard by the U.S. Supreme Court. Chief Justice Marshall had to decide if state law applied to the Cherokee Nation. The State of Georgia did not even appear in Court, refuting that the U.S. Supreme Court had jurisdiction to hear the case.

## All Intercourse with Indians Shall Be Carried on Exclusively by Federal Government

Chief Justice Marshall held that the Supremacy Clause of the U.S. Constitution, treaties and laws of the United States contemplated Indian territory as completely separated from that of states and further held that all intercourse with them shall be carried on exclusively by the federal government. Chief Justice Marshall extended this lack of extra-territorial jurisdiction of states over Indian territory to not only Indian Nations with federal treaties but to all Indian Nations. Under *Worcester*, within their boundaries, Indian Nations possessed rights with which no

State could interfere; the power of regulating intercourse with them was vested in the United States.

## Laws of Georgia Have No Force within Cherokee Nation

Chief Justice Marshall further held:

> ...Cherokee nation, then, is a distinct community, occupying its own territory, with boundaries accurately described, in which laws of Georgia can have no force, and which citizens of Georgia have no right to enter, but with assent of Cherokees themselves, or in conformity with treaties, and with acts of Congress. The whole intercourse between the United States and this Nation, is, by our Constitution and laws, vested in the Government of the United States.[1]

## *Worcester* Fashioned New Definition of Doctrine of Discovery

In *Worcester*, Chief Justice Marshall fashioned a new theory of the doctrine of discovery from his opinion in *Johnson* nine years previously that gave fee title to the 'discovering' sovereign. *He characterized the notion that Europeans had understood the 'discovery' of the continent and the settlement of the sea coast to give them authority over Indians and their lands an "extravagant and absurd idea..."*[2] (Emphasis added.) 'Discovery' did not vest fee title in the European countries nor did it thereby create an Indian occupancy right in their land. The preemptive right to purchase Indian land continued in the 'discovering' country, but not the divestment of the Indian's fee title.

Chief Justice Marshall further declared that upon 'discovery,' European colonizers simply possessed "the exclusive right of purchasing such lands as the natives were willing to sell."[3] He stressed that conquest as a justification for conversion of Indians to Christianity would be better accomplished "by conciliatory conduct and good example; not by extermination."[4]

America, separated from Europe by a wide ocean, was inhabited by a distinct people, divided into separate nations, independent of each other and of the rest of the world, having institutions of their own, and governing themselves by their own laws.

> It is difficult to comprehend the proposition that the inhabitants of either quarter of the globe could have rightful original claims of dominion over the inhabitants of the other, or over the lands they occupied, or that the discovery of either by the other should give the discoverer rights in the country discovered which annulled the preexisting rights of its ancient possessors.

> Did these adventurers, by sailing along the coast, and occasionally landing on it, acquire for the several governments to whom they belonged, or by whom they were commissioned, a rightful property in the soil, from the Atlantic to the Pacific, or rightful dominion over the numerous people who occupied it? Or has nature, or the great Creator of all things, conferred these rights over hunters and fishermen, on agriculturists and manufacturers?[5]

To avoid bloody conflicts which might terminate disastrously to all, the principle, allegedly adopted was "that discovery gave title to the government by whose subjects or by whose authority it was made against all other European governments, which title might be consummated by possession."[6]

> This principle, acknowledged by all Europeans because it was the interest of all to acknowledge it, gave to the nation making the discovery, as its inevitable consequence, the sole right of acquiring the soil and of making settlements on it. ... It regulated the right given by discovery among the European discoverers, but could not affect the rights of those already in possession, either as aboriginal occupants or as occupants by virtue of a discovery made before the memory of man. It gave the exclusive right to purchase, but did not found that right on a denial of the right of the possessor to sell.[7]

## Reason for New Interpretation of Doctrine of Discovery

Chief Justice Marshall was concerned with states asserting authority over Indians and wanted a reason why no state could assert such jurisdiction, regardless of whether there was a federal treaty that trumped state law under the U.S. Constitution's Supremacy Clause. He had to devise a theory to eliminate any claim of state title to Indian lands, without mentioning *Johnson*. He did not want to admit the Court was wrong in *Johnson* which would undermine its power in the political system. Under Chief Justice Marshall, the Court had taken the position it could review federal (*Marbury v. Madison* [5 U.S. 137 (1803)] and state laws (*McCulloch v. Maryland* [17 U.S. 316 (1819)]) and rule on their constitutionality. This made them a very potent political force. States were already angry with Chief Justice Marshall and he was trying to avoid minimizing the new Court's authority by not mentioning or overruling *Johnson* in *Worcester*.

## No Redemption for Chief Justice Marshall

Justice Story remarked: "Thanks be to God, the Court can wash their hands clean of the iniquity of oppressing the Indians and disregarding their rights."[8] This is an acknowledgment of the injustice perpetrated by the U.S. Supreme Court. It was too little, too late. Chief Justice Marshall's dismay that his opinions in *Fletcher* and *Johnson* led to numerous forced removals of Indian Nations could not be redeemed.

In a letter to George Ticknor, lawyer and historian, written five days after the judgment of the court was announced, Justice Story accurately portrayed the situation: "The decision produced a very strong sensation in both houses; Georgia is full of anger and violence.... Probably she will resist the execution of our judgement, & if she does I do not believe the President will interfere.... The Court has done its duty. Let the nation do theirs. If we have a government let its commands be obeyed; if we have not it is as well to know it at once, & to look to consequences."[9]

Justice Story's forecast was justified. Georgia scoffed at Chief Justice Marshall's opinion, flouting the mandate of the Supreme Court. "Usurpation!" cried Governor Lumpkin. He would meet it "with the spirit of determined resistance."[10] Georgia only released the imprisoned missionaries the day before the start of the next Supreme Court term so as to avoid a collision with the Court which President Jackson did not want to occur.

## U.S. Supreme Court's *Worcester* Ruling Ignored by State of Georgia and President Jackson

Georgia ignored the U.S. Supreme Court's ruling in *Worcester*. They would continue to rely on the Georgia Guard to harass and intimidate Cherokees—if the Cherokees refused to emigrate, they told them there was no federal government to protect them and state jurisdiction would apply to them. President Jackson refused to enforce the U.S. Supreme Court's *Worcester* ruling that Georgia had no extra-territorial jurisdiction over the Cherokee Nation or fee simple title to their land.

## Walter Echo Hawk Summarizes Aspects of *Worcester* which Need to be Respected

In his book, In The Courts of the Conqueror, Echohawk succinctly summarizes the aspects of *Worcester* which need to be respected:

> (1) Indian tribes enjoy a sovereign right of self-government free from interference by the states;

> (2) their treaties must be honored as the supreme law of the land;

> (3)the doctrine of discovery and edicts from Europe do not divest Indian land or sovereignty;

> (4) and reservation borders are barriers against hostile states and land-hungry settlers that are protected by the United States.[11]

Notes

1. *Worcester v. Georgia*, 31 U.S. 515, 561 (1832).

2. Ibid., p. 544.

3. Ibid., p. 545.

4. Ibid., p. 546.

5. Ibid., p. 543.

6. Ibid., pp. 543-544.

7. Ibid., p. 544.

8. Warren, Charles. *The Supreme Court in United States History: 1780-1821*. Vol. 1. Little, Brown, 1922: 216.

9. Letter from Joseph Story to George Tichnor, March 8, 1832, in 2 W. W. STORY 83.

10. Beveridge, Albert Jeremiah. *The life of John Marshall*. Vol. 4. Houghton Mifflin, 1916: 349.

11. Echo-Hawk, Walter. *In the Courts of the Conqueror: The 10 Worst Indian Law Cases Ever Decided*. Fulcrum Publishing, 2018: 433.

# 29

# CHEROKEE NATION DIVIDED

Despondent and divided, the Cherokee Nation broke into two factions, for and against removal. Chief John Ross led a larger group against removal. Major Ridge led a smaller group supporting removal. In 1835 Major Ridge signed the Treaty of New Echota with the U.S. government agreeing to removal in exchange for five million dollars. The federal and state governments were fully aware that Major Ridge did not represent the majority of the Cherokee Nation. President Jackson only cared that he had a legal document to remove the Cherokees.

Chief John Ross wrote a letter to President Jackson opposing the Treaty of New Echota:

> By the stipulations of this instrument (Treaty of New Echota), we are despoiled of our private possessions, the indefeasible property of individuals... Our property may be plundered before our eyes; violence may be committed on our persons; even our lives may be taken away, and there is none to regard our complaints.[1]

## Voluntary and Forcible Removal

Ten thousand Cherokees in favor of removal agreed to accept the federal government's support and move west on their own two years after the signing of the Treaty of New Echota in 1835. Seventeen thousand Cherokees refused to move. President Van Buren assigned General Winfield Scott to forcibly remove these Cherokees, employing U.S. Army and state militia totaling about 7,000 soldiers. General Charles Floyd commanded the Georgia Militia (aka "Georgia Guard"). Using

7,000 troops, Indian removal from Georgia was accomplished in 20 days.

The seventeen thousand Cherokees that refused to move were brutally rounded up and marched 2,200 miles to Indian territory in Oklahoma. As many as 4,000 died along the "Trail of Tears." The three signers of the Treaty of New Echota were murdered by the Cherokee Nation.

## Removal of 'Five Civilized Tribes' Accomplished

The Choctaw were removed in 1831 (Treaty of Dancing Rabbit Creek). The Seminole were removed in 1832 (Treaty of Payne's Landing). The Chickasaw were removed in 1837 (Treaty of Pontotoc). The Cherokee were removed in 1838 (Treaty of New Echota, 1833).

The Creek were removed in 1834 (Treaty of Washington). The Creek complained bitterly in 1825 that the Treaty of Indian Springs, which sold virtually all of their remaining land, had been signed by individuals not authorized to make such a sale. The federal government's negotiators were well aware of this. The Creek's senior leaders had refused to sell and left the negotiations. After the senior leadership had left, the negotiators turned to the few remaining minor chiefs and persuaded them to sign the Treaty. John Crowell, the U.S. Creek agent, was horrified at the transparent fraud and wrote to the Secretary of War. "[W]ith the exception of McIntosh, and perhaps two others, the signatures to this treaty are either chiefs of low grade, or not chiefs at all." Crowell lambasted the charade. He warned Calhoun if the Treaty was ratified, it would lead to catastrophe among the Creeks. Calhoun, soon to be the next vice president of the United States, remained silent.[2]

Thomas McKenney, the Superintendent of Indian Trade for six years, took the liberty of writing directly to President John Quincy Adams:

> "My little knowledge of the Indian character warrants me in believing, that it needed no agent to excite the Creek Nation, under the recent circumstances, to the perpetration of bloody deeds." The fact that the treaty had been conducted furtively, behind the backs of nearly all the legitimate leaders of the tribe, was quite enough.[3]

In examining the records of the four major Creek Treaties in 1814, 1818, 1821 and 1825, Superintendent of Indian Trade McKenney determined a similar pattern: Of the thirty Creek chiefs who signed the Treaty of surrender in 1814, only eight signed the Treaty of 1818; ten signed the Treaty of 1821; and, only nine signed the disputed Treaty of 1825—only four of whom, as far as Superintendent McKenney could discern, were chiefs of moderate or significant rank.[4] "The land that stands fast under the white people's feet," the Creek diplomat intoned, "keeps slipping from under the feet of the red people."[5] Under the specter of calumny, the Treaty of Indian Springs was nullified by the Treaty of Washington, signed on January 26, 1826. It admitted that the Treaty of Indian Springs had been made with only a portion of the Creek Nation, and that the signers had not been authorized to make a treaty, much less cede any Creek lands.[6]

### 1833 War Department Annual Report – Commissioner of Indian Affairs Elbert Herring – Creeks Being Treated Cruelly

Commissioner of Indian Affairs Elbert's report to the Secretary of War documented the fact that while the stipulations under the Creek Treaty were being implemented, the Creeks were being treated cruelly:

> all intruders were to be removed from the ceded land until the country was surveyed, and the stipulated selections were made. This has not yet been done, and, in the interim, repeated complaints of gross injustice, and cruel treatment towards the Creeks, were received by the department. It was represented that, in many instances, they were driven from the lands they had cultivated; that they were unmercifully beaten; that their dwellings were burnt, and that they were compelled to flee to the woods for safety.[7]

### Alexis de Tocqueville, French Diplomat, Political Scientist and Historian, Traveled across U.S. and Authored Democracy in America

> At the end of the year 1831, while I was on the left bank of the Mississippi, at a place named by Europeans Memphis, there

arrived a numerous band of Choctaws... These savages had left their country and were endeavoring to gain the right bank of the Mississippi, where they hoped to find an asylum that had been promised them by the American government. It was then the middle of winter, and the cold was unusually severe; the snow had frozen hard upon the ground, and the river was drifting huge masses of ice. The Indians had their families with them, and they brought in their train the wounded and the sick, with children newly born and old men upon the verge of death.

They possessed neither tents nor wagons, but only their arms and some provisions. I saw them embark to pass the mighty river, and never will that solemn spectacle fade from my remembrance. No cry, no sob, was heard among the assembled crowd; all were silent. Their calamities were of ancient date, and they knew them to be irremediable. The Indians had all stepped into the boat that was to carry them across, but their dogs remained upon the bank.

As soon as these animals perceived that their masters were finally leaving the shore, they set up a dismal howl and, plunging all together into the icy waters of the Mississippi, swam after the boat.[8]

## 1836 War Department Annual Report – Commissioner of Indian Affairs C. A. Harris – U.S. Knew Creek Indians Would Be Abandoned along Route or Die during Removal – Alabama Emigrating Company to Be Paid for Proportionate Amount of Their Journey[9]

The removal of the Creek Indians was made a military operation due to their resistance.

## Agreement for Removal of Creek Indians between U.S. and Alabama Emigrating Company, August 13, 1836

Several private individuals formed the Alabama Emigrating Company and agreed to remove the Creek Indians to the new country allotted to them. The individuals included James C. Watson, Edward Hanrick, Felix

G. Gibson, R. W. Williams, A. Abercrombie, Alfred Iverson, George Whitman, S. M. Ingersoll, James Abercrombie, William A. Campbell, William J. Beattie, John D. Howell, William Walker and T. Gilman. The agreement stated that the removal of the Indians was under the direction of the military authorities and Alabama Emigrating Company was not to coerce or use threats and violence against the Creeks and were to treat them with lenity, forbearance, and humanity.

Article VI provided the following for those unable to continue to the destination:

> That the sick, those enfeebled from age or other cause, and young children, shall be transported in wagons or on horseback; that those who may be pronounced unable to proceed, may be left on the route, at some proper place, and under the care of some person, at the expense of the United States.

It is uncertain who would take care of those unable to proceed or what and how consideration for their care would be paid. It is also uncertain whether they would be reunited with their families at a later date.

Article VII provided that the Alabama Emigrating Company would be paid twenty-eight dollars and fifty-eight cents a head and for those who may die or be necessarily left on the way, an amount in proportion to the distance travelled.

The U.S. was fully aware that some of the Creeks might die on the journey or be left behind.


## Cherokees - Fierce Dispute arose When Federal Government Refused to Allow John Ross or William S. Coodey to Hold Office

After removal of the Cherokees, a fierce dispute arose when the federal government refused to allow John Ross or William S. Coodey to hold office. The Cherokees, who arrived later due to their resistance to removal, had the upmost faith in him. To coerce the agreement of the 'late' Cherokees, annuities were withheld. The Cherokees eloquently proclaimed their right of sovereignty to select their own representatives:

It will destroy the very rights which it wishes to secure to our people - that of personal and political rights. It a right that we cannot (as true citizens in a free country) sanction when in the infancy of our knowledge of what constitutes the free enjoyment of life, liberty, and property nor can we yield our conviction that it is for our benefit or good to have our birthright privileges thus annihilated ...[10]

When the 'late' Cherokees were still unwilling to unite with the 'early' arrivals the federal government threatened to separate them and a suitable portion of the Cherokee lands and annuities.

### 1844 Cherokee Agency, Agent P.M. Butler

Agent Butler complained of the "harshness, prejudice and proscription" that some in the military displayed in their treatment of the Cherokee which he considered unnecessary. Some treated the Indians "as imbecile inferiors, to be awed into submission, and even degradation, by contempt and an air of assumed superiority." An act considered lawful one day, is the next day unlawful.

> "Arrests are made with a high hand; and fugitives pursued with a multitude of people, and under circumstances well-calculated to offend the national pride of the Indians. These irregularities and abuses of authority assume the character of caprice, are highly vexatious, producing deep irritation and an abiding discontent among those who are subject to them."[11]

### Jacksonian Supreme Court Ignores Part of *Worcester* Pertaining to 'Doctrine of Discovery,' Cites to *Johnson*

Chief Justice Marshall's change in the application of the doctrine of discovery was rejected in the 1835 Supreme Court term in *Mitchel v. United States,* 34 U.S. 711 (1835), followed by other cases. The majority of the Supreme Court Justices were President Jackson supporters/appointees. In *Mitchel*, there is no reference to *Worcester* and *Johnson* is cited as having received 'universal assent.' The Court ignored the precedence of a prior Supreme Court decision without regard to what is known as 'stare decisis.'

'Stare decisis' is Latin for "to stand by things decided. Courts defer to 'stare decisis' when a ruling has already been issued on the subject, even if the soundness of the decision is in doubt. Its purpose is to promote the evenhanded, predictable and consistent development of legal principles, to foster reliance on judicial decisions and contribute to the actual and perceived integrity of justice.

Notes

1. https://americanindian.si.edu/nk360/removal-cherokee/transcripts/papers-of-john-ross-original-text.html (accessed online November 11, 2020).

2. John Crowell to John C. Calhoun, February 13, 1825, ASP: Indian Affairs, 2: 583-4.

3. Thomas McKenney to John Quincy Adams, June 9, 1825, M21 2: 8.

4. Ibid., pp. 59-61.

5. Outline of an Interview between the Secretary of War and the Delegation of Creeks, November 30, 1825, M21 2: 270.

6. U.S. Statutes at Large, 7:286.

7. 1833 War Department Annual Report, Commissioner of Indian Affairs T. Hartley Crawford, Washington: Government Printing Office, 1834.

8. de Tocqueville, Alexis. *Democracy in America*. Vol. I & II. Regnery Publishing, 2003: 346.

9. 1836 War Department Annual Report, Commissioner of Indian Affairs T. Hartley Crawford, Washington: Government Printing Office, 1837.

10. 1840 War Department Annual Report, Commissioner of Indian Affairs T. Hartley Crawford, Washington: Government Printing Office, 1841.

11. 1844 War Department Annual Report, Commissioner of Indian Affairs T. Hartley Crawford, Washington: Government Printing Office, 1845.

# 30

# MONROE DOCTRINE, 1823;

# MANIFEST DESTINY, 1845

As the United States extended from sea to sea, President Monroe closed the country to any further colonization by any other countries. The Monroe Doctrine provided that the United States would not interfere in purely European affairs, nor in the affairs of existing colonies or dependencies in the Western Hemisphere. It warned that the United States would consider as unfriendly action any European intervention in the affairs of independent hemispheric nations that were recognized by the United States. Lastly, it declared that Europe should consider the Western Hemisphere 'out of bounds' for further colonization.[1] For Americans, this epitomized the declaration of a continental empire.

## Manifest Destiny, 1845

In an 1839 article in the Democratic Review, John O'Sullivan—a Democrat in the era of the expansionist hawk Andrew Jackson—had first articulated his early understanding of American Exceptionalism in 1839, outlining the contours of the new nation: "Its floor shall be a hemisphere—its roof the firmament of the star studded heavens, and its congregation an Union of many Republics, comprising hundreds of happy millions, calling, owning no man master, but governed by God's natural and moral law of equality, the law of brotherhood—of 'peace and good will amongst men.'"[2]

In 1845, he gave the doctrine of discovery a uniquely American flavor when he coined the term Manifest Destiny to defend U.S. expansion and claims to new territory:

> ... the right of our manifest destiny to over spread and to possess the whole of the continent which Providence has given us for the development of the great experiment of liberty... is right such as that of the tree to the space of air and the earth suitable for the full expansion of its principle and destiny of growth.[3]

It captured and consolidated longstanding concepts from the Crusades and the papal-sanctioned colonization process such as holy war, divine sanction, chosen people, promised land, terra nullius (if land was not being cultivated or put to good use it could be considered vacant, even if inhabited by indigenous peoples), and the proselytizing and conversion of heathens.

Three basic ideas underlie the concept of manifest destiny. First, the U.S.'s Christian moral values and institutions are superior. Second, the U.S. has been ordained to spread its Christian values for the benefit of the world and to fulfill God's wishes. Third, God has anointed the U.S. to succeed in this effort. Of course, if a government sees itself as appointed by God and carrying out God's mandate, then there is no questioning of its actual behavior.

The idea of Manifest Destiny, and the desire of Americans to fulfill their destiny, was an extremely powerful force. Thus, the Seven Years War, the Revolutionary War, the Louisiana Purchase, the U.S. Military Expeditions, the War of 1812, the annexation of Texas, the suspect War with Mexico, the settlement of the Oregon Territory and the Gadsden Purchase all opened the road to the domination of Indian Nations and to bringing them and their lands into the American continental empire. This would not have been possible without the complicity of the U.S. Supreme Court in rendering its decisions in *Fletcher, Johnson* and *Cherokee Nation* that thrust the country into a moral vacuum, permitting it to steal indigenous land and resources, engage in cost-benefit analyses of extermination of an entire race of people, and applaud the spurious "empire of liberty" created.

Senator Thomas Hart Benton's speech to Congress in 1846, epitomizes, in the most graphic, heinous and hideous exposition, the malevolence of the U.S.'s Manifest Destiny:

"It would seem that the White race alone received the divine command, to subdue and replenish the earth, for it is the only race that has obeyed it—the only race that hunts out new and distant lands, and even a New World, to subdue and replenish.

The Red race has disappeared from the Atlantic coast; the tribes that resisted civilization met extinction. This is a cause of lamentation with many. For my part, I cannot murmur at what seems to be the effect of divine law. I cannot repine that this Capitol has replaced the wigwam-this Christian people, replaced the savages-white matrons, the red squaws.... Civilization, or extinction, has been the fate of all people who have found themselves in the trace of the advancing Whites, and civilization, always the preference of the Whites, has been pressed as an object, while extinction has followed as a consequence of its resistance....

The van of the Caucasian race now top the Rocky Mountains, and spread down on the shores of the Pacific. In a few years a great population will grow up there, luminous with the accumulated lights of the European and American civilization. There presence in such a position cannot be without it influence upon eastern Asia....

The Mongolian, or Yellow race is there, four hundred millions in number spreading almost to Europe; a race once the foremost of the human family in the arts of civilization, but torpid and stationary for thousands of years. It is a race far above the Ethiopian, or Black-above the Malay, or Brown, (if we admit five races)-and above the American Indian or Red; it is a race far above all these, but still far below the White and like all the rest, must receive an impression from the superior race whenever they come in contact....

The sun of civilization must shine across the sea; socially and commercially the van of the Caucasians, and the rear of the Mongolians, must intermix. They must talk together, and trade together, and marry together.... Moral and intellectual superiority will do the rest; the White race will take the ascendant, elevating what is susceptible of improvement-wearing out what is not. ... And thus the youngest people, and the newest land, will become the reviver and the regenerator of the oldest....

It is in this point of view, and as acting upon the social, political, and religious condition of Asia, and giving a new point of departure to her ancient civilization, that I look upon the settlement of the Columbia river by the van of the Caucasian race as the most momentous human event in the history of man since his dispersion over the face of the earth.[4]

# Notes

1. https://millercenter.org/the-presidency/presidential-speeches/december-2-1823-seventh-annual-message-monroe-doctrine (accessed online November 11, 2020).

2. John L. O'Sullivan, "The Great Nation of Futurity," *The United States Democratic Review*, Volume 6, Issue 23, 1839, pp. 426-430. https://www.mtholyoke.edu/acad/intrel/osulliva.htm (accessed online November 21, 2020).

3. Ibid.

4. *Congressional Globe*, 29:1 (1846), 917-18.

# 31

## OREGON TERRITORY

## AND MEXICAN AMERICAN WAR

The U.S. and British contested claims for the Oregon Territory, which came to the brink of war, validate the lack of a clear interpretation or legal construction of the doctrine of discovery. Spain, England and Russia also claimed this area based on 'discovery.' Spain and Russia ended up renouncing their claims to the benefit of the United States. In 1846, Congress debated going to war with Britain over its claim to the Oregon Territory. If the doctrine of discovery was so clear cut how did two countries end up in 1846 still debating who had 'discovered' this Territory.

### Gallatin-American Argument for Claim to Oregon, Law of Nations Altogether Unsettled

America's response is their answer written by Gallatin—their sole justification: "For the Americans, Oregon is or will be home; for England, it is but an outpost."[1]

The United States relied on Lord Mansfield's axiom: "Possession is very strong, rather more than nine points of the law."[2]

Another U.S. argument as to who should win the Oregon territory was that they would provide a means for further English immigration, thus advancing an opportune justification for English acquiescence to the U.S. coming out victorious in its gamble for new territory.

> The United States and England are the only Powers who lay any claim to that country, the only nations which may and must inhabit

it. It is not, fortunately, in the power of either Government to prevent this taking place; but it depends upon them whether they shall unite in promoting the object, or whether they shall bring on both countries the calamities of an useless war, which may retard but not prevent the ultimate result. It matters but little whether the inhabitants shall come from England or from the United States. It would seem that more importance might be attached to the fact that, *within a period of fifteen years, near one million of souls are now added to the population of the United States by immigrations from the dominions of Great Britain; yet, since permitted by both Powers, they may be presumed to be beneficial to both. The emigrants to Oregon, whether Americans or English, will be united together by the community of language and literature, of the principles of law, and of all the fundamental elements of a similar civilization.*[3] (Emphasis added.)

To a similar purport the British Commissioners, Messrs. Huskisson and Addington, in the sixth conference held at London, December 16, 1826, maintained the uncertainty of a mere 'discovery' as giving any right to land:

The practice of European nations has certainly recognised in the nation which has first occupied the territory of savage tribes, that live by hunting, fishing, and roaming habits, the sole right of *acquiring the soil from the natives by purchase, or cession, or conquest,* for the purpose of establishing settlements. The more humane spirit of the modern code of nations seems disposed to reduce this right to a right of *pre-emption,* as against other European nations.[4] (Emphasis added.)

## United States Decides to Abrogate Oregon Convention with Britain and Claim Title to Oregon Territory Even if It Means War

While a Convention had been agreed to between the countries in 1818 and 1826 where they retained joint rights, President Polk directed the Secretary of State, in accordance with the joint resolution of Congress 'concerning the Oregon Territory,' to deliver the notice to the British Government for the abrogation of the Convention of August 6,

417

1827. Ending the Convention, instead of renewing it or continuing negotiations, meant the U.S. was ready to assert its sole rights to the Territory. Polk ran his Presidential campaign with the slogan 'Fifty-four Forty or Fight!' meaning he supported claiming the Oregon Territory to the 54th parallel for the United States and he was willing to go to war with the British to claim it.

There was Congressional opposition to the President's decision to send the dispatch. As Congressman Haywood voiced it, the President had decided to go for "All of Oregon.... No compromise. No negotiation!"[5]

Others supported the decision and were ready to go to war if necessary: Congressman Breese of Illinois was in favor of annulling the treaty of 1818 and sending the dispatch. The U.S. could then

> ... incorporate the country into our Union; protect the emigrant on his way to its fertile plains, and pledge to all who seek them, the honor and faith of the Government that they shall be made secure in their possessions by perfect grants of land, at the earliest period within the competency of the Government to act... We should all be Americans in deed; and heart and hand, in cordial union, rally as one man around our country's standard. A war, sir, will not proceed from us. It must come from the other quarter; and if it does come, it will be a war of aggression, unsustained by the sense of justice, or the sympathies of other nations. We never will, we cannot become an aggressive Power; but when an assault is made upon us, sir, the whole land will rise as the mighty man armed, and with a vigorous and united effort, overwhelm the aggressor.[6]

Despite the posturing, neither country really wanted to fight what would have been the third war in 70 years against the other. England caved in because it lacked the finances necessary for another war. The 1846 Oregon Treaty, resolving the dispute, divided the territory west of the Continental Divide along the 49th parallel to the Georgia Strait in favor of the United States, with all of Vancouver Island remaining under British control. This border today divides British Columbia from neighboring Washington, Idaho and Montana.

This claim of ownership to the present-day states of Oregon, Washington and parts of Idaho, Montana and Wyoming, under the doctrine of discovery gave absolutely no consideration to the numerous Indian

Nations who had lived in the Oregon Territory from time immemorial. As reported in Robert Gray's journal, the land along the Columbia River was inhabited by "vast numbers of natives," who were "eager to trade." Similarly, each day of this journey, Gray noted "many natives alongside," always curious and willing to trade furs; on some days he reported "many natives from different Indian Nations." [7]

To encourage settlement, Congress passed the Distribution-Preemption Act of 1841, which recognized squatters' rights and allowed settlers to claim 160 acres of land in the new territory. After residing on the property for 14 months, a claimant could purchase the property at $1.25 an acre.

On September 27, 1850, the Donation Land Claim Act of 1850 offered 320 acres at no charge to qualifying adult U.S. citizens (640 acres to married couples), subject to occupying their claims for four consecutive years. Members of Indian Nations were not U.S. citizens and therefore could not own land under the law, although Section 4 of the Act allowed "American half-breed Indians" of legal age who were citizens of the United States (or declared to be) to participate.

When Congress passed the Oregon Donation Land Claim Act of 1850, it broke promises made in the 1787 Northwest Ordinance. Federal officials never approached Indian Nations to negotiate for land cessions until 1853. The aptly titled Oregon Donation Land Claim Act promised "Free land! Gold in the rivers! Settlers and miners streamed into the valley carrying more than baggage. Many brought with them intense prejudice toward the Indians whose land they were invading."[8]

**Might Makes Right**

It's about might makes right.

> So—grab, grab, grab.[9] There was one obstacle only. Many of the more fertile meadows and river bottoms were in regions claimed by the Indians or else they were unpleasantly close to the routes the savages traveled from North to South.

The United States didn't succeed against England in this dispute because of its 'discovery' being paramount over England.

It wasn't about Robert Gray's first 'discovery' of the mouth of the Columbia River, thereby allegedly gaining the entire River drainage basin under an obscure axiom of the Law of Nations. England would challenge this as an individual accomplishment, not sanctioned by the sovereign United States, thus resulting in no valid U.S. claim.

It wasn't about Lewis and Clark's acts of symbolic possession on their Military Expedition. England would oppose mere branding of trees and posting of proclamations of their presence as far short of the requisite possession.

It wasn't about Jacob Astor establishing Fort Astoria as a trading post. England would denigrate his activity as that of an individual merchant and that mere establishment of a mercantile center did not constitute the level of occupancy or settlement required under the Law of Nations.

Certainly, the presence of multitudes of Indian Nations, reported on by Lewis and Clark, was wholly irrelevant to England or the United States.

*It was about the willingness of the United States to go to war with England to win another part of the continent.* Winning what are now the states of Washington, Oregon and Idaho, along with parts of Montana and Wyoming, was about building an empire.

## Mexican American War, 1846–1848

The Mexican American War, fought from 1846-1848, was the climax of America's quest for new territory. Mexico had allowed American settlers to claim land in order to augment its population. Settle they did. Enough so, that they declared themselves independent from Mexico in 1836, although Mexico never officially recognized their new republic. When the United States annexed Texas as a state in 1845, Mexico considered it an act of aggression. President Polk sent John Slidell to Mexico, offering $20 million in exchange for California and the New Mexico territories. Mexico refused to sell.

In the summer of 1846, thousands of American volunteers were authorized by Congress for twelve-months of military service and arrived in the lower Rio Grande Valley shortly thereafter. Most Americans resolutely supported the war. Approximately 75,000 men

420

eagerly enlisted in volunteer regiments raised by the various states. Thousands more enlisted in the regular U.S. Army. There was no need for a draft.

The U.S. Army sent troops commanded by General Zachary Taylor to the Nueces River to defend against a fallacious threat of a Mexican invasion. It was clear that President Polk's plan to use shock and awe military tactics was intended to favorably influence the U.S. position in negotiations for its proffered purchase of Mexico's southwest territory. The dominant military display was to demonstrate to Mexico that it didn't stand a chance against a U.S. war which would result in its complete physical destruction.

The Nueces River was the accepted U.S. boundary under the Louisiana Purchase. Generating no Mexican military response from its baiting, General Taylor moved his troops to the Rio Grande River, inside Mexico. Mexican soldiers crossed the River and fired on American troops. President James Polk proclaimed, "American blood had been shed on American soil."[10] He asked Congress to declare war, which it did on May 13, 1846. Just 25 years young, Mexico was ill prepared to fight a large-scale conflict with the U.S. Her government was still unsettled; she lacked the financial capital to engage in war; and her military did not have the technological resources the United States did. Many felt she had been duped into starting an unwinnable war.

At the Battle of Palo Alto, the United States successfully employed light artillery, a novel strategy. Field guns and cannoneers mounted on horseback moved with such speed that the eye could scarcely follow their movement. Working in conjunction with heavy U.S. 18-pounder siege cannon, they wreaked havoc in the opening battle. Marching south, the U.S. continued to win battle after battle in northern Mexico. They took New Mexico without a shot and faced small skirmishes in California which they put down. Still, the Mexican government refused to surrender.

General Winfield Scott, commander of all American forces, felt that the only way to force a surrender would be to occupy Mexico City. To do so he proposed an amphibious assault on Veracruz, then an overland march of less than 200 miles from there to Mexico City. The campaign for Mexico City proved to be costly, for this time Mexicans were defending the heart of their homeland. Winfield Scott's army captured the Mexican capital on September 13, 1847.

The Treaty of Peace, Friendship, Limits, and Settlement, better known as the Treaty of Guadalupe Hidalgo, was signed in 1848, and ended the Mexican American War. It increased the land mass of the U.S. by 50 percent and offered citizenship to the 100,000 Mexican nationals within the territory. Though the Treaty guaranteed religious freedom, property rights and the practice of Mexican culture and traditions, they were largely ignored. The Treaty protections were often overturned in legal cases or not recognized by the state and local governments. The mineral resources from the territory conquered created an economic boom for the U.S.

General U. S. Grant, who had served as a young Lieutenant in the War, later commented on it as follows:

> I do not think there was ever a more wicked war than that waged by the United States on Mexico. ... I had a horror of the Mexican War, and I have always believed that it was on our part most unjust. The wickedness was not in the way our soldiers conducted it, but in the conduct of our government in declaring war. ... We had no claim on Mexico. Texas had no claim beyond the Nueces River, and yet we pushed on to the Rio Grande and crossed it. I am always ashamed of my country when I think of that invasion.[11] (Emphasis added.)

## Gadsden Purchase, 1853–1854

James Gadsden was President of the South Carolina Railroad. President Franklin Pierce appointed him as the United States Minister to Mexico to negotiate to purchase a third of Mexico. When that failed, Gadsden succeeded in extracting enough land for his transcontinental railroad. General Santa Ana accepted $10 million for a strip of territory south of the Gila River, which is now southwestern New Mexico and southern Arizona (about the size of Pennsylvania). The continental puzzle was complete.

Notes

1. Gallatin, Albert, The Oregon Question. New York: Bartlett & Welford, 1846. Number III: 27.

2. Gerhart, Eugene C. *Quote It! Memorable Legal Quotations: Data, Epigrams, Wit and Wisdom from Legal and Literary Sources*. William Hein & Company, 1987: 499.

3. Gallatin, Albert, The Oregon Question. New York: Bartlett & Welford, 1846. Number V: 27.

4. Twiss, Travers. *The Oregon Territory, Its History and Discovery: Including an Account of the Convention of the Escurial: Also, the Treaties and Negotiations Between the United States and Great Britain, Held at Various Times for the Settlement of a Boundary Line: and an Examination of the Whole Question in Respect to Facts and the Law of Nations*. New-York: D. Appleton, 1846, Chap. XVI: 121.

5. Speech of Hon. William H. Haywood, of North Carolina, on the Oregon question: Delivered in the Senate of the United States, March 4 & 5, 1846.

6. Speech of Hon. S. Breese, of Illinois, on the Oregon question. Delivered in the Senate of the United States, Monday, March 2, 1846.

7. Deur, Douglas. "Empires of the Turning Tide A History of Lewis and Clark National Historical Park and the Columbia-Pacific Region." (2016: 40)

https://www.nps.gov/lewi/learn/historyculture/upload/Empires.pdf (accessed online November 11, 2020).

8. https://www.nps.gov/cali/learn/historyculture/upload/No-Land-is-Free-10-11-16.pdf (accessed online November 11, 2020).

9. Freeman, Douglas Southall. *George Washington, a biography*. Vol. 1: 12-1.

10. American Blood on American Soil, U.S. History.

https://www.ushistory.org/us/29c.asp (accessed online November 11, 2020).

11. Around the world with General Grant: a narrative of the visit of General U. S. Grant, ex-President of the United States, to various countries in Europe, Asia, and Africa, in 1877, 1878, 1879 to which are added certain conversations with General Grant on questions connected with American politics and history, John Russell Young, 1879: 448.

# 32

## CATACLYSMIC CHANGE—
## OWNERSHIP TO OCCUPNCY

Starting in the very late 1700s, a cataclysmic change occurred in the nature of Indian ownership of their land—Indian land title morphed from ownership to occupancy. States sold huge amounts of land occupied by Indians to speculators who were willing to wait for Indian removal—preemptive rights. Land was thus being sold right out from under the feet of the Indian owners. The prominent land speculators engaged in these sales wielded substantial political clout and needed to protect their purchases and accelerate their vesting of title. They needed to invent a basis of ownership other than a mere right of preemption to Indian lands and states were willing to go along. Cash-strapped states needed to fortify their suspect land marketing scheme of selling preemptive rights. The new republic was afraid to engender a battle with the states to protect Indians, challenging a fragile union.

**Factors Leading to New Concept of Indian Occupancy Rights**

Several factors underscored this radical transformation:

1. As a result of Britain's victory over France in the Seven Years War (aka French and Indian War, 1756–1763), France ceded its claims to lands in the Ohio River Valley. The British then used the Treaty of 1763 which ended the War as the basis for their claim to the Northwest Territory, replacing their prior claim that the English controlled the land by the right of conquest of the Iroquois. The

426

region included present day Ohio, Illinois, Indiana, Kentucky and West Virginia. As many as five Indian Nations also claimed this land—the Wyandotte, Delaware, Mingo, Miami and Shawnee.

2. The British Proclamation of 1763 ended the private purchasing of Indian land. When the Indians were no longer allowed to sell their land to buyers of their own choosing, it eliminated the right of disposition, a primary aspect of a fee simple absolute. It became possible to think of the Indians' property rights as something less than full ownership.

3. British colonists considered the Proclamation an unlawful impediment to acquiring Indian land. England's set aside of a huge amount of land as an Indian Reserve was wholly unpalatable. Colonists flagrantly violated it.

4. During the American Revolution, many Indian Nations allied with the losing side. Many Americans considered the Revolution as a war of conquest, with their victory entitling them to the Indians' land. The Continental Congress adopted and enforced this policy against Indian Nations, confiscating vast amounts of their land without compensation. While it was officially abandoned in 1793 by President Washington due to the fear of it generating more Indian hostilities and war, it lingered in the popular consciousness resulting in a huge westward surge of settlers who brazenly squatted on Indian land. In the absence of a federal force to remove them or assure their permanent removal, settlers flaunted their ability to intrude on Indian lands. If troops were sent to remove them, they would simply return after the troops left. If their crops were destroyed and their homes demolished, they simply replanted and rebuilt.

5. The huge war debt totaling approximately £165 million left the Continental Congress strapped for cash, its currency bogus. Precluded from taxing the country's citizens, its sole recourse was to divest Indians of their land and sell it. In New York alone, land sales had accounted for 2.5% of state revenue in 1790; by 1791, this percentage ballooned to 48.3%.

6. Immigration surged resulting in unprecedented demographic

changes. Between 1750 and 1770, the population doubled with 2.3 million settler colonists in 1770 and more on their way. Land was in acute demand and Indians weren't interested in selling out. In 1803 in a message to Congress, President Jefferson pointed out the southern Indians absolute refusal to further diminish their land base.

7. President Jefferson advocated for the assimilation of Indians. Changing Indians from alleged hunters to farmers was not a civilization effort but a façade to free up additional Indian land. Christianizing them was also a ruse. A transition to farming would lessen the amount of land needed by Indians such that it would justify reducing their land base. Alternatively, there was no need for a separate land base for Indians assimilated into the general society. In fact, by the time of President Monroe's administration, it was wholly disavowed as federal policy.

8. An unemployed military after the Revolutionary War seethed with resentment over unfulfilled promises of land, with the presence of Indians a continual irritant, as many had sided with the British in the War.

9. The growth of the image of the stereotypical savage Indian was used as a tool to characterize Indians as aggressive, war-mongering hunters who did not stay in any one place long enough to develop property rights in land. It made it easier to justify stealing Indian land when Indians were characterized, by powerful governmental authorities such as U.S. Supreme Court Chief Justice John Marshall, as "fierce savages, whose occupation was war, and whose subsistence was drawn chiefly from the forest."[1] As agricultural eastern Indian communities disintegrated, settler colonists facilely embraced an image of Indians as "dirty, draggle-tailed, blanketted, half human Squaws, or the filthy ferocious half naked Savages."[2]

10. Philosophers such as John Locke who equated ownership of land with cultivation and enclosure concretized ideas amenable to government officials desperate to obtain Indian land. Vattel, widely read by our founding fathers, expressed his philosophy that idle hunters that usurp more land than is reasonable had no reason

to complain "if other nations, more industrious, and too closely confined, come to take possession of a part of those lands."[3] Adam Smith, the father of capitalism, objectified Indians as hunters who had no knowledge of ownership of land.

11. Chief Justice Marshall was well aware of the purchase of the Louisiana Territory in 1803 which included all or part of 15 present-day states and two Canadian provinces. Numerous Indian Nations inhabited the region. President Jefferson wrote to John Milledge, Governor of Georgia, on November 22, 1803, that the U.S. now had the power to induce the eastern Indians to move west. President Jefferson disingenuously claimed that the Indians had only rights of occupancy in the soil and self-government. Previously, he had stated the U.S. only had a right of preemption.

12. The notion of a limited title and status as 'tenants-at-will' would make removal easier and also reduce the costs of purchasing the vast Indian lands in the Louisiana Territory. For example, the trusted Indian agent, William Clark, Lewis' co-captain on the Expedition, used his influence to wrangle a treaty with the Osage Indians in the Louisiana Territory: in return for ceding 50,000 square miles of their prized hunting grounds—almost all of Missouri—thereby ruining their fur-based economy, the Osage were given $1,400 in gifts, an $1,800 annuity, the services of a blacksmith, some farm tools and the use of a gristmill. Osage land purchased by the government for 10 cents per square mile was later resold for $1 to $2 per acre.

13. After the Louisiana Purchase, President Jefferson ceased to use the phrase "Friends and Brothers" when communicating with Indians. Instead, he addressed the Indians as "My Children" and he was "Your Great Father." As Children, Indians would be under the control and responsibility of the President, the Great Father, a Father that wanted to remove them west of the Mississippi River. A guardian could legally make decisions for its wards, such as compelling the sale of their land and removal.

14. President Jefferson used exploratory military expeditions to solidify the U.S. 'discovery' to interior parts of the country. A pronounced doctrine of discovery would buttress the U.S.

competing discovery claims. The military expeditions also included obtaining information about the Indians, their names, numbers, relations with other Indian Nations (alliances or feuds), capacity for war (Indian warrior capacity and location) and armaments and state of morality and religion. This data gave the United States a decision-making advantage in negotiations for acquiring lands or going to war.

15. The U.S. needed the doctrine of discovery in its arsenal to solidify its claims to the Oregon Territory and the west, inhabited by multitudes of Indian Nations. Spain, Russia and England's competing claims threatened adding this land to our continental empire. England considered going to war to protect its 'discovery.'

16. Of critical import, which simply cannot be understated, was the Northwest Ordinance which promulgated a pattern of westward expansion that would result in laying out state after state from coast to coast, a landman's dream. From President Washington on, it was a foregone conclusion that America's legacy was a continental empire. Indians were a mere obstacle to be eliminated or moved out of the way of the settlers. The settlement and creation of permanent non-Indian family-sized farms, without any regard for Indian rights, would go unchecked. Land subsidies and preemptive rights for squatters were used as tools for compact settlement of lands. This created advantages in extinguishing Indian claims at a lower cost. Compact settlements made defense against Indians easier which reduced the cost to the government of having to provide military services. It increased the ability to clear lands and eliminate game habitat for Indian hunting, compelling the removal of Indians. It made the migration of a group of settlers possible, rather than having them migrate singly. This facilitated the development of settler communities which in turn encouraged the migration of additional settlers. It made land more valuable by increasing the safety and security of these settlers. It helped the federal government reduce their national debt and accumulate capital for its own use and as collateral for credit. The federal government would reserve townships for their future sales. The increase in land values rewarded the initial settlers as their equity value in their properties was augmented which could be used for

private collateral for credit and further investment opportunities. What couldn't be done on a large scale privately, was made possible in a win-win scenario for the federal government and settlers who could economically benefit from initial lower land prices, paving the way for continental expansion.

17. In spite of the War of 1812 ending up in a stalemate between Britain and the U.S., the undisputed hegemony of the U.S. over the Ohio Valley culminated in displacing several American Indian Nations from their homelands. Spain's hold on its North American empire was so weak that it was only a matter of time before the various pieces of that empire—its claims to parts of Georgia, Alabama and Mississippi and East and West Florida—would 'fall like ripe fruit 'piece by piece' into American hands.' Under the 1819 Adams-Onis Treaty, Spain relinquished its claims to the U.S. to Spanish Florida (British East Florida and West Florida). All of its colonies in Mexico, Central and South America were clamoring for independence.

18. The most important blow to Indian landownership may have been the growing practice on the part of state governments of granting fee simple title to white settlers to identifiable parcels of Indian land, still inhabited by Indians, before the land had been purchased from the Indians.

a. This was partly a product of the Revolution, as state officials in the late 1770s and early 1780s set aside land inhabited by Indians for compensating military veterans, as they had no cash to pay them for their service.

b. State courts in Pennsylvania and North Carolina promulgated a new theory of the doctrine of discovery. The Pennsylvania Supreme Court postulated that the Indians never owned their land. "From the first discovery of the continents or islands of America these Aborigines were not considered as having any right, not being Christians, but mere heathens and unworthy of the earth."[4]

c. Under political pressure to grant land to settlers, and unable to purchase that land from the Indians, the states continued granting preemptive rights to settlers to assume ownership when the Indians were removed or they ceded it to the federal government.

d. In 1810, the Yazoo disputed land case finally made its way to the U.S. Supreme Court. Chief Justice Marshall stated in dicta (a mere side comment) that as a result of the Revolution, the states actually owned the fee simple title to all of the land within their boundaries. Any grant they made vested a fee simple estate, even if the land was inhabited by Indians. Indians only had an occupancy interest. This decision was wholeheartedly embraced and used to vindicate preemptive right sales as vesting the fee simple estate in the purchasers. This position contradicted President Washington's policy expressed in 1793 that Indians owned their land. Most likely, Chief Justice Marshall would have been aware of this significant policy change as he authored a biography of former President Washington in 1803. The consequences of Chief Justice Marshall's dicta were disastrous and horrendous for Indians. States had the leeway for 22 years to confiscate Indian lands. His decision in *Worcester v. Georgia* in 1832 would be wholly ignored by federal and state governments, without any untoward consequences.

e. Since under *Fletcher*, the states held fee title to all land within the state, it led the southern states to enact legislation incorporating Indian land into their counties and totally abrogating their sovereignty. They would be citizens of the state and subject to its laws.

f. Secretary of State Jefferson's opinion on the preemptive right of the federal government to purchase Indian lands was taken a step further by the states—the underlying Indian title being purchased was no longer a fee simple estate, but that of a tenant, a right of occupancy which could be stripped by ousting the tenant.

g. It made it possible for the federal government to secure state cession of their western lands which the federal government needed to raise revenue through sales. Georgia would not cede its western lands without an agreement that the United States would, at its expense, extinguish, for the use of Georgia, as early as the same could be peaceably obtained, on reasonable terms, the Indian title to lands within the state. As the southern Indians in Georgia later refused to sell their lands, the federal government was in a quandary, having made a legally binding compact it could not fulfill. The fourteen Cherokee Treaties guaranteed the Georgian lands to the Indians and under the Treaties they could not be forced to sell their lands.

h. The federal government faced the real threaten of state sectionalism, a full-blown civil war, undermining federalism. States impugned the republic's delay in removing the Indians and warned of their willingness to wage war against the Indians. Indian rights would be put on the back burner to fester.

i. A mutation of Indians from sovereign owners of their land to tenants of the state/federal government would make it easier to violate the sacred, solemn treaties entered into with sovereigns, binding under the Law of Nations. The Report of the Committee on Indian Affairs stated that that the treaties entered into by the federal government with Indians were not really treaties, but rather "a stately form of intercourse."[5] Violating a 'form of intercourse' would not incur the same censure that violating a treaty would provoke.

j. A tenant would be easy to oust under common law; no reason was required.

k. An occupancy interest would be cheaper to buy versus a fee simple title.

l. As revealed by Representative Henry Storrs—The reason Georgia wanted Indian lands was that her citizens didn't have the money to pay taxes and her debt made her situation precarious. This was true also of a new 'continental' republic that had no money for paying off the state war debts it assumed, forming a military, establishing a new government, conducting diplomacy or constructing much needed infrastructure, transportation services and paying any other costs.

m. Diminishing the value of Indian lands made it possible to acquire vast tracts, millions and millions of acres. Circumscribing the area held by Indians made it easier to control and exclude them. Removing them from their homelands resulted in a dispersal of Indians and a weakening of their status as sovereigns. Again, land expropriation and mineral exploitation would be easier.

n. Jeopardizing the ability of Indian Nations to sustain themselves through a loss of culture, land, game, flora and fauna, natural resources and valuable minerals, along with imposing brutal economic sanctions, would ultimately result in a loss of lives and sovereignty.

o. As pronounced by John Adams there was no common law regarding colonization. Chancellor Kent, renowned jurist and author of a landmark treatise on American common law, confirmed this understanding of the common law. In a precarious, unsettled, tripartite government, without established judicial rules or ethical procedures, a conservative, self-interested Chief Justice could propound the law as he desired it to be.

Chief Justice Marshall's acceding to the alleged 'discovery doctrine' in *Johnson* resulted in the federal government's receipt of fee simple title to the entire continent. The preemption rule which it established as between the federal government and Indian occupants resulted in the monopsonistic purchase of Indian lands grossly reduced in value as a plethora of one-sided government policies. Thus, the U.S. acquired an empire at fire sale, rock-bottom prices, facilitated by Chief Justice Marshall's collusion in two fraudulent cases.

The cataclysmic change in land tenure of Indians led to ethnic cleansing on an unparalleled scale encompassing the entire empire of the United States. The initial states/territories requesting presidential extinguishment of Indian title in their areas were: Georgia, Illinois, Indiana, Kentucky, Michigan Territory, Mississippi, Missouri, New York, North Carolina, Ohio, South Carolina and Tennessee. The same action would be followed by western states, including the southwest which had been part of Spain's and later Mexico's claimed territory, as a result of a papal donation. An ethnically homogenous geographic area was a highly desirable state.

# Notes

1. *Johnson v. M'Intosh*, 21 U.S. 543, 590 (1823).

2. "To James Madison from Americanus, 13x0 April 1816," *Founders Online,* National Archives, https://founders.archives.gov/documents/Madison/03-10-02-0380. [Original source: *The Papers of James Madison*, Presidential Series, vol. 10, *13 October 1815–30 April 1816*, ed. Angela Kreider, J. C. A. Stagg, Mary Parke *Johnson*, Katharine E. Harbury, and Anne Mandeville Colony. Charlottesville: University of Virginia Press, 2019, pp. 364–368.] (accessed online November 21, 2020).

3. de Vattel, Emerich. *The Law of Nations or the Principles of Natural Law Applied to the Conduct and to the Affairs of Nations and of Sovereigns*. Carnegie Institution of Washington, 1916. Book I, Chap. VII, §81.

4. *Thompson v. Johnston*, 6 Binn. 68, 75 (1813), Sept. 11, 1813, Supreme Court of Pennsylvania.

5. House Committee on Indian Affairs, H.R. 227 (1830), 11.

# 33

# DOCTRINE OF DISCOVERY - LEGAL FICTION

In a report to Congress by the Department of the Interior, dated 1929, the 'discovery doctrine' is set forth quoting *Johnson* for its validity, recognizing only an Indian land title of occupancy, a 'tenancy in common.' Incorporating a new element, it purported to further limit that right to land "actually possessed by them." It postulated that American Indians "had no conception of the private or exclusive ownership of land."

> III. In general, the United States recognizes in the Indian Tribes the right to perpetual occupancy, possession, and use of the lands claimed and actually possessed by them, the Tribe holding as tenants in common. The fee to such lands remains, however, in the United States as successor to the rights of the original European discoverers, and the Indian possessory right can be sold by them only to the United States. There are exceptions to this rule, hereinafter to be noted. ...

> The American Indian had no conception of the private or exclusive ownership of land. The only right the Indian understood and claimed was the right of perpetual user, occupancy, and possession, by the tribe, as tenants in common. Under the law of nations, as recognized by the United States, a change of sovereignty, occurring by reason of the acquisition of new territory by cession, makes no change as to private law or private rights in the new territory so acquired, but changes only the public law or political law in such territory. The Indian right to occupancy and possession of his

436

lands is further recognized by the acts of the British government, by acts of the Continental Congress, and by the Congress of the United States in its general enactments in regard thereto and in certain of the treaties of cession made with foreign powers.[1]

## Twenty First Century Scholars' Analyses

Numerous twenty first century scholars have pointed out how the doctrine of discovery adopted into federal law by the United States Supreme Court in *Johnson* is a disastrous legal fiction. Chief Justice Marshall wholly denied the common practice of European monarchs and colonists purchase of Indian land and regard for Indian sovereignty in his biography of George Washington and in the *Johnson* decision. There never was a customary or 'uniform' concept of the doctrine of discovery.

Among these scholars are government officials, prominent leaders and businessmen, along with legal scholars, from the colonial period and thereafter, that documented Indian land ownership as a predicate to purchase of such land. The policy changed from indigenous ownership with purchase of their land, to confiscation in an era of retribution, to a preemptive right on the part of United States to purchase native land after the Revolution. Nonetheless, empty state and federal coffers desperately needed the revenue that would come from the sale of Indian lands after the War, so a novel theory of Indian land title land was forged. Also, the nation needed land for its growing population. The doctrine of 'mere occupancy' would facilitate the removal of Eastern Indian Nations. Each formula was a matter of convenience for politicians and colonists who craved Indian land.

In analogizing the Supreme Court's *Johnson* decision to a con artist Jessica Buckelew writes:

> Discovery is a legal fiction, which has been perpetuated time and again to champion political ends, to the detriment of the aboriginal populations of the planet. In 1823 this legal fiction was indoctrinated into black letter law as the United States hurtled toward Manifest Destiny.[2]

Howard Berman, a lawyer concludes:

> Marshall seized upon this controversy to establish a judicial mythology that would rationalize the origin of land titles in the United States. ... By the early 19th century, therefore, discovery alone was no longer valid as a distributional principle. Indeed, it is questionable if it ever was totally accepted as a sufficient basis for dominion. As a distributional principle it was given limited recognition and various definitions by the European states...

Also:

> The equation of discovery to conquest amounts to a nimble transmutation of definition that itself stands as a conquest by judicial fiat. The historical record is quite clear that most of the lands alienated to the United States were acquired by purchase rather than by warfare. Marshall provided no historical context for the derivation of the conquest theory. He simply characterized the status quo, without analysis.[3]

Kent McNeil debunked Chief Justice Marshall's theory about Indian land title:

> The Marshall Court created "an Indian interest unknown to the common law, the definition of which has understandably eluded judges ever since."[4]

Blake Watson, Samuel A. McCray Chair In Law, at Dayton School of Law, also discounts Chief Justice Marshall's claim regarding the 'doctrine of discovery:'

> European views of Indian land rights during "the age of discovery" were by no means as uniform as Marshall intimates in *Johnson v. McIntosh*. The Spanish, French, Dutch, Swedish, and English views of Indian land rights varied considerably in their emphasis on discovery, papal authority, royal grant, feudal right, possession, and purchase.[5]

David Wilkins and Tsianina Lomawaima assert that "[t]he thrust of the Court's message in *M'Intosh* was that indigenous peoples did not have the natural right exercised by 'civilized' nations to sell their property to whomever they wished," and that the doctrine of discovery when defined ... to mean that the federal government holds the fee-simple title to all the Indian lands in the United States, is a clear legal fiction that needs to be explicitly stricken from the federal government's political and legal vocabulary.[6]

Steven Newcomb posits that "*Johnson* was premised on the ancient principle of Christian dominion and a distinction between paramount rights of 'Christian people' and subordinate rights of 'heathens' or non-Christians."[7]

Others have described the 1823 Supreme Court decision as "conquest by judicial fiat,"[8] "a tortured rationale,"[9] "a tool of efficient expropriation of Indian lands,"[10] "corrupt,"[11] "an extra-constitutional fiction ... developed ... to rationalize the subjugation of the Indian nations as a matter of law,"[12] "fraught with incoherence and ad hoc rationalizations"[13] and a "cruel joke."[14]

Robert Miller, an acclaimed and distinguished Indian legal scholar, queries what to do about the 'discovery doctrine:'

> But one thing seems clear, the United States and American citizens must face squarely the fact that many principles of federal Indian law and the modern day treatment of tribes and Indians are based on the Doctrine of Discovery and on religious and ethnocentric prejudices that are many centuries old. These lamentable relics of our past should not and cannot continue to be perpetuated or tolerated. They should have no place in the modern-day relationship between tribal nations, Indian people, and the United States.[15]

## Doctrine of Discovery Applied in Other Countries

The highest courts in Canada, Australia and New Zealand have also relied, explicitly or implicitly, on the doctrine of discovery enunciated without authority in *Johnson*. In Conquest by Law, Professor Lindsay Robertson states that the reach of the *Johnson* decision "has been global." He continues: "In its 1984 decision in *Guerin v. The Queen*, for example, the Supreme Court of Canada, after citing *Johnson*, held that 'Indians have a legal right to occupy and possess certain lands, the ultimate fee to which is in the Crown'. Under Canadian law, as under U.S. law, the tribes lost ownership of their lands by virtue of discovery". Robertson then mentions that the High Court of Australia cited *Johnson* in a remarkable opinion—*Mabo v. Queensland*—which, while recognizing for the first time land claims of indigenous Australians, nevertheless limited those claims under a variation of the doctrine of discovery.[16]

## Doctrine of Discovery Still Current Law

Even though it is now known that *Johnson* was based on deception and self-interest, violating the U.S. Constitution itself, it is still controlling law. Not only is the doctrine of discovery still very real, the law of prescription is used to justify it. Chancellor Kent, in his Commentaries on American Law (1826-30), portended this in his opinion that the *Johnson* decision was founded on pretense, yet would be undisputable after Chief Justice Marshall's pronouncement .

> The rule that the Indian title was subordinate to the absolute, ultimate title of the government of the European colonists, and that the Indians were to be considered as occupants ... was founded on the pretension of converting the discovery of the country into a conquest, and it is now too late to draw into discussion the validity of that pretension, or the restrictions which it imposes. ... The country has been colonized and settled, and is now held by that title. It is the law of the land, and no court of justice can permit the right to be disturbed by speculative reasonings on abstract rights.[17]

Implausibly, the U.S. Supreme Court in 2006 would agree. The Onondaga Nation was unjustly denied recovery of lands due to yet another judicially fashioned precept: the equitable doctrine of laches applicable to Indian land treaty claims. Three specific factors were identified foreclosing remedies: (1) "the length of time at issue between an historic injustice and the present day;" (2) "the disruptive nature of claims long delayed:" and (3) "the degree to which these claims upset the justifiable expectations of individuals and entities far removed from the events giving rise to the plaintiffs' injury."[18]

In *City of Sherrill v. Oneida Indian Nation*, 544 U.S. 197 (2005), the U.S. Supreme Court. further eroded Indian rights, stating:

> ...equitable doctrines, such as laches, acquiescence, and impossibility, can, in appropriate circumstances, be applied to Indian land claims, even when such a claim is legally viable and within the statute of limitations.[19]

Recognizing that the Onondaga Nation claims may never be addressed favorably due to the new judicial purported equity doctrines applicable to Indian treaty claims, the Onondagas filed a Petition in the Organization of American States Inter-American Commission on Human Rights. The Petition charges the United States with human rights violations based upon: (a) the original, illegal takings of the lands, (b) the lack of any remedy in United States Courts for treaty violations; and (c) the environmental destruction that has been allowed by the outside governments of the Onondaga lands and waters.[20]

Notes

1. Kappler, Charles Joseph, ed. *Indian Affairs: Laws and Treaties,* Vol. 4. US Government Printing Office.

2. Buckelew, Jessica (2015) "The Man Who Sold the World: The Long Con of Discovery," *American Indian Law Journal*: Vol. 3: Iss. 2, Article 1: 359.

3. Berman, Howard J. *The Concept of Aboriginal Rights in the Early Legal History of the United States*, 27 *Buff. L. Rev.* 643, 648 (1978).

4. McNeil, Kent. *Common law aboriginal title*. Clarendon Press, 1989: 236-237.

5. Watson, Blake A. "John Marshall and Indian Land Rights: A Historical Rejoinder to the Claim of Universal Recognition of the Doctrine of Discovery." 36 Seton Hall L. Rev. (2005): 482-483.

6. Wilkins, David Eugene, and K. Tsianina Lomawaima. Uneven ground: American Indian sovereignty and federal law. University of Oklahoma Press, 2001:63.

7. Newcomb, Steven T. "The Evidence of Christian Nationalism in Federal Indian Law: The Doctrine of Discovery, *Johnson v. McIntosh*, and Plenary Power." 20 N.Y.U. Rev. L. & Soc. Change (1992): 304.

8. Berman, Howard R. "The concept of aboriginal rights in the early legal history of the United States." *Buff. L. Rev.* 27 (1977): 637, 648.

9. Frazier, Terry W. "Protecting ecological integrity within the balancing function of property law." 28 *Envtl. L.* (1998): 53, 79 n.94.

10. Kades, Eric. "The Dark Side of Efficiency: *Johnson v. M'Intosh* and the Expropriation of American Indian Lands." *University of Pennsylvania Law Review* 148.4 (2000): 1065, 1080.

11. Norgren, Jill. "Protection of What Rights They Have: Original Principles of Federal Indian Law." *NDL Rev.* 64 (1988): 73, 94.

12. Skibine, Alex Tallchief. "Braid of Feathers: Pluralism, Legitimacy, Sovereignty, and the Importance of Tribal Court Jurisprudence." (1996): 557, 565.

13. Green, Shelby D. "Specific Relief for Ancient Deprivations of Property." Akron Law Review, Vol. 36: 264 (2003).

14. Miller, Robert J., Presentation at the Indigenous Peoples Forum on the Doctrine of Discovery, March 23, 2012, Arizona State Capitol House of Representatives.

15. Miller, R. J. (2005). The doctrine of discovery in American Indian law. Idaho Law Review, 42:96.

16. Robertson, Lindsay G. *Conquest by law: How the discovery of America dispossessed indigenous peoples of their lands*. Oxford University Press, 2005: 144.

17. 3 J. KENT, COMMENTARIES ON AMERICAN LAW 381 (rev. ed. New York 1889) (1st ed. New York 1826).

18. Heath, Joseph J. "The Doctrine of Christian Discovery: Its Fundamental Performance in United States Indian Law and the Need for Its Repudiation and Removal." *Alb. Gov't L. Rev.* 10 (2017): 143-144.

19. *City of Sherrill v. Oneida Indian Nation,* 544 U.S. 197 (2005).

20. Petition to the Inter-American Commission on Human Rights submitted by The Onondaga Nation and The Haudenosaunee against the United States at 37, *Onondaga Nation v. U.S.*, Case No.: P-624-14 (2014).

# 34
# DAMAGES RESULTING FROM DOCTRINE OF DISCOVERY

One of the most serious results of colonial strategies is the transfer of wealth between Indians and settler colonists by dispossessing indigenous peoples of valuable land, water and natural resources which generate revenue and capital through long-term investment.

Also, as stated by Walter Echo Hawk In The Courts Of The Conqueror: The 10 Worst Indian Law Cases Ever Decided, the justice afforded to Indians is not even-handed. The manner in which the United States Supreme Court views Indian peoples impacts not only the case they are addressing but future cases as well. It is important to understand how the United States Supreme Court has viewed Indians in order to be aware of the extent of its ignorance when it comes to Indian peoples. Indians become prisoners of the judicial systems' stereotypes.

**Impact of American Agricultural Land Policy**

American land policy, from the start, was designed to bolster the settlement and creation of permanent non-Indian family-sized farms, without any regard for Indian rights. The Land Act of 1800 gave settlers the right to purchase the land on which they had squatted at the minimum price. Their chronic indebtedness and lack of hard cash, along with the popular belief that the squatters were doing a national service by clearing the land and extending the area of civilization, led to rewarding them for their illegal squatting. Few farmers could raise $640 to buy a wilderness farm site, even with four years to pay. The Land Act of 1820 abolished the credit system but it revised purchase regulations to make it possible for anyone with $100 to buy an 80-acre tract. The price was still beyond the reach of thousands of debt-ridden farmers, so they simply squatted where they chose without title to the land.

By allowing generous credit terms in spreading out payments for land over four years, purchasing land became more feasible. This policy choice by the U.S. served the purpose of getting the land promptly settled in the Ohio River Valley and the Great Lakes as a buffer against British aggression.

More distressing was the policy to use the settlers as 'hired guns,' mercenaries, a military force against the Indians. Settlers were certain to vigorously protect their alleged land rights. Preemption and homesteading established a large population on a given piece of the frontier. Settlers presented the Indians with a large local militia that made the odds of a victorious attack so low that, realizing their weakness, the tribes sold out cheaply. However, opposed the common law tradition might be to squatters, these settlers played an important role in expropriating Indian lands at minimal cost.[1]

This policy required the United States to protect settlers from Indian violence-even when they provoked it. Without this assurance, settlers would not have been as willing to populate those areas where the U.S. needed them as a buffer against unwanted incursions by the British and their Indian allies or the Indians acting alone. Unable to protect or prevent Indians from lawlessness or punish the violators, the government instituted a policy of paying money damages to the Indians for their grievances, including the loss of lives.

## Squatters Rewarded by Government Inaction and Leniency

In a letter to President Madison from Edward Coles, November 6, 1815, Coles warned the President about Governor William Clark, Missouri territorial governor (of Lewis and Clark fame), approving the inclusion of an area within the state's territory that was given by Treaty to the Sacs and Foxes. Coles was President Madison's personal secretary, A Virginian, he had been a neighbor and associate of Presidents Jefferson and Monroe. A farmer and politician, he was elected as the second

Governor of Illinois from 1822 to 1826.

> Many settlers were moving to this disputed region as squatters in hopes that the federal government would require the Indian land to be ceded and they would later be granted it by pre-emption and the per acre cost would be reduced from $10 to $4-6. He advised the President all of the good land had been so secured, with the further proviso:

> Thus all the advantages of a sale by auction are lost to the Nation, and persons who in the face of the law will squatt themselves on lands, to which they know they have no right, become rich, first by means of the neglect, and then by the false indulgence of the Govt. ... We have seen how the lubberly Squatters are benefitted by the lenity and liberality of the Govt., we will now see how the keen speculators fatten upon its most charitable and praiseworthy liberality.[11]

### European Investment Aided in Indian Land Dispossession

European capital was highly sought after by U.S. land speculators and investors who sent influential Americans to generate interest. As François Furstenberg notes in his probing analysis of the role of European capital in frontier America:

> ...the funneling of European capital into the northern and northwestern [American] backcountry may well be one of the most important—and most overlooked—features of the post-Revolutionary era. ... It was European capital, not American, that began to integrate the northern U.S. backcountry into the Atlantic world's trade networks.[2]

### Colonial Legacy of Natural Resource Predation and Extraction

Natural resource-endowed Indian Nations served as feedstock for predatory colonial powers. Discovery of gold or other valuable natural resources resulted in decimation and removal of indigenous peoples. This occurred not only in the United States, but also in New Zealand,

Australia, Canada and in other Central and South American and African countries. In the 1500s 85% of the global supply of silver came from Spain's exploitation of Mexico. The impact of the Colorado gold rush on the Ute Indian Nations is, also, a prime example of this. The lingering impact of the 'discovery doctrine' on indigenous coal can be seen in the Navajo's twice unsuccessful case against Peabody Coal.

## 1827 War Department Annual Report – Secretary of War James Barbour – Valuable Agricultural and Mineral Indian Lands Must Be Purchased for Benefit of U.S.[3]

In his 1827 Annual Report, Secretary of War Barbour confirmed the importance of purchasing the land encompassing the Upper Mississippi Valley Lead-Zinc area which included northwest Illinois, southwest Wisconsin, and northeast Iowa. The expected annual supply of lead was equal to 10,000,000 pounds. One critical use at the time was for the manufacturing of bullets.

Archaeological records indicate that galena, a lead-sulfide mineral and primary lead ore, was utilized through placer mining by pre-Columbian Native American populations in eastern North America for nearly 10,000 years as a pigment, for ornamentation and extensive trade in the Southeastern and Midwestern United States.

## 1842 Annual Report of The Commissioner of Indian Affairs, Treaty with Wyandot (Huron); Treaty with Sac and Foxes, Treaty with Chippewas[4]

On March 17, 1842, the Wyandot (Huron) agreed to relinquish all claims to land in Ohio and Michigan. This territory consisted of approximately 114,140 acres of land, with most of it in the northwestern corner of Ohio. To compensate the Wyandot, the United States government agreed to provide 148,000 acres of land west of the Mississippi River. In addition to the land, government officials also agreed to provide the Wyandot with a yearly payment of 17,500 dollars. It marked the ramping up of the strategic removal of Indians to lands west of the Mississippi River.

The U.S. valued the lands at $20,000 but appraisers appointed under the

Treaty valued the land at $125,937. The U.S. then asked for a second appraisal which lowered the value to $66,941.

By the Treaty with the Sac and Foxes, 10 million acres were ceded. A "land unsurpassed in beauty and fertility," would be open to white settlement.

As reported by Michigan Superintendent Robert Stuart, by the Treaty with the Chippewa Indians of the Mississippi and Lake Superior, dated on the 4th October, 1842, a "valuable mineral region" and the southern shore of Lake Superior is secured to the U.S. The soil was of "excellent quality." There were copper ores of the "purest quality;" silver ores; and the fisheries on Lake Superior and its island would result in a "considerable source of revenue" to the white settlers.

The Chippewas of Lake Superior challenged the Isle Royale of having been included in a past Treaty. In order to avoid a possible war, the U.S. decided to purchase Isle Royale for 24 cents/acre for acreage known to be valuable in copper. The U.S. also paid $400 worth of gunpowder and $100 worth of fresh beef."

**Depletion of Water Resources**

The federal government defers to states to allocate certain public water resources within each state. However, the federal government maintains certain federal water rights, though, which exist separate from state law, e.g., water allocation related to federal lands, including Indian reservations. The majority of Indian Nations do not have a sovereign right to use water but must litigate or enter into water settlement agreements with states and others. This is due to (1) the application of the 'doctrine of discovery;' (2) the legal status of tribes as domestic dependent nations completely under the dominion and sovereignty of United States and thereby subject to federal property and water law; and (3) due to the federal water law vacuum prior to the 1900s, settlers developed their own customs, laws and judicial interpretations to administer allocation of public water resources within states. Indian water rights were not considered until the 1900s. As of February 2017, thirty-six Indian water rights settlements have been federally approved with 40 individual Indian tribes. Many more await legal review.

## Ecological Changes

Even when settlers respected Indian boundaries, large-scale colonial settlement produced dramatic ecological changes that could be devastating to traditional Indian life. English agricultural practices thinned the population of deer that the Indians relied on for subsistence. English husbandry changed the landscape—cows and pigs ate Indian crops, as well as the grass that supported wild game. English demand for fur drove the beaver and seal and other fur bearing game close to extinction. English mill dams threatened Indian fishing. The colonization of the eastern seaboard saw natural forest cover depleted. Grain farming replaced forest and grasslands in the western interior. Logging and the growth of industry changed the northwestern landscape as well.

As traditional ecosystems gradually vanished, land became less valuable to the Indians than it had been when it provided a sustenance base for them. The less the Indians' land was able to support traditional ways of life, the more the Indians would have been willing to sell it. Ecological change was thus an indirect catalyst for reducing the value of land and prompting sales that would not have otherwise occurred.[5]

Clearing and settling land inured to the benefit of the government by maximizing the benefits: it destroyed animal habitats, it intruded on Indian land and at times circumscribed it leading to the Indians willingness to move; and it brought a ready military force to curb Indian aggression against unlawful squatting. The government lacked the will or the forces to monitor a frontier hundreds of miles long.

> President Washington argued that [western lands] could not "be so advantageously settled by any other class of men as by the disbanded officers and soldiers of the army," for this plan of colonization "would connect our government with the frontiers, extend our settlements progressively, and plant a brave, a hardy and respectable race of people as our advanced post, who would be always ready and willing in case of hostility) to combat the savages and check their incursions."

> He further argued that the presence of military men "would be the most likely means to enable us to purchase upon equitable terms of the Aborigines their right of preoccupancy; and to induce them to relinquish our Territories"[6]

Unbridled land speculation led to exploring and surveying an area, obtaining, holding and selling of land, establishing settlement patterns, building homes, clearing and planting, using pristine resources, launching towns, developing transportation and communication systems, carrying on trade and introducing industry.

The Catawbas' chief complained to colonial officials in 1763: "His land was spoiled." The English had simply settled nearby, but in so doing "they have spoiled him 100 Miles every way."[7]

## Species Destruction

English demand for fur drove the beaver and similar animals close to extinction. The French concentrated on the St. Lawrence Valley, along the Mississippi River, and around Great Lakes. The British focused on the Hudson Bay and the Atlantic Coast. The Dutch for a short time traded in present-day New York.

The near total annihilation of bison was a "systematic slaughter" occurring primarily from 1830 to 1838. The herds had been driven to the west in previous centuries by encroaching settlers. From 1870 to 1880, over 3.5 million buffalo were killed, of which 3.2 million were killed by "professional" non-Indian hunters.

The scene witnessed by Meriwether Lewis, on September 17, 1804, would not be repeated:

> ...from this plane I had an extensive view of the river...and creek... this senery already rich pleasing and beatiful, was still farther hightened by immence herds of Buffaloe deer Elk and Antelopes which we saw in every direction feeding on the hills and plains. I do not think I exagerate when I estimate the number of Buffaloe which could be [observed] at one view to amount to 3000.[8]

In a study by the Sierra Club, it was determined that many of the species described by the U.S. Military Expedition are now extinct or face extinction.[9]

## Damages to Indian Spirituality, Culture and Social Identity

In A Public Declaration to the Tribal Councils and Traditional Spiritual Leaders Of the Indian and Eskimo Peoples of the Northwest, November 1997, the Bishops and Denominational Executives from churches in the U.S. Pacific Northwest, offered to [Indians and Alaskan Natives], on behalf of the Christian churches they represent, an apology for long-standing participation in the destruction of traditional Indian spiritual practices.

As leading social pioneers in the study of colonial trauma, Ms. Yellow Horse Brave Heart and Ms. DeBruyn have found the following:

> American Indians and Alaska Natives are plagued by high rates of suicide, homicide, accidental deaths, domestic violence, child abuse, and alcoholism, as well as other social problems (Bachman, 1992; Berlin, 1986; Indian Health Service, 1995; May, 1987). Racism and oppression, including internalized oppression (Freire, 1968), are continuous forces which exacerbate these destructive behaviors. We suggest these social ills are primarily the product of a legacy of chronic trauma and unresolved grief across generations. It is proposed that this phenomenon, which we label historical unresolved grief, contributes to the current social pathology, originating from the loss of lives, land, and vital aspects of Native culture promulgated by the European conquest of the Americas. The American Indian Holocaust: Healing Historical Unresolved Grief, Maria Yellow Horse Brave Heart, Ph.D. and Lemyra M. DeBruyn, Ph.D.

As is evident from the material herein, Indians and Indian Nations have experienced racism in all of its various forms: institutional racism, blatant racism (stereotypes), unaware racism (unconscious attitudes about minorities acted out), cultural racism (dominant group's culture mores are accepted standard) and most insidious—internalized racism and (brainwashing with stereotypes and negative messages about a group such that an individual believes what they have been taught is correct—heathen, savage Indian view).

## United Nations Summary of Damages to Indigenous Peoples as Identified by the United Nations

"...multiple threats and obstacles continue to hinder Indian social, economic, political and legal development, including discrimination and marginalization; lack of rights to land and natural and productive resources; denial and lack of access to justice; violations of cultural rights; denial of the rights to legal recognition, political representation and participation; lack of access to basic social services; denial of the right to existence and self-development; violence against indigenous individuals and communities, including rape and death of indigenous women; and multiple-impact land conflicts arising from development and conservation projects that fail to take into account the rights and interests of indigenous peoples.

Extractive industries, infrastructure projects, large-scale agriculture or hydroelectric dams and the promotion of new technologies such as improved seeds, chemical fertilizers and pesticides, the introduction of cash-crop cultivation and large plantation schemes" all negatively impact indigenous ecosystems.[10]

Notes

1. Kades, Eric. "The Dark Side of Efficiency: *Johnson v. M'Intosh* and the Expropriation of American Indian Lands." *University of Pennsylvania Law Review* (2000).

2. https://www.raremaps.com/gallery/detail/34312/a-new-map-of-the-western-parts-of-virginia-pennsylvania-ma-hutchins (accessed online November 8, 2020).

3. 1827 War Department Annual Report, Commissioner of Indian Affairs T. Hartley Crawford, Washington: Government Printing Office, 1828.

4. 1842 War Department Annual Report, Commissioner of Indian Affairs T. Hartley Crawford, Washington: Government Printing Office, 1843.

5. Cronon, William. "Changes in the Land: Indians. Colonists, and the Ecology of New England." (New York: Hill and Wang, 1983).

6. "From George Washington to Elias Boudinot, 17 June 1783," *Founders Online,* National Archives, https://founders.archives.gov/documents/Washington/99-01-02-11469 (accessed online November 8, 2020).

7. Banner, Stuart. *How the Indians lost their land: Law and power on the frontier.* Harvard University Press, 2005: 55.

8. http://xroads.virginia.edu/~Hyper/JOURNALS/lewis9.html (accessed online November 8, 2020).

9. See Sierra Club list in What's Lost, sierraclub.org/lewisandclark (accessed online November 8, 2020).

10. www.un.org/development/desa/indigenouspeoples/mandated-areas1/environment.html (accessed online November 22, 2020).

# 35

# "UTTER EXTIRPATION"- U.S. BLACK LEGEND

While Professor Kades does not acknowledge a malevolent force to the actions of the U.S. in settling Indian lands, he does analyze in depth the effect of 'muscular economics,' ... the other way to obtain (if not create) wealth: expropriation of that which others possess, via "crime, war, and politics."[1]

In a letter from Benjamin Franklin to Sir William Johnson, September 12, 1766, the outright murder of Indians is dismally portrayed:

> It grieves me to hear that our Frontier People are yet greater Barbarians than the Indians, and continue to murder them in time of Peace. I hope your Negociations will prevent a new War, which those Murders give great Reason to apprehend; and that the several Governments will find some Method of preventing such horrid Outrages for the future.[3]

In a 1794 Report on Indian Affairs by Secretary of War Knox, the seizure by force or fraud of Indian lands is set forth as well as the "utter extirpation of nearly all the Indians in most populous parts of the Union."

> The desires of too many frontier white people to seize by force or fraud upon the neighbouring Indian lands has been and still continues to be an unceasing cause of Jealousy and hatred on the part of the Indians ... The irritated passions on account of savage cruelty are generally too keen in the places where trials are had, to convict and punish for the killing of an Indian. ... *It is a melancholy reflection that our modes of population have been*

*more destructive to the Indian natives than the conduct of the conquerors of Mexico and Peru. The evidence of this is the utter extirpation of nearly all the Indians in [the] most populous parts of the Union.*[4] (Emphasis added.)

In a January 12, 1805, letter to President Thomas Jefferson from Henry Dearborn, Secretary of War, Dearborn calculated the purchase price of Indian lands as follows:

*...the average price we have paid and engaged to pay for Indian cessions, does not amount to quite one quarter of a cent per acre; and that, exclusive of the purchase from the Sacs and Foxes, the remainder will fall a little short of one cent per acre, taking into the account all the expenses of Treaties.*[2] (Emphasis added.)

In a frightening assessment of the condition of the Indians by Secretary of War Calhoun in 1818, he pronounced the inevitable outcome for Indians if they did not assimilate—their inevitable extinction. Time was running out for the Indians in the incursion of settlers moving west.

In fact, the neighboring tribes are becoming daily less warlike, and more helpless and dependent on us, through their numerous wants. They have, in a great measure, ceased to be an object of terror, and have become that of commiseration. The time seems to have arrived when our policy towards them should undergo an important change. They neither are, nor ought to be, considered as independent nations. Our views of their interest, and not their own, ought to govern them. By a proper combination of force and persuasion, of punishments and rewards, they ought to be brought within the pale of law and civilization. It is only by causing our opinion of their interest to prevail, that they can be civilized and saved from extinction. The Indians are not so situated as to leave it to time and experience to effect their civilization.[5]

Calhoun's pronouncements gained a ready audience in the U.S. With Indians viewed as stubborn impediments to westward expansion, the assertions that they were not independent nations or capable of acting in their own best interests or capable of assimilation were welcome words. With the nation deep in an economic depression, reducing every dollar spent in negotiating with every Indian Nation was laudatory.

455

The House's standing Committee on Indian Affairs in 1824 left two alternatives for Indians—civilization or extermination:

> The Indians are not now what they once were. They have partaken of our vices more than our virtues. ***Such is their condition, at present, that they must be civilized or exterminated; no other alternative exists.*** He must be worse than the savage who can view, with cold indifference, an exterminating policy. All desire their prosperity, and wish to see them brought within the pale of civilization.[6] (Emphasis added.)

Immediately after the conclusion of the fraudulent Treaty of Washington in 1826, Secretary of War Barbour under President John Quincy Adams, drafted a prospectus, in the form of a letter to the House Committee on Indian Affairs, delineating the current state of American-Indian relations:

> That the Native inhabitants of North America had been grievously wronged for a dozen generations Barbour had no doubt. What right, after all, did the original European settlers of the continent have to dispossess the American Indians? It was an important question, but he thought perhaps also a moot one. For the early settlers, might made right, and "fraud and force [were] perfectly legitimate in the acquisition of territory."[7]

More deploringly, William Clark in 1826, dismally described the impact of the settler colonists on Indians:

> ...Clark had become convinced that the survival of the Indians depended upon moving them out of the reach of whiskey-selling traders and land-hungry settlers. ***"Their power has been broken, their warlike spirit subdued, and themselves sunk into objects of pity and commiseration,"*** he wrote to his superiors in Washington. ***"While strong and hostile, it has been our obvious policy to weaken them; now that they are weak and harmless, and most of their lands fallen into our hands, justice and humanity require us to cherish and befriend them."***[8] (Emphasis added.)

In an 1828 address commemorating the first settlement of Salem, Massachusetts, Justice Story wrote the following:

What can be more melancholy than their history? By a law of their nature, they seem destined to a slow, but sure extinction. Everywhere, at the approach of the white man, they fade away. We hear the rustling of their footsteps, like that of the withered leaves of autumn, and they are gone forever. They pass mournfully by us, and they return no more .... But where are they? Where are the villages, and warriors, and youth; the sachems and the tribes; the hunters and their families ... The wasting pestilence has not alone done the mighty work. No,—nor famine, nor war. There has been a mightier power, a moral canker, which hath eaten into their heart-cores—a plague, which the touch of the white man communicated—a poison which betrayed them into a lingering ruin.[9]

The negative impact of colonization is again repeated by Chancellor Kent. It is more than obvious that exploiting Indian lands and resources also resulted in the decimation of Indian peoples:

This affords some consolation under a view of the melancholy contrast between the original character of the Indians, when the Europeans first visited them, and their present condition. We then found them, a numerous, enterprising, and proud spirited race; and *we now find them, a feeble and degraded remnant, rapidly hastening to annihilation. The neighborhood of the whites seems, hitherto, to have had an immoral influence upon Indian manners and habits, and to have destroyed all that was noble and elevated in the Indian character.*[10] (Emphasis added.)

Alexis de Tocqueville, a French diplomat, political scientist and historian, traveled across U.S. and recorded a very somber description of what occurred in the legal and systematic removal of the Indians and dispossession of their lands:

The white citizens of the United States, however, "have accomplished this twofold purpose with singular felicity; tranquilly, legally, philanthropically, without shedding blood, and without violating a single great principle of morality in the eyes of the world."[11]

Around 1832, the following states/territories requested presidential extinguishment of Indian title in their areas: Georgia, Illinois, Indiana, Kentucky, Michigan Territory, Mississippi, Missouri, New York, North Carolina, Ohio, South Carolina and Tennessee. This meant they did not want any Indians remaining in their areas.[12]

The purpose of the states' petitions, to the highest level of authority, the President of the United States, for removal of Indians was a blatant, calculated scheme of ethnic cleansing. "Ethnic cleansing" is the attempt to get rid of (through deportation, displacement or even mass killing) members of an unwanted ethnic group, in order to establish an ethnically homogenous geographic area.

These twelve states and later additional western states such as Colorado and New Mexico wanted to cleanse their states of a race of people, similar to what Spain did in 1492 when it expelled all Jews and Moors. The aim of ethnic cleansing is to establish ethnic homogeneity, a purity of blood, referred to in Spain as "limpieza de sangre." These states wanted to get rid of Indians.

### Reports of the Commissioners of Indian Affairs

The Reports of the Commissioners of Indian Affairs focused year after year on the Indian's paganism, debauchery, indolence and their utter lack of regard for women.

### 1838 War Department Annual Report - Commissioner of Indian Affairs T. Hartley Crawford - Paternalism of Federal Government – Improving Morality and Mind of Indians; Condescending New Commissioner Reveals Attitude of His Office – Allotment Mandatory to Cast off Savagism[13]

In 1838, the new Indian Commissioner T. Hartley Crawford, in a condescending manner, expressed again the role of the federal government to assume the paternal authority of improving the morality and mind of Indians by teaching them the mores of American society - how to farm or to assume the position of a vocational laborer at the very bottom of the pay scale. To do otherwise, was to enable idleness and vice.

If you would win an Indian from the waywardness and idleness and vice of his life, you must improve his morals, as well as his mind, and that not merely by precept, but by teaching him how to farm, how to work in the mechanic arts, and how to labor profitably ... Unless some system is marked out by which there shall be a separate allotment of land to each individual whom the scheme shall entitle to it, you will look in vain for any general casting off of savagism. Common property and civilization cannot co-exist.

To him, communal property ownership was an indicator of 'savagism.'

### 1839 War Department Annual Report – Commissioner of Indian Affairs T. Hartley Crawford – Barbaric and Ignorant Indians – Their Fate – Extinction; American Exceptionalism[14]

Again in 1839, Commissioner T. Hartley Crawford testified to the outcome of the Indians contact with whites: "The whole history of the race bears testimony to the fact that the contact of the white man is death to them."

In theorizing why this was, Commissioner Crawford continued in his blatant condemnation of Indian culture which he delineated as barbaric, ignorant and unable to avoid the vices introduced by whites:

Whether it be that barbarity necessarily recedes before civilization, that ignorance timidly retires before science and the arts, instead of improving; by them, or that the pursuit of game carries them further into the forest, and the vices they learn of us sicken and kill them – certain it is that, without advancing in any degree worthy almost of mention, we find, after ages of exertion by benevolent men, they are not less vicious, are diminishing gradually in number, and tending rapidly, by all the signs which precede it, to extinction. This has been the fate of many powerful tribes.

Commissioner Crawford, with his prejudice against those he was appointed to protect, passively announced their fate: extinction, as had been the destiny of many powerful tribes. Again and again, we have the highest ranking federal official whose role was to serve as the liaison between the tribes and the U.S. government affirming the genocidal outcome of that relationship – 'deliberately inflicting on the group conditions of life calculated to bring about its physical destruction in whole or in part.'

## 1840 War Department Annual Report, Commissioner of Indian Affairs T. Hartley Crawford – Washington Territory's Superintendent of Indian Affairs Advocated Taking Children Away from Their Parents, by Compulsion or by Compensation[15]

In Washington Territory, the Superintendent of Indian Affairs advocated taking children away from their parents, by compulsion or by compensation. He said:

"I am satisfied that many of the Indians would really part with their children for a small compensation in blankets and presents."

## 1841 War Department Annual Report, Commissioner of Indian Affairs T. Hartley Crawford – Contact with Whites Deadly to Indians; Liquor Problems[16]

### Sub-Agency for Chippewas

D. P. Bushnell:"An overfree intercourse with the whites, however, is fraught with so many ills to the unsophisticated Indian, that he must be secured against it, or his destruction is inevitable. To this cause may be attributed, the extinction of some of the most powerful tribes of this continent ..."

### Turkey River Sub-Agency, D. Lowry, Sub-Agent

Winnebagoes: "It is evident they must soon be numbered with the nations that have been" due to the ravages of alcohol.

At the white man's feet the red man lies, all prospects shrouded in the deepest gloom, and every day sinking lower and lower under the deadly action of his unfeeling master. Even the supplies of Government, intended for the Indians relief, mock his misery, serving only to bring him in closer conflict with the over-reaching advance of those of another color. And what adds still higher aggravation to the wretched condition of these wild children of the forest is, both church and state are ready to give them up.

What can you promise these Indians by removal? Will not the same white population follow them, and continue the present work of death: Has it not always been the case?

Obstacles to their improvement, growing out of an unsettled state, are most natural. And would produce the same effect on us which is felt by them....

I will only add, that what we must do for the aborigines of our country must be done quickly. They are rapidly melting away. The causes which operate in their destruction are every day increasing. In a few years the commercial cities of our people will border the Pacific as they now do line the Atlantic, and over the whole land from sea to sea will be scattered towns and villages, and the various improvements of civilized man. Where will be the home of the present wandering children of the forest?

Sac and Fox Agency – John Beach Indian agent:

On my first acquaintance with them in 1832, intoxication was rare among them, and I doubt if a confirmed or habitual drunk belonged to their nation; while at this time, except when far distant upon their hunting grounds, the whole nation, without distinction of age, race or sex, exhibits a continual scene of the most revolting intoxication.

## St. Peter's Agency, Iowa Territory, Amos J. Bruce, Agent

These Indians, depending on the fulfillment of said treaty stipulations, have neglected the usual precautions to secure the means of subsistence, and their situation is most deplorable. The corn crops having almost entirely failed, and game being too scarce in the country to furnish food for so large a number, unless some means is placed at the disposal of this agency for the succor of those in distress, there is much reason to fear that many will perish from actual starvation.

## St. Louis – D.D. Mitchell, Superintendent

Preying upon the Indians are "crowds and daily increasing crowds, of depraved white men, who have taken up their abode in the Indian country. This worse than savage population is composed of deserters from the fur traders …, renegades from Santa Fe and discharged soldiers and fugitives from justice."

## Council Bluffs Agency, Daniel Miller, Agent

The Omahas were suffering from misery and starvation which must shortly overtake them.

## 1843 War Department Annual Report, Commissioner of Indian Affairs T. Hartley Crawford – Turkey Creek Sub-Agency[17]

Agent John Chambers warned that the existing system of trade and intercourse with the Indians is destroying them and stressed the dire need for Congressional corrective action.

Agent Benjamin Terrill stated that Indians were discouraged from building homes due to their possible future removal. He advised that their excessive drinking was understandable due to their continued "perplexity" and "anxiety."

## 1845 War Department Annual Report, Commissioner of Indian Affairs – Manifest Destiny at Work – Liquor Problem; Religion[18]

The liquor problem has increased and is reported in all Agency reports. The Council Bluffs Sub-Agent, Richard S. Elliott reported as follows:

> ... the authority of the government is openly contemned by the whisky dealers and horse thieves, who hover along the frontier like ill-omened birds of prey, to seize the property of the Indians by any means that will place it in their power. ... The grog shops ... furnish the Indians as much as they desire ... for when an Indian gets into one of those grog shops, literally "dens of thieves," he does not get away until he has got rid of horse, saddle, blanket, gun, and whatever property he may have with him, if the dealer can possibly make him drunk enough to carry on the plunder effectually.

John Beach, the Indian agent at the Racoon River Agency reported as follows:

> Our religion appears to consist in knowing how most effectually to cheat them; our civilization in knowing how to pander to the worst propensities of nature and then beholding the criminal and inhuman results with a cold indifference—a worse than heathen apathy: while our religion is readily summed up in the consideration of dollars and cents.

1846 - War Department Annual Report, Commissioner of Indian Affairs William Medill.[19]

The Miamies were indebted to traders such that their annuities for the next five years would incur a deduction of $12,500.

## 1848 War Department Annual Report, Commissioner of Indian Affairs William Medill – Gross Carelessness or Worse in Giving Citizenship to Indians – They Could Then Sell Land[20]

In certain treaties, the U.S. would provide for citizenship to tribal members. At such time as they were deemed qualified for citizenship, they would receive patents for their lands which they were then free to sell, and their pro rata share of the funds of the tribe, and become citizens of the United States. The process below for the Pottawatomie Tribe would be repeated over and over across the country:

> Under this provision about 150 applications for patents, &c., have been made to this office; but on careful inquiry it was found that gross carelessness (or worse) had occurred in furnishing the certificates of good conduct, sobriety, and ability to conduct their own affairs, which certificates were a necessary preliminary to naturalization....

Professor Kades is right on point on the wholesale deprivation of Indian rights by Americans:

> Even with the advantages of Indian alcoholism, vulnerability to disease, and inferior military technology, the Spanish, as noted by de Tocqueville, were "unable to exterminate the Indian race by those unparalleled atrocities which brand them with indelible shame, nor did they succeed even in wholly depriving it of its rights." The Americans, despite resorting less often to atrocities, did manage to deprive the Indians of their rights, virtually exterminating them. The difference between the two colonial methods was simple: the Americans engaged in widespread agricultural settlement; the Spanish generally did not. As a result, "[s]ettlers, who ultimately would prove to be the most effective conquerors of North America, were by far the weakest of the ... elements" in Spain's invasion of the 'New World.'[21]

It leads us to Washington Irving's question:

> The [gigantic] question which has thus suddenly arisen, is, what right had the first discoverers of America to land, and take possession of a country, without asking the consent of its inhabitants, or yielding them an adequate compensation for their territory?[22]

Notes:

1. Kades, Eric. "The Dark Side of Efficiency: *Johnson v. M'Intosh* and the Expropriation of American Indian Lands." *University of Pennsylvania Law Review* 148.4 (2000): 1131.

2. "To Thomas Jefferson from Joseph Anderson and William Cocke, 5 March 1801," *Founders Online,* National Archives, https://founders. archives.gov/documents/Jefferson/01-33-02-0136. [Original source: *The Papers of Thomas Jefferson*, vol. 33, *17 February–30 April 1801*, ed. Barbara B. Oberg. Princeton: Princeton University Press, 2006, pp. 174–175.] (accessed online November 18, 2020).

3. "Enclosure: Report on Indian Affairs, 29 December 1794," *Founders Online,* National Archives, https://founders.archives.gov/ documents/Washington/05-17-02-0223-0002. [Original source: *The Papers of George Washington,* Presidential Series, vol. 17, *1 October 1794–31 March 1795*, ed. David R. Hoth and Carol S. Ebel. Charlottesville: University of Virginia Press, 2013, pp. 328–332.] (accessed online November 18, 2020).

4. "From Benjamin Franklin to Sir William Johnson, 12 September 1766," *Founders Online,* National Archives, https://founders.archives. gov/documents/Franklin/01-13-02-0146. [Original source: *The Papers of Benjamin Franklin*, vol. 13, *January 1 through December 31, 1766*, ed. Leonard W. Labaree. New Haven and London: Yale University Press, 1969, p. 416.] (accessed online November 18, 2020).

5. The Works of John C. Calhoun Volume 5. United States, Jazzybee Verlag:11.

6. "Civilization of the Indians," January 22, 1822, ASP; Indian Affairs, 2: 458.

7. James Barbour to John Cocke, "Preservation and Civilization of the Indians," February 3, 1826, ASP: Indian Affairs, 2: 647.

8. Civilization of the Indians," March 23, 1824, ASP: Indian Affairs, 2: 458.

9. Story, Joseph. The Miscellaneous Writings of Joseph Story .... United States, C. C. Little and J. Brown, 1852: 462–63.

10. Kent, James. Commentaries on American Law: 3. United States, Little, Brown and Company, 1867: 505.

11. de Tocqueville, Alexis. Democracy in America, Vols. I & II. Trans. Henry Reeve (New York: Bantam, 2000), Chapter XVIII: Future Condition Of Three Races, Part III: 411-412.

## 12. GEORGIA

"To James Madison from Georgia Legislature, 2 December 1816," *Founders Online,* National Archives, https://founders.archives.gov/documents/Madison/99-01-02-5597 (accessed online November 18, 2020).

## ILLINOIS

"To James Madison from Thomas Worthington and Others, 18 March 1814," *Founders Online,* National Archives, https://founders.archives.gov/documents/Madison/03-07-02-0328. [Original source: *The Papers of James Madison*, Presidential Series, vol. 7, *25 October 1813–30 June 1814*, ed. Angela Kreider, J. C. A. Stagg, Mary Parke Johnson, Anne Mandeville Colony, and Katherine E. Harbury. Charlottesville: University of Virginia Press, 2012, pp. 375–378.] (accessed online November 18, 2020).

## INDIANA

"To James Madison from Benjamin Lenover and Others, [ca. December 1815]," *Founders Online,* National Archives, https://founders.archives.

gov/documents/Madison/03-10-02-0055. [Original source: *The Papers of James Madison*, Presidential Series, vol. 10, *13 October 1815–30 April 1816*, ed. Angela Kreider, J. C. A. Stagg, Mary Parke Johnson, Katharine E. Harbury, and Anne Mandeville Colony. Charlottesville: University of Virginia Press, 2019, pp. 62–63.] (accessed online November 18, 2020).

## KENTUCKY

"To James Madison from Matthew Lyon and Others, 20 February 1811 (Abstract)," *Founders Online,* National Archives, https://founders.archives.gov/documents/Madison/03-03-02-0232. [Original source: *The Papers of James Madison*, Presidential Series, vol. 3, *3 November 1810–4 November 1811*, ed. J. C. A. Stagg, Jeanne Kerr Cross, and Susan Holbrook Perdue. Charlottesville: University Press of Virginia, 1996, pp. 175–176.] (accessed online November 18, 2020).

## MICHIGAN TERRITORY

"To Thomas Jefferson from Elijah Brush, 11 December 1805," *Founders Online,* National Archives, https://founders.archives.gov/documents/Jefferson/99-01-02-2799 (accessed online November 18, 2020).

## MISSISSIPPI

"To James Madison from the Mississippi Territorial Legislature, 22 November 1809 (Abstract)," *Founders Online,* National Archives, https://founders.archives.gov/documents/Madison/03-02-02-0101. [Original source: *The Papers of James Madison*, Presidential Series, vol. 2, *1 October 1809–2 November 1810*, ed. J. C. A. Stagg, Jeanne Kerr Cross, and Susan Holbrook Perdue. Charlottesville: University Press of Virginia, 1992, p. 78.] (accessed online November 18, 2020).

## MISSOURI

"To James Madison from Edward Hempstead, 31 March 1814," *Founders Online,* National Archives, https://founders.archives.gov/documents/Madison/03-07-02-0357. [Original source: *The Papers of James Madison,* Presidential Series, vol. 7, *25 October 1813–30 June 1814,* ed. Angela Kreider, J. C. A. Stagg, Mary Parke Johnson, Anne Mandeville Colony, and Katherine E. Harbury. Charlottesville: University of Virginia Press, 2012, pp. 402–403.] (accessed online November 18, 2020).

## NEW YORK

"From James Madison to Alexander J. Dallas, 31 July 1815," *Founders Online,* National Archives, https://founders.archives.gov/documents/Madison/03-09-02-0483. [Original source: *The Papers of James Madison,* Presidential Series, vol. 9, *19 February 1815–12 October 1815,* ed. Angela Kreider, J. C. A. Stagg, Mary Parke Johnson, and Anne Mandeville Colony. Charlottesville: University of Virginia Press, 2018, p. 496.] (accessed online November 18, 2020).

## NORTH CAROLINA

"To Thomas Jefferson from Joseph Anderson and William Cocke, 5 March 1801," *Founders Online,* National Archives, https://founders.archives.gov/documents/Jefferson/01-33-02-0136. [Original source: *The Papers of Thomas Jefferson,* vol. 33, *17 February–30 April 1801,* ed. Barbara B. Oberg. Princeton: Princeton University Press, 2006, pp. 174–175.] (accessed online November 18, 2020).

## OHIO

"To James Madison from the Ohio Congressional Delegation, 3 February 1816," *Founders Online,* National Archives, https://founders.archives.gov/documents/Madison/03-10-02-0213. [Original source: *The Papers of James Madison,* Presidential Series, vol. 10, *13 October 1815–30 April 1816,* ed. Angela Kreider, J. C. A. Stagg, Mary Parke Johnson,

Katharine E. Harbury, and Anne Mandeville Colony. Charlottesville: University of Virginia Press, 2019, pp. 207–208.] (accessed online November 18, 2020).

## SOUTH CAROLINA

"To James Madison from Henry Middleton, 31 December 1810," *Founders Online,* National Archives, https://founders.archives.gov/documents/Madison/03-03-02-0105. [Original source: *The Papers of James Madison*, Presidential Series, vol. 3, *3 November 1810–4 November 1811*, ed. J. C. A. Stagg, Jeanne Kerr Cross, and Susan Holbrook Perdue. Charlottesville: University Press of Virginia, 1996, pp. 88–89.] (accessed online November 18, 2020).

## TENNESSEE

"To James Madison from the Tennessee Congressional Delegation, 17 April 1816," *Founders Online,* National Archives, https://founders.archives.gov/documents/Madison/03-10-02-0401. [Original source: *The Papers of James Madison*, Presidential Series, vol. 10, *13 October 1815–30 April 1816*, ed. Angela Kreider, J. C. A. Stagg, Mary Parke Johnson, Katharine E. Harbury, and Anne Mandeville Colony. Charlottesville: University of Virginia Press, 2019, pp. 397–398.] (accessed online November 18, 2020).

13. 1838 War Department Annual Report, Commissioner of Indian Affairs T. Hartley Crawford, Washington: Government Printing Office, 1839.

14. 1839 War Department Annual Report, Commissioner of Indian Affairs T. Hartley Crawford, Washington: Government Printing Office, 1840.

15. 1840 War Department Annual Report, Commissioner of Indian Affairs T. Hartley Crawford, Washington: Government Printing Office, 1841.

16. 1841 War Department Annual Report, Commissioner of Indian Affairs T. Hartley Crawford, Washington: Government Printing Office, 1842.

17. 1843 War Department Annual Report, Commissioner of Indian Affairs T. Hartley Crawford, Washington: Government Printing Office, 1844.

18. 1845 War Department Annual Report, Commissioner of Indian Affairs T. Hartley Crawford, Washington: Government Printing Office, 1846.

19. 1846 War Department Annual Report, Commissioner of Indian Affairs T. Hartley Crawford, Washington: Government Printing Office, 1847.

20. 1848 War Department Annual Report, Commissioner of Indian Affairs T. Hartley Crawford, Washington: Government Printing Office, 1849.

21. Kades, Eric. "The Dark Side of Efficiency: *Johnson v. M'Intosh* and the Expropriation of American Indian Lands." *University of Pennsylvania Law Review* 148.4 (2000): 1146.

22. Washington Irving, A History of New York. New York: 1809 [Book I, chap v].

# 36

# CLIMATE CHANGE LEADS TO RESURGENCE
# OF DOCTRINE OF DISCOVERY

A new race to explore, conquer and acquire another 'new world' is on. Climate change is shrinking the Arctic icecap and opening new sea lanes, fisheries, oil fields and mineral caches for exploitation. Barren islands are suddenly valuable. Countries and companies are already planning how to exploit climate impacted land in the Arctic. Such planning is not unusual. Large companies have the management and organizational skills to develop procedures, budget, staff, employ resources and pander influence, along with the persistence and patience to wait for the opportune time to strike. Unlike most Indian Nations who lack revenue to pay for substantial litigation, companies will pool their money to retain legal representation, reducing the individual costs.

The Arctic plays host to substantial natural resources. A 2008 report released by the United States Geological Survey estimated that the Arctic holds around 1,670 trillion cubic feet of natural gas, 44 billion barrels of liquid natural gas, and 900 billion barrels of oil—the vast majority of these being offshore. As more territory becomes accessible, excess reserves of gold, zinc, nickel and iron, already found in part of the Arctic, may be discovered.

The American opposition to acting on climate change was not all-encompassing, though, because the *Trump administration viewed melting Arctic ice to be an economic opportunity.*[1]

On May 6, 2019, U.S. Secretary of State Pompeo offered that characterization during a wide-ranging speech in Finland today in which he also warned against China's increased Arctic presence, saying it threatens North American security and could be harmful to the environment.[2] Pompeo also warned Russia and China activities in Arctic, says Canada's claim over Northwest Passage 'illegitimate.'[3]

"The U.S. has a long-contested feud with Canada over sovereign claims through the Northwest Passage." "The Americans insist it's an international strait, open to vessels from any country, like the Strait of Gibraltar, or the English Channel, and Canada says no, these are internal waters, subject to the full force of our jurisdiction and control."[4]

### Russia Plants Flag on Arctic Seabed

On August 2, 2007, Russia planted a titanium flag on the floor of the Arctic Ocean purportedly to establish a claim for the estimated ten billion tons of oil and gas underlying the surface. The Arctic Indigenous Peoples consider land within the Arctic Circle their home. In addition, there are eight countries with territory inside the Arctic Circle that claim part of it based on 'discovery'—Canada, Norway, Sweden, Finland, Denmark (Greenland), Iceland, Russia and the U.S. (Alaska).[5]

Russia believes its Siberian shelf is directly linked to the Lomonosov ridge, an underwater mountain crest that runs 1,240 miles across the polar region. In 2001, Moscow submitted research findings to that effect to the United Nations, but they were rejected.

As noted by Sergei Balyasnikov, a spokesman for the Russian Arctic and Antarctic Institute: "This is a serious, risky and heroic mission ... It's a very important move for Russia to demonstrate its tential in the Arctic. It's like putting a flag on the Moon."[6]

The flag-planting ritual, as an element of symbolic possession, and the thinking behind the Russian's territorial claims have their roots in the development and use of the doctrine of discovery by European and American explorers from the 15th through the 21st centuries. When it comes to applying the 'discovery doctrine' in the 21st century, Russia is hardly alone. If there was no cause to consider Russia's flag planting the seed of a discovery claim, Canada's Foreign Minister would not have publicly contested their action.

## Canada Mocks Russia's Flag Planting Ploy

Russia's flag planting ploy, an element of the European doctrine of discovery, concerned Canada's Foreign Minister, Peter MacKay, who stated: "This isn't the 15th century. You can't go around the world and just plant flags and say: 'We're claiming this territory.'"[7]

The history of Canadian claims over the Northwest Passage stretches back to at least 1946. At that time, Lester Pearson, a future prime minister then serving as ambassador to the United States, asserted that the Canadian Arctic included "not only Canada's northern mainland, but the islands and the frozen sea north of the mainland between the meridians of its east and west boundaries, extended to the North Pole."[8]

## Arctic Indigenous Peoples' Caucus

Aqqaluq Lynge, speaking for the Arctic Indigenous Peoples' Caucus before the United Nations reminded them: "The world needs to know that the Arctic is already inhabited; it is not a scientific laboratory; it is not a museum. It is our home."[9]

*For now, the passage remains a challenge for conventional ships and efforts are being made to prevent frozen waterways that the local Inuit population depends on for travel from being opened up.* Tourism and other forms of economic development are already under way.[10]

## China and the South China Sea

Also, China in 2010 planted their flag on the floor of the South China Sea to claim sovereignty over this area and the assets under the sea-beds.

## Hans Island Claimed by Canada and Denmark

Canada is also facing off against Denmark over tiny Hans Island near northwestern Greenland. In 1984, Denmark's minister for Greenland affairs landed on the island in a helicopter and raised the Danish flag, buried a bottle of brandy and left a note that said "Welcome to the

Danish Island." Canada was not amused. In 2005, the Canadian defense minister and troops landed on the island and hoisted the Canadian flag and left a bottle of Canadian whisky. Denmark lodged an official protest. Periodically, each country visits and replaces the other's markers with their own.[11]

## Northwest Passage Sea Route

The Northwest Passage Sea Route, which links northern Europe to north-east Asia, is just one of three passages that Arctic countries and a host of non-polar nations are looking to exploit, according to Dr. Marc Lanteigne, expert in Arctic security. "Up until 20 years ago, the North-West Passage, a trans-Arctic waterway claimed by Canada as internal waters, would have been seen as impossible to breach. Now, however, with global warming making an impact, a handful of cruise ships have begun using the route for a few months of the year. In two decades' time, we could see it being used more extensively," he says.[12]

Scientists predict the Northwest Passage will be largely ice free in the summer by 2050 if current levels of warming continue.[13]

The United States and Canada are in a dispute about Canadian claims that an emerging Northwest Passage sea route is in its territory. "The strange legal limbo of the Northwest Passage can be traced back to 1985 when the US Coast Guard icebreaker, the Polar Sea, started navigating through the passage without asking Canada's permission. The routine resupply mission was quickly seen in Canada as a threat to Canadian sovereignty." The U.S. insists that the waters are neutral and open to all, but Canadian Prime Minister Stephen Harper states that he will place military icebreakers in the area "to assert our sovereignty and take action to protect our territorial integrity."[14]

Last year, Secretary of the Navy Richard Spencer said the U.S. would need to undertake more "freedom-of-navigation" voyages in the region—journeys to demonstrate that a nation has both the right and the ability to travel there.[15]

As stated by, Derek Burney, a longtime Canadian diplomat and government official. "There's always been a lot of tension about the borders up into the Arctic. ... We even had planes flying over [the U.S. icebreaker], dropping Canadian flags on it, just to make a statement."[16]

Russia and China are already hard at work to establish their claims.

## Finland

After 24 days at sea and a journey spanning more than 10,000 kilometres (6,214 miles), the Finnish icebreaker MSV Nordica set a new record for the earliest transit of the fabled Northwest Passage.[17]

## China

"China knows that the potential for shipping is profound. A vessel heading for Europe from Shanghai could cut several thousand kilometres off the southern route by using the Arctic waterway instead, which would represent a huge cost-saving," says Dr. Lanteigne. Dr. Lanteigne explains: "Both China and Russia are prepared to play the long game.[18] They know that sea ice is retreating at record levels and in 20 or 30 years the route will become much more useable. As an added contingency measure, in addition to the ports and railways they wish to develop, both are investing in ice-hardened liquefied natural gas container ships and state-of-the-art icebreakers. Ahead of meetings by the Arctic Council, a group of nations that border the area, raised suspicions about China's ambitions for the region and slammed Russia's "pattern of aggressive behaviour" there—and took a swing at Canada."[19]

## United Nations Arctic Council

The Arctic Council is made up of Canada, Finland, Denmark (Greenland), Iceland, Norway, Russia, Sweden and the United States (Alaska). Of these, Canada and Russia hold the most territory. Being a party to the United Nations Convention on the Law of the Sea (UNCLOS), which states that a country's Exclusive Economic Zone extends 200 nautical miles offshore, Russian claims over approximately 40% of the Arctic.

## Importance of Military Exploration

It is important to notice that the icebreakers are all military ships. In the dispute between the United States and Great Britain over the Oregon Territory, Great Britain refused to admit the validity of the 'discovery' by Captain Gray as an act by the United States as a sovereign. Captain Gray was not traveling on a national ship or under national authority. He had only been on an enterprise of his own, as an individual.

## Notes

1. https://globalnews.ca/news/5249435/arctic-climate-change-pompeo-economic-opportunity (accessed online November 29, 2020).

2. https://globalnews.ca/news/5246154/northwest-passage-canada-pompeo/ (accessed online November 29, 2020).

3. Ibid.

4. https://globalnews.ca/news/5256532/northwest-passage-canada-us-claim-challenge/ (accessed online November 29, 2020).

5. https://www.theguardian.com/world/2007/aug/02/russia.arctic (accessed online November 29, 2020).

6. https://www.nytimes.com/2007/08/03/world/europe/03arctic.html (accessed online November 29, 2020).

7. https://uk.reuters.com/article/uk-russia-arctic-canada-idUKN0246498520070802 (accessed online November 8, 2020).

8. https://globalnews.ca/news/5256532/northwest-passage-canada-us-claim-challenge/ (accessed online November 29, 2020).

9. Doctrine of Discovery, Used for Centuries to Justify Seizure of Indigenous Land, Subjugate Peoples, Must Be Repudiated by United Nations, Permanent Forum Told, May 8, 2012, United Nations, Economic and Social Council HR/5088, Department of Public Information, News and Media Division, New York, Permanent Forum on Indigenous Issues, Eleventh Session

https://www.un.org/press/en/2012/hr5088.doc.htm (accessed online November 8, 2020).

10. https://globalnews.ca/news/3634272/msv-nordica-sets-new-standard-for-earliest-crossing-of-northwest-passage/ (accessed online November 29, 2020).

11. https://www.nytimes.com/2016/11/08/world/what-in-the-world/canada-denmark-hans-island-whisky-schnapps.html (accessed online November 8, 2020).

12. https://www.raconteur.net/finance/northern-sea-route (accessed online November 29, 2020).

13. https://www.chicagotribune.com/news/environment/ct-climate-change-northwest-passage-20170729-story.html (accessed online November 29, 2020).

14. https://www.pri.org/stories/2017-09-04/who-controls-northwest-passage-its-debate (accessed online November 29, 2020).

15. https://globalnews.ca/news/5256532/northwest-passage-canada-us-claim-challenge/ (accessed online November 29, 2020).

16. https://www.pri.org/stories/2017-09-04/who-controls-northwest-passage-its-debate (accessed online November 29, 2020).

17. https://globalnews.ca/news/3634272/msv-nordica-sets-new-standard-for-earliest-crossing-of-northwest-passage/ (accessed online November 29, 2020).

18. China's Xinhua News Agency, Thursday, Sept. 27, 2012.

19. https://globalnews.ca/news/5256532/northwest-passage-canada-us-claim-challenge/ (accessed online November 29, 2020).

37

# CURRENT EFFORTS TO REPUDIATE
# DOCTRINE OF DISCOVERY

## Long March to Rome

Many are committed to overturn the doctrine of discovery at its roots by
having the Pope revoke the Inter caetera bulls of 1493. In 2016, eleven
indigenous representatives made the "Long March to Rome." They
met Pope and Archbishop Silvano Tomasi, chairman of the Pontifical
Council for Justice and Peace.[1]

## Pope Francis' Visit to Peru, January 2, 2018

On his visit to Peru, the Pope stated: "The native Amazonian peoples
have probably never been so threatened on their own lands as they are
at present ..." He decried the "pressure being exerted by big business
interests" seeking petroleum, gas, lumber and gold and plundering
"supplies for other countries without concern for its inhabitants."[2]

Edwin Vásquez, the Peruvian representative of the pan-Amazonian
alliance of indigenous organisations Coica, believed that "The pope is
a means to make our demands heard by the state." ... "The [regional
governments] do absolutely nothing to help us, in fact they blame us
for opposing development," said Vásquez, a Huitoto member of a
delegation representing more than 400 indigenous Amazonian peoples.
The group hoped the Pope would call on the Peruvian state to grant
them formal land titles for some 200,000 sq km of land, it said, as well

as urge the government to clean up rivers poisoned with mercury used in illegal gold mining.[3]

## Pope: Ensnared by Colonialism

In speaking to the indigenous peoples of the Amazon on January 19, 2018, the Pope declared: "Special care is demanded of us, lest we allow ourselves to be ensnared by ideological forms of colonialism, disguised as progress, that slowly but surely dissipate cultural identities and establish a uniform, single ... and weak way of thinking ..." Yet the Pope never referenced what started this—the Church's Papal Bulls.[4]

## United Nations Declaration on the Rights of Indigenous Peoples ("UNDRIP")

Indigenous peoples and the World Council of Churches have petitioned the U.N. for assistance in repudiating the 'discovery doctrine.' It took 25 years of deliberation to enact the United Nations Declaration on the Rights of Indigenous Peoples ("UNDRIP"). The problem is the dominance in the U.N. of the four countries who voted against it— Canada, the U.S., New Zealand and Australia. They later endorsed it as 'aspirational' and non-binding.

## Concern of Colonial Powers—Land Disputes and Natural Resource Extraction

Canada, USA, New Zealand and Australia have similar settler colonial histories and shared common concerns. They argue that autonomy recognized for indigenous peoples was problematic and would undermine sovereignty of their own states, particularly in the context of land disputes and natural resource extraction.

## Blame Game

Indigenous peoples are in the way of this blood thirsty drive for domination so they will continue to experience the 'blame game' at its worst. The Blame Game's rules, techniques, and advanced strategies describe picking a Target of Blame (TOB)—"the scapegoat, the stooge, the meal on the table."[5] They then blame the target for its failure to solve its problems. The inability of the target to accomplish the outcome is not considered, only the failure in their eyes. The blamer, such as the federal government, will complain—we tried Indian self-determination to give them as much control as we could and it hasn't worked. We knew they couldn't manage themselves; what a stupid waste of time and money. Whose idea was it anyway?

A skilled player can follow the Chain of Blame (COB) all the way back to the 'discovery' of the 'New World.' Settler colonists can blame General Amherst, Commanding General of British forces in North America during the Seven Years War, and Colonel Bouquet, for not doing a better job on spreading smallpox among the Indians.

One letter from General Amherst to Colonel reads:

> You will do well to try to inoculate the Indians by means of blankets, as well as to try every other method that can serve to extirpate this execrable race. I should be very glad your scheme for hunting them down by dogs could take effect, but England is at too great a distance to think of that at present.[6]

Then one from Colonel Henry Bouquet to General Amherst in 1763: "I will try to inoculate the Indians by means of blankets..."[7]

Significantly, in a discussion regarding the unofficial use of Lord Jeffrey as a mascot started a century ago, the Amherst College Trustees' stated:

> ... a central reason [to dislike the symbolism of Lord Jeff] has always been his suggestion, in wartime correspondence, that smallpox be used against Native Americans. Nothing may have come of his proposal, defenders counter; they add, for context, that harsh tactics were employed by both sides in the conflict.[8]

Amherst College is not named after General Amherst but the town it is located in is.

The College renamed the Lord Jeffery Inn, a campus hotel owned by the college, to the Inn on Boltwood.

To separate the College from Lord Amherst, it is important to recall its President's actions in challenging the Indian Removal Act. Heman Humphrey, the second president of Amherst College from 1823-1845, was against removal which he saw as a plan...

> "...to drive 70,000 unoffending people from the soil on which they were born, into distant wilds, where most of them will perish. ... What? Tell the Indians 'We want your country and you had better leave it,-You can never be quiet and happy here?' and then, because they do not take your advice, cut it up into counties, declare all their laws and usages, after a certain day, to be null and void, and substitute law, which it is known they cannot live under; and then turn round and coolly tell the world, 'O we mean no compulsion!' The farthest in the world from it! If these people choose to stay, why by all means let them remain where they are."[9]

## The End Game of the Settler Colonist

The Creeks in Georgia referred to the English as "Ecunnaunuxulgee," which translates as "People greedily grasping the land of the Red people."[10]

Aaron Bird Bear, a citizen of the Mandan-Hidatsa-Arickara Nation, defines settler colonialism as follows:

> Invasion is a structure not an event. Colonialism is suggested to be the policy or practice of acquiring full or partial political control over a nation, occupying it with settlers, and exploiting it economically. Additionally, settler colonialism aims for the dissolution of indigenous societies by establishing a new colonial society on seized land with the elimination of native societies as an organizing principal. Settler colonialism annihilates to supplant. North American settler colonialism exploited indigenous peoples over the past 500 years, and as twenty-first century conflicts over sovereignty, dominion over land, parameters of Indian law, natural resource extraction, treaty rights, and access to health care, education and welfare needs illuminates, the U.S. continues to exploit the land, resources and cultural knowledge that indigenous societies still possess.

Given any major economic upheaval, the settler colonist will conjure up a justification once more and turn for its rescue to Indian land and resources. Also, the continuing tension between Indian Nations and states is but the continuing issue of an 'imperium in imperio.' No state wants another state within its boundaries.

## "Small Doses of Death"

Representative Everett profoundly recognized the death grip of Georgia's entrenched legal and judicial systems oriented to demoralize peoples—"small doses of death" that structure the everyday life of individuals. This applies as well to political, economic and military control today.

> ... I say again, then, that legal force is the most efficient and formidable that can be applied. It is systematic, it is calculated and measured to effect its end. The sovereign power sits calmly in its council chamber, and shapes its measures most effectively to the desired object. Actual physical force is either tumultuary, as that of the mob, and of consequence, transitory; or it is that of the military arm of the Government, which, from the nature of things, is put forth only at a crisis, and to meet the exigency of an occasion. But force embodied in the form of law, a compulsory legislation, a code beneath which I cannot live, a duress which surrounds me, and pursues me whithersoever I travel, wherever I abide; ever acting by day, ever watchful by night, co-extensive with the land in which I live; Sir, I submit to this Congress of reasonable men, that it is the most effectual, and the most appalling form in which force can be applied; the most disheartening. All other force awakens a manly courage of resistance. But this deadly influence of an unfriendly legislation; this cold averted eye of a Government, which has checks and restraints for you, but no encouragements nor hopes: in short, this institution of things which is intended to depress, harass, and prostrate you, beneath which you feel you cannot live, and which drives you as an outcast from your native land; this is the force which every freeman would most deprecate.[11]

In the House of Representatives debates on the Indian Removal Act, Representative Evans ended with the following eloquent justification for standing up for the oppressed which applies just as much today:

> If I could stand up between the weak, the friendless, the deserted, and the strong arm of oppression, and successfully vindicate their rights, and shield them in their hour of adversity, I should have achieved honor enough to satisfy even an exorbitant ambition; and I should leave it as a legacy to my children, more valuable than uncounted gold—more honorable than imperial power.[12]

Notes:

1.https://indiancountrytoday.com/archive/face-to-face-with-pope-francis-to-get-the-inter-caetera-papal-bull-revoked-Gcv8Hgpd2EC6ydjMJWiaFA (accessed online November 8, 2020).

2. James Ayre, January 24, 2018

https://planetsave.com/2018/01/24/pope-francis-calls-amazon-protected-big-business-consumerist-greed/ (accessed online November 8, 2020); https://www.theguardian.com/world/2018/jan/19/pope-francis-amazon-indigenous-people-threat (accessed online November 8, 2020).

3. Ibid.

4. http://w2.vatican.va/content/francesco/en/travels/2018/outside/documents/papa-francesco-cile-peru_2018.html (accessed online November 8, 2020).

5. Farber, Neil E. *The Blame Game: the Complete Guide to Blaming: how to play and how to quit*. Hillcrest Publishing Group, 2010.

6. https://www.umass.edu/legal/derrico/amherst/34_41_114_fn.jpeg

(accessed online November 8, 2020).

7. https://www.umass.edu/legal/derrico/amherst/34_40_305_fn.jpeg (accessed online November 8, 2020).

8. https://www.amherst.edu/amherst-story/facts/trustees/statements/node/627738 (accessed online November 8, 2020).

9. https://www.wcu.edu/library/DigitalCollections/CherokeePhoenix/

Vol3/no01/indians-page-1-column-1-4.html (accessed online November 8, 2020).

10. https://www.cmich.edu/library/clarke/ResearchResources/Native_American_Material/Treaty_Rights/Pages/New-Section---The-Land.aspx (accessed online November 8, 2020).

11. Everett, Edward. Speech of Mr. Everett, of Massachusetts, on the Bill for Removing the Indians from the East to the West Side of the Mississippi: Delivered in the House of Representatives, on the 19th May, 1830. United States, Gales & Seaton, 1830: 7.

12. Speeches on the passage of the Bill for the removal of the Indians, delivered in the Congress of the United States, April and May, 1830. United States, Perkins & Marvin, 1830: 176.

# ACKNOWLEDGMENTS

This work would not have been possible without the outstanding research and scholarship done by so many on the Doctrine of Discovery. The list is much longer than this. For anyone who has written on this topic, thank you.

European Countries and Colonial Practices

Banner, Stuart. *How the Indians Lost Their Land: Law and Power on the Frontier*. Cambridge: Belknap-Harvard UP, 2005.

Royce, Charles, Indian Land Cessions in the United States in J. W. Powell (Ed.) Eighteenth Annual Report of the Bureau of American Ethnology to the Secretary of the Smithsonian Institution, 1896-97. Washington, DC: Smithsonian Institution

Historical Documents

Cherokee Phoenix

Lehigh University Students, Literature of Justification Project

National Archives, Founders Online, National Historical Publications and Records Commission and The University of Virginia Press

Oxford Historical Treaties, 1648 through 1919

https://opil.ouplaw.com/page/oht-about/about

Yale Law School, Lillian Goldman Law Library, Avalon Project, Documents in Law, History and Diplomacy

Books

Fuentes, Carlos, *The Buried Mirror*

Robertson, Lindsey A., *Conquest by Law: How the Discovery of America Dispossessed Indigenous Peoples of Their Lands*, 2005.

Articles

Colonial Settler Analysis

Natsu Taylor Saito, Tales of Color and Colonialism: Racial Realism and Settler Colonial Theory, 10 Fla. A & M U. L. Rev. 1 (2014).

History

National Park Service

Land Speculation

The Great American Land Bubble: The Amazing Story of Land-Grabbing, Speculations, and Booms from Colonial Days to the Present times, A.M. Sakolski

Music

Indigie Femme

Food

Tocabe Restaurant

## Family

Nobody has been more important to me in the pursuit of this project than the members of my family. They generously provided me with the protected academic time to pursue this project. They also made sure that whatever resources and assistance I needed for this project were available. Their encouragement and support were invaluable. Thank you to my most beloved husband, Dag, my Mom and Dad, my sons, D.J. and Aaron, my daughter-in-laws, Malin and Marianne, and my grandchildren—Hadlie, Callan, Sander, Kennedy and Cooper, whose love provide such joy in my life.

## The Truth Tellers

Representative Evans language in The Debates and Proceedings in the Congress of the United States on the Indian Removal Act, applies to all of you.

"If I could stand up between the weak, the friendless, the deserted, and the strong arm of oppression, and successfully vindicate their rights, and shield them in their hour of adversity, I should have achieved honor enough to satisfy even an exorbitant ambition; and I should leave it as a legacy to my children, more valuable than uncounted gold—more honorable than imperial power."

—Representative Evans, speaking on S. 102, on May 18, 1830, 21st Cong., 1st sess., Register of Debates in Congress 1049.

## Charts Credits

Chart, Main Treaties Ceding Indian Lands in Ohio, Ohio Lands Book.

Chart, John J. McCusker, Population of Colonies, "The Rum Trade and the Balance of Payments of the Thirteen Continental Colonies, 1650-1775 (Ph.D. diss., University of Pittsburgh, 1970, appendix B, 548-552.

Chart, Terms of Sale under Various U.S. Land Acts 1785-1862, Ohio Lands Book.

Chart, Revenue from Public Land Sales, The Great American Land Bubble: The Amazing Story of Land – Grabbing, Speculations, and Booms from Colonial Days to the Present Times, A. M. Sakolski, p. 267.

Chart, New York State Revenues from Indian Land Sales, 1790-95, The Divided Ground: Indians, Settlers, and the Northern Borderland of the Northern Borderland of the American Revolution, Alan Taylor, p. 201.

Chart, Value of Furs Exported to England by British Continental Colonies: 1700–1775 (Extract), Colonial and Pre-Federal Statistics, Chapter Z, Series Z 418-431, p. 1188.

Chart, Terms of Sale under Various U.S. Land Acts 1785-1862, Ohio Lands Book.

CPSIA information can be obtained
at www.ICGtesting.com
Printed in the USA
LVHW091623010822
724892LV00004B/382